Baltic Yearbook of International Law, Volume 18 (2019)

Baltic Yearbook of International Law

VOLUME 18, 2019

Editors-in-Chief:

Lauri Mälksoo, Ineta Ziemele, Dainius Žalimas

(TARTU) (RIGA) (VILNIUS)

Managing Editor:

Ligita Gjortlere, M.Sci.Soc., Riga Graduate School of Law

Language Editor:

Christopher Goddard, M.Ed.

Editorial Board

Egidijus Bieliunas (Former Judge at the General Court of the Court of Justice of the EU) – *Tanel Kerikmäe* (Professor at Tallinn University of Technology) – *Egils Levits* (President of the Republic of Latvia, former Judge at the Court of Justice of the EU) – *Mārtiņš Mits* (Judge at the European Court of Human Rights) – *Rein Müllerson* (Member of the *Institut de droit international*; Professor Emeritus of Tallinn University) – *Vilenas Vadapalas* (Attorney at Law; former judge of the General Court of the Court of Justice of the EU) – *Pēteris Zilgalvis* (Head of Unit, Digital Innovation and Blockchain, Digital Single Market Directorate, DG CONNECT)

The titles published in this series are listed at *brill.com/balt*

Advisory Board

Gudmundur Alfredsson (Professor, University of Akureyri; Visiting Professor, University of Strasbourg) – *Theo van Boven* (Professor Emeritus of International Law, University of Maastricht)– *James Crawford* (Judge at the International Court of Justice, the Hague) – *Andrew Drzemczewski* (Visiting Professor at Middlesex University; former staff member of the Council of Europe) – *John Dugard* (Professor Emeritus of Public International Law, University of Leiden; Professor Emeritus of Law, University of the Witwatersrand, Johannesburg) – *Asbjørn Eide* (Founder of the Norwegian Institute of Human Rights, University of Olso) – *Christine Gray* (Professor Emeritus in International Law, University of Cambridge) – *Mahulena Hofmann* (Professor, Chair at the University of Luxembourg) – *Göran Melander* (Professor Emeritus of International Law, University of Lund) – *Allan Rosas* (Former Judge at the Court of Justice of the EU) – *Bruno Simma* (Arbitrator, Iran-United States Claims Tribunal; Former Judge, International Court of Justice) – *Brigitte Stern* (Professor Emeritus of International Law, University of Paris I) – *Pietro Sullo* (Rector of the Riga Graduate School of Law) – *Rüdiger Wolfrum* (Professor, Former Director, Max Planck Institute for Comparative Public Law and International Law)

Baltic Yearbook of International Law, Volume 18 (2019)

Edited by

Lauri Mälksoo
Ineta Ziemele
Dainius Žalimas

BRILL
NIJHOFF

LEIDEN | BOSTON

Typeface for the Latin, Greek, and Cyrillic scripts: "Brill". See and download: brill.com/brill-typeface.

ISSN 1569-6456
E-ISSN 2211-5897
ISBN 978-90-04-43860-6 (hardback)

Copyright 2021 by Koninklijke Brill NV, Leiden, The Netherlands.
Koninklijke Brill NV incorporates the imprints Brill, Brill Hes & De Graaf, Brill Nijhoff, Brill Rodopi, Brill Sense, Hotei Publishing, mentis Verlag, Verlag Ferdinand Schöningh and Wilhelm Fink Verlag.
All rights reserved. No part of this publication may be reproduced, translated, stored in a retrieval system, or transmitted in any form or by any means, electronic, mechanical, photocopying, recording or otherwise, without prior written permission from the publisher. Requests for re-use and/or translations must be addressed to Koninklijke Brill NV via brill.com or copyright.com.

This book is printed on acid-free paper and produced in a sustainable manner.

Contents

Editorial Note   ix
   Ineta Ziemele

Guest Editorial   x
   Inese Freimane-Deksne

The "Thick" Rule of Law and Mutual Trust in the European Union   1
   Juha Raitio

The Impact of Digital Autonomous Tools on Private Autonomy   18
   Thomas Hoffmann

Powerful Private Players in the Digital Economy: Between Private Law Freedoms and the Constitutional Principle of Equality   32
   Peter Rott

Big Data and International Politics   52
   Juan Luis Manfredi Sánchez

Big Data and Competition Policy in the European Union   72
   Éva Miskolczi-Bodnár

Antitrust After Big Data   87
   John M. Yun

Big Data Ownership: Do we Need a New Regulatory Framework?   117
   Andris Tauriņš

Development of Consumer Collective Redress in the EU: a Light at the End of the Tunnel?   134
   Ana Vlahek

Consumer Protection in the EU Conflict-of-Laws Framework   169
   Carlos Llorente

Geo-blocking Regulation: Antitrust or Consumer Protection?   194
   Klemen Podobnik

Elements of Practices of the Baltic States in International Law

Republic of Estonia Materials of International Law 2017–2018   211
  Edited by René Värk

Republic of Latvia Materials on International Law 2017–2018   246
  Edited by Kristaps Tamužs

Republic of Lithuania Materials on International Law 2018   293
  Edited by Andrius Bambalas and Saulius Katuoka

Editorial Note

Volume 19 of the Baltic Yearbook of International Law is the second volume of the Yearbook appearing under the auspices of cooperation between the Riga Graduate School of Law and Brill Publishers. This volume is devoted to highlighting the reflections aired in Riga when the Law School was implementing the Jean Monnet Project in 2017–2019. These reflections broadly focused on the law of the European Union. However, two specific issues – separate yet related – were asked. The first of these was about the impact of the digital era on the consolidation of European Union law. The second concerned the impact of fundamental rights in the development of European Union law in the digital era. It is clear that the legal landscape within the European Union continues to represent a unique experiment where international law has emerged into a supranational legal system within one region. Examination and analysis of how such a legal system reacts to new challenges is also capable of providing broader ideas relevant to the development of international law in a digital world of the future.

Reports on the practice of the three Baltic States in international law cover the years 2017 and 2018. These provide interesting testimony on the importance of the rules of international law in all three States. It is evident that their national courts follow the decisions of the European courts and take them on board in good faith. Indeed, these decisions form an important part of the reasoning of the national courts. The three Baltic States continue to be active in promoting the rule of law in international relations. This is attested to by the positions adopted by their governments on difficult international issues such as the conflicts in Syria or Ukraine, the ability of the UN Security Council to deal with conflicts affecting international peace, or codification of international law.

The editors of the Baltic Yearbook are certain that the EU-law perspective will be of interest to international lawyers across the world, whether as an option or as an idea as to what the international legal order might look like with ever growing globalization and migration of the world's people.

Ineta Ziemele[*]

---

[*] Ph.D. (*Cantab.*) Professor of International and Human Rights Law, Riga Graduate School of Law; Judge of the Court of Justice of the European Union.

Guest Editorial

Papers published in this volume of the *Baltic Yearbook of International Law* emerged from a series of four conferences convened in the framework of the Erasmus+ Jean Monnet project entitled "Fundamental Rights at the Frontiers of the European Union" (2017–2019). A European Union (EU) grant was awarded to the Riga Graduate School of Law (RGSL) which was the first academic institution in Latvia to implement the Jean Monnet project. Conferences were held on such topics as: "*Consumer Protection and Fundamental Rights*" (18–19 June 2018), "*Competition, Big Data and Fundamental Rights*" (6–7 December 2018), "*Constitutional Law and Fundamental Rights*" (25–26 April 2019), and "*Fundamental Rights at the Frontiers of the European Union – Looking for a New Balance*" (20–21 June 2019), organized as the follow-up conference to the project.

The purpose of the project was to enrich legal discourse on fundamental rights in a multidisciplinary and holistic way, taking into account the changing EU integration environment and development of new technologies. During the conferences, leading academics from throughout Europe and the United States, judges of constitutional courts and of the Court of Justice of the EU (CJEU), Advocates General, along with public and private sector representatives explored the spillovers and crossovers between the public and private law dimensions of fundamental rights; between Big Data, competition law and consumer protection; and between common European values and national sovereignty. The conclusion was that, although not all areas require new legal regulation, an undoubted need exists for a new balance and for reinforced interaction between national, European, and international legal orders.

Over time, the EU has evolved from an organization based solely on common market objectives to a union of common values, based on respect for human rights, the rule of law and democracy – as set out in Article 2 of the Treaty on European Union (TEU). The Lisbon Treaty granted legally binding status to the Charter of Fundamental Rights, while Article 7 TEU operates as a trigger mechanism against any EU Member State that violates common values. At the same time, interpretations differ and appeals to democracy, the rule of law, and human rights continue to divide as much as to unite the EU Member States and the EU institutions. Faced with internal and external challenges, some EU Member States are returning with reinforced calls for respect of their national sovereignty. In parallel, an uneasy dialogue between national constitutional courts and the CJEU continues on the scope of "constitutional identity" (Article 4(2) TEU) and "common constitutional traditions" (Article 6(3)

TEU) as well as on their interlinkages with "common values". Juha Raitio argues that common European values – the rule of law, democracy and human rights – are interconnected and their observance is a precondition for mutual trust between the EU Member States, good governance and a well-functioning EU. To this end, both the EU and its Member States should engage in sincere and mutually respectful cooperation in advancing a value-based European legal order.

The development of new technologies and artificial intelligence brings with it a growing tension between the established value system in a democratic society and the demands of the digital economy. While people claim to be concerned about their privacy, at the same time they disclose their personal data comprehensively to third parties. To address this "privacy paradox", the EU adopted the General Data Protection Regulation. Thomas Hoffmann analyses the impact of digital autonomous tools on private autonomy and asserts that the "privacy paradox" in data protection applies to private autonomy as well, highlighting the need for respective protection mechanisms.

Another phenomenon is that States are no longer the main data retainers. Big Data is mostly processed by powerful private players (such as Facebook, Google, or Amazon). As a result, a change has occurred in the classic relationship between the State and the individual in the protection of fundamental rights. The question arises whether and to what extent fundamental rights should be applied in a horizontal relationship between two private parties. Peter Rott argues that with power comes responsibility and examines to what extent constitutional law – and in particular the constitutional principle of equality, including such procedural rights as the right to be heard and the right to be given reasons – applies to powerful digital players.

At the same time, Big Data continues to shape public policies, decision-making and international politics. Juan Luis Manfredi Sánchez discusses the ways in which Big Data affects international politics and points to the asymmetry between current reality (globalization, digitization and the crisis of sovereignty, among other key aspects) and the evolution of public international law.

Processing of Big Data has also created challenges to competition law, testing existing legal concepts and their enforcement. John M. Yun considers that Big Data is fundamentally about innovation and, as such, does not represent an inevitable obstacle to competition. Éva Miskolczi-Bodnár explores how competition law can be adapted to the specifics of the digital market and whether privacy concerns might be covered by the scope of competition law. It seems that the key issue is again about finding an appropriate balance – between competition objectives and promotion of innovations, and between protection of competition and protection of privacy as a fundamental right of individuals.

Additionally, Andris Tauriņš raises a highly pertinent question on the ownership of Big Data and explores the idea of a new semi-right in data, which is proposed by the EU Commission in its White Paper on "Data Ownership".

Digitization and globalization have expanded opportunities not only for traders, but also for consumers, leading to lower prices and to a greater range of choices. At the same time, consumers are faced with increased risks in terms of rights protection in complex digital and cross-border transactions. The EU has adopted both material and conflict-of-laws rules to address these concerns. However, not all areas are covered equally and challenges of interpretation and mutual interaction between those rules still affect their effective implementation. Klemen Podobnik explores the EU Geo-blocking Regulation as a legislative instrument of consumer protection and points to the need to separate it from competition law. Ana Vlahek analyses how consumer collective redress has developed in the EU and how this tool contributes to guaranteeing effective access to justice – an essential element of the rule of law as one of the core values of the EU. Carlos Llorente recalls that consumer protection has even been recognized as a kind of a fundamental right in the legal instruments of the EU and its Member States and explores possible improvements in the interaction between the EU conflict-of-law rules governing consumer contracts.

Fundamental rights cut across different subject areas and different jurisdictions. Although subject to challenges and intense debate, they still maintain their status as a core constitutional value of both the EU and its Member States, along with democracy and the rule of law. Even in the era of Big Data and global markets, public and private law rules should be interpreted in the light of these core European values, and innovative approaches should be sought through complementarity rather than competition. We hope that this volume and the Jean Monnet project, implemented by RGSL, will provide a useful contribution in this regard.

Inese Freimane-Deksne*

---

* Ph.D. researcher in law at the European University Institute.

The "Thick" Rule of Law and Mutual Trust in the European Union

*Juha Raitio**

Abstract

The concept of the rule of law has lately become a topical and controversial issue. For example, the existence of effective judicial review is an inseparable part of the rule of law and some problems in this respect have been analysed. This article advocates for a thick concept of the rule of law. This refers to the idea that the rule of law has both material and formal content. The controversial part seems to be the question of material content and whether it obscures the essential meaning of the rule of law as a requirement of legality. However, the material aspect of the rule of law can be linked to the value-base of the European Union. For example, during its EU Presidency, Finland strongly emphasized the significance of the value base and the rule of law in Article 2 TEU for the development of the EU.[1] Democracy, the rule of law, and the actualisation of fundamental and human rights in particular are connected together, combined in a trinity where all the components form preconditions for the others. This stance is not a novelty in Finland, since Jyränki, for one, two decades ago already maintained that human rights protect the individual's position and thus belong to the sphere of the material concept of the rule of law.[2] I have employed the metaphor of a musical triangle. A triangle can only make a sound if all three of its corners are connected to each other, thereby connecting the sides of the triangle. Observance of the core values of the EU is a precondition for mutual trust between Member States, which in turn is necessary for a well-functioning European Union and good governance.

Keywords

rule of law – democracy – human rights – values of the EU – mutual trust – independence of the judiciary – Venice Commission

---

* Professor of European Law, University of Helsinki.
1 Presidency conclusions, Council document 12044/19 and *e.g.* the home pages of the president state <www.eu2019.fi>.
2 Jyränki, A. (2002) 'Oikeusvaltio ja demokratia' in A. Aarnio and T. Uusitupa (eds), *Oikeusvaltio* (Helsinki, Lakimiesliiton kustannus) p. 23. Antero Jyränki is the former professor of Constitutional law of the University of Turku.

1 The Material and Formal Elements of the Rule of Law

Let's start by trying to define the concept the of rule of law, although an attempt to define it is most likely doomed to fail at least to a certain extent. The rule of law is associated with the deepest layers of law, the layer of moral considerations.[3] It represents the fundamental and unwaivable values of the Member States and relates, therefore, to both legal culture and legal norms.[4] Another starting point is that the rule of law is not only a formal principle. In contemporary legal literature, especially in the field of EU law, one can refer to the 'thick' conception of the rule of law, which contains both formal and material elements.[5] Protection of individual rights seems to strengthen the interpretation of the 'thick' rule of law.[6]

Based on legal literature, the 'thick' concept of the rule of law seems to be controversial, especially with regard to how the material dimension of the concept the of rule of law should be regarded. In Sweden in the 1990s Frändberg described the concept of the rule of law as a 'rhetorical balloon' that one can, in a way, fill up, including in it everything possible that is felt to be positive.[7]

---

3 *See e.g.* Raitio, J. (2003) *The Principle of Legal Certainty in EC Law*, (Dordrecht, Kluwer Academic Publishers), pp. 301–304 and Klami, H.T. (1994) *Methodological Problems in European and Comparative Law*, (Helsinki, University Press), pp. 10–12.

4 Tuori, K. (2007) *Oikeuden ratio ja voluntas*, (Helsinki, WSOYpro) p. 222 and Tuori, K. (2011) *Ratio and Voluntas, The Tension Between Reason and Will in Law* (Farnham, Ashgate) p. 208. Tuori has somewhat similarly separated the Constitution into explicit, written norms and constitutional culture, which refers to constitutional theories, concepts and principles, as well as ways of dealing with these, *i.e.* patterns of constitutional argumentation.

5 *See e.g.* Pech, L. (2013) 'Promoting the rule of law abroad: on the EU's limited contribution to the shaping of an international understanding of the rule of law', in Kochenov, D., Amtenbrink, F. (eds.) *EU's Shaping of the International Legal Order*, (Cambridge, Cambridge University Press), pp. 108–129 or McCorquodale, R. (2016), Defining the International Rule of Law: Defying Gravity?, *International & Comparative Law Quarterly*, part 2, pp. 277–304, at pp. 284–285 (McCorquodale 2016): "Thus the approach taken in this article is to define the international rule of law in terms of the objectives of a rule of law Defining the International Rule of Law, and thereby provide a definition appropriate to the distinctive nature of the international system. The definition offered in this article of the international rule of law is a 'thick' one and includes the following elements or objectives: legal order and stability; equality of application of the law; protection of human rights; and the settlement of disputes before an independent legal body".

6 *See e.g.* Von Bogdandy, A., Antpöhler, C., Ioannidis, M. (2017), 'Protecting EU values, Reverse *Solange* and the Rule of Law Framework' in Jacab, A., Kochenov, D. (eds.), *The Enforcement of EU law and Values*, (Oxford University Press) pp. 218–233, at p. 226 (Von Bogdandy – Antpöhler – Ioannidis 2017).

7 Frändberg, Å. (1996) 'Begreppet rättsstat' in F. Sterzel (ed.), *Rättsstaten – rätt, politik, moral*, (Stockholm, Rättsfonden) pp. 21–41, at pp. 22–23.

Frändberg's argument reflects a fear according to which the rule of law, if interpreted too broadly, is in danger of becoming blurred as a concept and losing some of its expressiveness. In his more recent work Frändberg has studied 'law-state thinking' and clarified his idea of the 'watering-down of language'. According to Frändberg this tendency manifests itself mainly in the smoothing over of tensions and conflicts between different values and principles. He finds that including two or more different values or principles in one and the same concept hides the fact that they might be potentially contradictory. He advocates for 'minimal law state-thinking' in which only a few narrowly defined values are defined and applied in practice.[8] In the same tone Raz has warned against confounding the concept of the *rule of law* with a wide range of values, principles or goals that are characteristic of a good legal system.[9]

Although the concept of the rule of law is ambiguous, a legal interpretation is always contextual, so that labelling the concept of the rule of law as a rhetorical balloon is hyperbole.

Crucially, merely democratic legitimacy for legislation is not enough, since some sort of substantive acceptability of legal rules is also a prerequisite for legitimacy. This kind of demand for substantive acceptability of law is clearly difficult to define or describe, but Fuller succeeded in illustrating its main features by telling the fascinating allegory of King Rex, who failed to make law in eight different ways.[10] For example, laws cannot be obscure or require the impossible. They cannot be changed frequently, since lack of stability causes many problems. They cannot be made to contradict each other, in that one rule may not allow something that another rule prohibits. This reference to Fuller is not as novel an idea as it may seem, since Kilpatrick recently referred to Fuller in her article which relates to managerialism connected to taming the

---

8   Frändberg, Å. (2014) *From Rechtsstaat to Universal Law-State, An Essay in Philosophical Jurisprudence*, (Dordrecht, Springer) pp. 30–32.
9   Raz, J. (1979) *The Authority of Law, Essays on Law and Morality*, (Oxford, Clarendon Press) p. 211.
10 Fuller, L.L. (1969) *The Morality of Law* (New Haven and London: Yale University Press) pp. 33–38. King Rex wanted to reform his administration of justice, which was expensive, the judges were slow and corrupt, and the language used in court was old-fashioned and clumsy. As a solution, legislator and monarch Rex stipulated that all laws were to be abolished. Thereafter, the administration of justice was based on ad hoc judgments, which in the long run were expected to form a legal praxis that would guide the administration of justice. Judgments could not, however, be generalized in this way without legislation existing in the background, so the reform project was not successful. He decided to make seven other alterations, which all turned out to be failures.

sovereign debt crisis in the EU.[11] All in all, trying to define the rule of law is not merely a waste of time, but instead it seems to be an ever-topical task, which is worth studying from various angles. Having stated my inclination to rely on the 'thick' concept of the rule of law, let us consider how the rule of law can be perceived in EU law.

2   Rule of Law, Judicial Review, Adequate Reasoning and the Independence of the Judiciary

Even before the principle of the rule of law was separately mentioned in the EU Treaty, the European Court of Justice had stated in 1986 in its *Les Verts* judgment that the then European Economic Community is a community of law, because both its Member States and its institutions are under supervision aimed at compatibility between measures implemented by them and the document corresponding to the Constitution, namely the EU Treaty.[12] The *Les Verts* case essentially involved implementation of the requirement for an effective legal remedy in connection with an action for annulment. As a registered political party Les Verts (*parti écologiste*) was a legal person and not just an open category of an indeterminate group of citizens. The applicant had no other alternative remedy. It was held in the judgment that a decision by the European Parliament may be appealed despite the fact that the European Parliament was not mentioned in Article 263 TFEU concerning annulment. Rule-of-law thinking is illustrated by the fact that all acts by EU institutions that produce legal effects are subject to judicial oversight.

In the same tone, the Court of Justice has stressed in its subsequent case law that access to justice forms an element of the rule of law. That is, the right to an effective judicial remedy may play a significant role when it determines *locus standi* in the framework of Article 263 TFEU. However, the right to an effective judicial remedy is not a like trump card that always wins, since procedural prerequisites must be taken into consideration, which is surely not against the rule of law. For example, the former Court of First Instance held the application in the *Greenpeace* case[13] to be inadmissible, since none of the members of the Greenpeace organization in question could claim to have been directly and

---

[11] See Kilpatrick, C. (2015) 'On the Rule of Law and Economic Emergency: The Degradation of Basic Legal Values in Europe's Bailouts' 35:2 *Oxford Journal of Legal Studies* pp. 345–347.
[12] 294/83 Parti écologiste *"Les Verts"* v. *the European Parliament* (1986) ECR 1339, para. 23.
[13] T-585/93 *Greenpeace* (1995) ECR II-2205 and the affirmation of the position adopted in case C-321/95 P, *Greenpeace* (1998) ECR I-1651.

individually concerned as required by Article 263 TFEU. On the other hand, bearing in mind the contemporary political climate as regards protection of the environment and horizontal Article 11 TFEU, one might wonder whether the Court's position would be less restrictive today. In the field of environmental law the requirement of direct and individual concern makes it inherently difficult to provide adequate judicial review against EU actions affecting the environment. In this context it is also relevant to note that the preliminary ruling procedure is not to be used as a substitute for annulment actions based on Article 263 TFEU, although the timeframe of two months is relatively short for initiating proceedings.[14]

The Court of Justice has also underlined that legal decisions must contain adequate reasons so that the addressee of the decision is able to determine whether the decision contains a defect allowing its legality to be challenged.[15] This requirement of adequate reasoning can be linked to the principles of good (sound) administration, legal certainty as well as the rule of law. However, one may enquire whether the reasoning of the Court of Justice is always satisfactory from the perspective of diverse stakeholders or other courts. For example, in the *Ajos* case[16] the Danish Supreme court did not accept the Court's reasoning as regards discrimination on grounds of age in the context of the case. In the *Ajos* case, however, the reasoning of the Court of Justice does not appear to be inadequate.

For me the problem of inadequate reasoning relates to competition law cases in which the level of fines is involved.[17] The Commission's wide-scale discretion in determining competition-related fines came to the fore at the beginning of the millennium, since the likely fines were 1000 euros to 1 million euros in the case of minor infringements and from 1 to 20 million euros in serious infringements on grounds of the then valid guidelines.[18] Such a scale

---

14 *See e.g.* C-188/92 *TWD* (1994) ECR I-833, para. 24.
15 *See e.g.* 69/83 *Lux* (1984) ECR 2447, paras. 32–36.
16 *See* ECJ case C-441/14 *Ajos*, ECLI:EU:C:2016:278 as well as articles Neergaard, U. & Engsig Sørensen, K. (2017) 'Activist Infighting among Courts and Breakdown of Mutual Trust? The Danish Supreme Court, the CJEU, and the Ajos Case' 36 *Yearbook of European Law* pp. 275–313 and Nielsen, R. & Tvarnø, C. (2017) 'Danish Supreme Court Infringes the EU Treaties by Its Ruling in the Ajos Case' *Europarättslig Tidskrift*, 303–326, at p. 303, in which it was stated: "In its judgment in the Ajos-case, the Court of Justice of the European Union (CJEU) upheld its findings in Mangold and Kücükdeveci. The Danish Supreme Court defied the CJEU and did the opposite of what the CJEU had held it was obliged to do".
17 *See e.g.* Raitio, J. (2018), 'Rule of Law, Legal Certainty and Efficiency in EU Competition Law', *Rechtstheorie*, pp. 479–495.
18 *See e.g.* the Guidelines on the method of setting fines imposed pursuant to Article 15(2) of Regulation N:o 17 and Article 65 (5) of the ECSC Treaty, *OJ* C 9, 14.01.1998, p. 3.

offered too much discretion, although it seems that the Court of Justice has taken a different stance on this.[19] It is not at all unusual that the level of competition fines continues to cause legal debate even today, since even the contemporary guidelines are relatively obscure as well.[20] Article 23(4) of Regulation 1/2003 simply imposes a rigid upper limit for fines imposed by the Commission, namely 10 % of the total turnover of the undertaking concerned in the preceding business year. The basic amount of the fine will be related to a proportion of the value of sales, depending on the degree of gravity of the infringement, multiplied by the number of years of infringement.[21] As an example, one can refer to the Commission's so-called tax planning practices in State Aid cases.[22] From the perspective of legal certainty and the principle of proportionality, it is interesting that the EU General Court has lately made competition fines ordered by the Commission more reasonable due to their incorrectly defined subjective gravity, which in turn is related to inadequate reasoning at least to a certain extent.[23]

Judicial review and its relation to the rule of law has therefore been not that clearly stressed in older case law, whereas in more recent case law the connection between judicial review and the rule of law has been expressed clearly in the wording of the reasoning.[24] For example, in *Rosneft* the Court stated as follows:

> It may be added that Article 47 of the Charter, which constitutes a reaffirmation of the principle of effective judicial protection, requires, in its first paragraph, that any person whose rights and freedoms guaranteed by EU law are violated should have the right to an effective remedy before

---

19 See e.g. C-501/11 P, *Schindler*, ECLI:EU:C:2013:522, paras. 58, 59 and 75.
20 Council Regulation (EC) No 1/2003 of 16 December 2002 on the implementation of the rules on competition laid down in Articles 81 and 82 of the Treaty, *OJ L* 1, p. 1 and the Opinion of Advocate-General Wahl in case C-617/17 *Powszechny Zakład Ubezpieczeń na Życie S.A. v. Prezes Urzędu Ochrony Konkurencji i Konsumentów*, ECLI:EU:C:2018:976, paras. 56–57 and the ruling in case C-617/17 *Powszechny Zakład Ubezpieczeń na Życie S.A. v. Prezes Urzędu Ochrony Konkurencji i Konsumentów* ECLI:EU:C:2019:283, paras. 37–39.
21 Guidelines on the method of setting fines imposed pursuant to Article 23(2)(a) of Regulation No 1/2003, para. 19, *OJ C* 210, 1.9.2006, p. 2.
22 Commission decision SA.38375, *FIAT*, Commission decision SA.38374, *Starbucks* and Commission decision SA.38373, *Apple*.
23 See, e.g., T-418/10 *Voelstalpine*, ECLI:EU:T:2015:516 and T-389/10 and T-419/10 *Siderurgina Latina Martin*, ECLI:EU:T:2015:513.
24 C-562/13 *Abdida*, ECLI:EU:C:2014:2453, para. 45, C-362/14 *Schrems*, ECLI:EU:C:2015:650, para. 95 and C-72/15 *Rosneft*, ECLI:EU:C:2017:236, para. 73.

a tribunal in compliance with the conditions laid down in that article. It must be recalled that the very existence of effective judicial review designed to ensure compliance with provisions of EU law is of the essence of the rule of law.[25]

Nowadays, the rule of law is rather often seen in EU law as having material content. This partially explains the fact that the rule of law has begun to be applied as a legal settlement argument in EU courts. As a practical example, the Court has had to take a stance in defence of the rule of law, especially in contexts relating to the impartiality of the courts.[26] To illustrate, in relatively recent case law the Court has stressed the importance of the independence of judicial systems in the following way:

> In that regard, it must be pointed out that the requirement of judicial independence forms part of the essence of the fundamental right to a fair trial, a right which is of cardinal importance as a guarantee that all the rights which individuals derive from EU law will be protected and that the values common to the Member States set out in Article 2 TEU, in particular the value of the rule of law, will be safeguarded.[27]

Thus it is safe to conclude that the existence of effective judicial review is an inseparable part of the rule of law.[28] It is also relevant to point out that the Commission initiated the proceedings specified in Article 7(1) TEU against Poland in December 2017,[29] and the Parliament did the same with Hungary in

---

[25] C-72/15 *Rosneft*, ECLI:EU:C:2017:236, para. 73.

[26] See e.g. case Portuguese judges C-64/16 *Associação Sindical dos Juízes Portugueses v. Tribunal de Contas*, ECLI:EU:C:2018:117, sec. 30, 36 and the issues concerning Poland C-216/18 PPU, *LM*, ECLI:EU:C:2018:586, sec. 48, C-619/18, *Commission v. Poland*, ECLI:EU:C:2018:910, sec. 21, C-619/18 R, *Commission v. Poland*, ECLI:EU:C:2018:1021, C-192/18 *Commission v. Poland*, ECLI:EU:C:2019:924 and in the context of Art. 4(2) TEU in C-715/17 *Commission v. Poland*, ECLI:EU:C:2019:917, paras. 224–227, (Opinion of Advocate General Sharpston delivered on 31 October 2019). Claims relating to the rule of law are pending for Hungary, referring here to cases C-78/18 *Commission v. Hungary*, C-66/18 *Commission v. Hungary* and C-718/17 *Commission v. Hungary*.

[27] C-216/18 PPU, *LM*, ECLI:EU:C:2018:586, para. 48 and C-619/18, *Commission v. Poland*, ECLI:EU:C:2018:910, para. 21.

[28] C-72/15 *Rosneft*, ECLI:EU:C:2017:236, para. 73 and C-64/16 *Associação Sindical dos Juízes Portugueses v. Tribunal de Contas*, ECLI:EU:C:2018:117, para. 36.

[29] Proposal for a Council Decision on the determination of a clear risk of a serious breach by the Republic of Poland of the rule of law, COM (2017) final.

September 2018.[30] In legal literature these Polish and Hungarian developments have recently been labelled as 'illiberal democracy'.[31]

3   The Triangle of Rule of law, Democracy and Human Rights

Another aspect of this discussion based on EU law is the relationship between the rule of law, democracy and human rights. This European 'triangle of values' is not a novelty at all. For example, the following citation from German legal theorist *Radbruch* illustrates:

> Though democracy is certainly a praiseworthy value, the Rechtstaat is like daily bread, the water we drink and the air we breathe; and the greatest merit of democracy is that it alone is adapted to preserve the Rechtstaat.[32]

Somewhat later *Hayek* not only referred to this sentence by Radbruch but also added that democracy will not exist long unless it preserves the rule of law.[33]

As far as the European Union and its values are concerned, it is relevant to point out that observing the rule of law is also a condition for being a member of the European Union. In 1993, the European Council clarified the conditions that countries seeking EU membership must fulfil. In accordance with these so-called Copenhagen criteria, all European countries that adhere to the principles of freedom, democracy, human rights, respect for fundamental freedoms and the rule of law may apply for membership. Today, respecting the principle of the rule of law as a condition for membership is manifested in the Treaty because in accordance with Article 49 TEU a European state that respects and promotes the values defined in Article 2 TEU can apply for

---

30   European Parliament resolution of 12 September 2018 on the proposal calling on the Council to determine, pursuant to Art. 7(1) of the Treaty of European Union, the existence of a clear risk of a serious breach by Hungary of the values on which the Union is founded, 2017/2131 (INL).

31   See e.g. Bugarič, B. (2016) 'Protecting Democracy inside the EU: On Article 7 TEU and the Hungarian Turn to Authoritarianism', in C. Closa and D. Kochenov (eds.), *Reinforcing Rule of Law Oversights in the European Union*, (Cambridge, Cambridge University Press) pp. 82–101.

32   Radbruch, G. (1950) *Rechtsphilosophie* (Stuttgart, K.F. Köhler) p. 357.

33   Hayek, F.A. (1960) *The Constitution of Liberty* (London, Routledge & Kegan Paul) p. 248.

membership of the European Union.[34] It is characteristic of the EU legal concept of the rule of law to include, as does Article 2 TEU,[35] democracy, human rights, equality and the concept of the rule of law as part of the same entity, which is aptly described by the following quote from the *Kadi* case:

> It is also clear from the case-law that respect for human rights is a condition of the lawfulness of Community acts (Opinion 2/94, paragraph 34) and that measures incompatible with respect for human rights are not acceptable in the Community.[36]

Therefore, there are indications in the case law of the Court of Justice that, in its legal context, the concept of the rule of law includes certain material prerequisites for legal decision-making.[37]

In addition, there is reason to highlight the procedure of Article 7 TEU[38] to oversee the integrity of values in accordance with Article 2 TEU from the perspective of EU law and the operating framework of the Commission published in 2014, with which systemic – that is, system-level – threats are tackled in the Member States.[39] From a wider European viewpoint, the framework, for its part, is meant to advance achievement of the goals of the Council of Europe and also take into account the expertise and views of the European Commission for Democracy through Law, the so-called Venice Commission, on the principle of the rule of law. In its report, the Venice Commission lists the following factors included in the concept of the rule of law:

---

34   *See e.g.* C-621/18 *Wightman*, ECLI:EU:C:2018:999, paras. 62–63.
35   Art. 2 TEU: "The Union is founded on the values of respect for human dignity, freedom, democracy, equality, the rule of law and respect for human rights, including the rights of persons belonging to minorities. These values are common to the Member States in a society in which pluralism, non-discrimination, tolerance, justice, solidarity and equality between women and men prevail".
36   C-402/05 P and C-415/05 P, *Kadi and Al Barakaat* (2008) ECR I-6351, para. 284 *and also* correspondingly C-112/00 *Schmidberger* (2003) ECR I-5659, para. 73.
37   *See* 8/55 *Fédéchar* (1955) ECR 292, especially p. 299 and cases related to the concept of rule of law concerning EU law's external liability 5/71 *Schöppenstedt* (1971) ECR 975, 59/72 *Wünsche Handelsgesellschaft* (1973) ECR 791, 20/88 *Roquette frères* (1989) ECR 1553, C-152/88 *Sofrimport* (1989) ECR I-2477, C-104/89 and C-37/90 *Mulder* (1992) ECR I-3061 and C-282/90 *Vreugdenhill* (1992) ECR I-1937.
38   *See, e.g.*, T-337/03 *Bartelli Gálves* v. *The Commission* (2004) ECR II-1041, which concerned the procedure of then Art. 7 EU now Art. 7 TEU.
39   Commission Communication to the European Parliament and Council, 'A new EU operating framework for strengthening the principle of rule of law', COM (2014) 158 final.

- the principle of legality, which refers to transparency, accountability, and the democratic nature and pluralism of the legislative process;
- legal certainty;[40]
- prohibition of arbitrariness of the executive powers;
- access to justice in independent and impartial courts;
- effective judicial review, which includes respect for fundamental and human rights, and
- equality before the law.[41]

The Commission's operating framework and the work of the Venice Commission have not been unimportant, because in January 2016 the Commission began a dialogue with Poland in accordance with the operating framework due to problems related to the position of the Polish Constitutional Court.[42] These elements of the rule of law listed by the Venice Commission were also brought up in the Commission communication dated 3 April 2019.[43]

A fairly unambiguous interpretation can be read from the Communication concerning the operating framework according to which in EU law the rule of law is a constitutional principle formed of factors concerning both form and content.[44] According to the Communication, this means that adhering to the rule-of-law principle is essentially connected to respect for democracy and human rights in such a way that democracy cannot exist and human rights cannot

---

40   *See* an attempt to define legal certainty in *e.g.* Raitio 2003, (*supra* note 3) p. 387: "The principle of legal certainty in EC law relates to the principle of non-retroactivity and the protection of legitimate expectations in particular, but more profoundly it can be related to the conceptual scale for weighing up and balancing between predictability and acceptability, between formal justice and material fairness, in legal decision-making".

41   European Commission for Democracy Through Law (Venice Commission), *Report on the Rule of Law, Adopted by the Venice Commission at its 86th plenary session*, Venice 25–26 March 2011, Strasbourg, 4 April 2011, Study No. 512/2009, CDL-AD (2011)003rev., para. 41.

42   Commission recommendation (EU) 2016/1374, delivered on 27 July 2016, on adhering to the principle of rule of law in Poland, EUVL, No L 217, 12 August 2016, pp. 53–68, (C/2016/5703), which refers to the Venice Commission's definition of the principle of rule of law in section 5 of the Introduction.

43   Communication from the Commission: Further strengthening the rule of law within the European Union, COM (2019) 163 final, pp. 1–2.

44   In support of the interpretation concerning both the formal and material dimension of the concept of rule of law *see, e.g.*, C-50/00 P, *Unión de Pequeños Agricultores* (2002) ECR I-6677, paras. 38 and 39 as well as C-402/05 P and C-415/05 P, *Kadi and Al Barakaat* (2008) ECR I-6351, para. 316. A corresponding policy on the substantive and material dimension of the principle of rule of law is also included in the case law of the European Court of Human Rights, on which see *Stafford v. the United Kingdom*, Judgment of 28 May 2002 (Application no. 46295/99), para. 63.

be respected if the principle of the rule of law is not adhered to.[45] It is also central to state that the trust of EU citizens and national authorities in the realization of the rule of law in other Member States is important, so that the EU can act as a "region of freedom, law and security that does not have internal borders".[46]

This mutual trust among the Member States has also received an especially prominent role in Opinion 2/13 of the Court of Justice of the EU (CJEU).[47] Similarly to the CJEU, with regard to trust among the Member States, we should emphasize that all of the Member States comply with Union law, especially with the fundamental rights recognized in EU law.[48] The concept of the rule of law thus receives interpretive content in EU law only in connection to how democracy and fundamental rights are realized and how the Member States can trust each other's legal systems.

As a counter-argument to this contextual and fairly broad interpretation of the concept of the rule of law we can return to the argument according to which the rule of law is in danger of becoming blurred as a concept and losing some of its expressiveness. Thus if the concept of the rule of law in a European context can be understood in relation to fundamental and human rights and democracy, then what is the content of its meaning and is consideration of a material and formal concept of rule of law a relevant question any longer? My interpretation is that the contextual interpretation of the concept of the rule of law in relation to, for example, fundamental and human rights, does not exclude assessing what elements constitute the rule of law.

4   Mutual Trust or Blind Trust?

The trust of EU citizens and national authorities in the implementation of other Member States' rule of law is important, in order for the EU to achieve its

---

45   *See, e.g.*, Broekman, J.M. (1999) *The Philosophy of European Union Law*, (Leuven, Peeters) p. 205.
46   COM (2014) 158 final, para. 2, "Why the principle of rule of law is decisively important for the EU".
47   Opinion 2/13, Opinion delivered pursuant to Art. 218(11) TFEU on 18 December 2014, not published in the ECR, paras. 168,191,192 and 258. The CJEU held that the planned agreement for the EU to join the European Convention on Human Rights is not in conformity with Art. 6(2) TFEU or Protocol No. 8 EU, because, *e.g.*, it does not prevent the danger that the principle of mutual trust that exists among Member States in EU law could be infringed.
48   *Ibid.*, para. 191.

key objectives and operate as a supranational legal system where the enforcement of EU law is mainly executed by the Member States' authorities.[49] Mutual trust has been seen to be a prerequisite for good governance.[50]

Recently the principle of mutual trust has caused academic debate about what it means and how it can be achieved.[51] According to Opinion 2/13, mutual trust can be associated with the specificities of European Union Law. First of all, EU law is based on an independent source of law formed by framework agreements, which have the status of primacy in relation to the Member States' law.[52] The key characteristics of the Union's law have formed a basis for creation of a network of principles, rules and legal relations which share a mutual dependency, which reciprocally binds the Union itself and its Member States. The European Union is built on the understanding that each Member State shares several mutual values with all the other Member States, as described in TEU Article 2. This starting point of mutually acknowledged values justifies that mutual trust can prevail between Member States. The legal structure as such also includes fundamental rights as they have been recognized in the EU Charter of Fundamental Rights, and which are interpreted in accordance with the Union's structure and objectives.[53]

The citation of Section 191 in Opinion 2/13 summarizes the above-mentioned ideology and also demonstrates the significance of mutual trust as follows:

> In the second place, it should be noted that the principle of mutual trust between the Member States is of fundamental importance in EU law, given that it allows an area without internal borders to be created and maintained. That principle requires, particularly with regard to the area

---

[49] See committee briefing to the European Parliament and Council of Europe, *New EU operational framework for strengthening the rule of law*, COM (2014) 158 final, Sec. 2, "Why is the rule of law of fundamental importance to the EU?".

[50] Cramér, P. (2009), 'Reflections on the Roles of Mutual Trust in EU law', in Dougan, M., Currie, S., (eds.): *50 Years of the European Treaties, Looking Back and Thinking Forward*, (Oxford, Hart Publishing) pp. 43–61.

[51] See e.g. Bieber, R. (2015), '"Gegenseitiges Vertrauen" zwischen den Mitgliedstaaten – ein normatives Prinzip der Europäischen Union?', in Epiney, A., Affolter, S. (hrsg.): *Die Schweiz und die Europäische Integration: 20 Jahre Institut für Europarecht*, Schulthess, pp. 37–55 (Bieber 2015) and Farturova, M. (2016), 'La Coopération Loyale vue sous le Prisme de la Reconnaissance Mutuelle: Quelques Réflexions sur les Fondements de la Construction Européenne', *Cahiers de Droit Européen*, pp. 193–219. The connection between the principle of mutual trust and the principle of sincere cooperation or loyalty is one further argument to justify it.

[52] 6/64 *Costa v. ENEL* (1964) ECR 585.

[53] Opinion 2/13, statement issued under TFEU Art. 218 Sec. 11, issued on 18th December 2014, not published in the ECR, ECLI:EU:C:2014:2454, Secs 166–171.

of freedom, security and justice, each of those States, save in exceptional circumstances, to consider all the other Member States to be complying with EU law and particularly with the fundamental rights recognised by EU law.[54]

In the above cited Section 191 of Opinion 2/13, the CJEU referred to its previous legal praxis, namely the *N.S.* and *Melloni* cases,[55] which is necessary particularly in demonstrating when exceptions can be made to the principle of mutual trust. Lenaerts has had reason to emphasise that mutual trust does not mean 'blind trust', but instead trust must be earned and be based on each Member State complying with the level of human rights protection required by the EU.[56] Paragraph 191 in Opinion 2/13 has also been referenced in legal literature when the need has arisen to emphasize the normative function of mutual trust.[57]

In the *N.S.* case the Court held that a Member State which according to the Dublin II Regulation is responsible for examining applications for asylum is also responsible for observing the fundamental rights of the European Union. Thereafter, the Dublin II Regulation was revoked, and nowadays according to Article 3(2) of the Dublin III Regulation (EU) N:o 604/2013[58] Member States may not transfer asylum seekers to the Member State responsible for processing asylum applications if shortcomings concerning the relevant Member State's asylum procedure and reception conditions are such that the asylum seeker would be treated in an inhumane and degrading manner, as referred to in Article 4 of the Charter of Fundamental Rights of the European Union. On

---

54 *Ibid*, Sec. 191.
55 C-411/10 & C-493/10 *N.S.* (2011) ECR I-13905, paras. 78–80 and C-399/11 *Melloni*, ECLI:EU:C:2013:107, paras. 37 and 63.
56 Lenaerts, K. (2017), 'La vie après l'avis: Exploring the principle of mutual (yet not blind) trust', 54 *Common Market Law Review*, pp. 805–840, at p. 838. Lenaerts emphasises that, in terms of the efficiency of the principle of mutual trust and protection of human rights, it is significant that the European Court of Human Rights, the CJEU and national courts of justice engage in constructive dialogue. On the other hand, both the EU and Member States must prepare trust-enhancing legislation, which maintains this mutual trust.
57 Bieber 2015, *supra* note 51, p. 38.
58 European Parliament and Council Regulation (EU) N:o 604/2013, issued on 26 June 2013, establishing the criteria and mechanisms for determining the Member State responsible for examining an application for international protection lodged in one of the Member States by a third-country national or a stateless person, *OJ L* 180, 29.6.2013, p. 31, esp. p. 41. Originally the so-called Dublin Agreement is in the background of the Dublin system, *i.e.* the Convention determining the State responsible for examining applications for asylum lodged in one of the Member States of the European Communities, *OJ C* 254, 19.8.1997, p. 1.

the other hand, in the *Melloni* case it is essential to recognize that relying on national constitutional laws cannot weaken the influence of EU law in the territory of that Member State. The national level of protection of people's fundamental rights can be applied in Member States, subject to the proviso that such application does not compromise the level of protection confirmed in the Charter of Fundamental Rights, or the primacy, uniformity and efficiency of EU law.[59]

In particular, German literature has demonstrated that rights inferrable from EU citizenship should be interpreted at a wider level as being part of the ensemble of EU human rights, and when EU citizens rely on their rights that are based on EU law, against national law, it is a case of reverse *Solange* doctrine.[60] Originally the *Solange* doctrine referred to a case where the German Constitutional Court, in connection with the *Internationale Handelsgesellschaft* case,[61] considered it was competent to assess the harmony of the economic community's legal regulations in comparison to the fundamental rights protected by the German constitution, to the extent that the integration of the economic community has progressed so far ('solange') as to community law including codification on fundamental and human rights that satisfies German fundamental rights.[62]

The reverse *Solange* doctrine is demonstrated by referring to the *Zambrano* case,[63] where the CJEU dealt with a permit to reside to a minor who had EU citizenship, in the Member State of which the minor had citizenship. In this case, the parents of the child were nationals of a non-member country. According to the CJEU, the position of a Union citizen is so "fundamental" that TFEU Article 20 prevents national procedures as would result in EU citizens not being able to exercise the majority of the rights that they have on the basis of EU citizenship (*genuine enjoyment test*).[64] In the *Zambrano* case, minors

---

59   C-399/11 *Melloni*, the judgment was issued on 26th February, not published in the ECR, ECLI:EU:C:2013:107, Secs 59 and 60.
60   Von Bogdandy – Antpöhler – Ioannidis 2017, *supra* note 6, at pp. 219–220.
61   11/70 *Internationale Handelsgesellschaft* (1970) ECR 1125.
62   See Solange I case *Internationale Handelsgesellschaft mbH* v. *Einfuhr- und Vorratsstelle für Getreide und Futtermittel*, 29 May 1974, (1974) 2 CMLR 540 and respectively 2 BvL 52/71, BVerfGE 37, 271 and Davies, B. (2017) 'Internationale Handelsgesellschaft and the Miscalculation at the Inception of the ECJ's Human Rights Jurisprudence', in Nicola, F., Davies, B. (eds.): *EU Law Stories, Contextual and Critical Histories of European Jurisprudence* (Cambridge, Cambridge University Press) pp. 157–177, at p. 163.
63   C-34/09 *Zambrano* (2011) ECR I-1177.
64   *Ibid.*, Sections 42–44 and C-434/09 *McCarthy* (2011) ECR I-3375, Secs 45–47 and Raitio, J (2016) *Euroopanunionin oikeus*, (Helsinki, Talentumpro), p. 519.

would have had to leave the European Union with their parents if the parents were not issued a residence or work permit. However, no far-reaching conclusions should be drawn on the reverse *Solange* doctrine, since it is connected to rights inferrable from EU citizenship and thus is not applicable to a very extensive ensemble of fundamental and human rights.[65] As such, it does, however, create a worthwhile perspective for the topical academic debate concerning the principle of mutual trust.

From more recent case-law, the *Aranyasi* case is an interesting example of where legal literature has assessed that the principle of mutual trust has regulatory significance as a projection of the values underpinning the area of freedom, security and justice.[66] The CJEU stated, in the context of the European Arrest Warrant, that the principle of mutual recognition is based on the Member States' mutual trust concerning the principle that national legal systems are capable of ensuring equal and efficient protection of their fundamental rights as recognized at a union level and particularly in the Charter of Fundamental Rights.[67] In the way of the CJEU, it is worth emphasising in terms of mutual trust between Member States that all Member States observe Union law, particularly fundamental rights recognized in EU law. Thus, the concept of the rule of law only acquires interpretive content in EU Law in connection with how democracy and fundamental rights are implemented, and how Member States can trust each other's legal systems.

The same requirement of mutual trust between Member States is also indicated in directives concerning the development of an area of freedom, security and justice. This is a question of the efficiency of enforcing EU judicial objectives, standards and decisions in Member States. For example, mutual recognition of decisions in criminal matters can only be efficiently achieved by

---

65 *See also* Von Bogdandy – Antpöhler – Ioannidis 2017, *supra* note 6 p. 220, which states that, as of now, the CJEU has not specifically linked rights inferrable from EU citizenship and human rights as required by the Solange doctrine.
66 Weller, M. (2017) 'Mutual trust within judicial cooperation in civil matters: a normative cornerstone – a factual chimera – a constitutional challenge', *Nederlands internationaal privaatrecht*, pp. 1–21.
67 C-404/15 & C-659/15 PPU, *Aranyosi*, ECLI:EU:C:2016:198, Sec. 77. It is to be mentioned that, in his lecture at the highest administrative court on 24 May 2017, CJEU President Lenaerts particularly emphasized the link between Sec. 191 of Opinion 2/13 and *e.g.* the *Aranyosi* case in the interpretation of the concept concerning mutual trust between Member States. This is also natural since Sec. 191 of Opinion 2/13 is cited in Para. 78 of *Aranyosi*.

relying on mutual trust. Both judicial authorities and other parties involved in the criminal process must be able to consider the decisions of other Member States' judicial authorities as equal to decisions in their own country.[68] It is also a case of trust in that another Member State should apply these key legal guarantees correctly, that is, observation must not simply be allowed to remain at the level of comparison of provisions. Strengthening mutual trust is subject to detailed provisions on the protection of procedural rights and warranties as defined[69] in the Charter of Fundamental Rights, the European Convention on Human Rights and the ICCPR.[70] In this respect, it is essential that a value base in accordance with Article 2 TEU is achieved in each Member State.

5 Conclusions

My intention has been to advocate a 'triangle of EU values', namely the rule of law, democracy and human rights. In this respect, there is reason to refer to the Venice Commission's report concerning the rule of law,[71] wherein the rule of law is strongly connected to democracy and the requirement of implementation of human rights. The discourse concerning the rule of law in the EU cannot, therefore, be separated from the democracy that creates an environment for interpretation of the rule of law, distribution of power and the legal principles and human rights that legitimize the judicial system. In this context, the principle of the rule of law is not merely a 'rhetorical balloon'. The concept of the rule of law becomes a type of value-based ideal, according to which the development of societies is measured.[72] In terms of this article, it is essential that the existence of the material concept of the rule of law has not been

---

68 Directive of the European Parliament and of the Council 2012/13/EU issued on 22 May 2012 on the right to information in criminal proceedings, OJ L 142, 1.6.2012, pp. 1–10, Introduction Sec. 4.
69 International Covenant on Civil and Political Rights, 8/1976.
70 Directive of the European Parliament and of the Council 2013/48/EU issued on 22 October 2013, the right to be assisted in criminal proceeding and in proceedings concerning the European Arrest Warrant as well as the right for their arrest or detention to be reported a third party and to be in contact with third parties and consular authorities during arrest or detention, OJ L 294, 6.11.2013, pp. 1–12, Introduction Sec. 9.
71 European Commission for Democracy Through Law (Venice Commission), Report on the Rule of Law, Adopted by the Venice Commission at its 86th plenary session, Venice 25–26 March 2011, Strasbourg, 4 April 2011, Study No. 512/2009, CDL-AD(2011)003rev.
72 McCorquodale 2016, *supra* note 5, pp. 284–285.

denied when recent legal literature has focused on the tensions between the formal and material concept of the rule of law.[73]

---

[73] Konstadinides, T. (2017) *The Rule of Law in the European Union*, (Oxford: Hart Publishing). pp. 55–61, where Konstadinides specifies the Rule of Law with the help of the pair of concepts: 'thin/thick Rule of Law'.

The Impact of Digital Autonomous Tools on Private Autonomy

*Thomas Hoffmann**

Abstract

Digitalisation had started to interfere with private autonomy long before digital tools became autonomous, but they influenced form rather than content. Digital autonomous tools, however, reach to the core of private autonomy – the right to shape one's legal environment of one's own accord. Just as with data, people tend to waive this right out of convenience when tempted by useful autonomous devices available. And just as the GDPR reacted to this phenomenon by establishing privacy-by-design requirements, the need for respective protection mechanisms for private autonomy may be arising as well. This paper analyses the impact of digital autonomous tools on private autonomy and aims to point out gaps in protection as well as possible measures to alleviate these shortcomings.

Keywords

private autonomy – digital autonomous tools/autonomous digital tools – software agents – algorithm-based decision making – GDPR – privacy by design

1   Introduction

In Estonian mythology, a Kratt is a magical creature made from hay and household items. Upon delivering three drops of blood to the devil, the devil would bring the Kratt to life, and the Kratt would from then on serve its creator by following all orders the master gave it. Anyhow, the Kratt has to be kept permanently busy, as otherwise it would turn on its master and kill him. Charging the Kratt with impossible tasks (like carrying water in a sieve) could prevent this outcome – and even lead to the self-destruction of the Kratt, as it would eventually catch fire once overworked.

---

* Dr.iur., LL.M., Professor of Private Law at the Tallinn Law School, Tallinn University of Technology.

Drawing wise parallels between the Kratt and Artificial Intelligence, "Kratt" is also the name of a cross-sectoral project[1] launched in 2018 by the Estonian Government Office and the Ministry of Economic Affairs and Communications aiming to analyse and prepare for implementation of fully autonomous information systems; this label refers to the expert group and their strategy as well.

The mythological Kratt was provided with autonomy – even to a deadly extent. This paper will not discuss whether autonomous legal tools based on algorithm-based decision-making should be simultaneously treated as autonomous actors or even bearers of proper rights, even though such classifications are no longer as far-fetched as they appeared from a traditional legal perspective – as demonstrated by a motion brought by the European Parliament in 2017, which raised the issue of introducing an electronic personality.[2]

But even without proper capacity as legal entities, today's autonomous decision-making tools already represent a considerable challenge to the legal order. Returning to the same Motion – specifically to point 12 of its *General principles concerning the development of robotics and artificial intelligence for civil use*, stating that "it must always be possible to reduce the AI system's computations to a form comprehensible by humans" – some autonomous legal tools even today hardly comply with those minimum standards, taking for example into consideration that Black Box architectures in deep learning ensembles contradict fulfilment of the above-mentioned requirement by their nature.

This paper provides an overview on interference by digital tools with private autonomy, before focusing on the impact of *autonomous* digital tools on private autonomy, especially on those used for digital transactions. In this context, their impact is juxtaposed to their effects on privacy protection, whereas violation of privacy (as outlawed for example by the EU GDPR[3]) is to this end not perceived as a special form of violation of general private autonomy interests: Privacy may in general "protect the individual interest in autonomy because it carves out a space around individuals in which they can direct their

---

1 Artificial Intelligence for Estonia <https://www.kratid.ee/in-english>, visited 13 April 2020. Within this expert group, Tallinn Law School together with attorney-at-law Jaanus Tehver headed the legal workgroup, and the expert group completed its work in April 2019.
2 Motion for a EU parliament resolution with recommendations to the Commission on Civil Law Rules on Robotics, 2015/2103(INL).
3 Reg. (EU) 2016/679 of the European Parliament and of the Council of 27 April 2016 on the protection of natural persons with regard to the processing of personal data and on the free movement of such data, and repealing Directive 95/46/EC (General Data Protection Regulation).

lives".[4] However, this paper focuses on private autonomy in contract law only. In private law terms, a privacy violation results in a violation of the *integrity* interest of the data subject, while violation of private autonomy in contract law is a violation of the *security* and *transparency* interest of the user of an autonomous digital tool.

2   The Impact of Digital Tools on Private Autonomy in General

The general impact of digital tools on private autonomy was already considerable before the advent of algorithm-based decision-making.[5]

2.1   *Search Engines as Gatekeepers*
Private autonomy requires a minimum scope of choices in order to compose specific contract content. While theoretically this autonomy is even maximized by the abundance of choices provided in online commerce, actual access to these options is considerably controlled and restricted by search engines, which in the Western world usually means Google.[6] Even though the user defines the search criteria and will ultimately choose the object/service to be contracted with, she does so from a limited range of offers composed by the search engine at its discretion (in practice, the first pages of the hit list provided by the search engine). In general, she is not aware of other options which may suit her interests better – and thus cannot access the offers of providers of goods or services in case she is not satisfied with the spectrum of offers presented to her. The search engine works as a gatekeeper.[7]

2.2   *Standard Business Terms as Standard for Online Transactions*
Once the user has decided in favour of a certain product/service offered online, options for any form of individual negotiations of specific contract

---

4   D. Mokrosinska, 'Privacy and Autonomy: On Some Misconceptions Concerning the Political Dimensions of Privacy', 37 *Law and Philos* (2018) pp. 117–143), at p. 118, <https://doi.org/10.1007/s10982-017-9307-3>.
5   For a comprehensive synopsis *see* J. Grapentin, 'Die Erosion der Vertragsgestaltungsmacht durch das Internet und den Einsatz Künstlicher Intelligenz', *Neue Juristische Wochenschrift* (2019) p. 181.
6   Immanent conflicts with competition law have been analyzed already in 2006 by S. Ott, 'Ich will hier rein! Suchmaschinen und das Kartellrecht', *Multimedia und Recht* (2006) p. 195. For the Chinese Baidu see T. Hoffmann, Zh. Wang, 'Enforcing Chinese Antimonopoly Law in the Internet Industry: An Analysis with Special References to Baidu.com', 2 (2) *China and WTO Review* (2016) pp. 223–256.
7   Ott, *supra* note 6, p. 195.

contents are scarce to non-existent, caused by the relative anonymity of the user (no option for personal/individual influence on contract term composition) and the sheer number of transactions.[8] Standard business terms are the standard design for agreements concluded for online sales and services, restricting any viable practice of private autonomy of the paying party in this aspect as well.

2.3 ADR as Standard for Online Transactions

Additionally, Fries recently pointed out[9] that the parties increasingly distance themselves from applicable national law and create their own regulatory regime. In case of conflict between provider and customer, it often amounts to a discretionary decision by the company's responsible employee (Fries uses PayPal as an example) to decide whether the legal grounds of previously unilaterally – that is, in the General Terms and Conditions – granted remedies have been fulfilled. It becomes irrelevant whether under national law for instance the legal requirements for the right of withdrawal, material defects or transfer of risk are given, even if these rights – or rights following from the fulfilment of these criteria – were not formally waived by the client.

Once the client does not agree with the company's legal interpretation of the conflict – for example, not recognizing the right of withdrawal – judicial control of this decision tends to be increasingly privatized as well, as the General Terms and Conditions usually include an arbitration clause, shielding the client not only from substantive but procedural national law as well. Again, many clients are not aware whether – and how much – their interests are less protected in private dispute resolution compared to state court procedures.

2.4 Provision of Digital Tools by the State and Other Public Bodies

Digital tools facilitating transactions among private persons (such as the digital signature) generate considerable synergies, safe human and economic resources and are in many cases more secure than traditional tools. In any case, as many tools require prior formalization of content, private autonomy can either be restricted in terms of content – as the document to be signed provides only certain options to be chosen from – or in terms of access to the tool, if for exampe certain software or hardware is required for digital signatures. Even though a manual signature is always available as an alternative to this tool, a factual restriction arises in legal environments where the electronic

---

8   Grapentin, *supra* note 5, p. 182.
9   M. Fries, 'PayPal Law und Legal Tech – Was macht die Digitalisierung mit dem Privatrecht?', *Neue Juristische Wochenschrift* (2016), p. 2860.

signature has already achieved the status of a general standard, such as in Estonian legal practice.[10]

3 Autonomous Legal Tools and their Impact on Declarations of Intent

The most essential impact on private autonomy derives from the use of any tools which directly interfere with or even autonomously generate declarations of intent on behalf of the user.

The interpretation of declarations of intent in online sales was already controversial before the advent of software agents, smart contracts, AI and the like, as illustrated by case BGHZ 195, 126[11] of the German Federal Court of Justice (BGH, *Bundesgerichtshof*), where no contract had been concluded between an airline company and a client who had left the name of the passenger blank while booking a flight and claimed the right to assign the flight to a person specified only later (which was then declined by the airline, arguing that no consent had been reached even though the system had confirmed the previous unnamed booking). The court argued that even though the human individual on the buyer's side knows that a computer program will interpret a declaration of intent, the declaration would have to be interpreted as if the "represented" airline company board of directors itself – hence, not a computer program – would have read this declaration, and who obviously would not have accepted the offer to buy a flight which did not yet specify any name.

3.1 *Smart Contracts*

Once issues of interpretation have been settled, the parties have to decide about a form for their agreement. This can be a simple exchange of declarations via online interfaces or, if self-execution is feasible digitally and of interest to the parties, also via a "smart contract",[12] a software-based log of actions which may have legal significance (in that case, it protocols a declaration of

---

10 T. Hoffmann, 'Schutz oder Beschränkung der Privatautonomie durch den digitalen Staat: Überlegungen am estnischen Beispiel', Conference proceedings to *Privatautonomie als grundlegendes Prinzip des Zivilrechts*, Tbilisi, 1.-2.11.2018, edited by GIZ (in publishing procedure).

11 H. Sutschet, 'Anforderungen an die Rechtsgeschäftslehre im Internet', *Neue Juristische Wochenschrift* (2014), pp. 1041–1047.

12 On the concept from a legal perspective in general *see* M. Giancaspro, 'Is a 'smart contract' really a smart idea? Insights from a legal perspective', 33 *Computer Law & Security Review* (2018), pp. 825–835.

intent) and which – if respectively programmed – effectuates an additional transaction.[13]

3.1.1 Contract Content

In terms of private autonomy, there is less interference by smart contracts on the content of declarations of intent as such, but rather by the inherent features of the blockchain architecture:[14] First of all, legal effects triggered by undetermined legal terms depend largely on the choice, 'calibration' and control of the respective oracle which feeds the triggering data into the smart contract. While a term such as 'within a reasonable time' is a standard undetermined legal term so far causing little controversy in terms of its interpretation, it requires a clear ex-ante specification and coherent implementation into the respective oracle when used as a criterion within a smart contract, and this specification will usually not be made by the user, but rather by the software engineer creating the respective smart contract.

Private autonomy is even more reduced by the emerging possibility to compose a proper smart contract by smart contract tools or modules provided free or for a fee in open-source code libraries, as determining the content of these modules is also done by the software engineer who wrote the module code. As with anything provided ready-made and in this case often for free, such modules will probably enjoy huge popularity among users having access to these libraries, and the *automation bias* will provide solid general trust in terms of the objectivity, lawfulness and appropriateness of these modules for the specific user's purposes.

Taking into account that few software engineers provide these modules for solely altruistic motives – even if made accessible as freeware – control over the content of these modules accumulates with those who employ and thus instruct the engineers and/or who control these code libraries and their content, and these usually will not be consumers. Indeed, smart contract code libraries may soon serve to protect corporate interests just as standard business terms do today already – but this time extended by their automatic execution. Due to the blockchain's pseudonymity, a smart contract by design does not foresee any measures to protect weaker parties such as consumers or minors,

---

13   T. Hoffmann, 'Smart Contracts and Void Declarations of Intent', in: C. Cappiello, M. Ruiz Carmona (eds.), *Information Systems Engineering in Responsible Information Systems*, 350 Lecture Notes in Business Information Processing (Heidelberg: Springer International Publishing) p. 174.
14   For a comprehensive overview *see* P. De Filippi, A. Wright, *Blockchain and the Law. The Rule of Code* (Harvard University Press, Cambridge/Massachusetts, 2018) pp. 72–88.

and even if in the latter case a contract concluded with a minor is – absent consent by the legal representatives – both a violation of the interests of the weaker party as well as even void, the automatic execution of the company's alleged claim via a smart contract makes this major flaw irrelevant in practice. Litigation endeavours by the minor (or any other weaker party who sees her rights violated) against execution or for return of any assets transferred via the smart contract is made virtually impossible by the pseudonomity of the other party.

Private autonomy is beyond that affected by the impossibility of adapting to change of circumstances once a smart contract has been activated – even if intended by both parties.

3.1.2 Contract Execution

As pointed out in detail by Levy, a far broader range of preferred actions can be taken by contract parties than ultimate performance of contractual duties, as contracts may serve as well as an indirect – but even more efficient – means of shaping or specifying legal relations between the parties by for example including *prima facie* unenforceable terms, by inserting purposefully underspecified terms into contracts or by willfully not enforcing enforceable terms.[15] A creditor may for example have a personal or even economic interest in not insisting on immediate performance by a long-time customer, as the customer's financial constraints may be only temporary, or as the economic value of the goodwill established over the years between the parties may be higher than the value of the performance owed.

While the general features of the digital ecosystem erode private autonomy mainly in terms of the choice of contract partners and contract contents, smart contracts expand this trend to the attitude towards non-performance of contractual duties. Although performance of these duties presumably seems to be the core interest of the parties, private autonomy also includes the option to not to perform a contract – for various legitimate reasons.

3.2 *Software Agents*

The term *software agent* partly overlaps with *intelligent-* or *autonomous agent*, but all terms refer to a computer program which is able to generate autonomous – namely, not user-determined – declarations of intent on behalf of the user on the basis of algorithms and/or other data input. In the framework of this paper, these are called *autonomous digital tools*. In contrast to

---

15   K. Levy, "Book-Smart, Not Street-Smart: Blockchain-Based Smart Contracts and the Social Workings of Law", 3 *Engaging Science, Technology, and Society* (2017) pp. 1–15.

mere computer declarations (as illustrated in the airline company case), the *essentialia negotii* are exclusively determined by the software itself, meaning that the software is able to activate/de-activate itself without any interaction with the user and to invoke tasks including contract content determination.

3.2.1 Contract Bots

If autonomous digital tools are used for contract conclusion, they do not simply calculate the outcome of criteria – defined in advance by the user – applied to certain data fed to the system, but they develop the respective decision autonomously (contract bots). An example of a simple calculation resulting in a traditional computer declaration would be a program autonomously buying the cheapest flight over a certain distance offered on a specific online marketplace during a specific period of time, while a task performed by a software agent – provided for example with the user's essential real-time health data via a portable wrist device – would be to buy 'any food that is good for the user today', or in a corporate environment to manage import/export with the sole aim of maximizing annual profit.

While none of these situations would, if performed by a human instead, in legal terms see the human as a mere messenger, but as a representative (also the choice of the cheapest flight offer requires a certain degree of autonomy, which a messenger does not have), it can still be argued whether the program in the first situation should not be seen as making a decision deduced clearly from objective criteria set in advance by the user, even if the outcome was not foreseeable when the task was given. It is also true that in general a person can be held accountable for legally significant actions which explicitly cannot be influenced/controlled by her – a person can throw dice, for instance, announcing beforehand that certain scores signify certain declarations of intent (for example, to buy an equivalent number of drinks for friends in a bar) – but in many legal systems gaming and betting contracts are not binding unless licensed, and additionally the range of options (and risks) is in all these imaginable cases clearly limited and as such much more comparable to the first case: They all boil down to essential contract content having been defined by the user beforehand and are thus not autonomous decisions taken by the system.

3.2.2 Deep Learning Ensembles

While this autonomous determination is technically practiced today already, the degree of autonomy is increasing considerably by the use of deep-learning ensembles. Deep learning operates in dimensions far more complex than the human mind is able to discern, rendering it impossible for a human observer to deduce exactly how the algorithm's heuristics lead to any decision or measure taken by the system. This *black box*, where the respective measure evolved works technically the same as neurons in the human brain, where merely design and interaction between individual neurons can be observed and described, while the exact logical steps depicting the exact method of decision-making are obscured. This is especially the case in *multi-agent-systems* where various *black boxes* interact with each other.

Even if deep-learning ensembles are at present rather used for decision-making in complex management systems such as those found in port logistics,[16] the complexity of online commerce and the speed and efficiency of these ensembles predestine them equally for contractual purposes – at least beyond the EU, where at present articles 13 II (f) and 14 II (g) GDPR entitle the data subject to be provided with and be granted access to (article 15 I (h) GDPR) personal data on "the existence of automated decision-making (…) and (…) *meaningful information* about the logic involved, as well as the significance and the envisaged consequences of such processing for the data subject",[17] whereas providing this *meaningful information* about the logic involved is by design severely hindered (if not impeded altogether) by any form of *black box*-decision-making.

3.2.3   Legal Qualification

The choice of foodstuff in the second case – and even less any decisions made in black box systems – can also in a broad interpretation no longer be considered as a declaration composed by a human making use of an algorithm; they clearly depict situations which under traditional private law concepts are regulated via agency. Applying agency instruments (directly or by analogy) to these declarations would, however, imply that the software is considered to be the author of the declaration of intent in the form of an *e-person* or other form of legal entity[18] (which is beyond the scope of the EP motion mentioned above

---

16   Deep learning ensembles are used in proactive process adaptation *e.g.* in the process management system of *Duisport* in Duisburg/Germany, the world's largest river port. For details *see* A. *Metzger*, A. Neubauer, P. Bohn, K. Pohl, 'Proactive Process Adaptation using Deep Learning Ensembles', in P. Giorgini, B. Weber (eds), *31st Int'l Conference on Advanced Information Systems Engineering (CAiSE 2019)*, Rome, Italy, June 3–7, LNCS vol. 11483, Springer 2019.
17   Supra note 3.
18   L. Specht, S. Herold, 'Roboter als Vertragspartner? Gedanken zu Vertragsabschlüssen unter Einbeziehung automatisiert und autonom agierender Systeme', *Multimedia und Recht* (2018) pp. 40–44.

and has not found much support among lawyers so far),[19] which would provide a wide range of problems in terms of liability for these entities or, if they are held liable themselves, in terms of their funding. The alternative to the agency model is to consider activating a software agent to perform certain transactions as a blank declaration of intent, which is filled with content by the software agent, which beyond that does not legally become visible.

Either way, both approaches have in common that the user's private autonomy is outsourced, while the degree of this waiver of autonomy depends on knowledge about the waiver as such and/or the technical possibilities to access information on the exact degree of waiver of autonomy.

In this context, it has to be pointed out that an actual violation of the private autonomy of a party – for example, making the party conclude a contract with content/and or under conditions she does not know about – in principle leads to mistake and thus primarily avoidability of declarations of intent issued on behalf of the user, even though national law differs considerably on the reasons for avoidance; Zimmermann summarizes "the will-theoretical model of most continental European countries, according to which a contract should be based upon the real intentions of the contracting parties, stands in contrast to the significantly more contract-friendly conceptions of the common law, Austrian law and the Scandinavian legal systems".[20]

The erosion of private autonomy which this paper focuses on refers less to these constellations where a contract party has 'dragged' the user against or without her intent into a legal relationship (which would make the declaration of intent avoidable), but – parallel to personal data disclosed to controllers via 'consent'-box clicks on interfaces – where the user has initially agreed to (yet unknown) contract content or conditions, either by activating the autonomous legal tool altogether (which usually includes consent to the terms and conditions) or by granting further consent within the course of its operation. In other words, it focuses on that scope of extending (or, economically speaking, outsourcing) private autonomy which among humans is archived via granting authority to a representative.

---

19   M. Heckelmann, 'Zulässigkeit und Handhabung von Smart Contract', *Neue Juristische Wochenschrift* (2018) pp. 505–510.
20   N. Jansen, R. Zimmermann, 'Contract Formation and Mistake in European Contract Law', 31 (4) *Oxford Journal of Legal Studies* (2011) pp. 625–662.

4 The Private Autonomy Paradox

Those cases where not the contract content itself but waived rights are involved (such as acceptance of standard business terms or ADR clauses) are very similar to disclosure of personal data in terms of procedure and awareness of the providing/waiving party. This also includes the aspect that people in many cases disclose their data as a 'collateral loss' which they sacrifice as they are interested in accessing information, goods or services they value more than their data, virtually having no other choice than making the requested clicks on the respective boxes on the company's interface, which is the same case with various rights waived by the user in online commerce or by autonomous legal tools in general.

The 'privacy paradox' in data protection, which addresses the phenomenon that people consistently indicate that they value their privacy but simultaneously disclose their private data comprehensively and for free, applies in terms of private autonomy just as well;[21] few people would be ready to admit that they would charge roboters to decide about their daily needs, but an increasing number do.

4.1 *Comparison with Personal Data Protection Mechanisms*

The EU addressed the data protection privacy paradox in the GDPR, which introduces in its article 25 the principle of *privacy by design* as a general concept, claiming that the "controller shall implement appropriate technical measures for ensuring that, *by default*, only personal data which are necessary for each specific purpose of the processing are processed". The GDPR thus protects all personal outbound data of the data subject by demanding technical measures to reduce disclosure of these data to the necessary minimum, protecting the *data security* (i.e. that personal data is not accessed by others) and *integrity* (i.e. that data is not manipulated) of the data subject.

Protecting the private autonomy of weaker parties has been established for decades in the form of laws establishing extensive information duties, for example towards consumers, compensating for the information disparity between the parties, even though many of these mechanisms have had little effect in online commerce.[22]

---

21 K.P. Berger, 'Institutional arbitration: harmony, disharmony, and the 'Party Autonomy Paradox', 34 *Arbitration International*, (2018), pp. 473–493, https://doi: 10.1093/arbint/aiy028.

22 N. Helberger, M. Loos, C. Mak, L. Pressers, 'Digital content contracts for consumers', 36(1) *Journal of Consumer Policy* (2013) pp. 37–57.

The maintenance of this traditional information disparity is partly facilitated by digital tools, as in the given example of waiving substantive or procedural rights by clicking on the respective boxes which signify acceptance of standard business terms and/or ADR clauses. Making use of *autonomous* digital tools, however, contributes to an information disparity not (primarily) between consumers and entrepreneurs, but between any user of an autonomous tool and the creator of the tool, or – in case of those black box architectures where the exact deduction of the decision remains also obscured to the software engineer creating/maintaining the program – the program itself. It is thus not only the private autonomy of weaker parties that may be in need of protection but the *transparency interest* of any party to a legal transaction.

4.2   Another Form of Knowledge Disparity

In contrast to the traditional knowledge disparity between consumers and entrepreneurs and to personal data protection issues, this disparity is not due to the lack of resources of the less informed party. A consumer may accept detrimental standard business terms mainly because she does not have the resources to maintain a legal department comparing the conditions of the terms with her rights established by national law. But a resourceful entrepreneur will also have essential difficulties in verifying which filters have been employed by search engines, depriving her of more favourable offers – or which criteria have been used in algorithm-based decisions affecting the company.

An information duty on the use of algorithm-based decisions has been established by the GDPR in the above-mentioned articles 13 and 14, but it does so solely in the context of data integrity interest protection of natural persons, that is, for data subjects in terms of article 4 I EU GDPR, and to the extent defined in article 22 GDPR. Beyond that, articles 13 II (f) and 14 II (g) EU GDPR only constitute an information duty towards the data subject on the facts *that* algorithm-based decisions are made and meaningful information on *how* they are made; they do not claim the establishment of any technical implementation measures, as does the privacy by design-concept in article 25 EU GDPR.

5   Private Autonomy by Design?

An imperative modelled after the privacy by design-concept of article 25 EU GDPR could prove to be a viable measure addressing this knowledge disparity. An option would be to demand technical measures providing unrestricted access to regularly updated information on exact and exhaustive details on all legal relationships generated by an autonomous legal tool on behalf of the user, including the exact causes which lead to them or will presumably lead to them in future.

5.1 *Extended Information Duties?*

But other than the privacy-by-default concept, which restricts the data flow between the data subject and the controller, such measures would rather further increase the amount of information addressing the user of an autonomous digital tool, who in practice is already overwhelmed by excessive information provided to her in standard business terms or as a consequence of consumer information duties performed by entrepreneurs. The effect could even be adverse if even more small-print and interface boxes to be clicked would drive users to providers applying attractive UX design, which may be smart and simple, but incomplete in terms of providing transparency.

5.2 *Certificates?*

A simpler and thus more user-friendly approach could be to grant certificates to autonomous tools which by design take the transparency interests of the user sufficiently into account. Certificates could be issued by state authorities equipped with experts in the field and expire after a certain period, similar to technical inspection authorities for vehicles. Establishing a general certificate was also proposed by the "study on the human rights dimensions of automated data processing techniques and possible regulatory implications" by the European Council of 2018, which suggests in point five of its concluding recommendations that "certification and auditing mechanisms for automated data processing techniques such as algorithms should be developed to ensure their compliance with human rights. Public entities and non-state actors should encourage and promote the further development of human rights by design and ethical-by-design approaches and the adoption of stronger risk-assessment approaches in the development of software".[23]

6 Conclusion

Digital tools had started interfering with private autonomy long before they became autonomous. The programming of search engines as gatekeepers, the

---

[23] European Council, Study on the human rights dimensions of automated data processing techniques and possible regulatory implications (2018) p. 45 <https://edoc.coe.int/en/internet/7589-algorithms-and-human-rights-study-on-the-human-rights-dimensions-of-automated-data-processing-techniques-and-possible-regulatory-implications.html#> visited 13 April 2020.

virtual impossibility to negotiate individual contract details by the consumer in online commerce and the standard inclusion of ADR clauses in business terms have restricted mainly consumer private autonomy by digital means. Interference by the very nature of novel digital tools first arose with computer declarations, resulting in interpretation horizon disambiguities, and even more with the advent of smart contracts, which by their nature considerably reduce private autonomy to choosing whether and how to perform or require performance of contractual duties.

Autonomous legal tools generate declarations of intent autonomously on behalf of the user to the same degree as a human agent acts on behalf of the persons represented, but as these tools are not legal entities themselves, the law on agency cannot be applied to resolve potential conflicts. Even though this partial distribution of private autonomy to these software agents can considerably affect the legal relations and rights of a user – and even though many users, if asked explicitly, would protest against being partially governed by robots – users tend to make ample use of the convenience offered by autonomous legal tools.

This private autonomy paradox resembles (except that it refers to both private and corporate users) the privacy paradox in personal data protection, which has been addressed by the EU GDPR, there especially by the privacy by design-principle in article 25 GDPR, which requires controllers to establish appropriate technical measures ensuring that only necessary data is obtained in the first place.

Whether a similar private autonomy-by-design principle would be necessary and – if so – technically feasible depends essentially on the scope of protection that private autonomy requires in these constellations, whereas it has to be taken into account that private autonomy includes the right to waive it. In terms of potential protection measures, it should be taken into account that complex paternalistic approaches may even more induce the choice of simple default company settings, leading to adverse effects. Certificates granted to verified autonomous digital tools by state agencies upon successful analysis of embedded transparency could prove useful, but would require a clear definition of both an autonomous digital tool itself as well as of specific criteria subject to investigation, which at present are not yet established.

Powerful Private Players in the Digital Economy: Between Private Law Freedoms and the Constitutional Principle of Equality

Peter Rott*

Abstract

The digital economy has been driven by countless start-up companies but also by extremely powerful players such as Facebook, Twitter, Google, Amazon, or Paypal. They have not only accumulated a significant if not dominant position in their relevant markets but they have also gained enormous relevance for the economic and social relationships of individual citizens or consumers, and even traders and politicians. At the same time, citizens are at risk of being denied access to their services, or of having to pay individualized prices, due to their personal circumstances or their shopping or credit history. This article shows that traditional concepts of contract law and also data protection law offer little help to these citizens. It therefore explores the application of the fundamental right to equality to powerful digital players and the legal consequences of such application, including the right not to be subjected to arbitrariness and the right to be given reasons for decisions.

Keywords

digitalization – social media – scoring – personalized pricing – freedom of contract – automated decision-making – right to equality

1   Introduction[1]

The digital economy has been driven by countless start-up companies but also by extremely powerful players such as Facebook, Twitter, Google, Amazon, or

---

*   Prof. Dr., University of Kassel.
[1] This article is partly based on previous work, in particular P. Rott, 'A Consumer Perspective on Algorithms', in L. de Almeida, M. Cantero Gamito, M. Durovic and K.P. Purnhagen (eds.), *The Transformation of Economic Law* (Hart Publishing, Oxford, 2019) pp. 43 ff., and P. Rott, 'Dynamische und personalisierte Preise zwischen Vertragsfreiheit und Willkür', in: J. Lamla, T. Hess, C. Ochs and M. Friedewald (eds.), *Die Zukunft der Datenökonomie* (Springer, Wiesbaden, 2019) pp. 285 ff.

Paypal, to name but a few. They have not only accumulated a significant if not dominant position in their relevant markets but they have also gained enormous relevance for the economic and social relationships of individual citizens or consumers, and even traders and politicians. For example, individuals may lose their Facebook 'friends' or their Twitter contacts and their visibility for these contacts if they are excluded from Facebook or Twitter. Likewise, they may lose visibility for the community if they cannot be found on Google (any more). Their access to goods and services may be impeded if they are blocked by Amazon or if they cannot use PayPal as a payment service provider. Or they may face different treatment than other consumers due to their personal situation, for example, due to their credit history, amounting in particular to higher prices or unfavourable payment conditions.

As will be shown in the first part of this article, current private law is of little use to remedy this situation, as it treats these powerful players as 'normal' private parties that enjoy the freedoms of private law, in particular, freedom of contract (2.1. and 2.2.). Data protection law is similarly unhelpful (2.3.). Therefore, in its second part, this article explores whether and to what extent constitutional law, and in particular the constitutional principle of equality, applies to such powerful players (3.). The analysis takes its starting point in the case law of the German *Bundesverfassungsgericht* (Federal Constitutional Court; FCC) and then moves on to the situation under the Charter of Fundamental Rights of the European Union as interpreted by the Court of Justice. The article concludes that powerful digital players have to comply with the principle of equality, and that this comes with procedural rights, in particular the right to be given reasons for a decision. Finally, it offers some reflections on a special legal framework for powerful digital players.

2 The Private Law Perspective: Freedom of Contract

2.1 *The Principle*

As a starting point, private law serves to guarantee private autonomy, one emanation of which is freedom of contract. In the German constitution[2] as well as under EU law in general[3] and under Article 16 of the Charter of Fundamental

---

[2] Freedom of contract is guaranteed by Art. 2 para. 1 *Grundgesetz* (Basic Law; GG).
[3] See ECJ, 16 January 1979, Case 151/78 *Sukkerfabriken Nykøbing Limiteret v. Ministry of Agriculture*, ECLI:EU:C:1979:4, at para. 20; ECJ, 5 October 1999, Case C-240/97 *Spain v. Commission*, ECLI:EU:C:1999:479, at para. 99. It was pointed out, however, that freedom of contract was weaker in European private law than in national private laws, see B. Heiderhoff, 'Vertrauen versus Vertragsfreiheit im europäischen Verbrauchervertragsrecht', 21 *Zeitschrift für Europäisches Privatrecht* (2003) pp. 769 ff.

Rights in particular,[4] freedom of contract is even a fundamental right; although freedom of contract may of course be limited so as to balance it with competing fundamental rights and with the public interest.[5]

Freedom of contract includes not only the guarantee, vis-à-vis the State, to regulate one's own affairs by means of concluding contracts with other individuals, but also the right to choose who to do business with[6] or, in a negative sense, the freedom not to conclude a contract with another individual if one does not want to, for whatever reason.[7]

Moreover, freedom of contract includes the right to determine the price for goods or services.[8] Indeed, in a decision of 1958 the German *Bundesgerichtshof* confirmed that freedom of contract includes the right to charge different customers different prices, unless special aggravating circumstances are in place.[9] The prospects of personalized pricing have of course massively increased in the meantime through profiling. Its lawfulness has just been confirmed at EU level. The new Directive (EU) 2019/2161 on better enforcement and modernization of EU consumer protection rules[10] introduces a new information obligation on traders, according to which they must inform the consumer, 'where applicable, that the price was personalized on the basis of automated decision making'. At the same time, recital (45) of that Directive confirms that '(t)raders may personalise the price of their offers for specific consumers or specific categories of consumers based on automated decision making and profiling of consumer behaviour allowing traders to assess the consumer's purchasing power'. Thus, the Directive offers consumers the opportunity to avoid traders

---

4   *See* the Explanations Relating to the Charter of Fundamental Rights, [2007] OJ C 303/17, Explanation on Article 16 – Freedom to conduct a business, and ECJ, 22 January 2013, Case C-283/11 *Sky Österreich GmbH* v. *Österreichischer Rundfunk*, ECLI:EU:C:2013:28, para. 42; ECJ, 18 July 2013, Case C-426/11 *Mark Alemo-Herron and others* v. *Parkwood Leisure Ltd*, ECLI:EU:C:2013:521, para. 32.
5   *See, e.g.*, ECJ, 6 September 2012, Case C-544/18 *Deutsches Weintor eG* v. *Land Rheinland-Pfalz*, ECLI:EU:C:2012:526, paras. 47 and 54; *Sky Österreich, supra* note 4, para. 46.
6   *See* ECJ, 10 July 1991, Joined Cases C-90/90 and C-91/90 *Jean Neu and others* v *Secrétaire d'Etat à l'Agriculture et à la Viticulture*, ECLI:EU:C:1991:303, para. 13.
7   *See, e.g.*, J. Basedow, 'Der Verordnungsentwurf zum Geoblocking – ein Trojanisches Pferd gegen die Vertragsfreiheit', 27 *Europäische Zeitschrift für Wirtschaftsrecht* (2016) p. 641, at p. 642.
8   *See* ECJ, 22 March 2007, Case C-437/04 *Commission* v. *Council*, ECLI:EU:C:2007:178, para. 51; ECJ, 19 April 2012, Case C-213/10, *F-Tex SIA* v. *Lietuvos-Anglijos UAB "Jadecloud-Vilma"*, ECLI:EU:C:2012:215, para. 45.
9   *See* BGH, 18 April 1958, I ZR 158/56, 60 *Gewerblicher Rechtsschutz und Urheberrecht* (1958) p. 487.
10 [2019] OJ L 328/7.

that personalize prices but does not itself do anything to prevent such practices.

2.2 Exceptions to Freedom of Contract in Contract Law

Exceptions only apply where the national or EU legislator has introduced them for imperative reasons of public interest or to accommodate the (fundamental) rights of other individuals that would be unreasonably affected by such negative or unfavourable decisions.

2.2.1 Obligation to Contract

The strongest exception to freedom of contract is an obligation to contract, which is often but not necessarily combined with equal conditions for all customers.

2.2.1.1 Services of General Interest

The main examples are services of general interest,[11] such as telecommunication services[12] and the supply of electricity,[13] gas and water, and more recently basic bank accounts.[14]

Digital services have not yet been fully recognized as services of general interest. Although 'functional internet access' forms part of the universal service obligations of telecommunication services providers under Directive 2002/22/EC, only a few EU Member States have made access to broadband internet a universal service that every citizen must be granted. The new Directive (EU) 2018/1972 establishing the European Electronic Communications Code[15] will improve the situation in that it requires Member States to ensure that all consumers have access at an affordable price to an available adequate broadband internet access service.[16] What exactly 'adequate' means in this context is

---

11 *See generally* P. Rott and C. Willett, 'Consumers and services of general interest', in G. Howells, I. Ramsay and T. Wilhelmsson (eds.), *Handbook of Research on International Consumer Law*, 2nd ed. (Edward Elgar Publishing, Cheltenham, 2018) pp. 267 ff.
12 Art. 20(2) no. 1 of the Telecommunications Universal Services Dir. 2002/22/EC, [2002] OJ L 108/51.
13 Art. 27 of the Electricity Market Dir. 2009/72/EC, (EU) 2019/944, [2019] OJ L 158/125.
14 *See* Art. 16 of Dir. 2014/92/EU on the comparability of fees related to payment accounts, payment account switching and access to payment accounts with basic features, [2014] OJ L 257/214; on which *see* P. Rott, 'Das Basiskonto nach dem Entwurf des Zahlungskontengesetzes', 30 *Verbraucher und Recht* (2015) pp. 3 ff.. For the classification of basic banking services as services of general interest, *see* the Commission's Communication 'A Quality Framework for Services of General Interest in Europe', COM(2011) 900, p. 12.
15 [2018] OJ L 321/36.
16 *See* Art. 84(1) of Dir. (EU) 2018/1972.

left to the Member States but the Directive specifies that adequate broadband internet access must be capable of supporting E-mail, search engines, basic training and education online tools, online newspapers or news, buying or ordering goods or services online, job searching and job searching tools, professional networking, internet banking, eGovernment service use, calls and video calls (standard quality) and social media and instant messaging.[17]

Thus, access to services that some of the powerful digital players provide, such as search engines (Google), buying or ordering goods (Amazon) and social media (Facebook), is indirectly recognized to be of relevance for people's social and economic life. The obligation to contract, however, only relates to internet access as such, rather than to the services themselves.

2.2.1.2 Anti-discrimination Law

If a trader bases the rejection of a contract on specific data relating to, for example, sex or religion, this may turn into discrimination in terms of anti-discrimination laws.

Discrimination in relation to the supply of goods and services is dealt with by Directive 2000/43/EC implementing the principle of equal treatment between persons irrespective of racial or ethnic origin[18] and by Directive 2004/113/EC implementing the principle of equal treatment between men and women in the access to and supply of goods and services.[19] Some national legislators have extended the prohibition on discrimination to other reasons. For example, the German legislator has extended the principle of equal treatment to religion, handicap, age, and sexual identity.[20] In contrast, poverty or political opinions are not relevant criteria. Clearly, this also applies where discrimination is hidden in an algorithm;[21] although the General Data Protection Regulation (GDPR) has not… GDPR[22] has not taken up this issue.[23]

---

17   *See* Art. 84(3) with Annex V of Dir. (EU) 2018/1972.
18   [2000] *OJ L* 180/22, in particular Art 3(1)(h).
19   [2004] *OJ L* 373/37.
20   *See* § 19 para. 1 *Allgemeines Gleichbehandlungsgesetz* (General Act on Equal Treatment; AGG).
21   *See* P. Hacker, 'Teaching fairness to artificial intelligence: Existing and novel strategies against algorithmic discrimination under EU law', 55 *Common Market Law Review* (2018) pp. 1143 ff.; S. Genth, 'Dynamische Preise: ein Gewinn für Handel und Verbraucher', 96 *Wirtschaftsdienst* (2016) p. 866; Sachverständigenrat für Verbraucherfragen, *Verbrauchergerechtes Scoring* (SVRV, Berlin, 2018), at pp. 135 ff.
22   Reg. (EU) 2016/679 on the protection of natural persons with regard to the processing of personal data and on the free movement of such data, [2016] *OJ L* 119/1.
23   Only recital (71) of the GDPR mentions the risk of discriminatory profiling, *see* P. Scholz, 'DSVGO Art. 22 Automatisierte Entscheidungen im Einzelfall einschließlich Profiling', in:

Another problem will lie in the detection and proof of discrimination,[24] as this will usually take the form of indirect discrimination.[25] Generally speaking, the burden of proof is with the claimant. Although EU law provides for reversal of the burden of proof in situations where a potential discrimination victim provides facts from which it may be presumed that direct or indirect discrimination has occurred,[26] the reversal of the burden of proof, however, only relates to the causation between the special characteristics of the potential victim (for example, religion) and the different treatment.

2.2.2   Obligation to Equal Treatment?

A different form of intervention in freedom of contract is the obligation to treat all customers equally. This is an obligation that we find again, with certain limitations, in the law of services of general interest[27] and in anti-discrimination law.

2.2.3   No Right to Know

Outside the area of services of general interest, where generally applicable prices must be published by the suppliers, the consumer has hardly any right or realistic possibility to find out how he or she is treated in comparison to other consumers. The above-mentioned new Directive on better enforcement and modernization of EU consumer protection rules only requires that consumers be informed pre-contractually that automated decision making is present but does not include an obligation to explain how this has played out for the consumer. And Article 9(2) of the Consumer Credit Directive 2008/48/EC only requires creditors to inform the consumer immediately and without charge of the result of consultation of a database (for the purposes of assessing the consumer's creditworthiness) if the credit application is rejected on that basis. Thus, the creditor does not have to explain to the consumer why he rejects a credit contract on the basis of that result.

2.3   *Limitations by Data Protection Law?*

Data protection law does not address the rejection of a contract or the personalization of prices as such but it does address profiling and automated

---

S. Simitis, G. Hornung and I. Spiecker (eds.), *Datenschutzrecht* (Baden-Baden, Nomos, 2018) para. 14.
24   *See also* Sachverständigenrat für Verbraucherfragen, *Verbraucherrecht 2.0* (SVRV, Berlin, 2016), at p. 70.
25   *See* Hacker, *supra* note 21.
26   *See* Art. 8(1) of Dir. 2000/43/EC and Art. 9(1) of Dir. 2004/113/EC.
27   *See, e.g.*, Art. 1 of Protocol No. 26 on services of general interest, as introduced by the Lisbon Treaty.

decision-making, which is often used when it comes to different treatment of customers.

2.3.1 Automated Decision-making

Automated decisions are, first of all, mentioned in Article 22 GDPR, which entitles the data subject not to be subject to a decision based solely on automated processing, including profiling, which produces legal effects that – or otherwise similarly operates to – significantly affect him or her. The basic aim of this provision is related to human dignity and fundamental rights: the exercise of fundamental freedoms by human beings should not be subjected to the decision of an algorithm but a decision with legal effects should always be made by a natural person.[28]

Article 22 GDPR has some requirements and provides for some exceptions, though, that seriously limit its application. Where a contract is actually concluded, the exception of Article 22(2)(a) is involved, whereby automated decisions are allowed if 'necessary for entering into, or performance of, a contract between the data subject and a data controller'. This exception applies where the consumer's personal circumstances, in particular his or her creditworthiness, are relevant for the contract; this is obvious when it comes to credit[29] but also to long-term contracts such as rent or energy supply,[30] and finally – in terms of optimal use by the trader of the consumer's willingness to pay by way of personalized pricing – to all contracts.

Where no contract is concluded, the first hurdle to overcome is Article 22(1) GDPR. Whether or not rejection of conclusion of a contract produces a 'legal effect' in terms of Article 22(1) GDPR is a controversial issue.[31] At least, one could argue that it 'similarly significantly affects' the consumer.[32] Even then, however, the exception of Article 22(2)(a) GDPR is said to apply, for the reasons explained above. Overall, Article 22(1) GDPR is of little help to the consumer.

---

28   See Scholz, *supra* note 23, para. 3.
29   According to Art. 8 of the Consumer Credit Dir. 2008/48/EC as well as Art. 18 of the Mortgage Credit Dir. 2014/17/EU, a creditor must assess aconsumer's creditworthiness before making a decision on concluding a credit contract. To this end, the creditor shall consult the relevant databases containing information about the consumer's credit history.
30   See Scholz, *supra* note 23, para. 43, with further references.
31   For legal effect: M. Helfrich, 'DSVGO Automatisierte Entscheidungen im Einzelfall einschließlich Profiling', in: G. Sydow (ed), *Europäische Datenschutzgrundverordnung*, 2nd ed. (Baden-Baden, Nomos, 2018) para. 48; against Scholz, *supra* note 23, para. 34.
32   See Scholz, *supra* note 23, para. 35. *See also* recital (71) para. 1 GDPR.

2.3.2 A Right to Know?

The right to know about personal data that are collected from a data subject is subject to Article 13 GDPR, a provision that also addresses profiling and automated decision-making. According to Article 13(2)(f) GDPR, the data controller must, at the time when personal data are obtained, provide the data subject with information concerning the existence of automated decision-making, including profiling, referred to in Article 22(1) and (4) and, at least in those cases, with meaningful information about the logic involved, as well as the significance and the envisaged consequences of such processing for the data subject. The same applies, according to Article 14(2)(g) GDPR, to personal data that has not been obtained from the data subject. Finally, under Article 15(1)(h) GDPR, the data subject is entitled to obtain from the controller confirmation as to whether or not personal data concerning him or her are being processed, and, where that is the case, access to the personal data and information on the existence of automated decision-making, including profiling, referred to in Article 22(1) and (4) and, at least in those cases, meaningful information about the logic involved, as well as the significance and the envisaged consequences of such processing for the data subject.

The crucial question is what 'the logic involved' entails. Whereas it is clear that the data subject must be informed about data included in calculating the score, that information is only meaningful if one also knows how the pieces of information are weighed and what comparison groups are used.

The same issue was subject to debate in Germany, in relation to a now-repealed provision of the *Bundesdatenschutzgesetz* (Federal Data Protection Act; BDSG), according to which the consumer was entitled to be informed about the type of data used for calculating the score and the coming into being and the relevance of the score in the individual case and in plain and intelligible language.[33] The view that the consumer had the right to know about the weighing of pieces of information and of comparison groups was rejected by Schufa, which relied on protection of its business secrets; a decision that the *Bundesgerichtshof* confirmed in 2014.[34] In other words, the consumer does not have the right to know what the algorithm does with his or her data.[35]

Authors that had been unhappy with the above-mentioned decision of the *Bundesgerichtshof* maintain that the 'logic involved' in the terms of Article

---

33 § 34 para 2 BDSG of 2009.
34 *See* BGH, 28 January 2014, VI ZR 156/13, 67 *Neue Juristische Wochenschrift* (2014) pp. 1235 ff.
35 *See* T. Weichert, 'Scoring in Zeiten von Big Data', 47 *Zeitschrift für Rechtspolitik* (2014) p. 168, at p. 169.

13(2)(f) GDPR includes weighing the factors used for calculating a score.[36] Even disclosure of the score formula is thought to be necessary in exceptional cases, if this is the only way by which the person concerned can avoid and rectify an incorrect calculation.[37]

The prevailing view, however, is that the requirements of Article 13(2)(f) GDPR are even weaker than those of the former German data protection law.[38] This view is also taken outside Germany.[39] Thus, Article 13(2)(f) GDPR is of little help in explaining the decision in the individual case.[40]

3 The Constitutional Law Perspective: the Principle of Equality

The sheer power of some digital players as well as their relevance for people's lives begs the question as to whether these players have become so State-like that they must observe fundamental rights, including the right to equality. This question is, of course, not entirely new and has, for example, been posed – and mainly answered in the negative – in relation to large multinational corporations in public international law. Nevertheless, law is dynamic, and there is reason to revisit that issue in relation to powerful digital players. To that end, we shall first reconsider the reasons why the State is bound by fundamental rights whereas private companies are normally not; where exceptions to that rule have been made in the past; and whether it is now time to broaden the scope of application of fundamental rights towards powerful digital players.

3.1 *German Law*
3.1.1 The Principle: no Obligations on Private Players
According to Article 3 paragraph 1 GG, the fundamental rights of the *Grundgesetz* are binding on the State, including all its emanations. In contrast,

---

36 *See* A. Dix, 'DSGVO Art. 13 Informationspflicht bei Erhebung von personenbezogenen Daten bei der betroffenen Person', in Simitis, Hornung and Spiecker (eds.), *supra* note 23, at para. 16.

37 *See* Dix, *supra* note 36, at para. 16; A Roßnagel, M Nebel and P Richter, 'Was bleibt vom Europäischen Datenschutzrecht? – Überlegungen zum Ratsentwurf der DS-GVO', 5 *Zeitschrift für Datenschutz* (2015) p. 455, at p. 458.

38 *See* J. Taeger, 'Scoring in Deutschland nach der EU-Datenschutzgrundverordnung', 49 *Zeitschrift für Rechtspolitik* (2016) p. 72, at p. 75.

39 *See, e.g.*, S. Wachter, B. Mittelstadt and L. Floridi, 'Why a right to explanation of automated decision-making does not exist in the General Data Protection Regulation', 7(2) *International Data Privacy Law* (2017) pp. 76 ff.

40 *See also* I. van Ooijen and H.U. Vrabec, 'Does the GDPR Enhance Consumers' Control over Personal Data? An Analysis from a Behavioural Perspective, 42 *Journal of Consumer Policy* (2019) p. 91, at p. 97.

according to the established case law of the *Bundesverfassungsgericht* (Federal Consitutional Court; BVerfG), they are not directly binding on private players.[41] The middle ground is the famous doctrine of the indirect effect of fundamental rights that courts, as emanations of the State, have to consider when they apply the law in litigation between private parties.[42] This doctrine has been applied to a number of fundamental rights, including the personality right,[43] the general freedom to act,[44] and also the right to free speech[45] (see also *infra*, at 3.1.3.2.). It is, however, a controversial issue whether that doctrine can also be applied to the principle of equality as equality is not a value as such but needs something to relate to. Thus, recognizing the principle of equality in private law would mean recognising the direct rather than indirect effect of that principle in private law relationships.[46]

3.1.2   Labour Law

In the 1980s, the *Bundesarbeitsgericht* (Federal Labour Court; BAG) applied Article 3 directly to the parties to collective agreements that factually govern contracts between employers and employees.[47] This case law has been criticized in academic writing ever since,[48] and while the *Bundesverfassungsgericht* left the question of direct application open,[49] the BAG itself, in a later decision of 1998, denied the direct effect of Article 3 GG.[50]

---

41   *See, e.g.*, Bundesverfassungsgericht (Federal Constitutional Court; BVerfG), 11 April 2018, 1 BvR 3080/09, 71 *Neue Juristische Wochenschrift* (2018) p. 1667, at p. 1668.

42   Established case law since BVerfG, 15 January 1958, 1 BvR 400/57, 11 *Neue Juristische Wochenschrift* (1958) pp. 257 ff.

43   Established case law since BGH, 25 May 1954, I ZR 211/53, 7 *Neue Juristische Wochenschrift* (1954) pp. 1404 ff.

44   *See, e.g.*, BVerfG, 19 October 1993, 1 BvR 567/89 et al., 47 *Neue Juristische Wochenschrift* (1994) pp. 36 ff.

45   *See, e.g.*, BVerfG, 12 December 2000, 1 BvR 1762/95 and 1787/95, 54 *Neue Juristische Wochenschrift* (2000) pp. 591 ff.

46   See A. Hellgardt, 'Wer hat Angst vor der unmittelbaren Direktwirkung?', 73 *Juristenzeitung* (2018) pp. 901 ff.; F. Michl, 'Situativ staatsgleiche Grundrechtsbindung privater Akteure', 73 *Juristenzeitung* (2018) pp. 910 ff.

47   *See, e.g.*, BAG, 13 November 1985, 4 AZR 234/84, 3 *Neue Zeitschrift für Arbeitsrecht* (1986), pp. 321 ff.; BAG, 25 February 1987, 8 AZR 430/84, 4 *Neue Zeitschrift für Arbeitsrecht* (1987), pp. 667 ff.

48   See only M. Herdegen, 'GG Art. 1 Abs. 3', in: T. Maunz and G. Dürig (eds.), *Grundgesetz*, vol. 1, del. 87 (Munich, C.H. Beck, 2019), para. 114.

49   See BVerfG, 22 February 1992, 1 BvL 21/85 and 4/92, 90 *Entscheidungen des Bundesverfassungsgerichts* (1992) pp. 46 ff.

50   See BAG, 25 February 1998, 7 AZR 641/96, 15 *Neue Zeitschrift für Arbeitsrecht* (1998) pp. 715 ff.

3.1.3 An Exception Based on Power and Need?

3.1.3.1 The Bundesliga Case

The debate on the application of fundamental rights in private law relationships has been revived through a recent decision of the *Bundesverfassungsgericht*; which has in the aftermath been taken up by civil courts in relation to powerful players in the digital world.

The *Bundesverfassungsgericht* had to decide on the lawfulness of a ban on a football fan from all *Bundesliga* games. While the *Bundesverfassungsgericht* held that the fundamental right to equality did not amount to a *general* obligation of private players to treat all private persons equally, this is different where a private player offers goods or services to the public at large and makes far-reaching decisions on the participation of others in social life. In this situation, private players must not exclude others arbitrarily from access to their goods or services. Instead, they must provide objective reasons that justify their decisions. According to the *Bundesverfassungsgericht*, this is connected with procedural requirements. In the instant case, these included a hearing of the football fan concerned. Moreover, the private party must give reasons so as to allow the person concerned to enforce his rights.[51]

In German academic writing, the *Bundesverfassungsgericht* decision has become a hot topic, as it deviates from previous case law and from the previous consensus between constitutional lawyers. Some authors criticize the decision because, without laying it open, the *Bundesverfassungsgericht* has accepted, under certain circumstances, the direct effect of the principle of equality in private law relationships.[52] Others appear to agree, in principle, based on the fact that certain private players have become State-like.[53] There is some concern, however, about the demarcation between private players that are so powerful that they have to consider the fundamental rights of their (potential) customers, and those that are still below the threshold (see also *infra*, 3.1.3.3.). Moreover, authors have pointed out that due to market developments, the status can change, and previously State-like players may become less powerful

---

[51] See BVerfG, 11 April 2018, 1 BvR 3080/09, 71 *Neue Juristische Wochenschrift* (2018), pp. 1667 ff. In another football case, the football association had not provided any evidence for the football fan in question being dangerous (beyond a recommendation by the police to impose a Germany-wide ban on that fan). Thus, AG Frankfurt ordered that the ban be lifted; *see* AG Frankfurt, 20 September 2018, 30 C 3466/17, BeckRS 2018, 23376.

[52] See Hellgardt, *supra* note 46, at p. 908; Michl, *supra* note 46, at p. 916; A. Lang, 'Netzwerkdurchsetzungsgesetz und Meinungsfreiheit', 143 *Archiv des öffentlichen Rechts* (2018), p. 220, at p. 242.

[53] *See, e.g.*, S. Muckel, 'Mittelbare Drittwirkung des allgemeinen Gleichheitssatzes', 50 *Juristische Arbeitsblätter* (2018) p. 553, at p. 556.

due to the market entry of new players; which would change their legal obligations towards their customers.[54] At the same time, it should be noted that this phenomenon is not unique, as the same can happen in competition law where companies may gain or lose a dominant position, which is the crucial criterion for the application of one strand of EU competition law (see Article 102 TFEU). Finally, authors have criticized the procedural duties that the *Bundesverfassungsgericht* established, arguing that private parties would be upgraded to State-like entities.[55]

3.1.3.2 Application to Powerful Digital Players?

In the following, authors have transferred the logic of the *Bundesliga* judgment to the digital world,[56] and German courts have begun to apply fundamental rights rhetoric to powerful digital players. Decisions mainly relate to Facebook but there are also decisions on Youtube and PayPal. However, the situations concerned and the doctrinal approaches vary.

Most decisions concern (previously) existing contractual relationships (accounts), which are temporarily blocked or terminated or within which individual posts of users are deleted. The digital players thereby usually rely on their standard terms, according to which they can, for example, delete posts and ban accounts if the user engages in hate speech.[57] Indeed, in the German context digital players are even required by law to block and delete hate speech.[58] Users instead point to their fundamental right of free speech, which is protected under Article 5 paragraph 1 GG, and authors have warned against so-called 'overblocking'.[59]

All judgments have confirmed Facebook's right to sanction hate speech as well as the validity of the related standard terms but they have also required

---

[54] *See* U. Kischel, 'GG Art. 3', in: v. Epping and C. Hillgruber (eds.), *BeckOK Grundgesetz*, 41 ed. (Munich, C.H. Beck, 2019), at para. 93b.
[55] *ibid.*, at para. 93c.
[56] *See* A. Peukert, 'Gewährleistung der Meinungs- und Informationsfreiheit in sozialen Netzwerken', 21 *MultiMedia und Recht* (2018) p. 575. For an early contribution, *see* K.-H. Ladeur, 'Ausschluss von Teilnehmern an Diskussionsforen im Internet – Absicherung von Kommunikationsfreiheit durch „netzwerk-gerechtes" Privatrecht', 4 *MultiMedia und Recht* (2001) pp. 787 ff.
[57] *See also* M. Beurskens, '„Hate-Speech" zwischen Löschungsrecht und Veröffentlichungspflicht', 71 *Neue Juristische Wochenschrift* (2018) p. 3418, at p. 3420.
[58] *See* § 3 para. 2 *Netzdurchsetzungsgesetz* (Network Enforcement Act; NetzDG).
[59] *See, e.g.*, B. Holznagel, 'Overblocking durch User Generated Content (UGC) – Plattformen: Ansprüche der Nutzer auf Wiederherstellung oder Schadensersatz?', 34 *Computer und Recht* (2018) pp. 369 ff.; A. Schiff, 'Meinungsfreiheit in mediatisierten digitalen Räumen', 21 *MultiMedia und Recht* (2018) pp. 366 ff.

Facebook to consider the user's fundamental right to free speech when applying their standard terms. For example, the LG Bamberg came to the conclusion that, in the light of Article 5 GG, a particular Facebook post (dealing, among others with illegal immigration) did not meet the standard of hate speech that allows Facebook to delete the post.[60] Courts have, however, argued that private parties do not need to comply with the right to free speech in the same way as the State has to do, as long as constitutional values are observed and the decision is not arbitrary.[61]

All these cases involved the indirect effect of the right to free speech on the interpretation of Facebook's standard terms and on their application. Similarly, in a case involving a Youtube video the KG Berlin held that, in the light of the right to free speech, the video in question did not represent hate speech. Therefore, Youtube had no (contractual) right to take it down.[62]

The question whether or not Facebook is also bound by the principle of equality is currently pending before the *Bundesverfassungsgericht*. The case relates to the account of the right wing party "Der III. Weg". Because of a post that Facebook classified as hate speech, Facebook first blocked the account for 30 days, then deleted it. "Der III. Weg" took action in the civil courts and finally before the *Bundesverfassungsgericht*, their main line of argument asserting a violation of the principle of equality. The *Bundesverfassungsgericht* has not yet taken a final decision but in the fast-track procedure for interim decisions, it did not exclude that Facebook might be bound by the principle of equality and accepted the application for interim judicial protection because the ban deprived the applicant of an essential communication channel with potential voters in the critical phase before the elections to the European Parliament.[63]

3.1.3.3   Who is Sufficiently Powerful?

The question remains: which digital players are so powerful that they have to consider their users' or potential users' fundamental rights? For further

---

60   *See* LG Bamberg, 18 October 2018, 2 O 248/18, 22 *MultiMedia und Recht* (2019) p. 56.
61   See OLG Karlsruhe, 28 February 2019, 6 W 81/18, 7615 *Beck-Rechtsprechung* (2019); LG Heidelberg, 28 August 2018, 1 O 71/18, 23 *Zeitschrift für Urheber- und Medienrecht – Rechtsprechungsdienst* (2019) p. 72. For an advocate of different standards *see also* J. Lüdemann, 'Grundrechtliche Vorgaben für die Löschung von Beiträgen in sozialen Netzwerken', 22 *MultiMedia und Recht* (2019) pp. 279 ff.
62   *See* KG Berlin, 22 March 2019, 10 W 172/18, 9590 *Beck-Rechtsprechung* (2019).
63   *See* BVerfG, 22 May 2019, 1 BvQ 42/19, 38 *Neue Zeitschrift für Verwaltungsrecht* (2019) pp. 959 ff.

assessment in the case of the "III. Weg", the *Bundesverfassungsgericht* mentioned the criteria of the degree of the dominant position of Facebook, the orientation of the platform, the degree of dependence on the platform and the interests of the platform operator and other third parties.[64]

In relation to Facebook, courts have argued that Facebook had a 'quasi-monopoly' among social networks. Due to the high number of users, it has a position in public life that no other social network matches.[65] Commentators have noted that Facebook provided a 'digital universal service'[66] and that applying the equality principle to Facebook was the logical next step after the *Bundesliga* decision.[67]

In academic writing, Youtube and Twitter have been regarded as being State-like, next to Facebook.[68]

In a slightly different context, the LG Dortmund regarded Paypal as an essential payment service for an online ticket service, and freezing a Paypal account as an infringement of the fundamental right to an established and operating business (*eingerichteter und ausgeübter Gewerbebetrieb*).[69] A commentator pointed out that PayPal could have a dominant position in the market for online payment service providers.[70]

A most important candidate would seem to be the credit rating agency Schufa,[71] which rules the German credit rating market with a market share of 80 to 100% in certain sectors such as banking.[72] It is their scores that are used by all kinds of suppliers and service providers in their decision to conclude a contract or otherwise and to determine the conditions of such a contract. Thus, the Schufa score is absolutely crucial for the consumer's access to the market;[73] this suggests that the score must not be arbitrary and that, on demand, Schufa must give (real) reasons for the score, which is more than mere information about the data that went into the score.

---

64   *ibid.*, at para. 15.
65   *See* LG Bamberg, *supra* note 60, p. 56, and most recently BGH, 23 June 2020, KVR 69/19, in a competition law case.
66   *See* S.V. Knebel, 'Anmerkung', 22 *MultiMedia und Recht* (2019), p. 60; against Lüdemann, *supra* note 61, at 283 f.
67   *See* M. Seyderhelm, 'Anmerkung', 38 *Neue Zeitschrift für Verwaltungsrecht* (2019) p. 962.
68   *See* Kischel, *supra* note 54, at para. 93b.
69   *See* LG Dortmund, 15 January 2016, 3 O 610/15, 03046 *Beck-Rechtsprechung* (2016).
70   *See* R. Podszun, 'Paypal kann sich für Kontosperre nicht auf Kuba-Embargo stützen', 8 *Gesellschafts- und Wirtschaftsrecht* (2016) p. 211.
71   *See also* Michl, *supra* note 46, at p. 917.
72   *See* Wikipedia, *Schufa* (2018), <https://de.wikipedia.org/wiki/Schufa>.
73   *See also* Weichert, *supra* note 35, at p. 169.

3.2 The EU Charter of Fundamental Rights
3.2.1 Obligations on Private Parties?
The Charter itself is silent on whether or not it imposes obligations on private parties to comply with the fundamental rights stated therein.

From its Article 51(1), a minority opinion has concluded that private parties are not affected by the Charter, as that provision only mentions the institutions, bodies, offices and agencies of the Union and the Member States as addressees of the Charter.[74] The Advocates General have taken different views on the issue. Whereas AG Trstenjak rejected the idea of direct effect in the case of *Dominguez*,[75] AG Cruz Villalón advocated in the case of *Association de médiation sociale* in favour of direct effect.[76] The Court of Justice recently explicitly stated that Article 51(1) does not address the question whether those individuals may, where appropriate, be directly required to comply with certain provisions of the Charter and that this provision cannot, accordingly, be interpreted as meaning that it would systematically preclude such a possibility.[77]

Indeed, the Charter contains articles that are obviously geared towards conflicts between private parties.[78] Some of these relate to employment relationships where Member States have also made exceptions to the rule that private parties should not be bound by fundamental rights. Examples are the workers' right to information and consultation within the undertaking under Article 27,

---

[74] See, e.g., M. de Mol, 'Kücükdeveci: Mangold Revisited – Horizontal Direct Effect of a General Principle of EU Law', 6 *European Constitutional Law Review* (2010) p. 302; A. Hatje, 'Art. 51', in J. Schwarze (ed.), *EU-Kommentar*, 4th ed. (Nomos, Baden-Baden, 2019) para. 20; H.-P. Folz, 'GR-Charta Artikel 51', in C. Vedder and W. Heintschel von Heinegg (eds.), *Europäisches Unionsrecht*, 2nd ed. (Nomos, Baden-Baden, 2018) para. 16. More cautious but also advocating against direct horizontal effect: W. Kahl and M. Schwind, 'Europäische Grundrechte und Grundfreiheiten – Grundbausteine einer Interaktionslehre', 49 *Europarecht* (2014) p. 170, at pp. 175 ff.

[75] AG Trstenjak, 8 September 2011, Case C-282/10 *Maribel Dominguez* v. *Centre informatique du Centre Ouest Atlantique*, ECLI:EU:C:2011:559.

[76] AG Cruz Villalón, 18 July 2013, Case C-176/12 *Association de médiation sociale* v *Union locale des syndicats CGT and others*, ECLI:EU:C:2013:491.

[77] CJEU, 6 November 2018, Case C-684/16 *Max-Planck-Gesellschaft zur Förderung der Wissenschaften e.V.* v. *Tetsuji Shimizu*, ECLI:EU:C:2018:874, para. 76.

[78] See A. Seifert, 'Die horizontale Wirkung von Grundrechten', 22 *Europäische Zeitschrift für Wirtschaftsrecht* (2011), p. 696, at pp. 700 ff.; H.D. Jarass, 'Die Bedeutung der Unionsgrundrechte unter Privaten', 25 *Zeitschrift für Europäisches Privatrecht* (2017) p. 310, at p. 315; A. Schwerdtfeger, 'Charta Artikel 51 Anwendungsbereich', in: J. Meyer and S. Hölscheidt (eds.), *Charta der Grundrechte der Europäischen Union*, 5th ed. (C.H. Beck, Munich, 2014) paras. 57 ff.

protection in the event of unjustified dismissal under Article 30, and fair and just working conditions under Article 31. Another example is actions relating to children under Article 24(2), which explicitly addresses private institutions.

In the meantime, the Court of Justice has confirmed in several cases that Charter rights can take direct effect between private parties. Although in *Association de médiation sociale*, the Court denied direct effect to the workers' right to information and consultation within the undertaking of Article 27 of the Charter (because it considered that provision to be too unspecific), on the other hand it *obiter* maintained that the principle of non-discrimination on grounds of age, laid down in Article 21(1) of the Charter, was sufficient in itself to confer on individuals an individual right which they may invoke as such.[79] In the case of *Egenberger*, the Court confirmed this finding on Article 21(1), this time concerning non-discrimination on grounds of religion,[80] and added that Article 47 of the Charter on the right to effective judicial protection was also sufficient in itself and that national courts were required to ensure, within their jurisdiction, judicial protection for individuals flowing from Articles 21 and 47 and to guarantee the full effectiveness of those articles by disapplying if need be any contrary provision of national law.[81] In *Max Planck Gesellschaft*, the Court recognized the direct effect between private parties of the right to paid annual leave, as laid down in Article 31(2) of the Charter, noting that the right of every worker to paid annual leave entails, by its very nature, a corresponding obligation on the employer.[82]

The most important consequence of the recognition of the direct effect of Charter rights in private law relationships is, of course, that the Charter right prevails over national legislation that could not be interpreted in line with the Charter and therefore must be disapplied by the national court.[83]

After all, the capability of taking direct effect between private parties depends on the individual Charter right. In the words of AG Cruz Villalón: 'the horizontal effect of fundamental rights operates very differently for each right or, more simply, for the various groups of rights. There are rights which, by

---

79 CJEU, 15 January 2014, Case C-176/12 *Association de médiation sociale* v *Union locale des syndicats CGT and others*, ECLI:EU:C:2014:2, para. 47.
80 CJEU, 17 April 2018, Case C-414/16 *Vera Egenberger* v. *Evangelisches Werk für Diakonie und Entwicklung eV*, ECLI:EU:C:2018:257, para. 76; confirmed by CJEU, 6 November 2018, joined Cases C-569/16 and C-570/16 *Stadt Wuppertal* v. *Maria Elisabeth Bauer* and *Volker Wilmeroth* v. *Martina Broßonn*, ECLI:EU:C:2018:871, paras 85 ff.
81 *Egenberger, supra* note 80, paras 78 f.
82 *Max-Planck-Gesellschaft, supra* note 77, para. 79.
83 *Ibid.*, para. 80.

their very structure, are not addressed to individuals, just as there are rights whose relevance in relationships governed by private law it would be inconceivable to deny'.[84]

Of course, the court may, in a dispute between individuals, be called on to balance competing fundamental rights which the parties to the dispute derive from the provisions of the TFEU or the Charter, and may even be obliged, in the review that it must carry out, to make sure that the principle of proportionality is complied with. Such an obligation to strike a balance between the various interests involved has no effect on the possibility of relying on the rights in question in such a dispute.[85]

3.2.2 A Horizontal Right to Equality?

According to Article 20 of the Charter, everyone is equal before the law. The principle of equality before the law is a general principle of EU law which, according to the established case law of the Court of Justice, requires that comparable situations should not be treated differently and that different situations should not be treated in the same way, unless such different treatment is objectively justified. A difference in treatment is justified if it is based on an objective and reasonable criterion, that is, if the difference relates to a legally permitted aim pursued by the legislation in question, and it is proportionate to the aim pursued by the treatment.[86] In the case of *Microsoft Mobile Sales International*, relating to copyright law, the Court criticized the fact that the relevant legislation did not lay down *objective and transparent criteria* to be satisfied by persons required to pay fair compensation or by their trade associations for the purposes of concluding such agreement protocols.[87]

The question is whether or not the right to equality is among those Charter rights that can take direct effect between private parties. The wording 'before the law' seems to suggest otherwise, as private parties do not make laws; but the same applies to Article 3 paragraph 1 of the German *Grundgesetz*, and it has not stopped the *Bundesverfassungsgericht* from applying Article 3 paragraph 1 GG to private parties.

84　AG Cruz Villalón, *supra* note 76, para. 38.
85　*Egenberger*, *supra* note 80, para. 80, with further references.
86　See only CJEU, 10 November 2016, Case C-156/15 *Private Equity Insurance Group SIA v. Swedbank AS*, ECLI:EU:C:2016:851, para. 49.
87　CJEU, 22 September 2016, Case C-110/15 *Microsoft Mobile Sales International Oy and others v. Ministero per i beni e le attività culturali (MIBAC) and others*, ECLI:EU:C:2016:717, para. 48.

Indeed, the Court of Justice has treated private measures in the recent past on a par with State measures where they had a comparable effect on private parties. The best example is the case of *Fra.bo* concerning a breach of Article 34 TFEU (free movement of goods) by the German *Deutsche Vereinigung des Gas- und Wasserfaches eV* (DVGW).[88] In Germany, the DVGW offers the only possibility to obtain a compliance certificate for copper fittings with the relevant legal requirements on water supply. In the case at hand, DVGW had denied certification of copper fittings produced and distributed by the Italian producer Fra.bo, thereby effectively denying Fra.bo access to the German market (as almost all German consumers only buy copper fittings that have been certified by DVGW). Although DVGW is a private organization, the Court of Justice treated this as an obstacle to the free movement of goods. It reasoned that the DVGW, by virtue of its authority to certify the products, in reality holds the power to regulate entry into the German market of products such as the copper fittings at issue.[89]

To draw an analogy from the horizontal direct effect of fundamental freedoms with the horizontal direct effect of Charter rights seems appropriate, as the Court of Justice did exactly that in the above-mentioned case of *Egenberger*, where it referred to old case law on discrimination under the EEC Treaty and the EC Treaty, such as its decisions in *Defrenne* and *Angonese*.[90]

Similarly, one could argue that Facebook has the power to regulate access to social media through its standard terms and by way of applying them to potential or existing customers. In a recently leaked note relating to a potential successor instrument to the E-Commerce Directive 2000/31/EC, a 'Digital Services Act', the European Commission stated in the context of oversight over hate speech and the like that "many public interest decisions that should be taken by independent public authorities are now delegated to online platforms, making them de-facto regulators without adequate and necessary oversight, even in areas where fundamental rights are at stake".[91] The difference between DVGW and Facebook, however, is that DVGW has been given its power through a legislative act, while Facebook has simply acquired it by playing the market,

---

[88] CJEU, 12 July 2012, Case C-171/11 *Fra.bo SpA v Deutsche Vereinigung des Gas- und Wasserfaches eV (DVGW)—Technisch-Wissenschaftlicher Verein*, ECLI:EU:C:2012:453.
[89] For details, *see* H.-W. Micklitz and R. van Gestel, 'European Integration through Standardization: How Judicial Review is Breaking Down the Club House of Private Standardization Bodies', 50 *Common Market Law Review* (2013) p. 145.
[90] *Egenberger, supra* note 80, para. 77.
[91] *See* <https://cdn.netzpolitik.org/wp-upload/2019/07/Digital-Services-Act-note-DG-Connect-June-2019.pdf>, at 3.

and Facebook's position in the market for social media is less exclusive than the position of DVGW in certifying copper fittings.

4 The Fundamental Right to Know

The principle of equality prohibits arbitrary decisions. One essential emanation of the principle of equality is therefore the obligation of public authorities to give reasons for all their decisions. In numerous decisions, the German Federal Constitutional Court has pointed to the constitutional principle that a citizen who is affected by the decision of a public authority has the right to be given reasons for the decision, as he is only then able to defend his rights.[92] This right is also enshrined in Article 41(2)(c) of the Charter of Fundamental Rights. Consequently, the *Bundesverfassungsgericht* in the *Bundesliga* case required the Deutsche Fußballbund to give reasons for the stadium ban so as to allow the person concerned to enforce his rights.[93] The same would apply to powerful private players in the digital world that block, ban or reject a (potential) customer or that treat their customers differently.

The right not to be subjected to arbitrariness and the right to be given reasons for decisions includes the individual possibility to understand and to control the reasons given. Thereby, mere reference to an external score that is not explained in itself is insufficient, as it still does not allow the customer to understand the decision.

5 Conclusion

Some players in the digital economy have accumulated immense market power, and they keep growing. In their regulatory powers *vis-à-vis* the consumer, they have become State-like. With power comes responsibility, and in particular the duty to observe the principle of equality, as laid down in Article 3 GG and Article 20 of the Charter of Fundamental Rights; which includes procedural rights such as the right to be heard and the right to be given reasons. These rights limit the freedom of contract that private parties enjoy. This means not only that termination of an existing contractual relationship must be justified in the light of the fundamental rights of the person concerned but

---

[92] See, e.g., BVerfG, 16 January 1957, 1 BvR 253/56, 6 *Entscheidungen des Bundesverfassungsgerichts* (1957) p. 32, at p. 44.
[93] See *supra*, at 3.1.3.1.

also that an applicant for a contract can only be rejected for good reasons, and that differential treatment must be justified and explained. Ideally, these principles should be taken up and concretized by the legislator. Legislation on services of general interest could serve as a model for regulation of powerful private players in the digital economy.

Big Data and International Politics

Juan Luis Manfredi Sánchez*

Abstract

Big Data is a transformational avalanche of data-encompassing ideas, activities, standards, social behaviours and customs, plus related devices and platforms. This new environment changes the nature of public policies and decision-making. Big Data in International Politics refers to the intelligence provided to improve processes and results in world affairs. Applications and databases have become sources of authority at a moment when expert knowledge is under suspicion. Without data, decisions are less transparent and tend to be arbitrary. However, automation has also favoured the dissemination of propaganda. International Politics for Big Data promotes governance bringing together both political and technical aspects. Privacy, and Human Rights, and discourse on the common good appear as universal values. Big Data for International Politics is devoted to improving relations among international actors. The work agenda includes the refugee issue, global public health and combating climate change, an expression of humanitarian innovation and conflict prevention. Finally, the article refers to two unsettled issues: 1) the value of forecasts based on previous behaviours in a growing environment of complexity and 2) data politics, the political nature of data collection and its bias.

Keywords

big data – international relations – governance – artificial intelligence – propaganda – human rights – data politics

1   Introduction

Big data is currently a burning issue. There are many definitions of this concept that point in the same direction: using technology, a dataset is collected from different sources, before being processed and distributed for use. This new environment,[1] based on algorithms, computing and processing, is an

---

* University of Castilla-La Mancha, Spain.
1 A. de Mauro, M. Greco and M. Grimaldi, 'What is big data? A consensual definition and a review of key research topics', in G. Giannakopoulos, D. Sakas and D. Kyriaki-Manessi (eds.),

aggregate of physical components and intangible processes: "Rapid advances in instrumentation and sensors, digital storage and computing, communications and networks, including the advent of the internet".[2]

In the main, I advocate for a broader definition: following its own logic, the culture of big data encompasses ideas, activities, standards, social behaviours and customs, plus those devices and platforms that employ such data on a massive scale. Puyvelde, Coulthart and Shahriar Hossain consider that big data have affected the role of and the approach to analysis and employing prospective techniques: "Big data is not only about data, but also about the means, both technological and methodological, by which data are stored, processed and analysed".[3] The scale of the change in public policy and decision-making is gauged by the exponential aggregation of data, information and other similar assets that surpass the human ability to understand the environment without the support of computing. McNeely and Hahm contend that it is possible to regard big data as "datasets whose size is beyond the analytical capacities of most database software tools".[4] According to Ünver, "Big data gives us data granularity that enables micro-level approaches such as behavior, cognitive biases or worldview analysis, as well as the volume that can be scaled to meso-level (networks, collective action, ethno-nationalist movements) and macro-level (ideology, identity, systems research) simultaneously".[5]

The impact of big data is not linear, but transformational. The avalanche of data has saturated the capacity of institutions and citizens alike to receive, understand and leverage them. All of the studies performed to date on the big data phenomenon have underscored three key aspects, namely, volume, variety and velocity. The first two represent the structural characteristics of big data.[6] Any connected device manages information that can be shared, while social networking sites provide qualitative information on social behaviours. The sheer volume and variety of data are conducive to a better understanding

---

1644:1 *American Institute of Physics Conference Proceedings* (AIP Publishing, Melville, 2015) pp. 97–104.

[2] D. Van Puyvelde, S. Coulthart and M. Shahriar Hossain, 'Beyond the buzzword: big data and national security decision-making', 93:6 *International Affairs* (2017) p. 1387.

[3] *Ibid.*, p. 1403.

[4] C.L. McNeely and J.-on Hahm, 'The big (data) bang: policy, prospects, and challenges', 31:4 *Review of Policy Research* (2014) p. 305.

[5] H.A. Ünver, 'Computational International Relations. What Can Programming, Coding and Internet Research Do for the Discipline?', *All Azimuth: A Journal of Foreign Policy and Peace* (2019) p. 15.

[6] V. Mayer-Schönberger and K. Cukier, *Big Data: A Revolution that Will Transform How We Live, Work and Think* (John Murray, London, 2013).

of social customs. As to velocity, what is of interest here is the necessary methodological innovation in order to combine computational and qualitative analyses. Internet time differs from the social sciences kind: a trend (a trending topic, viewing a story on Instagram or other manifestation of ephemeral communication) cannot be collected as easily as data deriving from other sources. For this reason, the design of algorithms, computing techniques and forms of data processing affect research results.

These three Vs have shaped the predictive mantra of public policies, voting behaviour, consumption trends, business intelligence and crisis management, despite the fact that they ignore the noise. In research methods, volume is not correlated with the quality of the information that can be extracted. Thus, there is a need for new skills – not so much for data collection but for approaching, analysing and interpreting them. As stated by Clark and Golder, "Big data can help to the extent that it makes previously unobservable variables observable, thereby reducing the need for an instrument, or by making new potential instruments available".[7]

It is the three Vs that have been added to the construction and decision-making processes based on big data: veracity, variability and value.[8] The first requires methodological unity when collecting, exploiting and qualitatively interpreting data. Spreadsheets do not collect other types of information or intangible attributes such as reputation, influence or prestige. On social networking sites, the number of followers is not tantamount to possessing the power or capacity to influence public policies or the media agenda. Having an influence on social media, in terms of node value, does not mean having more followers, but centrality, in-degree and out-degree positions in the network. Variability refers to the origin of data, which can be linked to public or private institutions, of a personal nature or structured on databases or non-homogeneous intervals, among other examples. Each model or format creates value when it can be combined to obtain new information. The scalability of comparisons and the search for patterns, rather than for more information, fall into this category. Lastly, value is understood as the capacity to create new opportunities, provide innovative solutions and meet specific social or economic demands. Knowledge generated through the use of big data creates value not when data collection is multiplied, but when it resolves burning issues.

---

[7] W.R. Clark and M. Golder, 'Big Data, Causal Inference, and Formal Theory: Contradictory Trends in Political Science?' 48 *PS: Political Science & Politics* (2015) p. 67.

[8] A. Gandomi and M. Haider, 'Beyond the hype: Big data concepts, methods, and analytics', 35:2 *International Journal of Information Management* (2015) pp. 137–144.

Therefore, value is to be found in databases, which need to be processed and organized before being exploited.[9]

2 International Politics in the Data Age

Akaev and Pantin explain that major technological advances shaping the economy in successive waves have altered the world order. Each generation is governed by a political system constructed on the dominant technological and economic bases. For the period between 2020 and 2050, these authors claim that "biotechnology, advanced information technologies, new sources of energy"[10] will be the main driving forces behind change. For *The Economist*, that age has now begun inasmuch as "the world's most valuable resource is no longer oil, but data".[11] It has yet to be determined how that change will affect international relations and globalization.

International politics has become increasingly convoluted, characterized by the absence of a sole (hegemonic) power. In a multipolar scenario, there are different levels of capacity for and interest in exercising power, as well as new political and legislative balances.[12] So, the complexity lies in the greater number of actors, the dispersion of authority, the diversity of issues on the international agenda, and the lack of a universal legal corpus that substitutes the liberal model.[13] The 2030 Agenda for Sustainable Development, environmental risk reduction, conflict management, peacekeeping, nation-building, blockchain, financial transactions, biopolitics, caring for refugees, cybersecurity and social credit management – all are shaping this complex scenario. Political change is slow, non-hierarchical and non-linear, while the technological kind is immediate and has a global reach. It is a semi-open system in which influence is multidirectional. Hierarchy is not pyramidal, even though there are a limited number of actors with greater influence than others. Depending on the

---

9   O. Kwon, N. Lee and B. Shin, 'Data quality management, data usage experience and acquisition intention of big data analytics', 34:3 *International Journal of Information Management* (2014) pp. 387–394.
10 A. Akaev and V. Pantin, 'Technological Innovations and Future Shifts in International Politics', 58:4 *International Studies Quarterly* (2014), pp. 867–872.
11 *The Economist*, 8 May 2017.
12 J.G. Boulton, P.M. Allen, and C. Bowman, *Embracing Complexity: Strategic Perspectives for an Age of Turbulence* (Oxford University Press, Oxford, 2015); R.O. Keohane and D.G. Victor, 'The Regime Complex for Climate Change', 9:1 *Perspectives on Politics* (2011) pp. 7–23.
13 J.J. Mearsheimer, 'Bound to Fail: The Rise and Fall of the Liberal International Order', *43:4 International Security* (2019) pp. 7–50; G.J. Ikenberry, 'The Future of the Liberal World Order: Internationalism After America', 90:3 *Foreign Affairs* (2011) pp. 56–68.

environment, influence can be operationalized and is best explained in terms of political and economic geography than in thematic ones.

In the light of the new uncertainties, this work describes three possible ways in which the big data phenomenon will affect international politics, based on different categories.[14] The result is a map that should serve as a guide for scholars and professionals. Interest in mapping the relationships between big data and international politics is not statistical but structural, for the purpose of providing examples, identifying trends and avoiding mere statistical correlation. For this reason, connectivity has different densities and intensities that affect the object or content of those relationships, the channel or mechanism employed and the subject per se of the action.

3   Big Data in International Politics

The world affairs agenda needs data to make decisions and to broker agreements, namely, in order that these should be rational, solid and relevant. The higher the number of actors, decisions and data, the greater will be the complexity. International political information, economic analyses and forecasts, public policy and social leadership play an epistemic role in forming public opinion in open societies. Quality information improves processes and results. Big data fuel intelligence insofar as they not only draw from official statistics, but also from different sources, trends, social media sentiment and information deriving from connected devices. Gathering this type of information is even more relevant either when there is a lack of quality sources or when these serve the particular interests of a government. According to Donnay:

> While such indicators based on remote sensing technologies are usually imperfect, they can provide excellent proxies for local conditions in the absence of other highly granular statistics collected on the ground. These data are thus usually not meant to replace other more reliable measurements but can serve as highly granular subnational proxies for key covariates. By doing so, they provide invaluable insights into countries or

---

[14]   This follows the approach proposed by The Royal Society in 2009 to evaluate the impact of scientific development on diplomacy. We have adapted the conceptual categories to the particularities of big data, as a specific scientific area, which combines theoretical aspects with other idiosyncrasies affecting the economy, politics and social customs. *See* the original in The Royal Society, *New frontiers in science diplomacy: Navigating the changing balance of power* (The Royal Society, London, 2010).

regions where the local political or security situation does not otherwise permit the regular and/or granular collection of comparable statistics.[15]

The role of knowledge explains the production of international relations and their typical mechanisms. Work rules, intergovernmental routines, institutionalized procedures and international agreements are all expressions of that knowledge production, whether this be regulatory, non-regulatory or soft regulatory. Applications and databases have become sources of authority at a moment when expert knowledge is under suspicion. Big data affect both decision-making processes – analytical methods, planning, forecasting, information management, and the like – and products – the items on the world agenda.

This first proposal is in line with the growing demand for quality, evidence-based public information. According to the OECD:

> Governments and policy makers face increasingly complex and interrelated policy challenges that require fit-for-purpose solutions. There is a need for a trusted evidence-based knowledge infrastructure that underpins policy making with advice to resolve these challenges and bridge isolated silo approaches.[16]

This proposal structures the international governance and accountability of international actors. Without data, decisions are less transparent and tend to be arbitrary. Publication of evidence-based data enhances the results of political decision-making because it employs a comparative scientific method (data are comparable) and empowers policymakers.

As to diplomacy, the minimum unit of knowledge is disseminated via official (official gazettes, interviews, press releases, institutional websites, and so on) or unofficial (unofficial statements, propaganda, social networking sites, and the like) channels that influence international affairs. More information is available, although this does not mean to say that there are more points of agreement or interpretation. Making information available should not be confused with the analytical criteria that each and every subject possesses as regards international action. Diplomacy comprises an area that has institutionalized the intensive use of information to achieve its objectives because *pacta*

---

15   K. Donnay, 'Big Data for Monitoring Political Instability', 2017, *International Development Policy / Revue internationale de politique de développement*, para. 27, <journals.openedition.org/poldev/2468?lang=es>, visited on 13 June 2019.

16   *Government at a Glance 2017*, 2017, OECD, p. 119, <www.oecd.org/gov/government-at-a-glance-2017-highlights-en.pdf>, visited on 13 June 2019.

sunt servanda. The value of the written word resides in establishing points of agreement or disagreement through many different mechanisms: not only international treaties, agreements and accords, but also statements, consulting systems, non-regulatory agreements and – more recently – tweets and videos.

Information automation offers an obvious opportunity for reducing repetitive tasks with little value added, while 'depersonalising' recurrent ones, and errors (for example, in transcribing or translating meetings). However, potential human errors and conceptual deficiencies do not disappear but are transferred to the programmer, as Ünver indicates: "Whether AI can truly be freed from human error and ego is a hotly contested topic within computer science itself and its answers aren't necessarily convincing to the critiques of AI diplomacy".[17]

The epistemology of big data requires the consensus of public opinion, because this may favour a technocratic decision-making style. During the past decade, interest in accountability, governance, public information transparency and also international affairs has increased greatly. Such a change in demand has had an impact on the organization of public information. In times of crisis of legitimacy and representation, it is important to recall the participatory character of democracies and the political value of the liberal order. Action is taken in one direction or another not only because of the tyranny of data, but also because of a shared belief in a common project. The issues to be broached include identifying the key actors who create public opinion and shape information currents, both as information sources and as analysts of international reality.

At this point, it is worth mentioning the impact of big data on disinformation campaigns and propaganda,[18] above all when bearing in mind that automation has favoured the dissemination of content, regardless of its precision or veracity.[19] Terminological confusion (virtual reality, big data, algorithms, deep fakes, and so on) hinder the design of a strategy for combating disinformation on the part of the public authorities with the support of journalists, think tanks, platforms and other relevant tools for shaping public opinion. In the digital environment, this deliberate confusion undermines institutional

---

17 H.A. Ünver, 'Computational Diplomacy. Cyber Governance and Digital Democracy', 2017, edam, centre for Economics and Foreign Policy Study, p. 10, <www.researchgate.net/publication/331073991_Computational_Diplomacy_Foreign_Policy_Communication_in_the_Age_of_Algorithms_and_Automation>, visited on 13 June 2019.

18 S. Vosoughi, D. Roy and S. Aral, 'The spread of true and false news online', 359 *Science* (2018) pp. 1146–1151.

19 S. Woolley and P. Howard, 'Political Communication, Computational Propaganda, and Autonomous Agents', 10 *International Journal of Communication* (2016) pp. 4882–4890.

credibility and creates a sort of 'liar's dividend',[20] which has the advantage of the benefit of the doubt. As Ünver remarks, "Balance of power in computational propaganda – like cyber war – favors the offensive side as costs of defending against such attacks require greater resources and better coordination. Even when the defender is successful (i.e. corrects disinformation quickly), psychological processes of digital information consumption still linger on".[21] *In dubio, pro dubio.* Lastly, it is appropriate to review the crisis of expert knowledge,[22] which is leading to the irrelevance of the media, universities, think tanks and other conventional knowledge providers.

In the context of fake news, international relations professionals have the chance to recuperate spheres of influence and to exercise the power of mediation. In international affairs, a key and sensitive asset is trust, which is undermined by fake news and the deluge of propaganda in the shape of bots, trolls and the like.[23] International trust is built by defending a specific position, the veracity of technical information and the facts being conveyed and by speaking and acting coherently. Trust is not built through advertising campaigns or isolated tweets, but through continual participation on the international digital stage. In a context of uncertainty and specific or recurrent problems, international relations professionals are reliable conveyors of messages, bridges between public and private interests, creators of narratives and arguments. As to audiences, on the other hand, these professionals can contribute to their media education and literacy. Insofar as international affairs are complex, it is essential to identify sound sources, explain the technical specifications of products or services and employ an accessible language that is neither technical nor ambiguous. Versus the proliferation of alternative facts and the harmful use of artificial intelligence, this task should be performed across the board with the involvement of governments, high-tech multinationals, users and scholars.[24]

---

20 B. Chesney and D. Citron, 'Deep Fakes: A Looming Challenge for Privacy, Democracy, and National Security', 2018, SSRN, <https://papers.ssrn.com/sol3/papers.cfm?abstract_id=3213954>, visited on 13 June 2019.
21 Ünver, *supra* note 17, p. 7.
22 T. Nichols, 'How America Lost Faith in Expertise: And Why That's a Giant Problem', 96:2 *Foreign Affairs* (2017) pp. 60–73.
23 S. Bradshaw and P. Howard, 'Troops, Trolls and Troublemakers: A Global Inventory of Organized Social Media Manipulation', 12 *Oxford Project on Computational Propaganda* (2017) pp. 1–37.
24 J. Bullock and M. Luengo-Oroz, 'Automated Speech Generation from UN General Assembly Statements: Mapping Risks in AI Generated Texts', 2019, presented at the International Conference on Machine Learning, AI for Social Good Workshop, Long Beach, United States.

4 International Politics for Big Data

The asymmetry between current reality (globalization, digitization and the crisis of sovereignty, among other key aspects) and the evolution of public international law points to the need for a more in-depth examination of international relations. In order to understand international reality, it is essential to make new sources available, to identify actors with the ability to act on the basis of the facts, to analyse behaviours and practices with political or economic consequences and to open new lines of research.

Data governance is a political and technological matter based on a formula that leverages the benefits of the classic intergovernmental system. The international right-wing accepts the role of States in obliging citizens to meet a set of basic obligations, such as not committing wrongful acts and protecting infrastructures. This idea was further developed in the G7 Lucca Declaration (11 April 2017)[25] and in the United Nations General Assembly Resolution (A/RES/71/28, of 9 December 2016). There has been visible progress in countering disinformation, a pressing concern for liberal democracies. For its part, the European Union published the Action Plan on Disinformation, in which this activity is regarded as posing a direct threat to European stability.[26] Similarly, the impact of algorithms on human rights was debated in the Council of Europe.[27]

For the time being, international politics has offered conventional political solutions, based on cooperation, multilateral institutions and bilateral meetings. Distributed technological governance – without a hierarchical structure – does not correspond to reality. States still have exclusive competence in this respect and the singularity of data – such as privacy issues – can only be regulated by common consent. At any rate, the governance of digital affairs involves political and technological issues: "The solution to long-term challenges in Internet governance requires bringing together the political and the

---

25 G7 2017 Italia, *1G7 DECLARATION ON RESPONSIBLE STATES BEHAVIOR IN CYBERSPACE*, 2017, <www.mofa.go.jp/files/000246367.pdf>, visited on 13 June 2019.
26 European Commission, *JOINT COMMUNICATION TO THE EUROPEAN PARLIAMENT, THE EUROPEAN COUNCIL, THE COUNCIL, THE EUROPEAN ECONOMIC AND SOCIAL COMMITTEE AND THE COMMITTEE OF THE REGIONS: Report on the implementation of the Action Plan Against Disinformation*, 14 July 2019, <https://eeas.europa.eu/sites/eeas/files/joint_report_on_disinformation.pdf>, visited on 13 June 2019.
27 Council of Europe, *ALGORITHMS AND HUMAN RIGHTS: Study on the human rights dimension of automated data processing techniques and possible regulatory implications* (Council of Europe, Strasbourg, 2017) p. 12.

technical, rather than dismissing the technical as not politically constructed or the political as not technologically constrained".[28] New ways of protecting privacy should be explored in order to preserve it as a fundamental right of individuals.[29]

Versus the intergovernmental model, it is important to consider ethical alternatives resulting from the irruption of big data into international relations, whether these be codes of conduct, knowledge production or a basis for universal standards. There is no room for Barlow's Utopia,[30] which rejects state sovereignty over digital reality. However, the idea that technological issues allow for participation and a different governance model, with some opportunities for cooperation, has indeed caught on.[31] The European Union's Cybersecurity Strategy envisages the need for public institutions, private initiatives and citizens to share responsibilities, each with different capacities and goals.[32] Even though legacy diplomacy has retained control over the processes and has added value through institutional trust, third-party participation will require the transformation of work methods.

International governance is orientated towards political action for the common good as a universal value. It consists in the capacity to choose between policies that favour a greater number of people and institutions in order to extend the benefits. 'Data for good' refers, albeit imprecisely,[33] to improving "access to opportunity, especially for communities of individuals for whom opportunities have historically been limited".[34] The decision on what is good or positive for society is political. Technology is neither neutral nor impartial:

---

28   De Nardis, L., 'Five Destabilizing Trends in Internet Governance', 12 *I-S: A Journal of Law and Policy* (2015) p.132.
29   L. Andersen, *et al.*, Human rights in the age of artificial intelligence, 2018, accessnow.org, <www.accessnow.org/cms/assets/uploads/2018/11/AI-and-Human-Rights.pdf>, visited on 13 June 2019.
30   J. Barlow, 'A Declaration of the Independence of Cyberspace', 1996, Electronic Frontier Foundation, <www.eff.org/cyberspace-independence>, visited on 13 June 2019.
31   M. Raymond and L. DeNardis, 'Multistakeholderism: anatomy of an inchoate global institution', 7 *International Theory* (2015) pp. 572–616.
32   European Council, 'Reform of cybersecurity in Europe', <www.consilium.europa.eu/en/policies/cyber-security/>, visited on 13 June 2019.
33   S. Hooker, 'Why "data for good" lacks precision', 22 July 2018, *Towards Data Science*, <https://towardsdatascience.com/why-data-for-good-lacks-precision-87fb48e341f1>, visited on 13 June 2019.
34   A. Rediet, and K. Goldner, 'Mechanism Design for Social Good', 4:3 *AI Matters* (2018) pp. 27–34.

Like all forms of modeling, data science relies on defining the bounds of what is variable and what is fixed, what is of interest and what is immaterial, in order to analyze and make statements about the world. Such cordoning has allowed data science to realize remarkable accomplishments and amass prestige. Yet as data science is increasingly embedded within social and political contexts, the field has come up against the contradictions set within its models: by design, data science lacks the language and methods to fully recognize and evaluate its impacts on society, even as it is increasingly oriented around social impacts.[35]

Lastly in this section, it should be noted that big data management is a breeding ground for political economy in the face of the increasing privatization of spaces and problems relating to the privacy, radicalization and polarization of messages, plus a lack of transparency as regards tax obligations. The scientific literature indicates how advertising shapes mentalities and exploits memorable ideas, slogans and photographs for economic gain and creating new business opportunities. At present, this current identifies capitalism with the logic of appropriation of common goods of an immaterial nature, whether these be emotions, political slogans or knowledge production.[36] Critical theory contends that the substitution of data with political decisions is a conceptual error that promotes 'the end of theory'[37] and creates a mythology of the cognitive capacity of forecasts on the freedom of political decisions:

> This cultural mythology can be seen in city billboards promoting 'big data solutions', at highly profitable big data conferences, and in the many newspaper and magazine columns covering the advances brought about by big data science. The very term big data science is itself a kind of mythological artifact: implying that precepts and methods of scientific research change as the data sets increase in size.[38]

---

35   B. Green, 'Data Science as Political Action: Grounding Data Science in a Politics of Justice', *Working Paper* (2018) p. 45.
36   E. Illouz, *Cold intimacies: the making of emotional capitalism* (Polity Press, Cambridge, 2007).
37   M. Graham, 'Big data and the end of theory?', *The Guardian*, 9 March 2012, <www.theguardian.com/news/datablog/2012/mar/09/big-data-theory>, visited on 13 June 2019.
38   K. Crawford, K. Miltner and M. Gray, 'Critiquing big data: Politics, ethics, and epistemology', 8 *International Journal of Communication* (2014) p. 1664.

5   Big Data for International Politics

Big data could be used for improving relations either between countries or between these and other international actors. This would make it possible to reduce the inequality between actors, since the power deployed depends not only on military or economic force, but also on the ability to create new opportunities for development and forging relations. It is an asset for cooperation in world affairs: if data are shared, illicit digital practices can be detected – whose prosecution is complex – and illegal financial movements aimed at money laundering or tax evasion can be identified. It is an example of how technology can help "to level the playing field between the rich and the poor".[39] This power acquires a novel nature: the capacity to handle, order and create value with big data will ultimately lead to the emergence of a 'processing power', namely, the ability to exploit them.

International cooperation is the field in which a greater number of initiatives can be found, insofar as the relations between data scientists, solutions based on the efficient use of information and the exchange of experience can contribute to establish relations between countries defending very different positions. The work agenda includes the refugee issue, global public health and combating climate change. Big data increase the capacity to convert available public and private information into actionable policies, into real action proposals.

The UNHCR employs the expression 'humanitarian innovation'.[40] The use of data and algorithms has a substantial impact on the assessment of public policy and contributes to accountability. It is worth mentioning here the Global Pulse initiative of the United Nations Secretary-General, defined in the following terms:

> Global Pulse is a flagship innovation initiative of the United Nations Secretary-General on big data. Its vision is a future in which big data is harnessed safely and responsibly as a public good. Its mission is to accelerate discovery, development and scaled adoption of big data innovation for sustainable development and humanitarian action. The initiative was

---

39   G. Berridge, *Diplomacy: Theory and Practice* (Palgrave Macmillan, London, 2015) p. 201.
40   *ESSAYS FROM THE EDGE OF HUMANITARIAN INNOVATION*, 2018, UNHCR Innovation Service, <www.unhcr.org/innovation/wp-content/uploads/2018/01/InnovationYearInReview2017_web.pdf>, visited on 13 June 2019; *Humanitarian Innovation: The State of the Art*, 2014, 009 UNOCHA Policy and Study Series, <www.unocha.org/sites/unocha/files/Humanitarian%20Innovation%20The%20State%20of%20the%20Art_0.pdf>, visited on 13 June 2019.

established based on a recognition that digital data offers the opportunity to gain a better understanding of changes in human well-being, and to get real-time feedback on how well policy responses are working.

For Luengo Oroz, the chief data scientist at UN Global Pulse, "Measuring the impact of these data-driven decisions will help make the case for further investment in big data innovations. Once humanitarian practitioners understand the return on investment of big data innovations, we can start measuring the costs (financial and human) of not using these data, and we can begin to streamline scaling and adoption mechanisms".[41]

The aim of the Digital Humanitarian Network (DHN) is to form a consortium of Volunteer and Technical Communities (V&TCs), thus combining technological knowledge with first-hand humanitarian experience. It is an example of public and private coordination to improve the results of humanitarian action in emergency contexts. Its objective is the "real-time monitoring of mainstream and social media, rapid geo-location of event-data and infrastructure data, creation of live crisis maps for decision support, data development and cleaning, GIS and big data analysis, satellite imagery tagging and tracing and time-sensitive web-based research".[42] The aggregation of official sources and open ones (such as Twitter) makes it possible to take stock of an emergency situation expediently. This, in turn provides:

> ...a landscape of what information, tools and services have been developed and are currently available. These resources can be roughly divided by whether they are a source of information or whether they are a tool for structuring information. Resources in the latter category allow users a degree of control over information, either by providing a platform to input or structure data and information (tools) or by delivering a custom-made information source, such as a map or report (services). Information sources, meanwhile, present information to the user in a pre-structured format intended for a wide and usually public audience.[43]

---

41   *From big data to humanitarian in the loop algorithms*, 22 January 2018, United Nation Global Pulse, <www.unglobalpulse.org/news/big-data-humanitarian-loop-algorithms>, visited on 13 June 2019.

42   Digital Humanitarian Network, <http://digitalhumanitarians.com/>, visited on 13 June 2019.

43   *Resources for Situational Awareness in Humanitarian Emergencies: An Overview of Sources of Information, Tools and Services*, March 2018, Digital Humanitarian Network, <http://ow.ly/SrvU50p20Vf>, visited on 13 June 2019.

With this strategy, geographical information becomes a source of knowledge production applied to disaster prevention and management.

As to conflict management, big data are used to detect instability (social media sentiment analyses) and to anticipate economic movements. The study of the opinions of individuals and what decisions they make as a whole offers a precise aggregate of trends. The Global Database of Events, Language, and Tone (GDELT) project is "a realtime network diagram and database of global human society for open research".[44] Its data mines public information streams relating to television, audio-visual content, and press and information services in more than a hundred languages. The aggregation of data and its subsequent organization result in an "open data global graph over human society as seen through the eyes of the world's news media, reaching deeply into local events, reaction, discourse, and emotions of the most remote corners of the world in near-realtime and making all of this available as an open data firehose to enable research over human society".[45]

Duffield has proposed a critical review of 'humanitarian innovation'[46] whose aim is not to work towards eradication of inequality, but towards a non-humanitarian technological approach: "digital humanitarianism tends to reinforce the poverty and exposure that the neoliberal project demands. After half a century of failed terrestrial aid engagements, chronic poverty has been transformed into a challenge for remote engineering".[47] In the words of Burns, this poses a problem of an epistemological nature: "These epistemological limits are observed mostly by those working in formal humanitarian institutions, and contrast with how the digital humanitarian community envisions their own contributions".[48] Duffield has toughened his stance because he believes that "[i]n the absence of conventional social statistics, behavioural change and population movements are constantly mapped through combinations of data informatics, sensor feedback and remote satellite imaging".[49] Their diagnosis coincides with those of other authors. Read, Taithe and Mac

---

44   The GDELT Project, <www.gdeltproject.org/>, visited on 13 June 2019.
45   *Idem.*
46   M. Duffield, 'The resilience of the ruins: towards a critique of digital humanitarianism', 4:3 *Resilience* (2016) pp. 147–165.
47   *Ibid.*, p. 152.
48   R. Burns, 'Rethinking big data in digital humanitarianism: practices, epistemologies, and social relations', 80 *GeoJournal* (2015) p. 484.
49   M. Duffield, 'The Boomerang Effect', in E. Schwarz, A. McKeil, M. Dean, M. Duffield and D. Chandler, *Datafying the Globe: Critical Insights into the Global Politics of Big Data Governance*, 26 January 2019, *Big Data & Society*, <http://bigdatasoc.blogspot.com/p/essays-and-provocations.html>, visited on 13 June 2019.

Ginty criticize the fact that the 'data revolution' and 'technological enthusiasm' have not got to the root of the problem, but have only reproduced – with evident improvements – the structures.[50]

6 Two Unsettled Issues

Big data poses two problems. The first lies is the growing complexity of international politics and the relative value of forecasts based on previous behaviours. As Orsini suggests:

> Studying governance systems [...] as complex systems has a number of important implications. First, instead of focusing on individual institutions, attention is directed toward interactions and interconnections – that is, the physical/social nexus between governance approaches. Second, evaluating global governance systems needs to take into account the complexity of the system – that is, system level performance is not the same as additive performance. And third, because learning, adaptation, self-organization, and feedbacks play important roles in complex systems, we need to critically rethink assumptions about top-down steering and 'orchestrating' governance.[51]

It is precisely for this reason that the predictive capacity of data and their impact on the design and implementation of public policies can affect creativity and downplay the most innovative solution.[52]

Data collection creates scenarios that reduce uncertainty and establish the probability of an event happening. Nevertheless, spreadsheets are incapable of gathering social, emotional or propagandistic information, which requires action *in situ* using human capital. The tendency to believe that big data not only serve as tools but also offer political decision-makers solutions is a grave mistake. This problem takes the shape of the automation of decisions, without human presence or a developed ethics that assesses the external repercussions of the direct implementation of a decision. As Schwartz remarks:

---

50 R. Read, B. Taithe and R. Mac Ginty, 'Data hubris? Humanitarian information systems and the mirage of technology', 37:8 *Third World Quarterly* (2016) pp. 1314–1331.

51 A. Orsini, P. Le Prestre, P.Haas, M. Brosig, P. Pattberg, O. Wideberg, J-F. Morin, L. Gomez-Mera, N. Harrison, R. Geyer and D. Chandler. 'Complex Systems and International Governance', 5 *International Studies Review* (2019) p. 14.

52 E. Finn, *What Algorithms Want: Imagination in the Age of Computing* (MITPress, Cambridge, 2017).

Predictive and prescriptive architecture is not value free. As I highlight elsewhere, algorithms and data technologies in general are rarely neutral. They typically reflect the goals and intentions of their makers, and they have the unsettling capacity to normalise their position and priorities. They also alleviate decision-makers from moral responsibility by offering scientific-technological authority for judgment, wherein erroneous or incomplete information can be sanitised through an 'invisible machinery of faith'.[53]

The scientific literature on security issues has no doubt about the need to rely on human sources. The massive use of data at the expense of other intelligence-gathering tools will not improve the expected results: "decision-makers may put undue confidence in big data tools, mistakenly seeing technological solutions as a silver bullet that can resolve the complex dilemmas they face".[54] Stuenkel considers that the predictability of international developments, based on Google searches, social media posts or online shopping, gives rise to new ethical concerns since "[i]n an ideal world, the international community could use big data to help create a better early warning system and identify countries at risk. Conversely, genocidal regimes may have an easier time locating members of a certain minority, and repressive dictatorships may use big data to predict where and when subversive movements emerge".[55] There is no simple technical solution to this dual problem. Data disclosure to third parties for providing services (geolocation, social networking sites, streaming television, and so on) leads to the violation of privacy. It is the age of instant messaging versus privacy.

The second problem has to do with the very nature of data. Data collection, moreover, corresponds to a pre-existing condition, which predefines fields, searches and connections. Big data is also biased. According to Green:

> Biased data is certainly one piece of the story, but so are existing social and political conditions, definitions and classifications of social problems, and the set of institutions that respond to those problems; none of

---

[53] E. Schwarz, 'No Matter How Big, Data is Dumb', in E. Schwarz, A. McKeil, M. Dean, M. Duffield and D. Chandler, *Datafying the Globe: Critical Insights into the Global Politics of Big Data Governance*, 26 January 2019, *Big Data & Society*, <http://bigdatasoc.blogspot.com/p/essays-and-provocations.html>, visited on 13 June 2019.

[54] Van Puyvelde, *supra* note 2, p. 1399.

[55] O. Stuenkel, *Big Data: What does it mean for International Relations?*, 6 March 2016, Post-Western World, <www.postwesternworld.com/2016/03/06/mean-international-relations/>, visited on 13 June 2019.

these factors can be removed from politics and said to be neutral. And while data scientists are of course not responsible for creating these aspects of society, they are responsible for choosing how to interact with them. When engaged with aspects of the world steeped in history and politics, in other words, it is impossible for data scientists to not take political stances.[56]

In line with the Foucauldian tradition, data reflect a structure of knowledge and power. Data are politics. The ordering and deployment of data reveal a specific structure, in this case linked to States as principal data sources and providers. Public data, depending on States or, at best, on international organizations, control the population, demography, social customs and health trends. They offer a static vision of social behaviours and preferences. The interaction between power and knowledge occurs in a specific space – be it a motorway, a railway line, public television or postal mail – that shapes the exercise of power.[57] Under a monopolistic structure, both the message and the medium are controlled.

Technological development has diversified the type of data and infrastructure, but has not eliminated the practice of power and knowledge by leveraging data. In point of fact, the monopoly of data production has become a duopoly, this time by institutionalising the collection, monitoring and subsequent sale of private data of a dynamic nature. These are behaviours, political preferences, sexual orientation and practices, emotions and so on and so forth.[58] With respect to the spatial dimension, this duopoly is evinced in the ownership of the servers in which information is stored, the use of search engines and tools, the cable infrastructure itself and even the management of the Internet Corporation for Assigned Names and Numbers (ICANN).

With public or private ownership, with a monopoly or a duopoly, the institutionalization of big data demonstrates the existence of an inexorable relationship that could be called 'data politics'. This is how Bigo, Isin and Ruppert express the idea:

> What these examples illustrate is that data and politics are inseparable. Data is not only shaping our social relations, preferences, and life chances

---

56 Green, *supra* note 35, p. 18.
57 M. Foucault, 'Space, knowledge, and power', in M. Foucault and P. Rabinow, P. (eds.), *The Foucault Reader* (Penguin UK, London, 1991) pp. 239–256.
58 M. Arias Maldonado, 'La digitalización de la conversación pública: redes sociales, afectividad política y democracia', 173 *Revista de Estudios Políticos* (2016) pp. 27–54.

but our very democracies. And that is how we want to speak of data politics. However, a problem with these views on data politics is the subjects who are constituted as the addressee and are presumably the affected Internet subjects. This is the second shortcoming that has led us to articulate what we call data politics. It concerns atomism: often such pronouncements address atomized individuals who need to protect themselves from the dangers of the Internet and its manipulations. It is based on the ontological premise of 'hyper-individualism' whereby persons, events, and phenomenon are treated as independent and 'atomistic' entities (Lake, 2017). Data politics that emerges from this reaction is one of urging people to protect themselves as individuals.[59]

In a nutshell, the collection, organization and distribution of data do not occur in a vacuum: "data does not happen through unstructured social practices".[60] Indeed, data are politics: "The field of data science must abandon its self-conception of being neutral scientists to recognize how, despite not being engaged in what is typically seen as political activity, the products of its labors shape society".[61]

7 Conclusions

Big data is one of the major game changers in international relations. Their use will transform the relations between States, governments, citizen bodies and public opinion, non-governmental organizations (NGOs), news outlets, social movements and a multitude of actors on the international stage. Furthermore, big data have arrived on the scene at a moment when there is a need for new governance models in face of the threat posed by climate change. However, the liberal order and multilateral cooperation have seen better days. The rivalry between China and the United States, European vagueness and the aftermath of the crisis are not contributing to building mutual trust, but new physical or digital walls. It is thus a political and technological decision that, in the three dimensions analysed here, has given rise to opportunities and threats.

Regulation, standardization of legal systems and developing public regulation involve different consequences. In the international environment, the

---

59   E. Ruppert, E. Isin and D. Bigo, 'Data politics', *Big Data & Society* (2017) p. 3.
60   *Ibid.*, p. 2.
61   Green, *supra* note 35, p. 46.

logic of shared norms and values limits the power of actors interested in imposing rules and decision-making procedures. The European Union acts as a global regulatory power that aspires to a model based on guarantees and individual rights. Its global governance capacity is diminished by the lack of global companies and companies that boost such regulatory power. Google, Huawei, Microsoft, Xiaomi, América Móvil or other global companies may not share the European approach. This risk is reflected in an excess of technocracy and less innovation environment. China acts as a candidate for first technological power and moves away from European standards. China does not resist or reject the European regulatory framework, but proposes its own version. For instance, the questions related to property rights of privacy may differ substantially. And there is a risk consisting in the conflict with the European model and cosmopolitan ideals. In the case of the United States, its regulatory action responds to a model of deregulation and evaluation of the consequences (*ex post* regulation). The concern that governs American law is understood from the perspective of anti-monopolistic practices. Matters of individual freedom are not a priority in technological advances as big data. In total, it is concluded that there is no single example of norms, values and correction standards. It is not a phenomenon of deregulation or absence of norms, but a process of creating norms adapted to the different regional systems.

In relation to the 'big data in international politics' aspect, this article concludes that regulation and the creation of norms lead to the coercive imposition of the standards in which countries, companies, civil society and citizens operate. There are three different approaches. At the level of 'international politics for big data', multilateral activity requires regulatory consensus. This is an opportunity to anchor regulation to specific objectives: climate change, the fight against terrorism, prosecution of illicit or human trafficking. In these matters, isolated data has no effective value for the implementation of public policy. It is likely that the three models listed above can find multilateral accommodation. This is not supranational cooperation, like other intergovernmental decisions or even laws, because both China and the United States show their preference for the reaffirmation of state power in the face of possible interference. Tension here can occur in the regulation of propaganda and public diplomacy, as well as freedom of speech or hate speech. These are central elements of freedom of information, but clear limits are established in the local tradition. Lastly, "big data for international politics" raises the tension between the State and cosmopolitanism. Humanitarian affairs, crisis management, migration and refugees, inequality and numerous issues require a political response before their regulation. Within this framework, the 2030 Agenda seems like a minimum agreement to advance some specific aspects of equal opportunity.

In conclusion, regulation of big data is in an emerging phase: there is a lack of evidence about the consequences of regulation in one way or another. We do not assist in the transformation of a previous cosmopolitan normative system, but rather the dynamics of digital transformation have affected the very foundations of the international political dynamic.

The path will not be a smooth one. However, the time has come to standardize practices in order that cooperation for the sake of the common good should be rewarded – as far as possible. There is room for international cooperation without prejudice to national sovereignty in a digital, open and connected future. But the way ahead is fraught.

Big Data and Competition Policy in the European Union

*Éva Miskolczi-Bodnár**

Abstract

Because of the specific features of digital markets and the emergence of new business models in the digital economy, competition often takes on a rather distinctive form, challenging competition authorities in the assessment of merger controls and anti-competitive behaviour. Several competition authorities have concluded recently that although generically formulated competition law provisions can be adapted to the particularities of a data-driven market, big data may require the use of somewhat specialized tools and methods in law enforcement, especially in the assessment of market power during merger control proceedings. One particular issue is whether data protection concerns might be covered by the scope of competition law. Recent case law suggests that national law enforcers are becoming increasingly flexible regarding privacy policies as a non-price competition factor in merger control in order to prevent future anti-competitive practices and a general reduction of competition in the relevant market.

Keywords

big data – digital economy – mergers – data protection – non-price competition – notification thresholds – competition authority

1 Introduction

Recent developments in digital markets have led to the emergence of a number of firms that achieve extremely significant turnover based on business models which involve the collection and use of data and personal data. Marketing has always been based on some form of market research, which usually comprises systematic data collection, processing and analysis. However, the recent technological development of the digital economy has revolutionized possibilities to collect, process and commercially use 'Big Data' in almost

---

* Ministry of Justice of Hungary.

every business sector. Although there is no agreed definition of 'Big Data' as a legal term, it is defined in legal literature as "the information asset characterized by such a high volume, velocity and variety to require specific technology and analytical methods for its transformation into value".[1] The distinguishing features of Big Data, which is usually referred to as the '4 Vs' are accordingly the large dimension and variety of datasets, high-speed (and almost real time) analysis of those datasets and the exponentially increasing value that can be extracted from them as a result. This phenomenon has spurred new discussions about the role of data in economic relationships as well as in the application of competition law, in particular as regards assessment of data as a factor in defining a relevant market and establishing market power. High-profile competition cases, such as those involving Facebook, Microsoft, and Google, indicate that competition policy faces new types of challenges in cases related to the digital economy, compared to those in more traditional sectors. This study aims to describe those challenges and to explore how the specific characteristics of digital economy markets impact competition policy and law enforcement.

The rapid growth of the digital economy raises challenges for both policy makers and law enforcers. At the practical level, competition law enforcers must face the added complexity of evaluating the conduct of market players in a dynamic environment. There are still many uncertainties concerning this sector as to competitive pressures, the specific mechanisms operating in the markets, a well as the nature of possible harms affecting consumers and innovation, all of which have to be taken into account in the assessment.[2] The question inevitably arises whether existing competition legislation is sufficient in its current form or whether it must be updated by adding specific tools for assessing the digital market sector.

At policy level, the emergence of new business models, the widespread accumulation of data and the use of big data analytics question the normative scope of competition law, its optimal use, goals and correlation with other fields of law and policy. Ultimately, legislators have to decide whether competition law may consider other policies or whether it is even obliged to enforce them.

---

1   A. De Mauro, M. Greco and M. Grimaldi (2016), 'A Formal Definition of Big Data Based on its Essential Features', *Library Review*, Vol. 65, No. 3, pp. 122–135, <https://www.researchgate.net/publication/299379163_A_formal_definition_of_Big_Data_based_on_its_essential_features>,, visited on 23 July 2017.

2   Ariel Ezrachi, 'EU Competition Law Goals and the Digital Economy' (June 6, 2018). Oxford Legal Studies Research Paper No. 17/2018, p. 2. <www.beuc.eu/publications/beuc-x-2018-071_goals_of_eu_competition_law_and_digital_economy.pdf>, visited on 10 November 2018.

2   Does Big Data Call For New Legislation?

Policy makers should ensure that any *industry-specific* regulation to be introduced is indeed *necessary* and effective. It is of high importance to consider the costs and benefits of the proposed rules in order to ensure that they do not imply disproportionate administrative burdens or other restrictions and do not render implementation and enforcement unpredictable and intransparent. In order to decide whether new legislative measures are needed in competition law, it is necessary to examine whether using big data and big data analytics is a game changer that requires a different approach from the legislator.

There are two different views in the academic debate – one that sees big data as 'business as usual' and asserting that the existing competition law toolkit can work sufficiently well and is able to tackle mergers, collusions and abuses of market power in the data economy just as well as in any other sectors. Meanwhile, another group of scholars disagrees, pointing to those specificities of big data that render standard competition law analysis ineffective.[3]

2.1   *The Distinct Characteristics of Data-driven Competition*

To properly assess the antitrust implications, the legislator has to examine how companies utilize big data and whether this has any implications for competition among these entities. From the several trends that have been observed in that regard it is worth noting that at microlevel the value of data has changed the traditional relationship between consumers and producers. Sometimes the data itself is so valuable that service provider technology companies are willing to offer free services in order to obtain it. Consequently, data became an essential asset in terms of competition and market power and thus may provide a sizeable first-mover advantage, namely the competitive advantage gained by the initial significant occupant of a market segment.

In this regard, those scholars advocating against the differential treatment of the digital sector claim firstly that data is not finite and non-rivalrous; and secondly that it is reusable and replicable, so companies – even new players – can access, collect and analyze data that is also widely available, as users leave multiple digital footprints.

Those opposing this view, on the other hand, point out that the type of data must be examined as to its substitutability. Data that search engines or social

---

[3] Mira Burri, 'Understanding the Implications of Big Data and Big Data Analytics for Competition Law: An Attempt for a Primer' (June 27, 2018), in Klaus Mathis and Avishalom Tor (eds.), *New Developments in Competition Law and Economics* (Springer, 2019), p. 241, <www.ssrn.com/abstract=3203394>, visited on 4 November 2018.

networks need for their services is quite specific and unlikely to be readily available in the market.[4] Technology companies would certainly not invest in and provide free services for users in order to collect and analyze relevant information if the data was otherwise widely available.

Because of the specific features of digital markets, competition often takes on a rather distinctive form, challenging competition authorities in the assessment of merger controls and anti-competitive behaviour. As such, due consideration must be given to the following characteristics widely common in the digital sector as listed by the OECD.[5]

Digital firms often compete by developing new business models or platforms and in the meantime redefine the boundaries of the market they are competing on and for, or even create entirely new markets. Because of the versatility of digital markets, competition authorities should treat the relevant market as a dynamic concept, rather than as a static one when assessing market power. In order to do so, authorities should first focus on the business model of the firm under investigation and to identify what other companies or business models may influence its profits.

Platform competition often leads to a winner-takes-all outcome, or in other words the tipping of the market making market dominance a likely outcome of success.

Digital markets are often characterized by economies of scale and strong direct and indirect network effects whereby increases in usage increase the value of the network for the same or an interdependent group of users.[6] Regarding platforms, the larger the number of users of a platform, the more attractive it becomes for other potential users, advertizers or content providers to join. Both features reinforce the competition-to-dominance trait mentioned above, *inter alia* by constituting a barrier to entry.

Two-sided markets with zero-priced services, such as social networks, search engines or content sharing services, are typical within the digital market. Since charging end-users might not always be profitable even given a large user base, it is a more economically viable option to sell audience access to advertizers. The market for consumers' attention is highly competitive as consumers easily find alternative content. Thus, differentiation between the two sides of digital platforms has become a widespread method, where advertizers

---

4 Inge Graef, 'Market Definition and Market Power in Data: The Case of Online Platforms', 38 *World Competition: Law and Economics Review* (2015) p. 483.
5 Organisation for Economic Co-operation and Development (OECD) (13 February 2013) *The Digital Economy*, DAF/COMP(2012)22. Paris: OECD Publishing, p. 5.
6 Nicholas L. Johnson and Alex Moazed, *Modern Monopolies: What It Takes to Dominate the 21st Century Economy* (New York: St. Martin's Press, 2016) p. 95.

are charged for access to consumer data, while the service provided for consumers is either free or to be paid for by non-monetary means. Only in those cases where end-users are less inclined to search for alternatives (or alternatives are not available) is the service provider able to charge user fees in addition.[7]

As the digital economy becomes increasingly interconnected, a degree of co-ordination and co-operation between firms is unavoidable and often pro-competitive. On the other hand, highly concentrated and transparent markets are prone to collusion.[8]

Digital markets are characterized by high rates of investment and innovation, which leads to rapid technological progress in the sector.

2.2 National Reports on the Implications of Big Data

Lately, many competition authorities have issued reports or strategies on the implications of big data with regard to competition policy (for example, the relevant agencies of the United Kingdom,[9] France, Germany[10] and Hungary[11]) or opened sector-specific inquiries and public hearings (for example, France, Germany,[12] Italy[13] and the United States[14]). The majority of these reports conclude that existing competition rules can be applied in data-driven markets.

---

7   Directorate General for Internal Policies, 'Challenges for Competition Policy in a Digitalised Economy' study for the ECON Committee, (July 2015) IP/A/ECON/2014-12 p.23, <www.europarl.europa.eu/RegData/etudes/STUD/2015/542235/IPOL_STU%282015%29542235_EN.pdf>, visited on 10 May 2017.

8   German Federal Cartel Office, ,Big Data und Wettbewerb -Schriftenreihe „Wettbewerb und Verbraucherschutz in der digitalen Wirtschaft"', (Oktober 2017) p. 8, <www.bundeskartellamt.de/SharedDocs/Publikation/DE/Schriftenreihe_Digitales/Schriftenreihe_Digitales_1.pdf?__blob=publicationFile&v=3>, visited on 15 May 2019.

9   Competition and Markets Authority, *The commercial use of consumer data* (June 2015), <www.assets.publishing.service.gov.uk/government/uploads/system/uploads/attachment_data/file/435817/The_commercial_use_of_consumer_data.pdf >, visited on 20 May 2019.

10 French Competition Authority (FCA) and German Federal Cartel Office, *Competition Law and Data* joint report (May 2016), <www.autoritedelaconcurrence.fr/doc/reportcompetitionlawanddatafinal.pdf>, visited on 30 March 2019.

11 In September 2018 the Hungarian Competition Office published its medium term digital strategy and law enforcement agenda, announcing the start of a sector specific inquiry and launching proceedings in the digital sector as its priority.

12 The FCA subsequently opened a sector-specific inquiry into the online advertizing market, while the BKartA started investigations into the social media sector.

13 The Italian Competition Authority (AGCM), Data Protection Authority and Communications Authority launched a joint fact-finding survey on the implications of big data in May 2017.

14 Federal Trade Commission press release, *FTC Announces Hearings On Competition and Consumer Protection in the 21st Century* (20 June 2018), <www.ftc.gov/news-events/

The national competition authorities and the European Commission (hereinafter: Commission) have the necessary legal instruments needed to take measures against companies that abuse a dominant position or to block mergers that would result in a dominant position.[15] Competition law provisions are generically formulated and apply in a wide variety of factual circumstances. This allows competition authorities to adapt their instruments to the particularities of a data-driven market and to avoid rigidly applying prescribed methods. In addition, authorities emphasize the importance of relying on market forces rather than sector-specific regulation and state that firms should not be condemned merely because they are large or even dominant and possess valuable big data.

Regarding law enforcement, the main finding of the reports is that the fundamental aspects of the analytical framework – for example, market definition, market power, competitive effects – should continue to be applicable, although big data can raise new challenges that may require the use of somewhat specialized tools and methods. At the same time, these reports recognize that no universally valid conclusions can be drawn to offer categorical guidance without looking at the specific case involved, so that a case-by-case analysis is inevitable.[16]

Most often market power can result in prices above the competitive level as dominant firms abusing their bargaining power are able to profitably increase prices over marginal costs. As such, in most cases competition authorities have to assess those price effects that the firms under investigation have exerted on the market. In the digital sector with zero-priced services, however, market power might not have any impact on charging policy. Instead, market power may more likely lead to a reduction in quality or of the incentive to innovate, where suboptimal quality or avoided investment costs might result in excessive profit margins. Thus, one of the required changes of method is that enforcement should be able to address non-price effects as well. Quality is a leading example of the non-price dimension of competition; however, what constitutes quality will vary from case to case.[17]

---

press-releases/2018/06/ftc-announces-hearings-competition-consumer-protection-21st>, visited on 2 June 2019.

15   Dutch Ministry of Economic Affairs, Big data and competition, Rotterdam: ECORYS 2017, p. 13–14, <www.rijksoverheid.nl/binaries/rijksoverheid/documenten/rapporten/2017/06/13/big-data-and-competition/big-data-and-competition.pdf>, visited on 5 November 2018.
16   *See* Joint report, *supra* note 9, pp. 26–27.
17   *See* Competition Bureau Canada, Big data and innovation: key themes for competition policy in Canada (September 2017) p. 8, <www.competitionbureau.gc.ca/eic/site/cb-bc.nsf/eng/04342.html>, visited on 20 November 2018.

At least so far, competition agencies around the world have been cautious whenever cases with big data implications appear and have not intervened proactively,[18] taking rather a *laissez-faire* approach. Of course, certain costs are attached to antitrust intervention, as well as risks stemming from untimely or erroneus intervention. Therefore, in technologically dynamic markets in particular, the reluctance of authorities to intervene might be justified. One of the main conclusions deterring authorities from intervention is that the structure of dynamic markets at any point in time is likely to be in transition, so the elements of the competitive environment which competition authorities decide to investigate are likely to become outdated as the investigation proceeds.[19] Furthermore, temporary dominance is the prize for which firms compete and is not in itself prohibited by competition law. As such, enforcement that precludes market players from achieving market power may be counter-productive and slow innovation by eliminating incentives to invest in research of new technologies.

On the other hand, risks associated with large networks, data pools, platforms and their impact on competing innovators and market structure may call for greater scrutiny. Proper enforcement must strike the right balance between taking steps to prevent behaviour that truly harms competition and over-enforcement that chills innovation while unjustifiably protecting those market players who otherwise would fall out of the market while competing on the merits.

3   Mergers and Acquisitions in the Digital Sector

3.1   *Goals and Potential Effects of Mergers*

The adequacy of current merger control thresholds has recently been questioned in the context of increasing numbers of digital start-up takeovers. In many markets, a merger between an established undertaking and an innovative newcomer only has a low impact on the existing market structure because of the newcomer's low market share or even the absence of horizontal overlap. However, in data-related markets, such a merger could result in differentiated data access and increase the concentration of data related to that market if the

---

18   Roisin Comerford and D. Daniel Sokol, 'Antitrust and Regulating Big Data' 23 *George Mason Law Review* (2016), p. 1130.
19   Howard A. Shelanski, 'Information, Innovation, and Competition Policy for the Internet', 161 *University of Pennsylvania Law Review* (2013) pp. 1670–1671.

newcomer is already in possession of a large database.[20] This is an increasingly common phenomenon, with OECD data showing that mergers whose main purpose was to acquire datasets almost tripled over the 2008–2012 period.[21]

Additionally, in assessing possible restraints on competition resulting from a merger, competition authorities may have to cast a close look at the advantages the new entity will have by combining different sets of data. This could raise competition concerns, in particular if the combination of data makes it impossible for competitors to replicate the information extracted from it.[22]

Despite dynamic market interactions in the digital economy and the contestability of the market, there is a concern that successful digital firms tip the market and achieve considerable market power. Because network effects on digital markets lead to a winner-takes-all outcome, first-mover advantages may be significant. As such, it may be of high importance to prevent others from being the first to profitably exploit their new technologies or datasets, namely to prevent entry into future markets.[23]

A firm may achieve 'first entry' to a future market mostly by innovating on its own. The diversified and improved products or the efficiency gains achieved that are often passed on to consumers are clearly beneficial to end-users and does not raise competition concerns. Alternatively, a firm may acquire a company with an innovative technology or service and attract engineering talent. Such an acquisition can also benefit end-users and SMEs, firstly because the prospects of being acquired stimulate small companies and startups to innovate, and secondly since the combination of own and acquired technologies may enhance development even further. However, there is a risk that an acquisition has the sole purpose of eliminating the most threatening potential competitors while they are still small. That is why it is also referred to as a *preemptive merger*.

---

20 German Monopolies Commission (*Monopolkommission*), Special Report No. 68: *Competition policy: The challenge of digital markets* (2015) §§ 109, 478, <www.monopolkommission.de/images/PDF/SG/s68_fulltext_eng.pdf>, visited on 20 November 2018.
21 OECD, *Data-Driven Innovation: Big Data for Growth and Well-Being*, OECD Publishing, Paris (2015), <www.dx.doi.org/10.1787/9789264229358-en>, visited on 30 May 2019.
22 Bundeskartellamt, Study: Competition Law and Data (10th May, 2016) p. 16, <www.bundeskartellamt.de/SharedDocs/Publikation/DE/Berichte/Big%20Data%20Papier.pdf?__blob=publicationFile&v=2>, visited on 12 May 2017.
23 Directorate General for Internal Policies, *Challenges for Competition Policy in a Digitalised Economy* study for the ECON Committee, July 2015, IP/A/ECON/2014-12, p. 29, <www.europarl.europa.eu/RegData/etudes/STUD/2015/542235/IPOL_STU%282015%29542235_EN.pdf>, accessed on 10 May 2017.

3.2 Recent Legislation on Mergers

Innovative companies newly entering the market will often fail to generate high turnover at first. On the other hand, their corporate value may be significant as a result of their innovative products, the data sets they have compiled, and their market presence in terms of users.[24] This value causes a contradiction between low turnover and a high purchase price, which also indicates how the acquirer perceives the relevance of the firm in the market.

Considering the above mentioned new trends, in October 2016 the Commission launched a public consultation on potential reform of EU merger control thresholds. The consultation and proposed changes aimed to simplify and modernize the current functioning of merger control. One of the objectives of the consultation was to assess the effectiveness of the current turnover-based jurisdictional thresholds of the EU Merger Regulation,[25] particularly with regard to acquisitions in the digital and pharmaceutical sectors. Under the relevant law in force,[26] the Commission examines in principle only mergers with an EU dimension, where the merging entities reach certain world-wide and EU-wide turnover thresholds. Smaller mergers without an EU dimension may fall under the remit of Member State competition authorities instead, given that national turnover thresholds are met. One of the questions discussed was whether and if so how to capture mergers between established companies and new entrants with insignificant turnover, but with access to a valuable database instead.[27]

Only a minority of responding stakeholders participating in the public consultation perceived the existence of such an enforcement gap and are in favour of introducing complementary jurisdictional thresholds, fearing that in the digital sector EU merger control may fail to catch all competitively significant cross-border transactions. One group of Respondents proposed introduction of either a sufficiently high level of transaction value threshold or a notification

---

24 Victoria Moorcroft, Ariane Le Strat, *The rise of Big Data – Intersection between Competition law and customer data* (January 2018), <www.twobirds.com/en/news/articles/2018/uk/the-rise-of-big-data-intersection-between-competition-law-and-customer-data>, visited on 5 June 2019.
25 Council Regulation (EC) No. 139/2004 of 20 January 2004 on the control of concentrations between undertakings (the EC Merger Regulation), *OJ L* 24, 29.01.2004, p. 1–22.
26 *See* EC Merger Regulation Article 1, 4(5) and 22.
27 WilmerHale, *8-in-8 Recent Trends in European Law and Policy Alert Series: Competition and Big Data—Recent Developments in Europe* (July, 2018), <www.wilmerhale.com/en/insights/client-alerts/20180712-8-in-8-recent-trends-in-european-law-and-policy-alert-series-update-competition-and-big-data-recent-developments-in-europe>, visited on 2 May 2019.

requirement based on the number of consumers directly impacted by the merger.[28]

On the other hand, the vast majority of stakeholders did not perceive the need for any amendment to the EU Merger Regulation since high-value acquisitions of low-turnover targets are typically subject to merger review at the national level or, even if it might not be the case, national laws can usually be adapted more swiftly to add non-turnover-based notification thresholds. Furthermore, some pointed out the markedly higher resources required to investigate the increased number of cases, while others noted that the purchase price, being subjective, does not necessarily indicate the competitive significance of a transaction. This overwhelming rejection is probably one reason why the Commission have not published any conclusions or submitted any legislative proposals.

Meanwhile at EU Member State level, Germany and Austria introduced additional, value-based thresholds in 2017 similar to those proposed by the Commission. As a result even if turnover-based thresholds are not met, a merger may be notifiable if the value of transaction consideration exceeds 400 million EUR in Germany or 200 million EUR in Austria, and the target company has significant current domestic activities.[29] With the addition of such criteria the company's potential and therefore its competitive relevance might not be overlooked. To make application of the provisions transparent, in July 2018 the German Federal Cartel Office and the Austrian Federal Competition Authority published a joint guideline with instructions for interpreting the thresholds.[30]

3.3 Privacy Implications of Mergers

Recent mergers that took place in the EU have raised some serious concerns about potentially substantial harm to privacy in data-driven markets, where consumers surrender control over their data. As the new, merged entity accumulates different datasets, it significantly increases the risk that extensive information can be compiled about each individual consumer, facilitating profiling and automated decision-making. Its controversial nature goes to the very

---

28 Summary of replies to the Public Consultation on Evaluation of procedural and jurisdictional aspects of EU merger control (July 2017) p. 4, <www.ec.europa.eu/competition/consultations/2016_merger_control/summary_of_replies_en.pdf>, visited on 8 May 2019.
29 Section 35(1a) of the German Act against Restraints of Competition (GWB) and 9(4) of the Austrian Cartel Act (KartG), respectively.
30 Guidance on Transaction Value Thresholds for Mandatory Pre-merger Notification (Section 35 (1a) GWB and Section 9 (4) KartG) (July 2018), <www.bwb.gv.at/fileadmin/user_upload/Downloads/standpunkte/2018-07_Guidance_Transaction_Value_Thresholds.pdf>, visited on 1 May 2019.

question of the outer limits of competition law and how far this field of law should take into consideration broader, non-economic concerns.

At this point we must look back at our starting point to the second question: "Is this a competition problem?" Because even if the development of technology and business models gives rise to a clear need for a change in policy, an assessment is needed as to which field of law is the most suitable to tackle the problem. Nowadays, authorities and courts have ever more frequently to face the practical implications of the overlapping policies of competition law, consumer law, and privacy protection.

Data collection and use is subject to several legal constraints. Consumer protection rules and intellectual property (IP) rights might be applicable to both non-personal and personal data, while personal data are also subject to general data protection law and the fundamental right to privacy. The question arises whether competition law firstly has an adequate mandate to impose further constraints and obligations on data collecting firms, and secondly whether it has sufficient tools at its disposal to ensure compliance.

To decide whether competition policy is adept at addressing the issue, the main goals and values of competition law may provide some useful insights in order to determine its scope.

EU competition rules and values have been interpreted and clarified through case law, official publications, and legal literature. According to the Commission, competition in the market is protected "as a means of enhancing consumer welfare and of ensuring an efficient allocation of resources".[31] It must also be highlighted that these core values and Treaty-based competition rules do not exist in a vacuum and must be interpreted in the light of wider European normative values.[32] According to the Treaty on the Functioning of the European Union, "the Union shall ensure consistency between its policies and activities, taking all of its objectives into account".[33]

Ultimately, the goal of competition policy is to ensure that both businesses and consumers get a fair share of the benefits of growth and free market.[34] From the consumers' point of view these benefits may take the form of either

---

31 European Commission, 'Guidelines on the Application of Article 81(3) of the Treaty' [2004] *OJ C* 101/97, para. 13.
32 Ezrachi, *supra* note 1, p. 3.
33 Art. 7, Consolidated version of the Treaty on the Functioning of the European Union [2016] *OJ C* 202/47.
34 European Commission, 'Report on Competition Policy 2016' COM(2017) 285 final, p. 2, <www.ec.europa.eu/transparency/regdoc/rep/1/2017/EN/COM-2017-285-F1-EN-MAIN-PART-1.PDF>, visited on 8 May 2019.

cheaper or better products and services as these are the two ultimate dimensions – namely, price and non-price competition – in which companies compete with each other and customers evaluate and rank products. As we have seen above, in the digital environment, where the price is often ostensibly free for consumers, quality thus forms an important dimension of competition. It logically follows that in the absence of prices, the harm deriving from abuse of a dominant position will also appear in the form of quality degradation instead of a higher price level, to the detriment of consumer welfare. As a result, the digital market will increasingly require law enforcers to consider a range of unquantifiable variables as opposed to general cases where analysis of quantifiable price effects is sufficient.

Because of consumers' rising privacy awareness, it is arguable that consumers may view privacy as an important element of quality, particularly in the case of free technology services. As a result, the scale of privacy protection offered to consumers could be a relevant dimension of non-price competition between firms and, as such, it should become part of competition analysis. That way the frequent claim that data protection concerns are falling outside the scope of competition law – and as such competition authorities should not address this question in their decision – can be sidestepped and these matters can be assessed not as a distinct policy but as an aspect of quality. Although in legal literature this conclusion has become widely accepted,[35] nevertheless, it is yet to be seen whether enforcement agencies and courts will be willing to adopt this view and implement it into case law. Especially, since assessing whether, and if so, to what extent new forms of data collection and data processing constitute quality degradation and increase the risk of data security, extensive involvement of data professionals is required in the law enforcement process in the future.

4 EU Case Law of Data-driven Mergers

The argument that there may be overlaps between competition and privacy concerns is not entirely new, yet competition authorities have been very careful in mixing competition and other concerns. In 2006, the European Court of Justice in *Asnef-Equifax*[36] stated that privacy concerns raised by the big data

---

[35] *See also* Allen P. Grunes and Maurice E. Stucke, *Debunking the Myths over Big Data and Antitrust*. Competition Policy International Antitrust Chronicle (2015), p. 5.
[36] Case C-238/05 – *Asnef-Equifax* v *Asociación de Usuarios de Servicios Bancarios (Ausbanc)*, [2006] ECR I-11125.

phenomenon fall outside the scope of intervention by competition authorities. The dissenting statement in *Google/DoubleClick*[37] already suggested in 2008 that privacy could be "'cognizable' under the antitrust laws"[38] and that it should have been taken into consideration in market analysis. The Federal Trade Commission of the United States (hereinafter: FTC) has stated that antitrust laws do not provide a basis for blocking or imposing conditions on a merger purely to safeguard privacy. In Europe, the Commission's evaluation similarly followed a conservative route and focused solely on analyzing its competitive effects on price and market structure. Although the Commission did not address privacy concerns, it stressed nonetheless that the decision is without prejudice to the parties' separate obligations under EU data protection law.[39] This was confirmed in the subsequent *Facebook/WhatsApp* merger case,[40] where the transaction was cleared by both the FTC and the Commission without any conditions attached. The latter pointed out that "[a]ny privacy-related concerns flowing from the increased concentration of data within the control of Facebook as a result of the Transaction do not fall within the scope of the EU competition law rules but under EU data protection law".[41]

The Commission ignored the serious decrease in the strength of the terms of Whatsapp's privacy policy after acquisition which might have been assessed as a decrease in the quality of the service post-merger. Or, equivalently, in the sense that data has been identified as the 'new currency of the internet', an increase in the collection of private data could be compared to a price increase. In this case the Commission should have reached the conclusion that privacy considerations can fall within the ambit of non-price quality competition and, as such, competition law.[42]

By contrast, in their joint report in 2016, the French and German competition agencies pointed out that:

> privacy policies could be considered from a competition standpoint whenever these policies are liable to affect competition, notably when

---

37 Commission decision of 11 March 2008 in Case No COMP/M.4731, *Google/DoubleClick*.
38 Pamela Jones Harbour, Commissioner, FTC, Dissenting Statement regarding in re *Google/DoubleClick*, FTC File No. 071-0170, 20 December 2007, p. 10.
39 *Google/DoubleClick* decision, *supra* note 35, para.164.
40 Commission decision of 3 October 2014 in Case No. COMP/M.7217, *Facebook/WhatsApp*.
41 *Facebook/WhatsApp* decision, para. 164.
42 Kimmel, L. and J. Kestenbaum, (2014), 'What's Up with WhatsApp?: A Transatlantic View on Privacy and Merger Enforcement in Digital Markets', *Antitrust*, Vol. 29, No. 1, <www.connection.ebscohost.com/c/articles/102841624/whats-up-whatsapp-transatlantic-view-privacy-merger-enforcement-digital-markets>, visited on 20 November 2018.

they are implemented by a dominant undertaking for which data serves as a main input of its products or services. In those cases, there may be a close link between the dominance of the company, its data collection processes and competition on the relevant markets, which could justify the consideration of privacy policies and regulations in competition proceedings.[43]

Despite its previous position in Facebook/WhatsApp, the Commission has most recently acknowledged in *Microsoft/LinkedIn*[44] that although privacy concerns fell under data protection laws, privacy could be seen as a non-price competition factor in merger control assessment to the extent that consumers saw it as a significant factor in the quality of services offered.[45]

By accepting that the decisions of undertakings on the collection and use of personal data can have implications on the economic and competition dimension as well, the Commission's policy may be shifting toward a more holistic approach.

5 Conclusion

There is broad consensus among legislators, enforcers and scholars that the existing competition rules in force can be applied in data-driven markets, and the fast-growing technology sector does not as such constitute grounds for an immediate change of policy. A – not broadly supported – exception might be the broadening of notification thresholds in order to give due consideration to the transaction value and thus to the relevance of the acquired firm in merger cases. Nonetheless, competition authorities may need to adapt their instruments to the particular circumstances in a data-driven market which does not require amendment of legislation but rather of the methods employed in competition analysis. Moreover, the number of cases in which data plays a major role will likely increase, so that in order to understand the business model in its depth it becomes vital for regulators and enforcers to obtain expertise in data and computer science in the future.

Finally, since the dominance of a company, its data collection processes and the state of competition in the relevant markets are closely linked together, it should be accepted that some anti-competitive practices will inevitably

---

43   Joint report, *supra* note 9, pp. 22–23.
44   Commission decision of 16 December 2016 in case COMP/M-8124 *Microsoft/LinkedIn*.
45   *Ibid*, para. 350.

infringe more than one relevant area of law at the same time. This could justify consideration of privacy policies and regulations in competition proceedings and may call for closer cooperation between consumer, data and competition authorities in the framework of their investigations to address enforcement gaps.[46]

---

46 Anca D. Chirita, 'Data-Driven Mergers Under EU Competition Law' (June 20, 2018) In J Linarelli & O Akseli (eds.), *The Future of Commercial Law: Ways Forward for Harmonisation* (Oxford, Hart Publishing, 2019) p. 43, <www.ssrn.com/abstract=3199912>, visited on 3 November 2018.

Antitrust After Big Data

*John M. Yun**

Abstract

With the rise of digital markets, the conventional wisdom was that big data was a new economic phenomenon that would allow incumbent firms with market power to entrench their market positions, foreclose competitors, and serve as a virtually insurmountable barrier to entry. This led to calls for greater antitrust enforcement and regulation of big data practices. Since that time, with the benefit of substantial growth in the theoretical and empirical economic literature involving big data, it is appropriate to revisit our understanding of big data's implications for antitrust. This paper contributes to the discussion by detailing three things we have learned about big data as it applies to competition policy. First, we now have a better understanding of the role that big data plays in the production and innovation process. Second, it makes little sense to reflexively label big data as a barrier to entry. Competition policy is better served by considering actual entry conditions rather than basing competitive effects analysis on determining whether access to certain inputs are or are not barriers to entry. Third, competition authorities now have a sizeable level of experience in assessing big data in actual cases. It is notable that, thus far, big data alone has not fuelled a theory of harm that has led to an agency challenge in the U.S.A. or Europe. All these considerations suggest that we are perhaps in a new, more mature, era regarding big data in competition policy – not because big data is any less important to innovation – but because researchers and regulators have consistently found that big data in and of itself does not represent a relevant antitrust concern.

Keywords

big data – barrier to entry – network effects – digital platforms – competition policy – antitrust

---

* Associate Professor of Law and Director of Economic Education, Global Antitrust Institute, Antonin Scalia Law School, George Mason University. I thank Ken Heyer, Seth Sacher, and Joshua Wright for tremendously helpful comments.

1 Introduction

The phrase 'big data' likely first entered the economic lexicon in 2000, when economist Francis Diebold used the term in his paper, '"Big Data" Dynamic Factor Models for Macroeconomic Measurement and Forecasting'; although Diebold acknowledges that "credit for the term Big Data must be shared".[1] Regardless of its origin, most definitions of big data are similar to the one provided by the OECD: "Big Data is commonly understood as the use of large scale computing power and technologically advanced software in order to collect, process and analyse data characterized by a large volume, velocity, variety and value".[2]

Since those early days, according to Matt Turck, interest in big data reached its apex between 2011 and 2014 – at least in the world of venture capitalists (VC).[3] Since that time, VC interest has transitioned to the analytical tools needed to assess and unlock value from big data – namely, through machine learning and artificial intelligence. This shift prompted Turck to ask in 2016: "Is Big Data still a 'thing'?"[4]

While interest in big data had begun to wane among VCs, public interest in, and concern over, big data as a potential *competition issue* perhaps hit its apex in mid-2017 when *The Economist* contended that, in terms of its role in today's information economy, big data plays a role similar to that historically played by oil in powering the pre-information economy. Put succinctly, *The Economist* declared that big data is "the new oil".[5] Yet, well before that point, research into

---

1 Francis X. Diebold, 'On the Origin(s) and Development of "Big Data": The Phenomenon, the Term, and the Discipline', 13 February, 2019, <https://www.sas.upenn.edu/~fdiebold/papers/paper112/Diebold_Big_Data.pdf> at p. 2.
2 OECD Directorate for Financial and Enterprise Affairs Competition Committee, "Big Data: Bringing Competition Policy to the Digital Era", Background note by the Secretariat, 29–30 November 2016, at p. 2.
3 Matt Turck, "Is Big Data Still a Think? (The 2016 Big Data Landscape)", 1 February 2016, <http://mattturck.com/big-data-landscape> ("interest in the concept of 'Big Data' reached fever pitch sometime between 2011 and 2014. This was the period when, at least in the press and on industry panels, Big Data was the new 'black gold' or 'oil'. However, at least in my conversations with people in the industry, there is an increasing sense of having reached some kind of plateau. 2015 was probably the year when the cool kids in the data world (to the extent there is such a thing) moved on to obsessing over AI and its many related concepts and flavors: machine intelligence, deep learning, etc.").
4 *Id*. Certainly, a comparison of the frequency that users searched for the terms 'big data' and 'machine learning' on Google Search supports Turck's conjecture, which indicates that searches for big data peaked around 2014, and searches for machine learning have outstripped that of big data after 2016. *See* Google Trends at <https://trends.google.com/trends/?geo=US>.
5 The Economist, 'The World's Most Valuable Resource is No Longer Oil, But Data', 6 May 2017, available at <https://www.economist.com/leaders/2017/05/06/the-worlds-most-valuable-re-

whether big data truly represents an antitrust problem had already began with a number of foundational questions including: what exactly is big data?; do only big firms have it?; do you need it to enter and compete successfully in a digital economy?; is it a barrier to entry?; can it be a competition problem?; and can it generate efficiencies, enhance consumer welfare, and perhaps even promote competition? Some early conclusions, which we detail in Section 2, tended to suggest that competition agencies should use a strong presumption of harm when a firm with market power possesses big data.

Since those initial inquiries, there has been a flurry of research and commentary in a relatively short period of time – primarily, over a five-year period from 2013 to 2018. From this research, what has emerged are some key findings and insights that indicate we have moved into a new 'era' in how we consider big data in the context of antitrust. This is not to suggest that big data is no longer a consideration in antitrust review; it is. But rather, there is growing recognition that big data in and of itself is not a competition problem. In this paper, after discussing the primary antitrust concerns in Section 2, we detail the three findings that we believe support this new era conclusion.

First, as detailed in Section 3, we have a better understanding of the role that big data plays in the production and innovation process. Big data is one input, among many, that a firm uses to maximize profits, including through innovation. The success of a new product, new feature, or other types of innovation, whether from an entrant or an incumbent, relies on a mix of factors that the firm combines to help it take advantage of concurrent market opportunities, such as shifts in consumer preferences or changes in rivals' behaviour. Indeed, even with potential network effects and associated feedback effects from the use of big data,[6] the fundamental reality is that data lacks worth unless it is combined with ingenuity, skill, and market conditions to unlock its value. Nearly all research on big data has affirmed this central point.

Second, in competition analysis, there is often confusion regarding what is and what is not a barrier to entry – as evidenced by a lack of consensus

---

source-is-no-longer-oil-but-data>. The idea of data as the new oil was likely coined by UK mathematician Clive Humby (*see* Michael Palmer, 'Data is the New Oil', <https://ana.blogs.com/maestros/2006/11/data_is_the_new.html>).

6 The idea is that successful use of big data and analytics creates a positive feedback loop. For example, a greater volume of users can provide data to a search engine which, in turn, has a positive impact on search quality. A positive impact on search quality, in turn, can result in a greater volume of users. This can be labelled as 'data-driven indirect network effects'. *See* Cédric Argenton & Jens Prüfer, 'Search Engine Competition with Network Externalities *8 J. Competition L. & Econ.* 73 (2012) and Jens Prüfer & Christoph Schottmüller, 'Competing with Big Data', (*Tilburg Law School Legal Studies Research Paper Series* No. 06/2017, <http://ssrn.com/abstract=2918726>).

regarding its definition – which we explore in detail in Section 4. While big data frequently represents an important asset and resource that firms use, that fact, in and of itself, does not demonstrate that it constitutes a barrier to entry. As Tucker & Wellford (2014) state:

> The fact that some established online firms collect a large volume of data from their customers or other sources does not mean that new entrants must have the same quantity or type of data in order to enter and compete effectively ... [L]ack of asset equivalence should not be a sufficient basis to define a barrier to entry.[7]

There is also the fact that similar data may be available to entrants due to the non-rivalrous nature of information, rather than most of it being owned exclusively by the incumbents using it. Ultimately, we find that labelling big data an entry barrier does not necessarily make it so. Rather, a proper analysis of the role played by big data in impeding – or perhaps even facilitating – entry is better performed by examining actual entry conditions on a case by case basis. Competition policy is ill-served by prejudging the outcome of the analysis by resorting to labels rather than by a careful examination of the facts.

Additionally, as detailed in Section 5, competition authorities in the U.S.A. and Europe have now amassed considerable experience in assessing big data in actual cases and, thus far at least, it has yet to play a dominant role in any competition agency challenge – holding aside cases where data is the product itself.[8] What does this lack of agency challenge tell us? While it does not prove that big data is not a competition issue, it can support that proposition. Moreover, an assessment of the agencies' decisions that involve big data reveals a

---

[7] Darren S. Tucker & Hill B. Wellford, 'Big Mistakes Regarding Big Data', *Antitrust Source*, December 2014, at pp. 1, 7.

[8] *See* D. Daniel Sokol and Roisin Comerford, 'Antitrust and Regulating Big Data', 23 *Geo. Mason L. Rev.* 1129 (2016) at p. 1130 ("In reality, there is no challenge at all, as the arguments for antitrust intervention when Big Data has come up as an issue have never carried the day for any merger or decided conduct case in any Department of Justice Antitrust Division ('DOJ'), Federal Trade Commission ('FTC') or Directorate-General for Competition ('DG Competition') case to date."). *See also* Margrethe Vestager, 'Competition in a Big Data World', speech given 17 January 2016, <https://ec.europa.eu/commission/commissioners/2014-2019/vestager/announcements/competition-big-data-world_en> ("we shouldn't take action just because a company holds a lot of data. After all, data doesn't automatically equal power...The Commission has looked at this issue in two merger cases – Google's acquisition of DoubleClick, and Facebook's purchase of WhatsApp. In the particular circumstances of those cases, there was no serious cause for concern...We continue to look carefully at this issue, but we haven't found a competition problem yet.").

lack of basis to suggest that competition agencies and the courts have been systematically neglecting this possible issue.[9]

Finally, in Section 6, we explore the relevant legal aspects of big data in antitrust. Specifically, we focus on what the presence of big data should imply, in the context of a rule of reason analysis. We find there is little basis for a presumption of harm regarding big data – given the current state of the evidence. Conversely, there is growing evidence that big data can play a central role in realizing merger-specific efficiencies.

In totality, these considerations suggest that either we are in a new era regarding big data in competition policy – or we should be. In this new era, big data and analytics are considered just as important to innovation; yet, there is a recognition that big data is not anything unique when it comes to competition. It should be treated no differently than assets such as highly skilled labour, specialized capital, and R&D infrastructure. Thus, just as it is possible to formulate a theory of harm involving the foreclosure of a necessary input involving intellectual property and capital, it is also possible to formulate a theory of harm involving the foreclosure of vital data.[10] Yet, the same rule of reason paradigm applies, which is based on weighing alleged anticompetitive harms with potential procompetitive benefits using actual evidence. Therefore, the mere possession and use of big data, as well as the competitive advantages gained from big data and associated analytics, are neither necessary nor sufficient conditions for presuming harm, let alone for concluding it.

To slightly expand the point, there is a distinction between firms monopolizing data and firms collecting and utilizing data in their ordinary course of business. These are the not the same thing and should not be conflated with each other. Monopolizing data involves a firm engaging in anticompetitive means to exclusively control so much information that rivals are unable to effectively compete. Firms who collect a great deal of data and use the data to improve products are engaging, instead, in procompetitive conduct, suggesting

---

9   Of course, there are plenty of criticisms of the U.S. antitrust agencies' decisions to enforce and not to enforce. In support of this position, the most cited study is John Kwoka, *Mergers, Merger Control, and Remedies*, Cambridge (MA): MIT Press, (2015). The study, however, has a number of weaknesses. *See* Michael Vita & David Osinski, 'John Kwoka's Mergers, Merger Control, and Remedies: A Critical Review', *361 Antitrust Law Journal 82* (2018). We are not aware of Kwoka-like critiques of EC decisions.

10 Although Tucker (2019) argues convincingly that big data should not be considered an "essential facility". *See* Catherine Tucker, 'Digital Data, Platforms and the Usual [Antitrust] Suspects: Network Effects, Switching Costs, Essential Facility', *Review of Industrial Organization* 54 (2019), pp. 683–694 at p. 684.

that use or even ownership of lots of data need not necessarily lead to consumer harm.

2   The Rise of Big Data

Given that the use of data by suppliers to improve efficiency and gain a competitive advantage is certainly not a new concept,[11] when did the concern regarding big data as an *antitrust* problem begin? Certainly, the idea that possessing certain types of data can give firms a competitive advantage predates the digital era. Muris & Nuechterlein (2018) convincingly argue that concerns about the use of data were present even during the heyday of the Great Atlantic and Pacific Tea Company (A&P).[12]

What has unquestionably changed is the rise of the digital economy and the staggering volume, velocity, and variety of data generated virtually instantaneously.[13] IBM estimated that "2.5 quintillion bytes of data" is created daily with "90 percent of the world's data created in the last two years alone".[14] According to Domo, a software provider, "By 2020, it's estimated that for every person on earth, 1.7 MB of data will be created every second".[15] In 2018, IDC

---

11   See Canada Competition Bureau, 'Big Data and Innovation: Implications for Competition Policy in Canada', 2017 ("...the use of data is hardly new. General stores used to keep a record of information about customers located in their small town (including, for example, credit information). One of the first large-scale and systematic collections of data occurred in the mid-nineteenth century when the large American railroads began mandating regular, system-wide reports, which required the building of extensive comptroller departments, the hiring of full-time auditors, and the development of fundamental accounting concepts still in use today. At about the same time, mercantile agencies, such as precursors to the Dun & Bradstreet firm, began collecting and selling substantial amounts of credit reporting data", p. 5); Alfred D. Chandler Jr., *The Visible Hand* (Harvard University Press, 1977) pp.109–119. ("...a constant flow of information was essential to the efficient operation of these new large business domains. For the middle and top managers, control through statistics quickly became both a science and an art. This need for accurate information led to the devising of improved methods for collecting, collating, and analyzing a wide variety of data generated by the day-to-day operations of the enterprise. Of even more importance it brought a revolution in accounting...").

12   Timothy J. Muris and John E. Nuechterlein, 'Antitrust in the Internet Era: The Legacy of United States v. A&P', 54 *Review of Industrial Organization* (2018) pp. 651–681 at p. 657 ("A&P also succeeded because it did what many tech companies do today, albeit amid much controversy: use data to create greater consumer value".).

13   See OECD, *supra* note 2.

14   <https://www-03.ibm.com/press/us/en/photo/36002.wss>.

15   *Data Never Sleeps 6.0*, Domo, <https://www.domo.com/learn/data-never-sleeps-6>.

estimated the global volume of data to be 33 zettabytes, which is equivalent to 33 trillion gigabytes – forecasting it to grow to 175 zettabytes in 2025.[16] Focusing more on the consumer end, global smartphone app downloads exceeded 194 billion in 2018, which is 35 percent more than just two years before.[17]

Clearly, this colossal volume of data implies that greater resources are needed to collect, store, and manage the data. While this potentially increases the capital requirements to handle such large volumes of data, the ready availability of cloud computing services enables many firms to access and utilize big data without having to make large investments in capital and infrastructure.[18]

Additionally, the sheer size and opportunities provided by big data has led, perhaps not surprisingly, to conjectures and concerns regarding its antitrust implications. The thinking has been that big data represents something new and potentially quite valuable, particularly with the rise and prominence of multi-sided platforms. And when something is potentially quite valuable, concerns naturally arise about whether it can be abused by large marketplace players. Further, though not as obviously antitrust-relevant, serious concerns have been raised about the implications of big data for consumer privacy. The antitrust concerns are summarized in the following argument from Newman (2014), as applied to one particular user of big data:

> control of information has been skewed towards a few players with both the concentrated data processing power and supply of user data to dominate a particular sector. For example, as of 2012, Google processes sixty-five percent of U.S. search queries, and earns seventy-eight percent of U.S. search advertising revenue (and eighty-five percent of global search

---

[16] IDC (2018), *Data Age 2025, Digitization of the World, From Edge to Core*, p. 6, available at <https://www.seagate.com/files/www-content/our-story/trends/files/idc-seagate-data-age-whitepaper.pdf>.

[17] App Annie (2019), *The State of Mobile 2019*, available at <https://www.appannie.com/en/insights/market-data/the-state-of-mobile-2019>.

[18] *See* Ibrahim Abaker Targio Hashem *et al.*, 'The Rise of 'Big Data' on Cloud Computing: Review and Open Research Issues', 47 *Information Systems* (2015) pp. 98–115 at p. 99 ("Cloud computing is one of the most significant shifts in modern ICT and service for enterprise applications and has become a powerful architecture to perform large-scale and complex computing…Cloud computing can not only minimize the cost and restriction for automation and computerization by individuals and enterprises but can also provide reduced infrastructure maintenance cost, efficient management, and user access".); Amit Verma, "Big Data and Cloud Computing – A Perfect Combination", Whizlabs.com, July 21, 2018 at <https://www.whizlabs.com/blog/big-data-and-cloud-computing> ("Cloud enables customers for big data processing without large-scale big data resources".).

revenue). Thus, antitrust authorities around the world have with good reason targeted the company for its dominance.[19]

The implication is that the sheer volume of data that firms with high market shares regularly collect is *the reason* for their dominance and/or their maintenance of monopoly power. That logic is suspect. Even if data were the primary reason for a firm's dominance, this hardly implies that dominant firms are doing anything nefarious, or that there is a need for competition authorities to intervene. Ownership and/or use of big data by large firms, it has been alleged, is objectionable because "control of user data can entrench monopoly power and harm consumer welfare in an economy shaped increasingly by the power of companies collecting personal data".[20] Maybe it can, maybe it cannot. Theory alone does not lead to a single unambiguous conclusion, and available evidence does not do so either.

Grunes & Stucke (2015) argue that "these features of big data [volume, velocity, variety, and value] have several implications for competition policy, including raising barriers to entry and foreclosing access to essential inputs".[21] Besides:

> companies whose business model depends on securing a competitive advantage through big data, may also devise anticompetitive data-driven strategies. Such strategies may include preventing rivals from accessing the data (such as through exclusivity provisions with third-party providers) or foreclosing opportunities for rivals to procure similar data (such as making it harder for consumers to adopt other technologies or platforms).[22]

Further, Grunes & Stucke state that it is a 'myth' that "[t]he current antitrust tools fully address big data issues".[23]

---

19   Nathan Newman, 'Search, Antitrust, and the Economics of the Control of User Data', *31 Yale Journal on Regulation 401* (2014) at p. 403.
20   *Id* at 404. Newman later refines his argument and states that "[a]t the core of Google's aggressive expansion of control over user data in recent years has been its rapid extension into a wide range of related product lines where it could collect ever more personal information about online users to sell to its advertisers", p. 426.
21   Allen P. Grunes and Maurice E. Stucke (April 2015), 'No Mistake About It: The Important Role of Antitrust in the Era of Big Data', *Antitrust Source*, pp. 1–14 at p. 3.
22   *Id* at p. 3.
23   *Id* at p. 3.

There is also a strand in the literature that suggests that big data leads to a loss in privacy, which could intersect with antitrust concerns.[24] Katz (2019) notes that privacy could be considered an antitrust issue to the extent that it is part of the non-price dimension of competition.[25] He finds, however, "that viewing privacy as an element of product quality highlights the fact that it is not evident that competition promotes privacy or, indeed, that promoting greater levels of privacy is desirable".[26] Further, Cooper (2013), Feinstein (2015), and Ohlhausen & Okuliar (2015) argue convincingly that privacy and antitrust considerations are best considered separately.[27]

In sum, with the rise of digital markets in the 2000s and the subsequent collection of large volumes of data, a number of researchers began asking whether or not big data is a competition issue. Boiled down to its essence, the concerns regarding big data – holding aside, for the moment the privacy considerations – follow the standard litany of (a) creating and/or maintaining market power, (b) allowing for the foreclosure of rivals, and (c) serving as a barrier to entry that prohibits or severely hampers the entry of innovative firms. Where legitimate, these concerns, as suggested above and discussed below, apply to important inputs generally, not to big data specifically or especially.

Despite strong concerns expressed by several commentators, including those quoted above, a number of researchers and commentators have examined the arguments and evidence and found no basis for concluding that big data is a unique competition issue that is different from how antitrust agencies analyze ownership and use of any other important inputs. Central to these arguments are the following points. First, big data is one among a host of potential factors that may determine market success. There is nothing particularly

---

[24] *See, e.g.,* Dissenting Statement of Commissioner Pamela Jones Harbour, In the Matter of Google/DoubleClick, FTC File No. 071–0170, December 20, 2007, at p. 4 ("The transaction will combine not only the two firms' products and services, but also their vast troves of data about consumer behavior on the Internet. Thus, the transaction reflects an interplay between traditional competition and consumer protection issues. The Commission is uniquely situated to evaluate the implications of this kind of data merger, from a competition as well as a consumer protection perspective".).

[25] Michael L. Katz, 'Multisided Platforms, Big Data, and a Little Antitrust Policy', 54 *Review of Industrial Organization* (2019) pp. 695–716 at p. 707.

[26] *Id.*

[27] James C. Cooper, 'Privacy and Antitrust: Underpants Gnomes, the First Amendment, and Subjectivity', 20 *Geo. Mason L. Rev.* (2013) pp. 1129, 1133–34; Deborah Feinstein, 'Big Data in a Competition Environment', CPI *Antitrust Chronicle*, May 2015, at p. 1 ("Despite calls to use the merger review process to improve privacy protections for consumers, the FTC continues to examine competition and consumer protection issues separately".); Maureen K. Ohlhausen and Alexander P. Okuliar, 'Competition, Consumer Protection, and the Right [Approach] to Privacy', 80 *Antitrust Law Journal* 121 (2015).

'unique' about big data in its ability to predict market success. Moreover, current antitrust tools actually *are* sufficient to address anticompetitive concerns that might arise from an alleged misuse of data. Second, while big data can be a highly valuable asset that firms expend resources to collect and analyze, it does not follow that its ownership or use reduces social welfare or constitutes an entry barrier that prevents innovative entrants from participating in markets. Finally, we now have over a decade of agency decisions where big data was considered, either explicitly or implicitly, and there has yet to be a challenge predicated primarily on abuse of big data. In the following sections, we further detail each of these points and their relevance to the policy debate.

3 Role of Big Data in a Firm's Production and Innovation Process

The paradigmatic antitrust concern involving big data is when it is perceived as an essential and exclusive factor in the production of a final good or service – typically as it relates to multi-sided platforms and/or other digital markets. Yet, all assessments of big data must, at some point, address how big data fits into the larger production function of firms – whether in a digital or widget market. While there are instances where data is the final product, such as commercial databases,[28] this is not the primary concern in terms of competition policy as it relates to big data.[29]

Specifically, Turck states that "Big Data, fundamentally, is … plumbing. Certainly, Big Data powers many consumer or business user experiences, but at its core, it is enterprise technology: databases, analytics, etc: stuff that runs in the back that no one but a few get to see".[30] Similarly, in a commentary to the Canadian Competition Bureau's white paper on big data, Microsoft stated, "it also bears emphasizing that large sets of structured, unstructured, labeled or

---

28   *See, e.g.,* Nielsen-Arbitron merger at Nielsen Holdings, Inc., No. C-4439 (FTC complaint issued Sept. 30, 2013); *FTC* v. *CCC* Holdings, Inc., 605 F. Supp. 2d 26, 38–39 (D.D.C. 2009).

29   Joshua D. Wright and Elyse Dorsey (Dec. 2016), 'Antitrust Analysis of Big Data', *Competition Law & Policy Debate* 2, pp. 35–41 at p. 37 ("Consumer data, however, is predominantly used by firms as an input into a final product—but is not ever the product itself. In other words, firms are neither pricing consumer data nor otherwise competing to provide better consumer data".).

30   *Supra* note 3. *See also* Michael Palmer, "Data is the New Oil", ANA Marketing Maestros, <https://ana.blogs.com/maestros/2006/11/data_is_the_new.html> ("Data is just like crude. It's valuable, but if unrefined it cannot really be used. It has to be changed into gas, plastic, chemicals, etc to create a valuable entity that drives profitable activity; so must data be broken down, analyzed for it to have value".).

unlabeled data *may have no known value* in the development of ML [machine learning] or AI [artificial intelligence] applications and may in fact not have any significant value. Data is thus best viewed as an 'asset' that may or may not have value just like any other asset depending on its commercial utility".[31]

These statements highlight the central point that big data must be considered in the larger context of a firm's production function.[32] Further, it is not necessarily the relative size of the collected data that can confer a competitive advantage but the quality of the data and/or the quality of the data analytics.[33] It boils down to the fundamental reality that the *mere possession* of big data does not accord a competitive advantage to a firm.[34] As in almost every dimension of competition, firms differ, not only in the attributes of their final products, but in how they organize themselves – *including the extent and efficiency of their use of big data via analytics*.[35]

---

[31] Microsoft Corporation, "Microsoft's Comments re Big data and Innovation: Implications for Competition Policy in Canada", November 17, 2017, p. 2, available at <https://www.competitionbureau.gc.ca/eic/site/cb-bc.nsf/eng/04320.html>.

[32] *See* Marc Bourreau *et al.*, 'Big Data and Competition Policy: Market Power, Personalised Pricing and Advertising', Centre on Regulation in Europe, February 16, 2017, <https://cerre.eu/sites/cerre/files/170216_CERRE_CompData_FinalReport.pdf> at 37> ("The first principle is that data are one input, which is important but not unique, to develop successful applications and algorithms. Other inputs are also important such as skilled and creative labour force (in particular computer scientists and singers), capital and distribution channels. Above all, the skills and creativity of the labour force will make the success of the applications".).

[33] *See* Eliana Garces, 'Data Collection in Online Platform Businesses: A Perspective for Antitrust Assessment', *CPI Antitrust Chronicle*, May 2018, at p. 3 ("Access to data is not normally at the root of an online platform's success".).

[34] In fact, there are instances when big data gets stale. *See* Lockwood Lyon, 'The End of Big Data', *Database Journal*, 16 May 2016 ("As data ages it tends to become less relevant for the following reasons: Newly implemented operational applications will not have a data history; Older products are removed and replaced by new products; Older customers may no longer exist; As you apply maintenance to current operational systems, some analyses of 'old' behavior becomes irrelevant; Older data tends to be less accurate and sometimes is missing altogether; as operational systems are adjusted to fix these problems, inaccurate or missing historical data will skew analyses".).

[35] Global Antitrust Institute, Comment on the Canadian Competition Bureau's White Paper, "Big Data and Innovation: Implications for Competition Policy in Canada", November 17, 2017, available at <https://papers.ssrn.com/sol3/papers.cfm?abstract_id=3079763> ("The implication is that, when considering the role that big data plays in a given market, rivals might speciously suggest that a market leader is succeeding due to the leader's sheer volume of data, when it is not data which is scarce but the skill and talent needed to combine the data with other inputs to produce something of value", p. 3). *See* Lyon *supra* note 34 ("The next phase of big data is now here. Applications and analysts must now create value

What about the argument that, while big data might not be a sufficient condition to compete effectively in digital markets, it is perhaps a necessary condition? Again, this assertion misses the point that firms are differentiated, not only in their ability to unlock value from big data, but in terms of how reliant they are on big data to fuel innovation and quality products.[36] The classic economic production function is a paradigm where firms mix a variety of inputs, from labour, capital, technology, land, and, relevant for our purposes, data analytics to produce output with certain attributes including quality. How *exactly* firms mix their inputs to produce the final product will differ. For instance, a particular entrant could invest heavily in R&D and intellectual property to develop a differentiated product while others are more heavily reliant on iterative machine learning as its user base grows. Similarly, an entrant could choose to invest and utilize big data – but perhaps not to the extent that an incumbent does.[37] Thus, improving quality through innovation can be achieved through a

---

in two ways: by automating current analytical results to feed back into operational systems and by turning to analysis of unstructured and unmodeled data".). Consider the production of academic empirical economic studies using large datasets. For academics, what differentiates a successful publishing record from a poor one is not likely an inability to access data. While certain academics might have access to 'better' data or more unique data – that process is endogenous and could be a result of superior effort on the part of the academic to obtain or construct a dataset. The point is that academic success comes down to the skill, effort, and ingenuity of the researcher – not whether or not they have access to bigger and better data.

36 For example, there is evidence that in the mid-2000s, Yahoo fell behind Google in their ability to monetize via search ads – not because Yahoo had fewer advertisers or less data – but because Yahoo had inferior ad matching algorithms. See Danny Sullivan, 'Yahoo's Poor Ad Targeting & Thoughts on Google-Yahoo', 21 September 2008 <https://searchengineland.com/yahoos-poor-ad-targeting-thoughts-on-google-yahoo-14780>.

37 Although at least in one respect entrants may have an advantage over incumbents. Specifically, startups and new entrants are not burdened by legacy systems and digital infrastructure from a prior age; consequently, they can be as nimble, if not more so, than entrenched incumbents. See Turck, *supra* note 3 ("Other digital native' companies, including many of the budding unicorns, started facing similar needs as the large Internet companies, and had no legacy infrastructure either, so they became early adopters of those Big Data technologies".). Additionally, theoretical work by Farboodi et al. (2019) shows that entrants can overtake incumbents if they are more efficient in extracting value per unit of data. See Maryam Farboodi et al., "Big Data and Firm Dynamics", 14 January 2019 <https://papers.ssrn.com/sol3/papers.cfm?abstract_id=3334064>, at p. 2 ("We also learn that initial size is not the most important factor in the success of a firm. A small firm that uses data efficiently, meaning that it harvests more data per unit of production, may lose money initially while it builds up its data stock. But if the firm can finance this phase, it can quickly out-compete a larger, less data-efficient firm".).

number of different paths. Consequently, asset equivalence is not a necessary condition for entry.[38]

For instance, Spotify overtook iTunes in terms of being the leading platform for online music – not because it had a larger amount of data, but because it mixed its ingredients in a different way than Apple.[39] Similarly, between 2011 and 2012, Chrome overtook both Firefox and Internet Explorer as the predominant web browser even though Chrome had a less than 5 percent share at the start of 2010.[40] Given that web browsers collect a tremendous amount of data on user behaviour,[41] under the big data theory of entry barriers, iTunes, Firefox, and Internet Explorer should never have relinquished their market leading

---

38 *See* Nils-Peter Schepp & Achim Wambach, 'On Big Data and Its Relevance for Market Power Assessment', 7 *J. European Competition L. & Prac.* (2016) pp. 120, 122 ("[P]otential competitors do not necessarily have to build a dataset equivalent to the size of the incumbent ... They rather need to find ways to accumulate highly relevant data to build a competitive, not necessarily the same dataset".). *See also* Xavier Boutin and Georg Clemens (2018), "Big But Not Insurmountable? How the Definition of 'Big Data' Can Help in the Assessment of Entry", <https://www.compasslexecon.com/wp-content/uploads/2018/04/Big-Data-Expert-Opinion.pdf> at p. 3 ("The evidence from data-related markets shows that the possession of large data volumes alone rarely provides a competitive advantage.).

39 *See, e.g.*, Ingrid Lunden, "In Europe, Spotify Royalties Overtake iTunes Earnings by 13%", TechCrunch.com, <https://techcrunch.com/2014/11/04/in-europe-spotify-royalties-overtake-itunes-earnings-by-13>, 4 November 2014; Mark Mulligan, "Mid-Year 2018 Streaming Market Shares", Midia.com, <http://www.midiaresearch.com/blog/mid-year-2018-streaming-market-shares>, 13 September 2018. One might argue that Apple's iTunes is not exactly the same product as Spotify's streaming service – so it is not actually an apples-to-apples comparison (rather the proper comparison is with Apple Music). The fact that Spotify (and Apple Music) are streaming services and not exactly the same as iTunes actually *proves* the larger point that markets evolve in ways that are not easily forecasted. (Apple's recent decision to discontinue iTunes in favour of its Apple Music product, among others, further proves the point.) Nonetheless, if we wanted to focus on an early-mover in streaming music services, one example would be Pandora, which currently sits seventh in global market share – despite the fact that it entered before all six firms ahead of it. *See* Mulligan *supra* note 39.

40 *See* StatCounter GlobalStats, <">http://gs.statcounter.com/browser-market-share/desktop-mobile-tablet/worldwide/#monthly-200901-201904>. Of course, one could argue that Chrome's ownership by Google and its trove of data are responsible for its success. According to one research paper, however, Chrome's success was due to its sheer technical superiority. (*See* Jonathan Tamary and Dror G. Feitelson, 'The Rise of Chrome', *PeerJ Computer Science* (2015), <https://peerj.com/articles/cs-28>.) Further, even if big data was primarily responsible for this superiority, and it is not clear that it is, this would be a welfare enhancing use of big data to facilitate entry and create a superior product.

41 *See, e.g.*, Dan Price, "10 Types of Data Your Browser is Collecting About You Right Now", MakeUseOf.com, <https://www.makeuseof.com/tag/data-browser-collects-about-you>, October 12, 2018.

positions.[42] Moving to social media, Snapchat is used more intensely per user than all other social media messaging apps in the U.S.A., including Facebook, Instagram, Messenger, and Pinterest.[43] The point of these examples is not to demonstrate that big data is unimportant, but to illustrate that firms can achieve tremendous market success, including overtaking incumbents, by using ingredients in different proportions based on their particular skills, sets of assets, and comparative advantages.

Of course, after entry, firms will likely adjust and re-optimize how they combine their various inputs to achieve their desired product features and levels of quality. For instance, a firm might have originally entered with lower costs or superior technology via a valuable patent or algorithm, but, over time, as it starts to gain users and data, it begins to incorporate the feedback and insights from the data into the design of its product and organization.[44] Similarly, an entrant might start with a basic product that fulfils a certain niche in the market but then proceeds to add new features; expand into adjacent markets; or change its overall business strategy.[45]

In sum, for the purposes of competition policy, it is critical to understand precisely *why* a product is successful. Even in the presence of big data, building

---

42 In Section 4, *infra*, we detail the use and abuse of the term 'barriers to entry'.

43 *See* App Annie ("2018, Top Social & Communication Apps by Average Monthly Sessions Per User"). Among users aged 12 to 17, Snapchat is the market leader with 16.8 million users, while Instagram and Facebook are second and third at 12.8 million and 11.5 million, respectively. *See* eMarketer, "Facebook is Tops with Everyone but Teens", 28 August 2018, <https://www.emarketer.com/content/facebook-is-tops-with-everyone-but-teens>.

44 An example would be Walmart. Although founded in 1962, today, Walmart analyzes a tremendous amount of data. Walmart processes 2.5 petabytes of data from 1 million customers every hour and uses big data to improve operational efficiency and increase online sales. *See* 'How Big Data Analysis Helped Increase Walmart Sales Turnover', Dezyre (23 May 2015), <https://www.dezyre.com/article/how-big-data-analysis-helped-increase-walmarts-sales-turnover/109>; Walmart Staff, '5 Ways Walmart Uses Big Data to Help Customers', Walmart Today (7 Aug. 2017), <https://blog.walmart.com/innovation/20170807/5-ways-walmart-uses-big-data-to-help-customers>.

45 The story of OpenTable is a case in point. Evans and Schmalensee detail how OpenTable originally attempted to sign up as many restaurants in as many cities as possible to participate on its restaurant reservation platform. After a few years of experience and uneven results, however, OpenTable decided to shift its focus to restaurants in four major cities: San Francisco, Chicago, New York, and Washington, D.C. The shift in strategy, based in part on observing user behavior, unlocked the cross-group effects it needed to achieve a critical mass of users and restaurants. *See* David S. Evans and Richard Schmalensee, *Matchmakers: The New Economics of Multisided Platforms* (Harvard Business Review Press, 2016) at pp. 10–11.

a better mousetrap is the foundational paradigm of competition.[46] The path to a better mousetrap can differ across markets and within firms in a given market. For example, network effects – both direct and indirect – could be the primary reason a product is successful in gaining and retaining consumers, rather than big data in and of itself.[47] And network effects can cause formerly leading products to lose their position quickly to new entrants with better products.

Even if the use of big data is the primary reason for one firm's success, a relevant question is whether comparable, but not necessarily equivalent, data are costly for a rival firm to acquire. In the decade or so since antitrust concerns over big data began in earnest, it is fair to say that the amount of data generated has further exploded and has been growing exponentially. Importantly, it is clear that multiple sources of data are often available to the same consumer and provided by multiple entities. The average consumer has over 100 apps on their smartphone with about 30–40 apps used per month.[48] Further, according to Deloitte, "estimates of the number of online accounts held by each individual across all online services range from 25 to 90, potentially

---

46 See *supra* note 11 (Canadian Competition Bureau) ("But competition policy in Canada does not, and should not, assume that 'big is bad'. Companies that achieve a leading market position – even a dominant one – by virtue of their own investment, ingenuity, and competitive performance should not be penalized for doing so. Imposing a penalty for excellence removes the incentives to pursue excellence".).

47 It is worth noting that, while big data and network effects are often discussed jointly and perhaps interchangeably, they are distinct concepts. *See supra* note 6. Ultimately, however, it is an empirical question regarding the strength of potential data-driven indirect network effects and whether or not there are diminishing returns. For instance, Chiou and Tucker (2017) find that large amounts of historical data may not be particularly useful for the relevancy of search results. See Lesley Chiou and Catherine Tucker, 'Search Engines and Data Retention: Implications for Privacy and Antitrust', NBER *Working Paper Series No. 23815* (2017). Further, Varian (2017) argues that improving search quality is more akin to learning-by-doing, rather than network effects. Varian challenges the presumption that collecting more data wondrously results in greater quality and this unlocks an unstoppable feedback loop. Rather, Varian states, "Though this is a convenient modeling shorthand, it can be somewhat misleading as it suggests that 'learning' is a passive activity that automatically happens as more output is produced. Nothing could be further from the truth. Learning by doing necessarily requires investment in data collection, analysis, and experimentation" (Hal Varian, 'Use and Abuse of Network Effects', <https://papers.ssrn.com/sol3/papers.cfm?abstract_id=3215488>, 17 September 2017 at p. 4). *See also* Tucker, *supra* note 10 at p. 684 ("I find little evidence that digital data augments market power due to either network effects or switching costs. Instead, digitization may have weakened these two economic forces, because it frees a user from a particular hardware system".).

48 App Annie, *supra* note 17.

increasing to around 200 in years to come".[49] Additionally, "[i]n the majority of categories included in the survey, most users use multiple providers rather than a single one, highlighting the ease with which people may access different services online".[50] In fact, the most common services where multiple providers are used include social and sharing platforms; online shopping; email, IM, video calling; travel; credit cards; and news.[51] Further, the Deloitte report concludes that "the same or similar data is often created across several providers" including browsing history, transaction data, location data, searches, and content viewed.[52] Thus, it is increasingly difficult to sustain a credible argument that what some firms or potential entrants in digital markets are missing today is access to big data. In fact, the problem is not how to get data but what to do with it.

Finally, when assessing the role that big data should play in competition policy, what must not be lost is that big data can lower a firm's costs through a more efficient production process and/or result in greater demand through higher quality or a greater matching to consumers' taste and preferences. This benefit is decidedly procompetitive and consumer welfare enhancing.[53] In some respects, big data's role is similar to that of R&D expenditures, learning-by-doing, and economies of scale. What can too easily be lost in the debate regarding the *potential* anticompetitive impact of large users of big data is the fact that big data and analytics are, to one degree or another, procompetitive assets that help drive innovation and otherwise benefit consumers.[54] While

---

49 Deloitte (2017), *The Data Landscape, A Report for Facebook*, p. 12, available at <https://www2.deloitte.com/uk/en/pages/technology-media-and-telecommunications/articles/the-data-landscape.html>.
50 *Id* at p. 23.
51 *Id* at p. 23.
52 *Id* at p. 26.
53 *See* Microsoft Corporation *supra* note 31 at p. 2 ("Using proprietary data to seek competitive advantage is economically efficient behavior that drives innovation".). *See, e.g.*, OECD (2015), Data-Driven Innovation, Big Data For Growth and Well-Being, https://read.oecd-ilibrary.org/science-and-technology/data-driven-innovation_9789264229358-en#page1 at p. 23 ("By collecting and analysing 'big data', a large share of which is provided by Internet users (consumers), Internet companies are able to automate their processes and to experiment with, and foster, new products and business models at much a faster rate than the rest of the industry. In particular, the advanced use of data and analytics enables Internet firms to scale their businesses at much lower costs than other ICT [information-communication technologies] firms, a phenomenon that goes much further than what Brynjolfsson et al. (2008) describe as *scaling without mass*".).
54 Importantly, the impact of data is not limited to digital platforms. Take, for instance, big data in the healthcare sector. Data is being used to forecast demand for inpatient admissions, epidemic outbreaks, and overall health outcomes. The OECD finds that data-driven

almost all serious scholarship acknowledges this fundamental reality, at least nominally, the debate over big data often focuses entirely on the *potential* for harm from big data, rather than on clear and documented evidence of the large benefits that it commonly provides. It would be as if computer operating systems were viewed with inherent suspicion simply because of the possibility that an owner of one might become dominant and then might engage in anticompetitive behaviour.[55] In the new era of big data, which we argue that competition policy has now entered (or should be entering), big data's procompetitive effects need to be afforded their proper weight – not only by competition agencies and courts but also by policymakers and scholars.

4   Big Data and Barriers to Entry

Related to the prior section's discussion is the question whether or not big data is a barrier to entry. Most commentators who favour aggressive antitrust enforcement as it relates to big data would argue in the affirmative.[56] We contend that it is important to consider how economists define barriers to entry and how this concept relates to the analysis of competitive outcomes. More importantly, rather than classifying big data, or other inputs, as barriers to entry – it is more relevant to detail what role big data plays in a particular market – both

---

innovation (DDI) is "a disruptive new source of growth that could transform all sectors in the economy. Even traditional sectors such as retail, manufacturing and agriculture are being disrupted through DDI", p. 27 OECD *supra* note 53. Further, "The analysis of 'big data', increasingly in real time, is driving knowledge and value creation across society; fostering new products, processes and markets; spurring entirely new business models; transforming most if not all sectors in OECD countries and partner economies; and thereby enhancing economic competitiveness and productivity growth". *Id* at p. 20. Also, from Deloitte *supra* note 49 at p. 9 ("A recent study for the European Commission estimated that the economic impact of data amounted to €300 billion in 2016 across EU28 countries, potentially rising to €430 billion by 2020. This includes the direct impacts in terms of revenues from big data, analytics and other data-related services, plus indirect impacts across sectors of the economy and induced impacts through increased economic activity".).

55   When this arguably happened, antitrust was certainly able to successfully intervene.
56   *See, e.g.,* Joshua Gans, "Enhancing Competition with Data and Identity Portability", Brookings Institute ("A firm's monopolization of data could harm consumers if it confers an incumbency advantage – supported by barriers to entry – that reduces the incentives for competing platforms to enter a particular market".); Terrell McSweeny & Brian O'Dea, 'Data, Innovation, and Potential Competition in Digital Markets – Looking Beyond Short-Term Price Effects in Merger Analysis', *CPI Antitrust Chronicle*, February 2018.

historically and in the present – in order to better forecast the hurdles that potential entrants must overcome to be an effective and viable competitor.

Scholarly discussions of barriers to entry inevitably start with Bain (1956), who defined barriers to entry as structural factors that allow incumbents to persistently price above the competitive level because they are not disciplined by a threat of entry.[57] Within this framework, economies of scale that require large capital expenditures, product differentiation, and absolute cost advantages would be considered barriers to entry. Viscusi et al. (1992) highlight a fundamental problem with Bain's definition, which is that "it is a tautology: A barrier to entry is said to exist if existing firms earn above-normal profit without inducing entry. In other words, Bain defines a barrier to entry in terms of its outcome".[58]

While Bain's definition offers a useful starting point, it tends to create a paradigm where economic concepts such as economies of scale and product differentiation are considered exogenous factors that then determine the competitiveness of an industry. This is a remnant of the prior structure-conduct-performance paradigm in industrial organization. A decade or so later, Stigler (1968) built off of Bain's definition and stated that a "barrier to entry may be defined as a cost of producing (at some or every rate of output) which must be borne by a firm which seeks to enter an industry but is not borne by firms already in the industry".[59] Two examples of this type of barrier to entry are patents and grandfathered government regulations. Economies of scale, on the other hand, would not be considered a barrier to the extent that an entrant has access to the same cost function – even if it operates on a different part of the same cost curve. One benefit of Stigler's definition is the explicit recognition that, if there is an asymmetry between incumbents and entrants – in that an entrant *must incur* a cost that an incumbent does not – this has the potential to confer, but does not guarantee, supra-normal profits to the incumbent in equilibrium.

Neither Bain's nor Stigler's definitions explicitly incorporate assessments of efficiency and economic welfare. Von Weizsäcker (1980) considers this a deficiency, given that "economists normally implicitly assume that barriers to

---

57 *See* Joseph Bain, *Barriers to New Competition* (Harvard: Harvard University Press, 1956) p. 3 ("A barrier to entry is an advantage of established sellers in an industry over potential entrant sellers, which is reflected in the extent to which established sellers can persistently raise their prices above competitive levels without attracting new firms to enter the industry".).

58 *See* W. Kip Viscusi *et al.*, *Economics of Regulation and Antitrust*, Fourth Edition (MIT Press, 2005) at p. 168.

59 *See* George J. Stigler, *The Organization of Industry* (University of Chicago Press 1983) p. 67.

entry are a distortion of the competitive process. They inhibit the proper working of the principle of the 'invisible hand', and thus imply inefficiencies".[60] In the face of this, Fisher (1979) and von Weizsäcker developed normative statements regarding barriers to entry.[61] Fisher found "a barrier to entry exists when entry would be socially beneficial but is somehow prevented".[62] Von Weizsäcker stated, "a barrier to entry is a cost of producing which must be borne by a firm which seeks to enter an industry but is not borne by firms already in the industry and which implies a distortion in the allocation of resources from the social point of view".[63] This is identical to Stigler, except for the last clause invoking welfare considerations. He uses economies of scale to illustrate his point. Namely, if capturing economies of scale can increase overall welfare *and* we associate entry barriers with inefficiencies, then, "in which sense can we speak of [exploiting scale economies to be] a barrier to entry?"[64] The virtue of von Weizsäcker and Fisher's formulation is that, when policy conclusions are on the line, it is imperative that welfare considerations are unequivocally stated.

What both Fisher and von Weizsäcker do is peel back the layers in defining and, more importantly, in understanding the role that market features such as economies of scale and product differentiation play in determining the market equilibrium. Fisher illustrates this idea when he states, "the right issue is not whether there are barriers to entry into the production of a particular mousetrap, but whether there are barriers to entry into innovation in mousetraps".[65] In other words, we should not be narrowly focused on a particular product or approach a firm uses, such as one that involves use of a certain volume or type of big data in particular ways, but on the larger question of whether other viable approaches to entry are hindered and, as stated earlier, whether this hindrance results in a loss of welfare.

In competition policy, the term 'barriers to entry' is generally used in one of two ways. Carlton (2008) summarizes this idea when he stated, "[t]rying to use 'barriers to entry' to refer to both the factors that influence the time it takes to reach a new equilibrium and to whether there are excess long-run profits is

---

60   C.C. von Weizsäcker, 'A Welfare Analysis of Barriers to Entry', 11 *The Bell J.Econ* (1980) at p. 399.
61   Franklin M. Fisher, 'Diagnosing Monopoly', 19 *Q. Rev. Econ. & Bus.* (1979) p. 7; von Weizsäcker *supra* note 60.
62   Fisher, *supra* note 61, at p. 23.
63   von Weizsäcker, *supra* note 60, at p. 400.
64   *Id.* at p. 401.
65   Fisher, *supra* note 61, at p. 57.

confusing".⁶⁶ The former definition is consistent, for instance, with the analysis of entry in the *U.S. Horizontal Merger Guidelines*.⁶⁷ The latter definition is more in line with the economic literature on barriers described above. The danger in labelling a factor as a 'barrier to entry' is a lack of clarity regarding which definition one is considering.

Entry into almost all high-value markets involves some hurdles that must be overcome and perhaps high costs that need to be incurred in order to compete successfully. Common examples include regulatory compliance costs, developing intellectual property, expenditures on specialized equipment, and hiring skilled labour. Labelling all these factors as barriers to entry effectively renders the term meaningless. Varian highlights this point when he states, "in starting a new business, is the problem with data or with knowledge? For example, I would like to enter the automobile manufacturing industry. Unfortunately, I know nothing whatsoever about how to build an automobile. Should that be considered a barrier to entry?"⁶⁸ Either the term 'barriers to entry' is explicitly stated and the welfare consequences evaluated, or, as Carlton recommends: "rather than focusing on whether an entry barrier exists according to some definition, analysts should explain how the industry will behave over the next several years ... [which] will force them to pay attention to uncertainty and adjustment costs".⁶⁹

For the reasons just discussed, it makes little sense to label big data as a barrier to entry and thereby treat it as an inevitable impediment to competition and consumer welfare.⁷⁰ First, big data is one of many potential factors that

---

66   Dennis W. Carlton, 'Barriers to Entry', 1 *Issues in Competition L. & Pol'y.* (2008) pp. 601, 606 See also Viscusi *et al., supra* note 58, at p. 168 ("There is perhaps no subject that has created more controversy among industrial organization economists than that of barriers to entry. At one extreme, some economists argue that the only real barriers are government related...At the other end of the spectrum, some economists argue that almost any large expenditure necessary to start up a business is a barrier to entry".).

67   U.S. Dep't of Justice & Fed. Trade Comm'n, Horizontal Merger Guidelines § 9 (2010) ("The Agencies examine the timeliness, likelihood, and sufficiency of the entry efforts an entrant might practically employ".).

68   Varian, *supra* note 47, at p. 9.

69   Carlton, *supra* note 66, at p. 615. Similarly, Demsetz (1982) observed that conditions frequently considered barriers to entry, such as scale economies, capital requirements, and advertising expenditures, are not the fundamental source of barriers; the fundamental barriers are rather the cost of information and the uncertainty that an entrant has to overcome. See Harold Demsetz, 'Barriers to Entry', 72 *Am. Econ. Rev.* (1982) p. 47.

70   Lambrecht and Tucker (2017) arrive at this conclusion through a slightly different approach. See Anja Lambrecht and Catherine Tucker, 'Can Big Data Protect a Firm from Competition?', *CPI Antitrust Chronicle*, January 2017, at p. 8 ("For a wide range of examples from the digital economy we demonstrate that when firms have access to big data, at least

influence "the timeliness, likelihood, and sufficiency of entry efforts an entrant might practically employ".[71] Certainly, effective investing in big data, machine learning, and artificial intelligence can create competitive distance between rivals, yet this distance is a by-product of competition on the merits and, as numerous examples confirm, is not necessarily an impediment to entry by firms clever enough to innovate a better mousetrap.[72] Rather than labelling big data as a barrier to entry, the focus should be on assessing what big data helps a firm accomplish, whether an incumbent's use of it furthers innovation and consumer welfare, and whether the incumbent's use of it actually prevents rivals from accessing it themselves or competing effectively in other ways.[73]

Finally, it is worth noting that if big data is a barrier to entry that lowers social welfare, then this idea is in some tension with related theories of harm involving incumbent firms, particularly digital platforms that are allegedly acquiring smaller potential or current rivals in order to pre-empt future competition.[74] If big data is such a significant barrier to entry, one might ask,

---

one, and often more, of the four criteria which are required for a resource to constitute a sustainable competitive advantage are not met".). *See also* Sokol and Comerford, *supra* note 8, at pp. 1135–1140.

71 Horizontal Merger Guidelines, *supra* note 67.

72 The Canadian Competition Bureau, *supra* note 11, at 14 ("Developing valuable data through competition on the merits does not run afoul of the Act even if it results in significant market power. For example, a firm can create market power by developing a high-quality product or an efficient production process[.]").

73 Further, significant expenditures on big data collection and analytics can result in high fixed costs; thus, merely observing that a firm is pricing above marginal cost and equating this with supra-competitive pricing is not properly considering the rate of return required to cover all the prior periods' expenditures on big data. *See* Michael L. Katz & Carl Shapiro, 'Systems Competition and Network Effects', 8 *J. Econ. Perspectives* (1994) pp. 93, 107 ("[M]erely observing a firm with a position of market dominance does not imply that the firm is earning super-normal profits: the firm's quasi-rents may merely reflect costs incurred earlier to obtain the position of market leadership".).

74 Facebook's acquisition of Instagram is considered the canonical example of an entrenched incumbent pre-empting future competition. Yet, this example likely suffers from a nirvana counterfactual fallacy. *See* Global Antitrust Institute, Antonin Scalia Law Sch., Geo. Mason Univ., Comment Submitted for the Australian Competition & Consumer Commission's Digital Platforms Inquiry, Preliminary Report, at p. 15 ("Central to the narrative that strategic acquisitions have entrenched market power is Facebook's acquisition of Instagram in 2012, from which some commentators have inferred that competition authorities are missing potential competition cases. At the time of the acquisition, Instagram had zero revenues and a handful of employees. Since Facebook's acquisition, Instagram has grown from 30 million users to well over one billion. During the same period, Facebook grew from approximately 900 million users to over two billion users. This substantial expansion in users and output is hardly indicative of an anticompetitive outcome. Of course, one could argue that, but for the acquisition, Instagram would have

how would these new entrants be able to threaten the incumbent acquirer's strong position in the marketplace? This line of inquiry leads to a number of critical implications. First, in markets characterized by big data, we should not expect to see entry that would be considered likely, timely, and sufficient. Second, in markets characterized by big data, nascent competitors (holding aside for the moment that their mere existence violates the prior implication) cannot be expected to represent a serious competitive threat to incumbents. Consequently, following this logic, acquisitions involving so-called 'nascent competitors' and incumbents employing big data are likely procompetitive. We can perhaps label this as the 'big data paradox'. The reality is that theories of harm based on data barriers to entry confuse data with knowledge.[75] Further, it illustrates the fundamental fragility of defining big data as a barrier to entry in the context of competition policy.

5 Big Data and Competition Matters

It has been at least a decade since the emergence of big data as a relevant competition issue. During that time, competition agencies in the U.S.A. and Europe have considered various aspects of big data in matters ranging from mergers to unilateral conduct by firms classified as 'dominant'. Yet, despite the flurry of policy research calling for antitrust condemnation of big data, competition agencies have yet to bring a challenge based primarily on big data considerations – other than as a tangential reference as a barrier to entry. What does this lack of agency challenge tell us? While it does not prove that big data cannot possibly present a competition issue, it is consistent with the idea that big data does not represent a unique competitive problem. Moreover, an assessment of the agencies' decisions in matters that involve firms utilizing big data fails to support the conjecture that competition agencies and the

---

been just as successful, if not more, and would have remained an independent competitor. While this type of 'nirvana' counterfactual is frequently asserted, without more it is not a sufficient basis upon which retrospectively to condemn an acquisition. To treat the success and associated output expansion of an acquired product as evidence of an anticompetitive acquisition severely twists the meaning of 'anticompetitive.'").

75 *See* Varian *supra* note 47 at pp. 9–10 ("Knowledge is a critical part of production. In economic models, knowledge is embedded in the production function but in the real world, knowledge is embedded in people. … Today's successful businesses had no data when they started, but nevertheless they were able to acquire sufficient expertise to gain a foothold, gather what data they could, and extract information and knowledge from that data to create competitive advantage over the incumbents".).

courts are falsely and systematically neglecting the issue entirely. Rather, in a number of cases, the agencies have fully considered big data issues and, ultimately, determined that they were an insufficient and inadequate basis upon which to issue a formal Complaint.

We examined a number of U.S. and European cases involving big data to better understand why it has not been the centrepiece of any antitrust challenge. The point is not to offer a comprehensive overview of all competition cases involving big data, but to identify a number of highly prominent and significant cases that can help inform the issue. Of course, there could be a big data challenge at some point in the future. Even so, it would only support the proposition that big data concerns can exist and be taken seriously, not that they are typical or frequent. Further, in contrast with the claims of some who have expressed great concern over big data and the ability of competition agencies to deal with it, Wright and Dorsey (2016) argue that, if there are legitimate concerns, they can be assessed with the standard tools that agencies employ.[76]

One of the world's largest commercial users of big data is Google. In 2011, the U.S. Federal Trade Commission (FTC) began to formally investigate whether Google was engaging in anticompetitive conduct with its online search engine. Specifically, the agency scrutinized Google's 'universal search' feature, which provides distinct, specialized search results in various categories such as for shopping queries, for instance, listing stores that sell a particular product, and local business queries, for example, providing a map of local florists and their addresses. These specialized search results were interspersed with the standard links to web sites, that is, 'blue links', to form a composite search results page. The allegation was that Google demoted links to competing web sites that offered similar specialized search information such as shopping and local business results. Further, the allegation was that Google unfairly promoted its own specialized search results at the top of the page, which deprived traffic to rival sites that offered similar content. There has been no shortage of commentary on the case, both before and after the FTC's ultimate decision to close the investigation.[77] Yet despite the fact that Google analyzes a staggering volume

---

[76] Wright and Dorsey, *supra* note 29, at pp. 35 ("the existing antitrust framework is well equipped with sophisticated tools and methods for analyzing just the kinds of issues big data presents".).

[77] *See e.g.*, Geoffrey A. Manne and Joshua D. Wright, 'Google and the Limits of Antitrust: The Case Against the Antitrust Case Against Google', 34 *Harv. J. L. & Pub. Pol'y* (2011) p. 3; Michael A. Salinger & Robert J. Levinson, 'Economics and the FTC's Google Investigation', 46 *Rev. Indus. Org.* (2015) p. 25; Richard J. Gilbert, 'U.S. Federal Trade Commission Investigation of Google Search', in John E. Kwoka, Jr. & Lawrence J. White (eds.), *The Antitrust*

of data, that fact alone – or even in combination with other concerns – proved to be an insufficient basis upon which to bring a complaint. In fact, the FTC concluded just the opposite, when it considered Google's implementation of universal searches to be procompetitive.[78] The lesson from the investigation is that competition cases require actual evidence of anticompetitive conduct and resulting harm.

In 2013, the U.S. Department of Justice (DOJ) challenged Bazaarvoice's acquisition of PowerReview, where "Bazaarvoice provides the market-leading R&R [rating & reviews] platform to manufacturers and online retailers".[79] In its complaint, the DOJ cited a document indicating that Bazaarvoice identified its "ability to leverage the data" as "a key barrier [to] entry".[80] After the court ruled in favour of the DOJ, the DOJ stated, "[t]he entry barriers identified by the Court include networks effects from syndication, switching costs, moderation, analytics, and reputation". While it is certainly true that the DOJ and the court considered data and analytics (presumably from big data) as a barrier to entry, they are only mentioned twice in these key DOJ documents; additionally, analytics is listed among a series of other 'barriers' including switching costs and reputation.[81] Rather, the deciding factors in bringing the case were the standard litany of potential harms from horizontal mergers including the fact that "PowerReviews' 'scorched earth approach to pricing' applied significant pressure to Bazaarvoice in competitive deals".[82]

Revolution (Oxford Univ. Press, 2013); John M. Yun, 'Understanding Google's Search Platform and the Implications for Antitrust Analyses', 14 (2) *Journal of Competition Law & Economics* (2018) pp. 311–329.

78 See Fed. Trade Comm'n, file no. 111–0163, Statement Regarding Google's Search Practices, in the matter of Google Inc. (3 Jan. 2013), <https://www.ftc.gov/system/files/documents/public_statements/295971/130103googlesearchstmtofcomm.pdf> at p. 2 ("quantitative evidence the Commission examined are largely consistent with the conclusion that Google likely benefited consumers by prominently displaying its vertical content on its search results page".).

79 Department of Justice, Competitive Impact Statement, *U.S.* v. *Bazaarvoice*, 24 April 2014, at p. 3.

80 Department of Justice, Complaint, *U.S.* v. *Bazaarvoice*, 10 January 2013, at p. 18.

81 Per Section 4 *supra*, the idea that switching costs and reputation are barriers to entry further supports the point made by von Weizsäcker, Fisher, and Demsetz that the use of the term 'barriers to entry' is generally used in a very imprecise manner and often divorced from dynamic welfare considerations.

82 DOJ Complaint, *supra* note 80, at p. 13. Further, if Bazaarvoice's ownership of big data served as a strong barrier to entry, how did the acquired firm manage to become such a threat? Rather, Bazaarvoice was successful because it was highly skilled in using the data that it collected.

In 2007, both the U.S.A. and Europe scrutinized, but eventually cleared, Google's acquisition of DoubleClick. The EC considered a theory of harm involving foreclosure based on the combination of Google and DoubleClick's assets. The essence of the theory was that combining Google's user data with DoubleClick's user data "would allow the merged entity to achieve a position that could not be replicated by its integrated competitors...Google's competitors would be progressively marginalized which would ultimately allow Google to raise prices for its intermediation services".[83] The EC also recognized that "[s]uch information could potentially be used to better target ads to users".[84] The EC ultimately concluded that "[e]ven if Google's and DoubleClick's data collections were available as input for DoubleClick it would therefore be unlikely that its competitiveness would be enhanced in a way that would confer on the merged entity a competitive advantage that could not be matched by its competitors".[85] This leads to the conclusion that "[f]rom this, it follows that the possible combination of data of Google and DoubleClick post-merger is very unlikely to bring more traffic to AdSense so as to squeeze out competitors and ultimately enable the merged entity to charge higher prices for its intermediation services".[86] Thus, it is clear that Europe explicitly considered and ultimately rejected a theory of harm where data played a central role – as the evidence did not support such concerns.

In the U.S.A., in a 4-1 Commission vote, the FTC cleared the Google-DoubleClick merger. In doing so, they explicitly considered and rejected "the theory that the combination of their respective data sets of consumer information could be exploited in a way that threatens consumers' privacy".[87] Relatedly, the Commission "assessed the suggestion that the combination of Google's database of user information and the data respecting users and competitive intermediaries collected by DoubleClick on behalf of its customers would give Google an overwhelming advantage in the ad intermediation market".[88] Ultimately, the Commission concluded that "the transaction is not likely to create, enhance, or facilitate market power".[89] In other words, big data considerations were explicitly considered but the evidence did not support such an action. In fact, the agency explicitly stated:

---

83 DG Comp, Google-DoubleClick, p. 359.
84 *Id* at p. 360.
85 *Id* at p. 364.
86 *Id* at p. 366.
87 Statement of Federal Trade Commission Concerning Google/DoubleClick, FTC File No. 071–0170, December 20, 2007, at p. 2.
88 *Id* at p. 12.
89 *Id* at p. 2.

At bottom, the concerns raised by Google's competitors regarding the integration of these two data sets – should privacy concerns not prevent such integration – really amount to a fear that the transaction will lead to Google offering a superior product to its customers. Yet, the evidence indicates that neither the data available to Google, nor the data available to DoubleClick, constitutes an essential input to a successful online advertising product. A number of Google's competitors have at their disposal valuable stores of data not available to Google.[90]

Similarly, in approving Facebook's acquisition of WhatsApp in 2014, the European Commission concluded that "regardless of whether the merged entity will start using WhatsApp user data to improve targeted advertising on Facebook's social network, there will continue to be a large amount of Internet user data that are valuable for advertising purposes and that are not within Facebook's exclusive control".[91] Additionally, for Microsoft's acquisition of LinkedIn in 2016, the EC concluded that "the Transaction does not raise competition concerns resulting from the possible post-merger combination of the 'data' (essentially consisting of personal information, such as information about an individual's job, career history and professional connections, and/or her or his email or other contacts, search behaviour etc. about the users of their services) held by each of the Parties in relation to online advertising".[92]

Finally, in 2008, while the EC ultimately cleared TomTom's acquisition of Tele Atlas,[93] DG Comp concluded that entry into navigable digital map databases was "unlikely" due to the "vast volumes of data [that] have to be collected from various sources and field survey teams".[94] That conclusion was

---

90   *Id* at p. 12.
91   DG Comp, Facebook-WhatsApp, p. 189.
92   DG Comp, Microsoft-LinkedIn, p. 176. *See also* p. 180 ("In the case at hand, however, the Transaction does not give rise to this type of concerns in relation to online advertising. First, Microsoft and LinkedIn do not make available their data to third parties for advertising purposes, with very limited exceptions. Second, the combination of their respective datasets does not appear to result in raising the barriers to entry/expansion for other players in this space, as there will continue to be a large amount of internet user data that are valuable for advertising purposes and that are not within Microsoft's exclusive control. Third, the Parties are small market players and compete with each other only to a very limited extent in online advertising and its possible segments".).
93   The EC found that the vertical transaction did not raise concerns of input foreclosure or a greater likelihood of anticompetitive coordinated conduct. *See* DG Comp, TomTom-Tele Atlas.
94   DG Comp, TomTom-Tele Atlas, 132.

soon to be proved by the market to be incorrect. As Boutin and Clemens (2018) highlight:

> [i]n fact, using its competitive advantages relating to variety and velocity, Google soon started to offer navigation for free. Google Maps Navigation integrated a series of features…using the data that was collected from Google's search engine. Moreover, it had the significant advantage of relying on the updates sent by its users. The combination of a high volume and variety of data updated at a high velocity caught incumbents such as TomTom off-guard.[95]

The EC inaccurately forecasted the future market environment because it believed big data insulated TomTom from competition; yet, it was a different type of big data that helped fuel Google's entry. This episode of disruptive entry further suggests that caution should be exercised when attempting to determine whether or not entry will be precluded by incumbent providers' access to and use of a specific type of big data.

6 Relevant Legal Aspects of Big Data

In this section, we explore the relevant legal aspects of big data on antitrust. Specifically, we focus on what the presence of big data should imply, in terms of presumptions, within the rule of reason framework. Should courts administer cases that involve considerations of big data differently? Should there be a stronger presumption of market power and, ultimately, of competitive harm?

Given the state of the current evidence – including the economic literature and the lack of prior cases and agency actions involving big data issues – we believe there is little basis for changing antitrust presumptions. Of course, this could change if the evidence mounts either in one direction or another. Yet, importantly, big data is fundamentally about innovation – as a firm cannot gain a competitive advantage without some degree of effort and ingenuity to turn raw data into something that provides value. Thus, the presence of big data should be treated in a manner similar to R&D and other innovative

---

95   Xavier Boutin and Georg Clemens (2018), "Big But Not Insurmountable? How the Definition of 'Big Data' Can Help in the Assessment of Entry", <https://www.compasslexecon.com/wp-content/uploads/2018/04/Big-Data-Expert-Opinion.pdf>, at p. 2.

activities. To the extent that these activities make it difficult for rivals to compete, then that is a potential consideration in terms of the degree of antitrust market power and the durability of that market power – but it does not, in and of itself, suggest competitive harm.

As emphasized in Section 4, reflexive labelling of big data as a 'barrier to entry' provides little guidance to courts as the term has no clear meaning in antitrust law. According to Lazaroff (2006):

> the Supreme Court has really never provided a comprehensive analysis of barriers to entry and their role in interpreting the Sherman, Clayton and Federal Trade Commission Acts. Rather, the Court has periodically referenced entry barriers in antitrust cases, resulting in a somewhat cryptic and uncertain message to lower courts, litigants and students of antitrust law.[96]

A brief survey of recent antitrust cases confirms Lazaroff's observation that the current treatment of entry barriers remains relatively perfunctory and lacking in clarity. For instance, conclusions about what constitutes an entry barrier verge on the contradictory.[97] Even in cases where discussion of entry barriers is more thorough, the lack of an accepted economic framework leaves courts with a great deal of uncertainty when it comes to deciding the question.[98] Thus, in terms of big data, courts should bypass labels and determine the precise role that big data plays in a given competition matter.

In terms of efficiencies, there are compelling arguments that mergers that bring together various data sets and/or improve the ability to analyze data should be recognized as cognizable efficiencies. Luib and Cowie (2020) detail a number of recent competition matters involving the recognition of big data

---

96 Daniel E. Lazaroff, 'Entry Barriers and Contemporary Antitrust Litigation', 7 *U.C. Davis Bus. L.J.* (2006) p.1, <https://blj.ucdavis.edu/archives/vol-7-no-1/Entry-Barriers-and-Contemporary-Antitrust-Litigation.html>.
97 Compare *GDHI Mktg. LLC* v. *Antsel Mktg. LLC*, No. 18-CV-2672-MSK-NRN, 2019 WL 4572853 at *9 n.5 (D. Colo. Sept. 20, 2019) ("The mere cost of capital is not a barrier to entry".) with *Philadelphia Taxi Ass'n, Inc* v. *Uber Techs., Inc.*, 886 F.3d 332, 342 (3d Cir. 2018) ("Entry barriers include … high capital costs".).
98 See *Buccaneer Energy (USA) Inc.* v. *Gunnison Energy Corp.*, 846 F.3d 1297, 1316–17 (10th Cir. 2017).

efficiencies.[99] The court in *AT&T-Time Warner* recognized that "the combined company can use information from AT&T's mobile and video customers to better tailor Time Warner's content and advertising to better compete with on-line platforms".[100] In *CVS Health-Aetna*, "[w]e were able to show that the combination of CVS Health and Aetna would lead to better-integrated medical and pharmacy data".[101]

In sum, the burden of production should remain with the plaintiff to demonstrate that the use of big data is a significant hindrance to the timeliness, likelihood, and sufficiency of entry and/or hinders the competitive process – as measured by the negative impact on consumer welfare. What should be avoided is a presumption that the mere presence of big data lowers the burden of production on the plaintiff to either meet its *prima facie* burden or its burden to rebut the defendant's efficiency justifications. In contrast, what recent competition cases have illustrated is that big data can play an integral role in realizing efficiencies post-merger.

7 Conclusion

Since initial concerns regarding big data were first expressed, experience has shown that big data is not a particularly scarce resource in the digital economy – but rather it is the ability to analyze it in a manner that unlocks value which can be in relatively short supply.[102] Given this, there is little justification for a presumption of harm when it comes to the collection and use of big data. Certainly, there could be instances when big data can play a role in a larger competition action, but that must be determined on a case-by-case basis. Further, it is important to recognize the potential role that big data can play in realizing cognizable efficiencies. Most certainly, calls to mandate

---

99 *See* Greg P. Luib and Mike Cowie, 'Big (But Not Bad) Data and Merger Efficiencies', ON-POINT / A legal update from Dechert's Antitrust/Competition Group, <https://info.dechert.com/10/13420/january-2020/big-(but-not-bad)-data-and-merger-efficiencies.asp>.
100 *Id.*
101 *Id.*
102 *See* Turck, *supra* 3 ("As Big Data continues to mature, however, the term itself will probably disappear, or become so dated that nobody will use it anymore. It is the ironic fate of successful enabling technologies that they become widespread, then ubiquitous, and eventually invisible".).

that data be shared, and that it be declared a sort of "essential facility", are wrought with further problems and would open a Pandora's box of unintended consequences – including those associated with setting appropriate terms and conditions under which sharing is to be performed – not to mention the likely conflict such policies may raise with intellectual property laws.

Big Data Ownership: Do we Need a New Regulatory Framework?

*Andris Tauriņš**

Abstract

Big data is the new oil – but who has the right to own it? Is the owner the creator of the individual data or the owners of data processing systems which add value to the mass of data – or should the information be shared for free with state institutions, for example, with the goal of limiting the amounts of traffic accidents in the city? This is one of the debates of our time. However, it seems that current frameworks, whether regarding IP law or trade secrets regulations, do not provide sufficient answers. Problems also arise with the offer of contractual relationships or licensing. That initiates the thought that a new type of regulation might be needed.

Keywords

big data – ownership of data – data creation – open source – data creation

1 Introduction

Only some ten years ago, entrepreneurs started to ask the question whether they can own the data processed within their systems. At that time, the answer was not clear. So the processing of data went on in a land of no rules. Now the perspective has changed: empowered with more information, users of data have started realizing their rights regarding data connected to them.

Now the question on data ownership has been raised by two sides: and each of them is fighting for an answer more favorable to them. At the same time, the scope of the issue has also developed: big data has come into the game. The question who can own big data is not a million-dollar question but rather a trillion dollars' worth: this the estimated value of the big data market to date.

As a result, the debate on whether we need new regulation for data ownership or whether existing laws are sufficient is the big question of our time.

---

* Senior associate, ZAB Sorainen.

2   The Definition of Big Data

Currently, no specific, universally approved legal definition of data exists – and even less so for 'big data'.

However, it can be noted that the first popular definition of *big data* was provided in 2001 by Doug Laney's model of the 'three Vs', referring to volume (the size and scale of data), velocity (speed of data generation and processing) and variety (the different forms and range of the data analysed).[1]

A more descriptive definition notes that big datasets are "large, diverse, complex, longitudinal, and/or distributed datasets generated from instruments, sensors, Internet transactions, email, video, click streams, and/or all other digital sources available today and in the future".[2]

According to the International Working Group on Data Protection in Telecommunications:

> Big Data is a term which refers to the enormous increase in access to and automated use of information. It refers to the gigantic amounts of digital data controlled by companies, authorities and other large organisations which are subjected to extensive analysis based on the use of algorithms.[3]

In practice, this means that we are speaking about vast exploitable datasets of unstructured and structured digital information,[4] that is, big masses of pseudonymized or anonymized data quickly collected by sensors and other devices.

Despite the descriptive definitions, questions and misunderstandings remain. Some argue that, theoretically, if big data is anonymized or pseudonymized, the pieces of data can no longer be connected to the original users. Others, however, talk about privacy within big data[5] and the user's involvement

---

1   D. Laney, *3D Data Management: Controlling Data Volume, Velocity and Variety*, 2001, Metra Group Research Note, p. 3, <http://blogs.gartner.com/doug-laney/files/2012/01/ad949-3D-Data-Management-Controlling-Data-Volume-Velocity-and-Variety.pdf>, visited on 10 September 2020.
2   National Science Foundation, *Core Techniques and Technologies for Advancing BigData Science & Engineering* (BIGDATA), 2012, <www.nsf.gov/pubs/2012/nsf12499/nsf12499.pdf>, visited on 20 May 2019.
3   International Working Group on Data Protection in Telecommunications, *Working Paper on Big Data and Privacy, Privacy principles under pressure in the age of Big Data analytics*, 55th Meeting, 5–6 May 2014, <https://www.datenschutz-berlin.de/fileadmin/user_upload/pdf/publikationen/working-paper/2014/06052014_en.pdf>, visited on 8 July 2019.
4   R. Kemp, *Legal Aspects of Managing Big Data*, October 2014, p. 2, <www.kempitlaw.com/wp-content/uploads/2014/10/Legal-Aspects-of-Big-Data-White-Paper-v2-1-October-2014.pdf>, visited on 20 May 2019.
5   J. Polonetsky, O. Tene, *Privacy and Big Data*, <www.stanfordlawreview.org/online/privacy-and-big-data-privacy-and-big-data>, visited on 20 May 2019.

in this mass. This distinction should be of vital importance when speaking about these masses of data, and it seems that at least two new definitions are needed.

For all cases, at least one thing is clear: big data has enormous value. For this reason, some call big data the 'new oil'[6] or 'new gold', or even something more valuable as this resource is infinitely renewable[7] and can be used by multiple actors for multiple purposes.[8] However, while theoretically extremely valuable, at the same time this 'gold' does not have any value at all – it is a sheer mass of data which cannot be used on its own. Here the description of volume – 'big' data, one of 'three Vs' – comes in.

Additionally, big data encompasses many types of stakeholders. These are not only companies working with data, such as ISPs, IT providers and data providers, for example, or marketplaces and data-driven services, but also – and most importantly – the consumers who create data.

Hence big data might be described as a large mass of data, which, firstly, is created through cooperation between several stakeholders and, secondly, is processed in isolation from the individuals from which the individual data arises and, thirdly, can be used for various purposes, such as development of new technologies and provision of new services.

3 Current Debate on Big Data

3.1 *Basis of the Discussion*

The discussion around big data has arisen for two main reasons: the development of technologies and the involvement of users. However, these reasons can be divided into even smaller segments.

---

6 'The world's most valuable resource is no longer oil, but data', 6 May 2017, *The Economist*, <www.economist.com/leaders/2017/05/06/the-worlds-most-valuable-resource-is-no-longer-oil-but-data>, visited on 10 September 2020; K. McBride, 'Monetizing Smart Cities: Framing the Debate', 28 March 2018, CIGI, Data Governance in the Digital Age Special Report, <www.cigionline.org/articles/monetizing-smart-city-data?utm_source=twitter&utm_medium=social&utm_campaign=data-series>, visited on 20 May 2019.

7 B. Marr, 'Here's why data is not the new oil', 5 March 2018, Forbes, <www.forbes.com/sites/bernardmarr/2018/03/05/heres-why-data-is-not-the-new-oil/#5d3aee183aa9>, visited on 10 September 2020. A. Schlosser, 'You may have heard data is the new oil. It's not', 10 January 2018, World Economic Forum, <www.weforum.org/agenda/2018/01/data-is-not-the-new-oil>, visited on 20 May 2019.

8 T. Scassa, 'Data Ownership', 4 September 2018, CIGI Papers No. 187, p. 1, <www.cigionline.org/publications/data-ownership>, visited on 20 May 2019.

3.1.1 Technological Perspective

Although the remarkable development of new technologies is a general basis for any internet-related debate, when speaking about data one must bear in mind recent trends.

Firstly, sensor technology has been installed in almost every device. This technology is used in virtually every industry, such as the motor industry,[9] traffic coordination (intelligent transportation[10]), household goods (including fridges, watches, and glasses), agriculture or healthcare;[11] even more – an actual term in urban planning is 'smart cities',[12] where data is gathered and assembled from literally every corner of the road and the household. Sensors in drones or robotic vehicles allow pinpointing of irrigation leaks, identify locations of pest infestation or take soil surveys whose results are immediately sent back to farmers and provide an insight on a possible problem in remote or dangerous locations.[13]

Secondly, the processing power of computers has increased phenomenally. This has an impact on the declining costs of data collection, storage, and processing, allowing the use of vast volumes of data. Already in December 2012, a long-range report by the U.S. National Intelligence Council 'Global Trends 2030: Alternative Worlds' declared: "[i]nformation technology is entering the Big Data era. Process power and data storage are becoming almost free; networks and the cloud will provide global access, and pervasive services"[14] – a tendency that has indeed continued.[15]

---

9   H. Barth, 'Big Data Analytics für Connected Cars', n: Prof. H., Fojcik T. (eds.) *Mobilität und digitale Transformation* (Springer Gabler, Wiesbaden, 2018) pp. 137–151.

10   H.V. Jagadish, J. Gehrke, 'Exploring the inherent technical challenges in realizing the potential of Big Data', July 2014, *Communications of the ACM*, Vol. 57, No. 7, p. 88, <www.db.ucsd.edu/wp-content/uploads/2015/07/p86-jagadish.pdf>, visited on 10 September 2020.

11   T.J. Farkas, 'Data Created by the Internet of Things: The New Gold without Ownership', 23 *Rev. Prop. Immaterial* (2017), pp. 5–17.

12   T. Scassa, *Who owns all the data collected by 'smart cities'?*, 23 November 2017, Toronto Star, <www.thestar.com/opinion/contributors/2017/11/23/who-owns-all-the-data-collected-by-smart-cities.html>, visited on 20 May 2019.

13   D. Wilson, *Intellectual property issues – big data, robotics and automation in precision agriculture*, April 2018, Norton Rose Fulbright, p. 4, <www.nortonrosefulbright.com/-/media/files/nrf/nrfweb/imported/cultivate---issue-15.pdf?la=en-de&revision=>, visited on 20 May 2019.

14   *Global Trends 2030: Alternative Worlds*, December 2012, The National Intelligence Council, p. 86, <www.dni.gov/files/documents/GlobalTrends_2030.pdf>, visited on 10 September 2020.

15   N.J. Shaba, *Big Data Database: Loopholes Regarding Ownership and Access to Data* (Uppsala Universitet, 2018) pp. 23–24, <www.diva-portal.org/smash/get/diva2:1218109/FULLTEXT01.pdf>, visited on 20 May 2019; Study on emerging issues of data ownership, interoperability, (re-) usability and access to data, and liability, 2018, The European Commission, pp. 340–341, <www.ec.europa.eu/newsroom/dae/document.cfm?doc_id=51486>, visited on 20 May 2019.

Thirdly, nowadays, almost everywhere in the developed world we can comfortably access network connections. It is expected that there will be more than 25 billion connected devices all over the world by 2021,[16] on average four devices for every one of us.

As a result, a new phenomenon has been developed: predictive analysis,[17] which allows processing of information across different platforms to identify an individual's behavioural trends. Through this tendency, research on causality connected to the past has shifted the study of predictions and modeling regarding the future[18] – who, when and how will do what. This is the basis for the value of big data and the time of 'informational capitalism'.[19]

When looking at other grounds for the debate and importance of this issue, the growing amounts of digital decision making and AI cannot be overlooked. Companies are interested in the use of big data and machine learning. This has also been recognized by Latvian state institutions.[20]

This phenomenon brings benefits to industries. Firstly, predictive maintenance allows meaningful forecasts of when and how equipment could malfunction. Secondly, the approach of equipment-as-a-service provides an option to pay for actual asset uptime – there is no need to own, manage, and maintain equipment as such. Thirdly, big data can be used to create new machine-learning-driven business models – for example, big data of sensor lines can help to predict which shipping lanes will be most useful during certain weather conditions.[21]

3.1.2   Economic aspects

In addition to its usefulness for specific companies, big data is currently at its peak of fame due also to expected impacts in the global market, leading to efficiency and cost reductions for end users.

---

16   K. Kundu, 25 Billion Connected Devices Expected By 2021, Thanks to IoT Revolution, 9 November 2018, Beebom, <www.beebom.com/25-billion-connected-devices-gartner>, visited on 20 May 2019.
17   J. Mauerer, *Was ist was bei Predictive Analytics?*, 11 December 2017, Computerwoche, <www.computerwoche.de/a/was-ist-was-bei-predictive-analytics,3098583>, visited on 20 May 2019.
18   R. Kemp, *Legal Aspects of Managing Big Data*, July 2014, p. 1, <www.kempitlaw.com/wp-content/uploads/2014/08/Legal-Aspects-of-Managing-Big-Data.pdf>, visited on 10 September 2020.
19   J.E. Cohen, 'The Regulatory State in the Information Age', *Theoretical Inquiries in Law* (2016) p. 17 (2).
20   Vides aizsardzības un reģionālās attīstības ministrija, Informatīvais ziņojums "Latvijas atvērto datu stratēģija", 2019, p. 5, <http://tap.mk.gov.lv/doc/2019_04/VARAMZin_180419.351.doc>, visited on 8 July 2019.
21   T.J. Ramsøy, *Why Data Ownership Matters in the Age of AI*, 14 September 2018, *Machine Design*, <www.machinedesign.com/industrial-automation/why-data-ownership-matters-age-ai>, visited on 20 May 2019.

The European Commission has recognized that "Big Data is a key economic asset in achieving competitiveness, growth and jobs due to its potential for impact and as an enabler for both horizontal and sector-specific gains".[22] In 2014, it was predicted that using this opportunity could mean up to 30% of the global data market for European suppliers, 100,000 new data-related jobs in Europe by 2020 and 10% lower energy consumption, better health-care outcomes and more productive industrial machinery.[23] However, to date, no compelling evidence exists to prove this prediction.

The same ideas have been pinpointed by the Organisation for Economic Cooperation and Development (OECD). They note that 'smart-grid' technologies, which are becoming ever more popular, are generating large volumes of data on energy and resource consumption patterns that can be exploited to improve energy and resource efficiency.[24] Therefore the OECD has recognized that large data sets are becoming a core asset in the economy.[25]

3.1.3 Growing Awareness of the Public

Another vital factor for the popularity of the debates on big data is the growing interest of users in activities connected to their data. One conclusion of the internet governance and data ownership survey was that 63 percent of respondents disagreed with this statement: "Share personal information with private companies online all the time and think 'It's no big deal' to do so".[26] As noticed by other authors, "nowadays with companies like Google and Facebook having built financial empires out of big data and mobile providers selling unlimited data plans, data is no longer an esoteric concept and data ownership has become a frequently debated topic".[27]

This is where a clash appears. Once it comes to light that companies have used data against the expectations of users,[28] it can mean high endangerment of reputation.

---

22 Fact Sheet Data CPPP, European Commission, <https://ec.europa.eu/research/industrial_technologies/pdf/factsheet-cppp_en.pdf>, visited on 8 July 2019.
23 *Ibid.*
24 Data-driven innovation for growth and well-being, OECD, <www.oecd.org/sti/ieconomy/data-driven-innovation.htm>, visited on 20 May 2019.
25 *Ibid.*
26 83% of Global Internet Users Believe Affordable Access to the Internet Should be a Basic Human Right, 24 November 2014, Ipsos, p. 3, <www.cigionline.org/sites/default/files/documents/internet-survey-2014-factum.pdf>, visited on 20 May 2019.
27 J. Harris, Who owns big data? March 26, 2015, <https://blogs.sas.com/content/datamanagement/2015/03/26/owns-big-data>, visited on 8 July 2019.
28 M. Day, G. Turner, N. Drozdiak, *Amazon's Alexa Team Can Access Users' Home Addresses*, 24 April 2019, Bloomberg, <www.bloomberg.com/news/articles/2019-04-24/amazon-s-alexa-reviewers-can-access-customers-home-addresses>, visited on 20 May 2019.

3.2 Example of the Complex Nature of Big Data

To gain a more in-depth insight into the practical side of big data processing, a useful illustration is the motor industry, which nowadays is one of the main stakeholders in the big data discussion.

The motor industry covers many actors: drivers, car producers, platforms, telecommunication providers. The first question that arises is whether data collection and processing within the smart technologies offered within a car are telecom services. The second question concerns the monetization of data: who owns data collected by the car with the help of specific platforms? If any of the actors are left out of this circle, the system will not work, and there would be no results and no data. Yet every party involved actively claims their rights 'for work done'.

Some legal systems support some of the property attributions. For example, in Germany, it is possible to argue that data is owned by those who technically created it.[29] However, instead of resolving the issue, it becomes entangled all the more.

Another important question concerns the general use of data. Is a tyre company allowed to use data gathered about a specific person? Theoretically, such activity would be in the interests of everyone involved as the company could produce safer and longer-lasting tyres with the help of data. The consumer, of course, would oppose the possibility of the tyre company obtaining his data for no remuneration, especially as the consumer would still need to buy those safer tyres for the full cost. Should this data be given to state institutions who could also learn more about driving patterns? Similar questions arise in parallel fields, such as smart homes or smart cities.

The information collected covers not only data about the driver but also – and more precisely – a lot of technical data regarding the movement and technical parameters of the car.[30] It is likely that such data are not covered by the GDPR[31] and therefore consumers have fewer rights.

---

29 T. Hoeren, 'Dateneigentum – Versuch einer Anwendung von § 303a StGB im Zivilrecht', *MultiMedia und Recht* (2013) p. 486.
30 J. Drexl, 'Designing Competitive Markets for Industrial Data – Between Propertisation and Access', 8 November 2016, *Max Planck Institute for Innovation and Competition Research Paper* No. 16–13, p. 10, <www.ssrn.com/abstract=2862975>, visited on 10 September 2020.
31 Regulation (EU) 2016/679 of the European Parliament and of the Council of 27 April 2016 on the protection of natural persons with regard to the processing of personal data and on the free movement of such data, and repealing Directive 95/46/EC, <https://eur-lex.europa.eu/eli/reg/2016/679/oj>, visited on 10 September 2020.

Finally, data collected by cars today is only a small part of the collection potential. In the future, connected vehicles most likely will collect data from smart cities, including traffic light information, weather services, public events, and road surface conditions.[32] How and why should the car industry 'own' the data, and what are the consumer's rights?

Sharing is only one aspect of data processing. However, the main questions arise regarding the tools needed to prove ownership of data.

4 Core Problem

4.1 *Insecurity for All Stakeholders*

Who has the right to monetize big data? This essential question causes substantial legal uncertainty. Due to this uncertainty, the issue has the potential to hinder investment in various sectors. It also creates a debate about data protection. According to the European Commission, "barriers to the free flow of data are caused by the legal uncertainty surrounding the emerging issues on 'data ownership' or control, (re)usability and access to/transfer of data and liability arising from the use of data".[33]

Legally speaking, to own something means to have property rights in it: that is, rights of possession, use, and enjoyment, which the owner can bestow, collateralize, encumber, mortgage, sell, or transfer, and the right to exclude everyone else from. In connection to data, Technopedia explains: "[d]ata ownership is the act of having legal rights and complete control over a single piece or set of data elements. It defines and provides information about the rightful owner of data assets".[34]

However, as many equal parties are involved in the creation of big data, who has these rights? As this is not strictly private data under the GDPR, data subjects or individuals are not the only owners. One can argue that data should be owned by the person who created it, namely, the consumer walking around with his mobile device. However, if someone did not know that his phone is collecting such data, can it qualify as his property? At the same time, big data

---

32 B. Darrow, 'The Question of Who Owns the Data Is About to Get a Lot Trickier', 6 April 2016, *Fortune*, <www.fortune.com/2016/04/06/who-owns-the-data>, visited on 20 May 2019.

33 B.V. Asbroeck, J. Debussche, J. César, 'Building the European Data Economy: Data Ownership', 1 January 2017, Bird&Bird, p. 3.

34 *Data Ownership*, IT Dictionary 'Techopedia', <www.techopedia.com/definition/29059/data-ownership>, visited on 20 May 2019.

is not directly owned by enterprises, as many data sources are from the outside, such as public places. A good deal of data is also computer-generated.[35]

The impossibility for all parties to own the masses of big data jointly created is apparent. This would create a clash between those rights due to conflicting interests.

Additionally, within the European Union, data are intangible, non-rivalrous goods and as such cannot be captured by the traditional definitions of property law,[36] which is based on fundamental rights. Finally, one should also not forget the possibility of big data being used for the public good – for example, for urban development,[37] for road safety[38] or for health system development.[39] This perspective also raises the question whether big data could and should be owned at all.

From the perspective of companies, data ownership is crucial regarding monopoly regulations. Several regulators have already drawn attention to competition issues concerning the excessive concentration of specific data.[40] Some regulators have even noted that, with their business models, some companies are limiting market access to their competitors. This aspect leads to a vicious circle as a company without market access cannot get access to data, but without data the business is meaningless.[41] However, who gives monopoly

---

35 P. Lambert, 'Computer-generated works and copyright: selfies, traps, robots, AI and machine learning', *E.I.P.R.* (2017) no. 1, pp. 12–20.

36 J. Drexl, 'Designing Competitive Markets for Industrial Data – Between Propertisation and Access', 8 November 2016, *Max Planck Institute for Innovation and Competition Research Paper* No. 16–13, <www.ssrn.com/abstract=2862975>, visited on 10 September 2020.

37 O. Rofman, *Can Big Data Solve The Urban Planning Challenge?*, 11 December 2017, techopedia, <www.techopedia.com/can-big-data-solve-the-urban-planning-challenge/2/33084>, visited on 22 May 2019.

38 M. Mills, '4 Ways How Big Data Will Improve Road Safety', 22 May 2017, *Datafloq*, <www.datafloq.com/read/4-ways-big-data-will-improve-road-safety/3127>, visited on 22 May 2019.

39 M. Lebied, 12 Examples of Big Data Analytics In Healthcare That Can Save People, 18 July 2018, the datapine Blog, <www.datapine.com/blog/big-data-examples-in-healthcare>, visited on 22 May 2019.

40 *Toronto Real Estate Board* v. *Commissioner of Competition*, 1 December 2017, the Competition Tribunal, FCA 236, no. A-174–16, <www.canlii.org/en/ca/fca/doc/2017/2017fca236/2017fca236.html>, visited on 20 May 2019; *Bundeskartellamt prohibits Facebook from combining user data from different sources Background information on the Bundeskartellamt's Facebook proceeding*, 7 February 2019, Bundeskartellamt, <www.bundeskartellamt.de/SharedDocs/Publikation/EN/Pressemitteilungen/2019/07_02_2019_Facebook_FAQs.pdf?__blob=publicationFile&v=5>, visited on 20 May 2019.

41 Bundeskartellamt prohibits Facebook from combining user data from different sources Background information on the Bundeskartellamt's Facebook proceeding, 7 February 2019, Bundeskartellamt, <www.bundeskartellamt.de/SharedDocs/Publikation/EN/Presse

companies the right to use all the data of users in a way identical to their trade secrets[42]?

The diversity of these questions shows the need for a broad range of answers.

4.2 Current Norms and Their Loopholes

The issue of data as property has been discussed since the 1970s[43] – without much success in terms of answers. A new academic debate has only now begun.[44] Unfortunately, practitioners do not have anything to offer: it has been recognized that from the theoretical perspective every stakeholder would have some rights to data, yet this answer has no practical use as no tools exist to protect those rights and even data as such. Laws provide other forms of protection to certain types of data, in particular the IP law area: database rights; copyright; and trade secrets. However, none of these provides adequate protection of ownership in big data.

4.2.1 Data Protection Laws

Laws dealing with data protection in the current situation do not provide a solution. These laws do not deal with non-personal data, which, in most cases, form the core of big data. Furthermore, the GDPR does not deal with the ownership of data at all. It only states the rights of data subjects, such as the right to control data.[45] However, a definition and terminology of ownership rights to data are lacking. Some authors hold the view that rights under Article 20 of the GDPR (the right to receive all data an enterprise has gathered about an individual in tangible form) could be seen as some form of ownership.[46] However,

---

mitteilungen/2019/07_02_2019_Facebook_FAQs.pdf?__blob=publicationFile&v=5>, visited on 20 May 2019.

42   G. Malgieri, '"Ownership" of Customer (Big) Data in the European Union: Quasi-Property as Comparative Solution?', *Journal of Internet Law* (2016) p. 1.

43   J.M. Fromholz, 'The European Union Data Privacy Directive', *Berkeley Technology Law Journal* (2000) p. 461.

44   B. Hugenholz, *Data Property: Unwelcome Guest in the House of IP" Paper presented at Trading Data in the Digital Economy: Legal Concepts and Tools*, 2017, <https://pure.uva.nl/ws/files/16856245/Data_property_Muenster.pdf>, visited on 10 September 2020. T.J. Farkas, 'Data Created by the Internet of Things: The New Gold Without Ownership?', *Revista La Propiedad Inmaterial* (2017) p. 5.

45   Regulation (EU) 2016/679, *supra* note 31.

46   T. Elliott, *Data Ownership: The Next Big Data Threat and Opportunity*, 16 July 2018, Timo Elliott's Blog, <www.timoelliott.com/blog/2018/07/data-ownership-the-next-big-data-threat-and-opportunity.html>, visited on 20 May 2019.

this right is restrictive as it firstly does not provide full ownership such as the right to sell the data, and, secondly, is only usable *post factum*.

4.2.2 IP Regulations

As for IP law, in comparison to objects of intellectual property norms, data cannot be seen as the intellectual creation of human beings. It can perhaps be better described as behaviour, technical or natural circumstances – with no involvement of creativity. Generally, copyright protection requires a human author. Works created by automated processes cannot be copyright-protected.[47] This means that laws regulating intellectual property lack the relevant tools needed for a big data world.

Further, more specific IP regulations which seem to be connected to data, such as the Database Directive,[48] are not a suitable solution.

This Directive provides the right to protect a database as an investment or as an original creation. However, in order to enjoy protection under the Database Directive a database must consist of a collection of independent works, data or other materials which (a) are arranged systematically or methodically; and (b) are individually accessible by electronic or other means. *Sui generis* rights to the database protect the investment to obtain, verify or present the contents of the database.[49] But ownership of rights to a database does not confer rights to individual data as such and are without prejudice to any rights subsisting in the content.[50]

Additionally, database rights only protect the database owner from a third party's "extraction and/or re-sutilization of the whole or of a substantial part"[51] of the database. This approach is not in line with the protection and ownership of individual data.[52]

In the literature, it is possible to find opinions that data could be licensed. For example, "legal ownership of personal data, in the broadest sense, must be vested in the person to whom it refers. That person may license the right to use

---

47 See, e.g., *Telstra Corporation Limited* v. *Phone Directories Company Pty Ltd*, 15 December 2010, Federal Court of Australia, FCA 44, no. VID 147 of 2010, <www.jade.io/article/204318>, visited on 20 May 2019., where the High Court of Australia found that there was insufficient human authorship in the automated process for creating telephone directories; Scassa, *supra* note 8, p. 10.
48 Directive 96/9/EC of the European Parliament and of the Council of 11 March 1996 on the legal protection of databases, <https://eur-lex.europa.eu/legal-content/EN/TXT/?uri=celex%3A31996L0009>, visited on 10 September 2020.
49 Malgieri, *supra* note 42, p. 4.
50 Directive, *supra* note 4.
51 Malgieri, supra note 42, p. 4.
52 *Ibid.*

some or all of this data to other parties – individual, commercial, and indeed governmental – under defined, binding, and enforceable conditions".[53]

However, when considering the amounts of data provided and processed every day, for example, within smart home systems or smart cars, it is clear that such a licensing system would be highly complicated.

The European Commission also acknowledges the lack of a comprehensive legislative framework regarding data created by computer processes or collected by sensors.[54]

4.2.3 Trade Secret Regulations

Trade secret regulations are not fit for defining ownership of big data either. This is so because these regulations apply only to information that meets the following requirements:

a) it is secret in the sense that it is not generally known to the public;
b) it has commercial value because it is secret;
c) it has been subject to reasonable steps to keep it secret under the circumstances by the person lawfully in control of the information.[55]

This means that a trade secret loses protection from the moment of disclosure. With big data, there is no need to keep it secret as all stakeholders have an interest in monetizing the information. Additionally, some stakeholders have the right to require others to disclose big data acquired. This makes trade secret regulations problematic for dealing with data ownership.

4.2.4 National and International General Legislation

National laws can only partly resolve the issue. Section 929 of the Latvian Civil Law states that the object of property can be all that has not been definitely removed from general circulation by law.[56] Theoretically, this broad norm can be interpreted so that data is the object of ownership. However, there is a risk

---

53 B. Devlin, *Who Owns Your Data?*, 25 July 2016, tdwi, <www.tdwi.org/articles/2016/07/25/who-owns-your-data.aspx>, visited on 20 May 2019.

54 The European Commission, *Legal study on ownership and access to data*, 2016, Osborne Clarke LPP, <https://op.europa.eu/en/publication-detail/-/publication/dobec895-b603-11e6-9e3c-01aa75ed71a1>, visited on 10 September 2020. The jurisdictions surveyed were: France, Spain, Germany, the UK, Italy, Belgium, the Netherlands.

55 Directive (EU) 2016/943 of the European Parliament and of the Council of 8 June 2016 on the protection of undisclosed know-how and business information (trade secrets) against their unlawful acquisition, use and disclosure, Article 2, <https://eur-lex.europa.eu/legal-content/EN/TXT/?uri=CELEX%3A32016L0943>, visited on 20 May 2019.

56 The Civil Law, Law of the Republic of Latvia, adopted on 28 January 1937, Section 929, <www.likumi.lv/ta/en/en/id/225418-the-civil-law>, visited on 20 May 2019.

of problems connected with enforcement of this norm if one actor wishes to claim absolute rights to big data.

The other EU Member States have less flexible laws. Germany, for example, has considered the principle that "data belongs to the generator".[57] Furthermore, opinions are even more polarized, as some may argue that the information has a public nature. If information about average speed on the roads is public, why should someone own the big data concerning the same information on car speed?

Finally, case law at EU level so far does not recognize ownership rights in data.[58]

This leads to the conclusion that none of the existing legal regulations resolve the issue of big data ownership. This, in turn, causes legal uncertainty, impacting decisions on investing in big data businesses. At the same time, it has been noted that a general property right would be superficial and could even be economically dangerous.[59]

5 The Dilemma of Regulation

Attorney-at-law Eric Le Quellenec has boldly stated that "after the protection of personal data, Europe's next big challenge is to achieve a uniform scheme for protection and exploitation of non-personal, machine-generated data".[60]

In 2015, the European Commission put forward the idea of a fifth EU fundamental freedom: the free flow of data.[61] This initiative addresses "the emerging issues of ownership, interoperability, usability and access to data"[62] with the

---

57 T. Hoeren, *Big Data and the Ownership in Data: Recent Developments in Europe*, 2014, p. 3, <www.rd-alliance.org/sites/default/files/Big_Data_and_the_Ownership_in_Data.pdf>, visited on 10 September 2020.
58 Asbroeck, Debussche, César, *supra* note 33.
59 *Arbeitsgruppe „Digitaler Neustart" der Konferenz der Justizministerinnen und Justizminister der Länder*, 15 May 2017, Justizportal des Bundes und der Länder, p. 93, <www.justiz.nrw.de/JM/schwerpunkte/digitaler_neustart/zt_bericht_arbeitsgruppe/bericht_ag_dig_neustart.pdf>, visited on 20 May 2019.
60 E.L. Quellenec, *A Call for a European "Civil Code" of Digital Data*, 12 September 2017, Euro Cloud, <www.eurocloud.org/news/article/a-call-for-a-european-civil-code-of-digital-data>, visited on 21 May 2019.
61 *Commission Staff Working Document on the free flow of data and emerging issues of the European data economy*, 10 January 2017, the European Commission, <www.ec.europa.eu/newsroom/dae/document.cfm?doc_id=41247>, visited on 22 May 2019.
62 *A Digital Single Market Strategy for Europe*, 6 May 2015, COM (2015) 192 final, the European Commission, <https://eur-lex.europa.eu/legal-content/EN/TXT/?uri=COM%3A2015%3A192%3AFIN>, visited on 10 September 2020.

ultimate goal being to 'build a data economy' which will concurrently "maximize the growth potential of the digital economy".[63] At the same time, the proposed Regulation on the Free Flow of Non-personal data[64] still does not address issues of ownership: instead, a right to data portability for non-personal data has been proposed,[65] thus showing similarities to Article 20 of the GDPR.

Without clear rules on ownership or the right to use big data commercially, the only answer to the ownership question seems to be a contractual relationship. This solution has been used by stakeholders so far. A clear example of that is the consensus found between organizations representing farmers and Agriculture-Technology Providers, such as John Deere, DuPont Pioneer, and Dow AgroSciences, in America.[66] They have signed the Privacy and Security Principles for Farm Data,[67] agreeing on how data is gathered, protected, or shared. Agrarian data generated from farming operations has been declared as the property of farmers. Yet, at the same time, it is the responsibility of the farmer to agree upon data use and sharing with other stakeholders.

But even this promising solution has its drawbacks. Firstly, parties must find a compromise on a wide range of issues, such as the scope of rights, internal use/onward dissemination, combination/use with other data; whether anticipated analysis of data is expressly permitted, what are the mechanisms for repurposing/adding new purposes, risk allocation, post-term use of data supplied in-term, derived data, and so on.[68] It is highly challenging to find a solution which would equally serve the interests of all parties involved.

---

63   Communication of the Commission of 6 May 2015 to the European Parliament, the Council, the European Economic and Social Committee and the Committee of the Regions—A Digital Single Market Strategy for Europe, COM(2015) 192 final, 14–15, Chapter 4.1., <https://eur-lex.europa.eu/legal-content/EN/TXT/?uri=COM%3A2015%3A192%3AFIN>, visited on 10 September 2020. J. Drexl, *Designing Competitive Markets for Industrial Data – Between Propertisation and Access*, Max Planck Institute for Innovation and Competition Research Paper No. 16–13, pp. 1–2, <www.ssrn.com/abstract=2862975>, visited on 20 May 2019.

64   Regulation (EU) 2018/1807 of the European Parliament and of the Council of 14 November 2018 on a framework for the free flow of non-personal data in the European Union, <https://eur-lex.europa.eu/legal-content/EN/TXT/?uri=CELEX%3A32018R1807>, visited on 10 September 2020.

65   *Ibid.*

66   M. Kassner, *Who owns the data once it becomes part of big data?*, 8 December 2014, TechRepublic, <www.techrepublic.com/article/who-owns-the-data-once-it-becomes-part-of-big-data>, visited on 20 May 2019.

67   Privacy and Security Principles for Farm Data, Farm Bureau, <www.fb.org/issues/technology/data-privacy/privacy-and-security-principles-for-farm-data>, visited on 20 May 2019.

68   Kemp, *supra* note 4, p. 18.

Secondly, technology companies might impose their power on users. However, it would be extremely burdensome for companies to regulate property issues contractually in a space where a myriad of data sources, storage as well as a countless number of actors exist at the same time. This comes in combination with the fact that contracts generally work *in personam*, meaning they are only enforceable against the contracting party. This challenge automatically creates either an extreme labyrinth of contracts between various parties – or ineffectiveness.

Finally, while taking into consideration the unavoidable international nature of data processing and big data, there is also a lack of harmonization of contract law in Europe.

Therefore this is not a final solution.

6 A Possible Acceptable Option for the Future

6.1 *The Creation of Semi-right*

A practical answer to the big data property issue seems to be a non-exclusive, flexible ownership right in data sets.[69] This is a proposal included in the white paper on 'Data Ownership',[70] issued within the Toreador Project (trustworthy model-aware analytics data platform – a three-year big data research project funded by the EU Commission[71]).

The non-exclusive nature of rights has been chosen because data – in comparison to several other resources – is "non-exhaustible and also non-rivalrous".[72] This means that several actors can use the same data at the same time, that is, there can exist "shared use of data by the different actors in the data value cycle, each on their own merits".[73]

In addition, the right to individual pieces of data leaves space for securing value even for the smallest pieces of data which already might be vital to their owners. Therefore, data is protected not only in bulk, as in databases, but also each smallest part individually, in small clusters and all together.

Finally, this form of data ownership can constantly change: "As soon as information is represented in a formalized manner suitable for communication,

---

69 F. Banterle, *"Data ownership" in the big data era: some thoughts on the new Bird&Bird White Paper – what's next for the EU?*, 24 February 2017, iPlens, <https://iplens.org/2017/02/24/data-ownership-in-the-big-data-era>, visited on 10 September 2020.
70 Asbroeck, Debussche, César, *supra* note 33.
71 Project 'Toreador', <www.toreador-project.eu>, visited on 20 May 2019.
72 Shaba, *supra* note 15, p. 22.
73 *Ibid.*

interpretation, or processing; it would qualify for protection under the new right".[74] Any performer could claim non-exclusive ownership of this data, regardless of whether they were the primary creator, collector, recorder, organizer or any other person involved.

In order to avoid a situation where several actors claim ownership of data without evidence of having worked with the data (having processed it), the authors of the project also offer to introduce a traceability obligation.[75] This innovation would mean a duty for all actors claiming ownership of data to show proof of having processed the data in the form of traceability logs. In the IT field, this should not be an issue – so, no new burdens are created for actors. At the same time, this obligation achieves other goals, such as the improved possibility for the data controller to respond to a data subject's requests regarding their data.

6.2   *The Future*

The offer has been recognized by other actors, noting that "[a]n exclusive right would risk blocking access to data. Access to data appears crucial in this data-driven economy. (…) Thus, a flexible approach to data is welcomed".[76]

The author of this article also welcomes the idea of a new semi-right as well as traceability obligations. In such a way, data could also be more effectively used for the common good – such as the development mentioned above of smart grids or enhanced security of smart cities.

The only room for doubt remains regarding the non-exclusive nature of this right. What seems to be lacking is any right to benefits – such as the right to receive compensation for the use of data primarily created by a private person.[77]

What is more, the issue of computer-generated data within this offer would not be entirely clear either. Some authors have considered that this data should be viewed as entirely within the public domain as computers do not need any incentives to promote innovation.[78]

Similarly, an issue arises on a final and unified definition of big data – as already noted above, there is still no clarity on a single umbrella term. That is

---

74   Asbroeck, Debussche, César, *supra* note 33, p. 124.
75   Asbroeck, Debussche, César, *supra* note 33, p. 125.
76   Banterle, *supra* note 69.
77   *Ibid.*
78   P. Samuelson, 'Allocating Ownership Rights in Computer-Generated Works', *University Of Pittsburgh Law Review* (1986) no. 47, p. 1185–1228.

also proven by 2016 research, where the countries involved provided at least nine different definitions of data.[79]

Additionally, the question of introducing this right in legal systems – as a single, unified right, identical in as many countries as possible – remains open.

So far, it is not known whether or when the European Commission will follow this advice – maybe the only chosen option will be the right to data portability. The idea of a non-exclusive ownership right would be a ground-breaking innovation in the current legal field. This seems to be an appropriate answer to the problems outlined. Yet one can also see a space for further research on an even better approach.

Acknowledgements

The author expresses his sincere gratitude to Madara Meļņika, his ex-colleague at the law firm Sorainen, for providing invaluable assistance in preparing this contribution in 2019.

---

[79] B. Sloot, S. Schende, *International and comparative legal study on Big Data*, 2016, <https://bartvandersloot.com/onewebmedia/WP_20_International_and_Comparative_Legal_Study_on_Big_Data.pdf>, visited on 8 July 2019.

Development of Consumer Collective Redress in the EU: a Light at the End of the Tunnel?

*Ana Vlahek**

Abstract

The development of collective redress in the EU started in the 1980s and first resulted in adoption of legislation on collective injunctive and declaratory relief for the protection of specific interests, in particular consumer interests, and later focused on expanding the rules in other areas of law as well as accompanying them with rules on collective compensatory redress. As in recent years ever more mass harm cases without a proper procedural framework for tackling them have been detected, the EU has intensified its collective redress regulation activities, in particular with a view to safeguarding consumers' interests. Although collective redress as such is generally perceived as a common feature of modern European judicial systems, the EU institutions have been tackling how best to regulate it in the European legal environment. They have produced a plethora of rather uncontrollable acts with different effects and scope of application that have introduced different and at times ambiguous definitions and concepts without enough valuable interpretation and insight into the reasons behind them. Referring to insufficient MS reaction to the 2013 Recommendation, in 2018 the Commission drafted a new, binding regime for consumer collective redress that may well require prudent MS that have already introduced compensatory collective redress to amend their recently adopted legislation. The paper presents the development of (consumer) collective redress in the EU by analysing four stages of legislative activity at the EU level and the principles and solutions of the relevant acts adopted within them.

Keywords

access to justice – effective judicial remedy – collective redress in the EU – collective action – collective settlement – consumer collective redress

---

* PhD, Associate Professor at the University of Ljubljana, Faculty of Law.

1 Introduction

The beginnings of filing collective actions in Europe date back at least to the Middle Ages.[1] In England, they evolved into the *Bill of peace* court practice, first enabling injunctive and declaratory redress that was available by 17th and 18th centuries at the latest, and later also compensatory collective redress.[2] Ideas on regulating and harmonizing collective actions in the modern legal environment of the European continent have, however, only emerged in the last couple of decades. The progress on the EU level that started in the 1980s has been slow and gradual and has to date not been completed. It first resulted in adoption of legislation on collective injunctive and declaratory relief for the protection of specific interests, in particular those of consumers, and later focused on expanding the rules in other areas of law as well as accompanying them with rules on collective compensatory redress. As more and more mass harm cases without a proper procedural framework for tackling them have been detected,[3] regulation of collective redress in the EU has become a priority in fostering access to justice. In recent years, this has focused on the introduction and harmonisation of compensatory relief throughout the EU, in particular with a view to protecting consumer interests. The optimal scope and the types of redress, rules on standing and other focal questions of collective redress regulation have, however, still not been fully decided upon.[4]

---

1 For further details, *see, e.g.*, W. Weiner, D. Szyndrowski, 'The Class Action, from the English Bill of Peace to Federal Rule of Civil Procedure 23: Is There a Common Thread?', 8 *Whittier L. Rev.* 935 (1986–1987); T.D. Rowe, Jr., 'A Distant Mirror: The Bill of Peace in Early American Mass Torts and its Implications for Modern Class Actions', 39 *Arizona Law Review* (1997); Court of Chancery, *Cases Argued and Decreed in the High Court of Chancery [1660–1697]* (Halsted, Grigg, New York, 1828); R.B. Marcin, 'Searching for the Origin of the Class Action', 23 *Catholic University Law Review* (1974); J. Sladič, 'Slovenian Law on Collective Actions: a Legal Transplant in Post-socialist Legal System', 3 *European Journal of Consumer Law* (2016) pp. 424–427.
2 *Ibid.* See also A. Vlahek, 'Razvoj kolektivnega varstva na področju antitrusta v Združenem kraljestvu', in M. Pavliha et al. (eds.), *Izzivi prava v življenjski resničnosti = Challenges of law in life reality: liber amicorum Marko Ilešič* (Pravna fakulteta v Ljubljani, 2017) pp. 541–554, 600–601.
3 *See* A. Galič, A. Vlahek, 'Zakon o kolektivnih tožbah', 2 *Pravosodni bilten* 2018, p. 25; D.R. Hensler, 'The Global Landscape of Collective Litigation', in D.R. Hensler, C. Hodges, I. Tzankova (eds.), *Class Actions in Context* (Edward Elgar, 2016) p. 4.
4 The original version of this article was submitted in early July 2019. As the Council had issued its general approach to the Commission's Proposal Directive (*see infra* note 93) before the article was reviewed, the article was subsequently amended so as to include analysis of the Council's amendments of November 2019.

2 Collective Redress as a Tool for Guaranteeing Access to Justice

Collective redress is perceived as a common feature of modern judicial systems.[5] It represents a tool for guaranteeing access to justice in the form of guaranteeing the right to access to the courts and the right to an effective remedy, the core fundamental rights of having a case heard in a court of law or other relevant authority and to obtain a remedy if it is found that the individual's rights have been violated.[6] The rights to an effective remedy and access to the court are protected, *inter alia*, by both the EU Charter (Article 47)[7] and the ECHR (Article 13[8] and, more importantly, Article 6 ECHR encompassing the right to access to the court[9] and also featuring the principle of equality of arms[10]). The guarantees set out in these articles are well established in global and regional human rights law[11] and constitute an important element of the rule of law being one of the founding values of both the Council of Europe and the EU.[12] They have long been recognized as general principles of EU law which underlie the constitutional traditions common to the MS.[13] The

---

5   Opinion of AG Jacobs in C-195/98 *Österreichischer Gewerkschaftsbund*, para. 47.
6   *Cf.* European Agency for Fundamental Rights, European Court of Human Rights, Council of Europe, *Handbook on European law relating to access to justice* (FRA and Council of Europe, Luxembourg, 2016) p. 16.
7   In accordance with the Charter's rules on its applicability. *See* S. Peers, T. Hervey, J. Kenner, A. Ward, *The EU Charter of Fundamental Rights, A Commentary* (Hart Publishing, 2014) p. 1199 ff; C-362/14 *Schrems*, para. 95.
8   Albeit only in cases of violations of rights and freedoms set out in ECHR. *See* P. van Dijk, F. van Hoof, A. van Rijn, L. Zwaak, *Theory and Practice of the European Convention on Human Rights* (Intersentia, 2006) p. 998 ff; R. White, C. Ovey, *Jacobs, White, Ovey, The European Convention on Human Rights* (Oxford University Press, 2010) p. 131 ff.
9   *See* D.J. Harris, M. O'Boyle, E. Bates, C. Buckley, *Harris, O'Boyle, Warbrick, Law of the European Convention on Human Rights* (Oxford University Press, 2014) p. 398 ff, referring to *Golder* v. *UK*, App. No. 4451/70; White, Ovey, *supra* note 8, p. 254 ff; A. Mowbray, *European Convention on Human Rights* (Oxford University Press, 2012), referring also to *Roche* v. *UK*, App. No. 32555/96, *et al.*, pp. 344, 383 ff.; Peers, Hervey, Kenner, Ward, *supra* note 7, p. 1205.
10 Harris, O'Boyle, Bates, Buckley, *supra* note 9, p. 413; White, Ovey, *supra* note 8, p. 261; Peers, Hervey, Kenner, Ward, *supra* note 7, p. 1263 ff; C. Grabenwarter, *Europaeische Menschenrechts-konvention* (C.H. Beck, 2009) p. 361.
11 D. Shelton in: Peers, Hervey, Kenner, Ward, *supra* note 7, p. 1200.
12 *See* C-362/14 *Schrems*, para. 95, and case-law referred to there; M. Klamert, D. Kochenov, T. Lock in M. Kellerbauer, M. Klamert, J. Tomkin, *The EU Treaties and the Charter of Fundamental Rights, A Commentary* (Oxford University Press, 2019) p. 28; Lock, D. Martin in Kellerbauer, Klamert, Tomkin, *supra* note 12, p. 2215. *Cf.* Harris, O'Boyle, Bates, Buckley, *supra* note 9, p. 399; White, Ovey, *supra* note 8, p. 242; Peers, Hervey, Kenner, Ward, *supra* note 7, pp. 1197, 1211.
13 *See, e.g.*, C-12/08 *Mono Car Styling*, para. 47, and case-law referred to there; Lock in Kellerbauer, Klamert, Tomkin, *supra* note 12, p. 2215, referring to, *inter alia*, 222/84 *Johnston*. *See also* Peers, Hervey, Kenner, Ward, *supra* note 7, p. 1197.

principle of effective enforcement of EU rights is also a reflection of the general EU principle of sincere co-operation laid down in Article 4/3 of the TEU and the obligation of the MS laid down in Article 19 of the TEU to ensure effective legal protection in the fields covered by EU law.[14]

However, the right to access to the court and the right to an effective remedy remain a dead letter in all those instances where only regular, individual redress is available to the victims of mass harm cases, in particular if they are in the position of the weaker party (also in terms of a one-shot litigant against a repeat player),[15] such as consumers or employees. In such cases, where harm has typically been dispersed among many individuals whose cost-benefit analysis of judicial redress does not favour filing actions (so-called individually non-recoverable claims),[16] effective enforcement of rights requires a different set of rules on standing, funding, procedural structure, and so on. Accessibility and effectiveness are in such cases best guaranteed through a collective redress mechanism. Although individual redress is – by law – fully available to victims, it can in fact impede the individual's access to the courts and thus not enable delivery of justice.[17] As has been emphasized in human rights law, the right of access to the court must not only exist in theory, it must also be effective,[18] and the limitations to which the right of access may be subject must not restrict the exercise of the right to such an extent that the very essence of the right is impaired.[19] Even the most detailed and optimal regulation

---

14   Peers, Hervey, Kenner, Ward, *supra* note 7, p. 1212.
15   A. Galič, 'Skupinske tožbe na področju potrošniškega prava', *Pravni letopis 2011* (2011), p. 215. *Cf.* U. Jeretina, A. Uzelac, 'Alternative Dispute Resolution for Consumer Cases: Are Divergences an Obstacle to Effective Access to Justice?', 4 *Mednarodna revija za javno upravo* (2014) p. 40. *See also Gorraiz Lizarraga and Others v. Spain,* App. No. 62543/00, where the ECtHR emphasized in para. 38 that "[...] in modern-day societies, when citizens are confronted with particularly complex administrative decisions, recourse to collective bodies such as associations is one of the accessible means, sometimes the only means, available to them whereby they can defend their particular interests effectively. Moreover, the standing of associations to bring legal proceedings in defence of their members' interests is recognised by the legislation of most European countries. [...] The Court cannot disregard that fact when interpreting the concept of "victim". Any other, excessively formalistic, interpretation of that concept would make protection of the rights guaranteed by the Convention ineffectual and illusory".
16   Galič (2011), *supra* note 15, p. 216. *Cf.* Jeretina, Uzelac, *supra* note 15, p. 40.
17   *Cf.* Harris, O'Boyle, Bates, Buckley, *supra* note 9, p. 399; Galič (2011), *supra* note 15, p. 216; P.H. Lindblom, 'Group litigation in Scandinavia' 1 *ERA Forum* 2009, p. 11.
18   White, Ovey, *supra* note 8, pp. 255, 135 ff, referring to, *inter alia, Steel and Morris v. UK,* App. No. 68416/01. *See also* Peers, Hervey, Kenner, Ward, *supra* note 7, p. 1214.
19   Peers, Hervey, Kenner, Ward, *supra* note 7, p. 1206, referring to *Ashingdane v. UK,* App. No. 8225/78.

of consumer rights or some other similar set of victims' rights has no meaningful effect without a proper procedural structure for their effective enforcement.[20] Without it, the overall and typically enormous harm caused to victims as a class is not addressed leaving the victims permanently deprived of their right to redress, whereas those in breach of victims' rights are enriched.[21] It is said that addressing such irregularities by strengthening private enforcement is also in the public interest due to the special and general prevention that cannot take place if judicial enforcement is in fact non-existent.[22] By avoiding numerous proceedings covering claims from the same mass harm case and thus eliminating likely backlogs in the courts, collective redress also contributes to efficient administration of justice.[23] At the same time, however, it must guarantee safeguards against potential abuse of claimants' rights to the detriment of the respondents.[24]

A concise description of collective redress is provided by AG Jacobs in his opinion delivered in *Österreichischer Gewerkschaftsbund* in 2000 when the regulation and application of collective actions in the EU had only started to emerge:

> Collective rights of action are an equally common feature of modern judicial systems. They are mostly encountered in areas such as consumer protection, labour law, unfair competition law or protection of the environment. The law grants associations or other representative bodies the right to bring cases either in the interest of persons which they represent or in the public interest. This furthers private enforcement of rules adopted in the public interest and supports individual complainants who are often badly equipped to face well organised and financially stronger opponents. The danger of abuse of such collective rights of action is again normally tackled by national procedural rules. Consequently, the Court has never objected to national rules providing for such collective rights of action and in practice often deals with questions referred in proceedings brought by interested associations.[25]

---

20 Galič (2011), *supra* note 15, p. 215. *Cf.* G. Howells, S. Weatherill, *Consumer Protection Law* (Ashgate Publishing, 2005) pp. 603 ff.
21 Galič, Vlahek (2018), *supra* note 3, p. 25.
22 *Ibid. Cf.* rec. 39 of the Preamble to Proposal Directive of 2018 (*see infra* Chapter 3.4).
23 Jeretina, Uzelac, *supra* note 15, p. 53. *Cf.* Galič (2011), *supra* note 15, p. 403.
24 Peers, Hervey, Kenner, Ward, *supra* note 7, p. 1226.
25 The AG referred in his opinion to C-470/93 *Verein gegen Unwesen in Handel und Gewerbe Köln*. The Court also referred to collective redress in C-199/08 *Erhard Eschig*. D. Ashton,

The growing reference to the importance of availability of collective redress throughout the EU goes hand in hand with the increase in the EU's powers in the Area of Freedom, Security and Justice, where the procedural rights are becoming increasingly important.[26] The development of EU regulation of collective redress has thus far undergone four stages. The EU has to date managed to harmonize collective injunctive and declaratory relief and is just about to harmonize collective consumer compensatory redress as well.

3   Stages of Development of Collective Redress in the EU

3.1   *First Stage: Regulation of Collective Declaratory and Injunctive Relief for the Protection of Specific Interests*

Collective redress mechanisms in the EU were first introduced in a set of directives prohibiting various commercial practices, such as misleading advertising,[27] unfair commercial B2C practices,[28] unfair contract terms in B2C contracts,[29] or laying down the rules on specific market behaviour, such as directives on consumer distance contracts,[30] consumers' rights,[31] medicinal

---

    D. Henry, *Competition Damages Actions in the EU: law and practice* (Edward Elgar Publishing, 2014) p. 136.
26 Lock in Kellerbauer, Klamert, Tomkin, *supra* note 12, p. 2213.
27 Council Directive 84/450/EEC of 10 September 1984 relating to the approximation of the laws, regulations and administrative provisions of the Member States concerning misleading advertising, *OJ L* 250, 19 September 1984.
28 Directive 2005/29/EC of the European Parliament and of the Council of 11 May 2005 concerning unfair business-to-consumer commercial practices in the internal market and amending Council Directive 84/450/EEC, Directives 97/7/EC, 98/27/EC and 2002/65/EC of the European Parliament and of the Council and Regulation (EC) No 2006/2004 of the European Parliament and of the Council ('Unfair Commercial Practices Directive') (Text with EEA relevance), *OJ L* 149, 11 June 2005.
29 Council Directive 93/13/EEC of 5 April 1993 on unfair terms in consumer contracts, *OJ L* 95, 21 April 1993, amended by Directive 2011/83/EU of the European Parliament and of the Council of 25 October 2011 on consumer rights, amending Council Directive 93/13/EEC and Directive 1999/44/EC of the European Parliament and of the Council and repealing Council Directive 85/577/EEC and Directive 97/7/EC of the European Parliament and of the Council, Text with EEA relevance, *OJ L* 304, 22 November 2011. See Ashton, Henry, *supra* note 25, p. 137.
30 Directive 97/7/EC of the European Parliament and of the Council of 20 May 1997 on the protection of consumers in respect of distance contracts, *OJ L* 144, 4 June 1997.
31 Directive 2011/83/EU of the European Parliament and of the Council of 25 October 2011 on consumer rights, amending Council Directive 93/13/EEC and Directive 1999/44/EC of the European Parliament and of the Council and repealing Council Directive 85/577/EEC and

products for human use,[32] and the like. Most of these directives were focused on protection of consumers' interests.[33] Part of their provisions lay down the rules on the enforcement of their substantive provisions. These directives, however, do not use terms such as 'collective redress' or 'collective actions'. Standing was typically given to persons or organizations regarded under national law as having a legitimate interest in protecting the specific interests covered by the directive in question. The courts or administrative authorities were given a plethora of powers to address infringements, such as a finding of infringement (declaratory relief), ordering cessation of an infringement or prohibiting it (such as an interim injunction or definitive injunctive relief),[34] and requiring publication of decisions in full or in part as well as of a corrective statement with a view to eliminating the so-called 'continuing effects of the infringement'. Some of these directives also set penalties for infringements and/or non-compliance with decisions by the courts or the authorities. These measures could be applied against different persons or groups of persons, such as traders from the same economic sector, or, if relevant, against a code owner. The directives allowed MS to adopt or retain the most stringent provisions in line with the TEC to ensure the maximum degree of protection of the specific interests covered by the directives.

In 1998, Directive 98/27 on collective injunctions for the protection of consumers' interests (the so-called Injunctions Directive)[35] was adopted. Its aim

---

Directive 97/7/EC of the European Parliament and of the Council Text with EEA relevance, OJ L 304, 22 November 2011.

[32] Directive 2001/83/EC of the European Parliament and of the Council of 6 November 2001 on the Community code relating to medicinal products for human use: Articles 86 to 100, OJ L 311, 28 November 2001.

[33] The EU legislator has also regulated different sorts of injunctive redress for the protection of collective interests in some other areas of law, such as intellectual property rights (Directive 2004/48/EC of the European Parliament and of the Council of 29 April 2004 on the enforcement of intellectual property rights (Text with EEA relevance), OJ L 157, 30 April 2004), environmental liability (see UNECE Convention on Access to Information, Public Participation in Decision-Making and Access to Justice in Environmental Matters (Aarhus Convention) and Directive 2004/35/EC of the European Parliament and of the Council of 21 April 2004 on environmental liability with regard to the prevention and remedying of environmental damage, OJ L 143, 30 April 2004) and data protection (Communication from the Commission on a comprehensive approach on personal data protection in the EU (COM(2012)609).

[34] In C-472/10 *Nemzeti Fogyasztóvédelmi Hatóság*, the CJEU assessed the effects of a judgment issued on the basis of an action for an injunction under Directive 93/13/EEC on unfair terms in consumer contracts. *See also* C-154/15, C-307/15 and C-308/15 *Gutiérrez Naranjo, Palacios Martínez, Banco Popular Español* on the temporal effects of a declaration of nullity of an unfair term.

[35] Directive 98/27/EC of the European Parliament and of the Council of 19 May 1998 on injunctions for the protection of consumers' interests, OJ L 166, 11 June 1998, in force from 1 July 1998.

was to protect the collective interests of consumers addressed in nine directives listed in an annex to the directive, with a view to ensuring the smooth functioning of the internal market. This was a general tool for injunctive relief that could, however, be applied only in cases of infringements of the listed directives. The MS could adopt or maintain in force provisions designed to grant more extensive rights to bring action at national level. This directive, too, did not provide a clear definition of collective redress as it merely stated somewhat ambiguously that "collective interests mean interests which do not include the cumulation of interests of individuals who have been harmed by an infringement".[36] In 2009, the Injunctions Directive was replaced by Directive 2009/22 (also called the Injunctions Directive)[37] which is still in force. The list in the annex to the directive was extended from the initial nine to thirteen directives, while otherwise the provisions of both directives are almost identical, including the definition of types of injunctive relief and entities qualified to bring an action. Directive 2009/22 requires the MS to designate the courts or administrative authorities competent to rule on proceedings commenced by 'qualified entities' seeking: (a) an order with all due expediency, where appropriate by way of summary procedure, requiring the cessation or prohibition of any infringement; (b) where appropriate, measures such as publication of the decision, in full or in part, in such form as deemed adequate and/or the publication of a corrective statement with a view to eliminating the continuing effects of the infringement; (c) in so far as the legal system of the MS concerned so permits, an order against the losing defendant for payment into the public purse or to any beneficiary designated in or under national legislation, in the event of failure to comply with the decision within a deadline set by the courts or administrative authorities, of a fixed amount for each day's delay or any other amount provided for in national legislation, with a view to ensuring compliance with decisions. These measures mirror to a large extent those provided by the sectoral directives presented above. A 'qualified entity' is defined as a body or organisation which, being properly constituted according to the law of a MS, has a legitimate interest in ensuring that the provisions of relevant consumer protection legislation are complied with, in particular: (a) one or more independent public bodies, in MS in which such bodies exist, specifically responsible for protecting the collective interests of consumers included in the directives listed in the annex; and (b) organisations whose purpose is to protect such collective interests of consumers, in accordance with the criteria laid down by

---

36 Rec. 2 of the Injunctions Directive.
37 Directive 2009/22/EC of the European Parliament and of the Council of 23 April 2009 on injunctions for the protection of consumers' interests (Codified version) Text with EEA relevance, *OJ L* 110, 1 May 2009.

national law. For the purposes of intra-Community infringements, and without prejudice to the rights granted to other entities under national law, the MS must, at the request of their qualified entities, communicate to the Commission their status, names and purpose. The Commission was tasked with drawing up, publishing and updating every six months a list of these entities and their purposes.[38] The MS were required to guarantee that qualified entities from other MS where the interests protected by those entities are also affected by the infringement have standing before their courts or administrative authorities, who in turn must accept the Commission's list as proof of the legal capacity of the entity, but can examine whether the purpose of the entity justifies its taking action in a specific case. Further, the directive allows the MS to require a party wishing to bring an action for an injunction to first consult the alleged infringer or both the infringer and the existing independent public body acting as a qualified entity. If the infringement does not cease within two weeks after the request, the party concerned may bring an action.

Both Injunctions Directives required the Commission to submit every three years a report on their application. The first report of 2008[39] showed that the MS amended their legislation to a greater or lesser extent in order to introduce the provisions of the first Injunctions Directive, but that use of measures in intra-Community cases had in particular been disappointing and was related to the high costs of bringing an action, as well as the complexity, length and limited scope of the procedure.[40] The second report was published in 2012[41] and concluded that despite its limitations, the injunctive action constitutes a useful tool for protecting the collective interests of consumers, and that qualified entities are gradually becoming aware of the possibilities under the

---

38 The latest list was published in a Commission Notification of 15 July 2019 (*OJ* C 237, 15 July 2019, pp. 3–68). Note that the Slovenian legislation referred to in the table (Consumer Protection Act) no longer applies as it was replaced by the new Collective Actions Act of 2017.

39 Report from the Commission concerning the application of Directive 98/27/EC of the European Parliament and of the Council on injunctions for the protection of consumers' interests, 18 November 2008, COM(2008) 756 final.

40 Report (2008), *supra* note 39, p. 5 ff.

41 Report from the Commission to the European Parliament and the Council Concerning the application of Directive 2009/22/EC of the European Parliament and of the Council on injunctions for the protection of consumers' interest (COM(2012) 635 final, 6 November 2012). A study on the application of Directive 2009/22/EC on injunctions for the protection of consumers' interests (former Directive 98/27/EC) was drafted for the Commission and published in 2011.

directive and gaining experience with its use. The Commission, however, detected important disparities among MS in the level of use of the tools and their effectiveness. The potential of injunctions was regarded as not fully exploited due to a number of shortcomings already detected in the first report. Similar conclusions were published in the 2017 Commission Fitness Check of EU consumer and marketing law,[42] and in the 2018 Report on the implementation of the 2013 Recommendation.[43] For these reasons, consumer injunctive collective redress is addressed in the 'New Deal for Consumers' package. Thus Directive 2009/22 might soon be repealed by the new Directive on representative actions for the protection of the collective interests of consumers, which is currently at the legislative stage.[44]

Collective interests of consumers as well as interim, injunctive and penalty measures for their protection are mentioned also in other pieces of EU legislation, such as Regulation 2006/2004 on consumer protection cooperation (CPC Regulation)[45] and its successor – the new CPC Regulation 2017/2394.[46] Although these regulations are without prejudice to the Injunctions

---

42   Commission Staff Working Document, Report of the Fitness Check of EU consumer and marketing law, 23 May 2017, SWD(2017) 209 final.

43   Report from the Commission to the European Parliament, the Council and the European Economic and Social Committee on the implementation of the Commission Recommendation of 11 June 2013 on common principles for injunctive and compensatory collective redress mechanisms in the Member States concerning violations of rights granted under Union law (2013/396/EU), 25 January 2018, COM(2018) 40 final.

44   Proposal for a Directive of the European Parliament and of the Council on representative actions for the protection of the collective interests of consumers, and repealing Directive 2009/22/EC (Text with EEA relevance) {SWD(2018) 96 final} – {SWD(2018) 98 final}, COM(2018) 184 final 2018/0089 (COD), 11 April 2018.

45   Regulation (EC) No 2006/2004 of the European Parliament and of the Council of 27 October 2004 on cooperation between national authorities responsible for the enforcement of consumer protection laws (the Regulation on consumer protection cooperation) Text with EEA relevance, OJ L 364, 9 December 2004.

46   Regulation (EU) 2017/2394 of the European Parliament and of the Council of 12 December 2017 on cooperation between national authorities responsible for the enforcement of consumer protection laws and repealing Regulation (EC) No 2006/2004 (Text with EEA relevance), OJ L 345, 27 December 2017. Communication of the Commission of 6 May 2015 titled 'A Digital Single Market Strategy for Europe', identified a priority need to enhance consumer trust through more rapid, agile and consistent enforcement of consumer rules. While a further Communication of the Commission of 28 October 2015 titled 'Upgrading the Single Market Strategy: more opportunities for people and business' reiterated that enforcement of EU consumer protection legislation should be further strengthened by the reform of Regulation (EC) No 2006/2004.

Directive,[47] as they both list only the authorities' investigative and enforcement powers in so-called cross-border cases,[48] they do regulate various interim, injunctive and penalty relief measures as well as various types of voluntary commitments by traders (but not compensatory relief claims and their enforcement).[49] Analysis of these acts shows that it is rather difficult to delimit their scope and understand the notions contained therein, and to thus fully grasp the EU system of collective redress.

3.2 Second Stage: First Attempts to Regulate Compensatory Collective Redress in Specific Areas of Law

In contrast to injunctive collective redress, compensatory collective redress has to date not been regulated in binding EU law. First attempts at regulation were focused on two specific areas of law, namely consumer protection and antitrust, where mass harm cases arise most often and where the claims are typically suitable for assessment in collective action proceedings.

The first set of Commission activities took place between 2005 and 2009 within initial attempts at regulating antitrust damages actions. In 2005, the Commission issued a Green Paper on antitrust damages actions which focused on questions of standing (in particular whether the victims themselves could file a collective action, that is, on whether to opt for the US-style class action) and distribution and quantification of damages.[50] After having analysed the responses,[51] in 2008 the Commission issued a White Paper on antitrust

---

47 Art. 2(5) of both CPC regulations.
48 'Intra-Community infringements' (plus 'widespread infringements' and 'widespread infringements with a Union dimension' as defined in the new CPC Regulation). *See also* Explanatory Memorandum in the 2018 Proposal Directive on consumer representative actions, pp. 4 ff, 14.
49 Art. 4 of the first CPC Regulation; rec. 46 of the Preamble and Art. 9 of the new CPC Regulation. *See also* L. Gorywoda, 'The Emerging EU Legal Regime for Collective Redress', in A. Nuyts, N.E. Hatzimihail, *Cross-Border Class Actions, The European Way* (Sellier European Law Publishers, 2014) p. 175.
50 Green Paper – Damages actions for breach of the EC antitrust rules {SEC(2005) 1732}, COM(2005)672. See Ashton, Henry, *supra* note 25, p. 139. *See* A.P. Komninos, *EC Private Antitrust Enforcement* (Hart Publishing, 2008) p. 234; D.P.L. Tzakas, 'Collective Redress Proceedings: Specific Issues Regarding Jurisdiction and Choice of Law', in M. Danov, F. Becker, P. Beaumont, *Cross-Border EU Competition Law Actions* (Hart Publishing, 2013) p. 239.
51 These, in particular industry, were largely against compensatory collective redress claiming it would overburden the economy and enable abuses.

actions.[52] The Commission considered that there is a clear need for mechanisms allowing aggregation of the individual claims of victims of antitrust infringements (be it by stand-alone or follow-on actions), and suggested a combination of two complementary mechanisms of 'collective redress': (1) representative actions brought by qualified entities, such as consumer associations, state bodies or trade associations, on behalf of identified or, in rather restricted cases, identifiable victims,[53] whereby these entities are either officially designated in advance or certified on an *ad hoc* basis by a MS for a particular antitrust infringement to bring an action on behalf of some or all of their members;[54] and (2) ambiguously termed 'opt-in collective actions', in which victims expressly decide to combine their claims for harm they suffered into one single action.[55] In 2009, the Commission published its Draft Proposal for a Directive on antitrust damages actions.[56] This went a big step further and provided for a proper US-style opt-out class action mechanism.[57] This mechanism was strongly criticized by the industry as well as the European Parliament[58] and the draft was eventually quashed.[59]

---

52   White Paper on Damages actions for breach of the EC antitrust rules, 2.4.2008, COM(2008)165.
53   Here, the Commission did not explain whether in the case of 'identifiable' victims, this would be an opt-in or an opt-out system. If the victims are fully identified at the outset of the proceedings, the only difference from a regular action is that instead of a joinder of individual parties, a representative entity files an action on behalf of the victims (who do not have standing, it is the entity who is formally the claimant party to the proceedings). In the case of identifiable victims, the representative entity files an action while the victims – depending on the system – opt-in or opt-out of the proceedings later in the course of collective proceedings in the sense of deciding whether they wish to be bound by the final judgment. A different understanding of these concepts is present in legal theory, *cf.* Anthanassiou, 'Collective Redress and Competition Policy', in Nuyts, Hatzimihail, *supra* note 49, p. 161 ff; Ashton, Henry, *supra* note 25, p. 131 ff, 140.
54   In contrast to other acts regulating collective redress, the White Paper did not address the issue of mutual recognition of the qualified entities. Ashton, Henry, *supra* note 25, p. 140.
55   These rules do not correspond to (better say understand) the typical rules on standing in typical collective actions. The opt-in mechanism as the Commission called it was, so it reads, designed as a regular multi-party action (joinder of parties), not as a proper collective opt-in action (in the latter case, the victims (or at least not all of them) would certainly not have the procedural position of a claimant). *Cf.* Anthanassiou, *supra* note 53, p. 161; Tzakas, *supra* note 50, p. 239.
56   The text of the proposal is no longer available on the internet.
57   *See* Arts. 3–6 of the proposal. *See also* Ashton, Henry, *supra* note 25, p. 141 ff; Tzakas, *supra* note 50, p. 243.
58   *See, e.g.*, European Parliament resolution of 26 March 2009 on the White Paper on damages actions for breach of the EC antitrust rules (2008/2154(INI)).
59   A. Fatur, K. Podobnik, A. Vlahek, *Competition Law in Slovenia* (Wolters Kluwer, 2016) p. 110.

The second field with active debate on collective redress (led by another DG) was consumer protection. In 2008, the Commission issued its Green Paper on consumer collective redress.[60] This is the first document revealing details of the Commission's position on how to best regulate collective redress in the EU. The Green Paper did not address collective redress for victims of EU antitrust infringements as this was to be covered by the antitrust damages regime that would enable relief to a wider group of victims, not only to consumers. The Green Paper stressed that there are barriers, in particular high litigation costs and complex and lengthy procedures, which *de facto* impede consumers from obtaining effective redress.[61] One of the options listed to address these problems was the judicial collective redress procedure. The Commission explained that it proposes a non-binding or binding EU measure to ensure that a collective redress judicial mechanism exists in all MS. It explained that this would ensure that every consumer in the EU would be able to obtain adequate redress in mass cases through representative actions, group actions, or test cases. This signalled that the Commission defined 'collective redress' broadly. 'Group actions' probably referred to a regular joinder of parties (not to a class action where the action is brought by some of the victims but has effects for the whole class depending on the opt-in or opt-out). This is confirmed by the definition of legal standing as only a representative action filed by a qualified entity such as consumer organisation or ombudsman was proposed. The issues to be decided within this option included financing of the procedure, prevention of unmeritorious claims, standing in court, the question of an opt-in or opt-out system and distribution of compensation. After receiving responses by the interested parties, in May 2009 the Commission issued a Consultation Paper for Discussion on the Follow-up to the Green Paper that listed redrafted reform options.[62] These legislative activities followed the Commission's 2007 Consumer Policy Strategy,[63] where it emphasized the importance of effective redress mechanisms for consumers and announced its intention to consider action on consumer collective redress. This was welcomed by the European Parliament, the Council and the European Economic and Social Committee.[64] As in 2011 the Commission decided to regulate collective redress horizontally, the drafting proceedings were discontinued.[65]

---

60 27 November 2008, COM(2008)794. *See* Gorywoda, *supra* note 49, p. 175 ff.
61 Green Paper, paras. 9, 13, 14.
62 *See* Gorywoda, *supra* note 49, p. 176.
63 COM (2007) 99 final.
64 Green Paper on Consumer Collective Redress, Ch. 1, para. 3.
65 Commentators report of the view of Commissioner Kuneva that on her watch, there will be no class actions. M. Danov, D. Fairgieve, G. Howells, 'Collective Redress Antitrust

The result of these failed attempts at regulating compensatory collective actions in the fields of antitrust and consumer protection was a decision by the Commission to regulate collective redress horizontally. In 2010 and 2011, commissioners Almunia, Dalli and Reding launched a public consultation "Towards a more coherent European approach to collective redress" and stressed that a general legal framework for collective redress would be drafted to correspond to the European legal tradition, perhaps allowing for specialized regulation of collective redress in certain specific fields, such as antitrust.[66] Collective redress was defined as encompassing both out-of-court mechanisms as well as representative or public authority-led collective injunctive and compensatory actions.[67] In 2011, the European Parliament's Committee on Legal Affairs (JURI) issued a draft report[68] which was not too lenient on the Commission's project. It emphasized that the Commission had not persuaded it of the need to regulate collective redress on the EU level. The report was finalized in 2012[69] and on its basis the European Parliament adopted a Resolution "Towards a Coherent European Approach to Collective Redress"[70] calling on the Commission to give reasons for regulation in the light of the principle of subsidiarity. It stressed the need for a horizontal approach to collective redress on the basis of common principles and paying due regard to national legal traditions and guaranteeing protective measures for the prevention of procedural abuses. Although the report focused on protection of consumers, the Parliament did not favour regulating collective redress separately for specific sectors. It promoted regulation of both injunctive and compensatory redress and continued to oppose the opt-out mechanism.[71] To avoid unmeritorious claims and misuse of collective redress and guarantee fair court proceedings, the European

---

Proceedings: How to Close the Enforcement Gap and Provide Redress for Consumers', in Danov, Becker, Beaumont, *supra* note 50, p. 252.

66 *Cf.* Gorywoda, *supra* note 49, p. 179 ff; Ashton, Henry, *supra* note 25, p. 142 ff.
67 *Ibid.*
68 Draft Report on 'Towards a Coherent European Approach to Collective Redress' (2011/2089(INI)).
69 Report on 'Towards a Coherent European Approach to Collective Redress' (2011/2089(INI)), A7-0012/2012.
70 European Parliament resolution of 2 February 2012 on "Towards a Coherent European Approach to Collective Redress" (2011/2089(INI)). *See* Ashton, Henry, *supra* note 25, p. 143 ff.
71 It is somewhat surprising how on the one hand, it is being stressed that, without collective redress mechanisms, victims with small claims would not have decided to file an individual action, while on the other hand, it is being stressed that the opt-out system would deprive them of this individual redress. Introducing appropriate rules on informing the victims about collective proceedings could surely solve this problem.

Parliament recommended the following safeguards: limited standing, full compensation for actual damage, access to evidence, the 'loser pays' principle and no third-party funding. It added that punitive damages and success fees are not appropriate. It also stressed the importance of alternative dispute resolution and the discretion of the judge to carry out a preliminary admissibility test (while the 2011 draft report of JURI, differently from its final version and the resolution, proposed a compulsory preliminary extrajudicial attempt to resolve the dispute). Following these events as well as taking into account that the stakeholders in the public consultation that took place in the preceding years raised the issue of inconsistencies between different Commission initiatives on collective redress,[72] the Commission decided to regulate collective redress coherently and horizontally without special regulation in specific fields of law.[73] This is also why Directive 2014/104 on antitrust damages actions has not touched upon collective redress.[74] The Commission also decided to address these issues in a soft-law instrument.[75] Having regard to the difficulties in pushing through the collective actions regime in the proposal for an antitrust damages directive, and the general controversy over many questions of regulation of collective proceedings, this move was certainly a wise one as it enabled some pressure on MS and offered at least minimal guidance if they decided to regulate collective actions.

3.3 Third Stage: Horizontal Soft-Law Approach to Regulating Collective Redress

In 2013, the Commission issued a Communication titled "Towards a European Horizontal Framework for Collective Redress".[76] Its aim was to report on the main views expressed in the public consultation over the preceding years, and to reflect the position of the Commission on some central issues regarding collective redress. A positive feature of the Communication – that can unfortunately not be detected in other Commission acts dealing with collective

---

72 Communication to the European Parliament, the Council, the European Economic and Social Committee and the Committee of the Regions titled Towards a European Horizontal Framework for Collective Redress, COM(2013) 401 final.
73 *Cf.* Gorywoda, *supra* note 49, p. 174.
74 Rec. 13 of the Preamble states that the directive should not require MS to introduce collective redress mechanisms for the enforcement of Arts. 101 and 102 TFEU.
75 *Cf.* Tzakas, *supra* note 50, p. 247; Danev, Fairgrieve, Howells, *supra* note 50, p. 273 ff. *See* a critique of such decision in Hess, 'Collective Redress and the Jurisdictional Model of the Brussels I Regulation', in Nuyts, Hatzimihail, *supra* note 49, p. 67 ff.
76 COM(2013) 401 final.

redress – is that it attempts to explain the meaning of 'collective redress' and some of its focal notions.[77]

The Communication was accompanied by a Recommendation on common principles for injunctive and compensatory collective redress mechanisms in the MS concerning violations of rights under EU law (2013/396/EU). In contrast to the injunctions directives, which cover only relief within specified areas of (mostly) consumer protection, this piece of soft law stresses that its principles should be applied horizontally and equally in all areas where collective claims in respect of violations of the rights under EU law would be relevant.[78] It adds, however, that it is without prejudice to the existing sectorial mechanisms of injunctive relief provided for by EU law.

The recommendations to the MS that are common to compensatory and injunctive collective relief cover standing, admissibility, information on a collective redress action, reimbursement of the legal costs of the winning party, funding, cross-border cases, and a registry of collective redress actions. The MS should designate representative entities to bring representative actions on the basis of clearly defined conditions of eligibility which should include at least the following: the entity should have a non-profit making character; there should be a direct relationship between the main objectives of the entity and rights under EU law that are claimed to have been violated and in respect of which the action is brought; and the entity should have sufficient capacity in terms of financial resources, human resources, and legal expertise, to represent multiple claimants,[79] acting in their best interest. The MS should ensure that representative actions can only be brought by entities officially designated in advance or certified on an *ad hoc* basis by MS national authorities or courts for a particular representative action. In addition, or as an alternative, the MS should empower public authorities to bring representative actions. These criteria vary to some extent from those set out in the Injunctions Directive.[80] The

---

[77] Unfortunately, it defines 'collective redress' very briefly and rather vaguely as "a procedural mechanism that allows, for reasons of procedural economy and/or efficiency of enforcement, many similar legal claims to be bundled into a single court action". More details are, however, available from the definitions of the 'opt-in' and 'opt-out' systems. The notions 'injunctive relief' and 'compensatory relief' are also briefly explained.

[78] It lists in para. 7 the typical areas where collective redress is of value: consumer protection, competition, environment protection, protection of personal data, financial services legislation and investor protection.

[79] More appropriately: victims (as the victims are not claimants and do not have standing in collective proceedings).

[80] It seems that the Recommendation defines 'standing' in a broader sense, but on the other hand lays down more detailed criteria for the qualification of entities.

Recommendation calls upon MS to enable dissemination of information about a claimed violation and the intention to file actions in that regard. It requires a certification phase. It sets out a loser pays principle, subject to the conditions provided for in the relevant national law. The Recommendation also regulates third party funding by requiring the claimant to declare to the court at the outset of the proceedings the source of the funds that it is going to use to support the legal action, and by laying down the criteria and safeguards for third party funding. The MS should ensure that in a cross-border dispute, a single collective action in a single forum is not prevented by national rules on admissibility or standing of foreign groups of victims or of officially designated representative entities. Finally, the MS should establish a freely accessible national registry of collective redress actions.

In addition to these principles common to both compensatory and injunctive collective redress, the Recommendation lays down specific principles relating to injunctive collective redress that mirror those of the Injunctions Directive. Expedient procedures are required for claims for injunctive orders and efficient enforcement of such orders. The MS should also establish appropriate sanctions against the defendant to ensure effective compliance with an injunctive order, including fines for each day's delay or some other amount provided for in national legislation.

Specific principles of compensatory collective redress include the rules on standing. The Recommendation states somewhat ambiguously that the claimant party should be formed on the basis of express consent by the natural or legal persons claiming to have been harmed, and refers to this as being the opt-in principle (it seems that this mechanism is a mere joinder of parties, not a collective action *stricto sensu*). It adds that any exception to this principle, by law or by court order, should be duly justified by reasons of sound administration of justice (thereby allowing, in principle, for real opt-in as well as opt-out (*sic!*) mechanisms). Persons claiming to have been harmed in the same mass harm situation should be able to join the claimant party at any time before judgment is given or the case is otherwise validly settled, if this does not undermine the sound administration of justice.[81] A member of the claimant party

---

81 It is not clear whether this system is supposed to be a mere multi-party action, a representative opt-in collective action or a class opt-in collective action. It seems that under collective redress, the Commission understands both 'real' collective actions (be it actions where the victims are not filing the action (representative or public actions) or actions where only one or some of the victims are filing the action (US-style class actions)) as well as various other mechanisms that are not real collective actions but serve the same purpose, i.e. to assess multiple claims in one proceeding (*e.g.* multi-party proceedings (joinder of claims), model case proceedings, grouping (joinder) of actions etc., where the

should also be free to leave the party at any time before final judgment is given or the case is otherwise validly settled, subject to the same conditions that apply to withdrawal in individual actions, without being deprived of the option to pursue the claim in another form, if this does not undermine the sound administration of justice. Rules on collective ADR and settlements are also laid down. The Recommendation favours follow-on collective actions. As to lawyers' fees, it states that MS should ensure that lawyers' remuneration and the method for its calculation do not create an incentive to litigation that is unnecessary from the point of view of the interest of any of the parties. The MS should not permit contingency fees that risk creating such an incentive whereas those MS that exceptionally allow contingency fees should provide for appropriate regulation in collective redress cases, taking into account in particular the right of the members of the claimant party to full compensation. Punitive damages should be prohibited. The 'loser pays' principle should apply. Third party funding is allowed but must be strictly regulated: the MS should ensure, that, in addition to the general principles of funding, for cases of private third party funding of compensatory collective redress, it is prohibited to base remuneration given to or interest charged by the fund provider on the amount of the settlement reached or the compensation awarded unless that funding arrangement is regulated by a public authority to ensure the interests of the parties. Despite the Preamble supplementing these recommendations, the reasons for the solutions set out in them are not satisfactorily presented. It is clear that on the one hand the Commission strove to build a system acceptable in the European legal environment free of any of the alleged pitfalls of US-style class actions that were constantly emphasised throughout the various drafting processes, but drafted the rules broadly enough so as to interfere as little as possible with the MS procedural framework. What is more, definitions of the basic notions are lacking or are not clear or apply vague terms that do not correspond well with the details of national civil procedure. Some of the rules are also ambiguous. This could be a hurdle for those MS wishing to implement the Recommendation and set up a coherent collective redress system that would fit the substance of claims.[82]

---

    victims must first file the actions themselves and the court then merely processes them more effectively than in the case of assessing each individual claim in separate proceedings).

82 For example, the Slovenian drafters of the new Collective Actions Act have faced this challenge and eventually copy-pasted some of the recommendation's provisions (*e.g.* on third party funding) without realising their potential negative effects. In the absence of the Recommendation, however, Slovenia would probably not (at least not that soon) have decided to regulate collective actions. It would also most probably not have based its

Although a soft-law act, the Recommendation stated that the MS should implement its principles by 26 July 2015. The Commission announced that it will assess the implementation of the Recommendation and decide if measures to consolidate and strengthen the horizontal approach reflected in it should be proposed. In January 2018, the Commission issued a Report on the implementation of the Recommendation,[83] and, already in April the same year, published a proposal for a new directive on consumer representative actions, signalling its discontent with MS reactions to the Recommendation.[84]

3.4 Fourth Stage: Directive on Consumer Representative Actions

After April 2017, when the European Parliament issued its Recommendation on *Dieselgate* calling on the Commission to propose legislation on a harmonised system of collective redress for EU consumers, based on best practices within and outside the EU,[85] and after May 2017, when the Study for the Fitness Check of EU consumer and marketing law[86] was published, Commission President Juncker in September 2017 announced a "New Deal for Consumers".[87] The Commission Work Programme for 2018[88] under the title "A New Deal for Consumers" announced a revision of EU consumer directives, including the Injunctions Directive. The initiative aimed to ensure that the planned revision of the directives laying down substantive rules for consumer protection is complemented by strengthened procedural rules for enforcing consumers'

---

regime on this soft-law instrument had it not offered so many options that could be adapted to the specifics of Slovenian civil procedure (*e.g.* allowing for contingency fees), and solutions fostering access to justice (*e.g.*, hybrid opt-in/opt-out, third party funding, broad rules on standing). See A. Galič, A. Vlahek, 'Challenges in Drafting and Application of the New Slovenian Collective Actions Act', in A. Uzelac, S. Voet (eds.), *Class Actions – The Holy Grail for (European) Civil Procedure?* (Springer, to be published in 2020).

83 See *supra* note 43. Data on MS regulation presented in the report is not entirely accurate (e.g., Slovenia had adopted its Collective Actions Act in September 2017 while the report merely mentions its drafting activities). The report also erroneously lists some MS among the MS having in place the rules on collective actions – the reason for this surely lies in the fact that the Commission has regarded instruments such as assignment of claims as instruments of collective redress. This again is proof that defining collective actions and collective redress is of utmost importance.

84 Explanatory Memorandum of the Proposal Directive (*see infra* note 89), p. 9.

85 European Parliament recommendation of 4 April 2017 to the Council and the Commission following the inquiry into emission measurements in the automotive sector (2016/2908(RSP)).

86 <https://publications.europa.eu/en/publication-detail/-/publication/f7b3958b-772b-11e7-b2f2-01aa75ed71a1/language-en>, visited on 30 June 2019.

87 State of the Union Address and Letter of Intent to the President of the Council and the EP, COM(2017)650 final of 24 October 2017, Annex II, point 8.

88 <https://ec.europa.eu/info/publications/2018-commission-work-programme-key-documents_en>, visited on 30 June 2019.

rights. As a result, in April 2018 the Commission adopted a Proposal for a Directive on representative actions for the protection of the collective interests of consumers, and repealing Directive 2009/22/EC[89] that was described by some as a light at the end of the tunnel.[90] Discussions during the first reading at the Council and its preparatory bodies started in April 2018,[91] while the European Parliament issued its position at the first reading in March 2019.[92] The two advisory bodies, namely the European Economic and Social Committee and the Committee of the Regions, gave their opinions in September and October 2018 respectively. Analysis of the latest documents issued within the Council, that is, the general approach as agreed at the Competitiveness Council on 28 November 2019,[93] shows that the initial text of the Proposal is being considerably reshaped. Both the Preamble to the Directive and its normative part have been almost entirely rewritten.

The Proposal of 2018 defines the subject matter of the directive as "setting out rules enabling qualified entities to seek representative actions aimed at the protection of the collective interests of consumers, while ensuring appropriate safeguards to avoid abusive litigation".[94] The Council's amendments added that these rules have as their objective the better functioning of the internal market taking as a base the achievement of a high level of consumer protection.

---

89   Proposal for a Directive of the European Parliament and of the Council on representative actions for the protection of the collective interests of consumers, and repealing Directive 2009/22/EC (Text with EEA relevance) {SWD(2018) 96 final} – {SWD(2018) 98 final}, COM(2018) 184 final 2018/0089 (COD), 11 April 2018. Once the directive is adopted, it is planned that MS are to transpose it in 18 months after its entry into force and it would then apply only after 6 months from its transposition. The latest Council's general approach amended these periods to 30 and 12 months respectively.

90   Conference on Consumer Protection and Fundamental Rights, Riga Graduate School of Law, 19 June 2018.

91   A series of documents within these discussions have been published in this period, including feedback from Czech, Swedish, Austrian and Portuguese Parliaments, a Joint declaration by Cyprus, Czechia, Latvia, Luxembourg and the Slovak Republic. *See:* <https://eur-lex.europa.eu/legal-content/EN/HIS/?uri=CELEX:52018PC0184>, visited on 24 January 2020.

92   <https://www.europarl.europa.eu/RegData/seance_pleniere/textes_adoptes/provisoire/2019/03-26/0222/P8_TA-PROV(2019)0222_EN.pdf>m, visited on 24 January 2020.

93   7877/18 + ADD 1 – 5, <https://eur-lex.europa.eu/legal-content/EN/TXT/PDF/?uri=CONSIL:ST_14600_2019_INIT&from=EN>, visited on 24 January 2020.

94   Art. 1/1 of the Proposal. It is interesting that safeguards against abusive litigation are mentioned in the definition of the scope of the directive having in mind that in comparison to the 2013 Recommendation these safeguards have to some extent been lowered as regards third party funding. For further details, *see* M. Djinović, A. Vlahek, 'Uncharted waters: analysis of TPLF funding in European collective redress' (U.S. Chamber, Institute for Legal Reform, 2019).

The Proposal does not explicitly set as its goal the guaranteeing of a fundamental right of effective judicial protection,[95] but the Preamble to and the substance of the Directive's provisions reveal that goal. Access to justice is explicitly mentioned in recital 4 of the Preamble with regard to the need to balance between access to justice and procedural safeguards against abusive litigation. Recital 0 explains that without effective means of obtaining redress, consumer confidence in the internal market is hindered, while recital 0a (like recital 0, inserted by the Council) mentions lack of effective means of enforcement of EU consumer law with regard to prevention of distortion of fair competition between infringing traders and compliant traders, and the smooth functioning of the internal market. Recital 2b (also inserted by the Council) asserts that effective and efficient representative actions available across the EU should boost consumer confidence, empower consumers to exercise their rights, contribute to fairer competition, and create a level playing field for traders operating in the internal market. Recital 3 lists examples of the obstacles that consumers face with individual actions: uncertainty about their rights and available procedural mechanisms, psychological reluctance to take action and a negative balance of the expected costs and benefits of an individual action.

According to the Proposal of 2018, the Directive would apply to domestic and cross-border infringements, including cases where those infringements have ceased before the start or conclusion of the representative action, but could apply only to infringements that started after the date of application of the directive (meaning, for example, that the Dieselgate infringements would not be covered[96]).[97] It must be stressed, however, that these rules on application of the new collective redress regime have been significantly amended by the Council.[98]

---

[95] The only part where a reference to Art. 47 has been made is rec. 7a (inserted by the Council) but it has not been referred to as the legal basis for introduction of the Directive's collective redress mechanism.

[96] It must also be stressed that any future Dieselgate would be covered only if the infringement fell under any of the acts listed in the annex to the Directive (or in national law).

[97] Art. 20 of the Proposal.

[98] Art. 20 now states that MS must apply the rules transposing the directive to actions brought on or after the date of application of the directive. This means that infringements that took place or started before that date would fall under the rules of the directive. The Council also added that MS must ensure that national rules on suspension or interruption of limitation periods transposing Art. 11 only apply to redress claims based on infringements occurring on or after the date of application of the directive. This will not preclude application of national provisions on suspension or interruption of limitation periods which were already applicable prior to the date of application of the directive to redress claims based on infringements occurring before that date. Cf. Art. 65 of the Slovenian

Fuelled by the European Parliament responding to the notorious Dieselgate by calling on the Commission to put forward a legislative proposal for the establishment of a collective redress system in order to create a harmonised system for EU consumers,[99] the Commission has shifted from its (and the Parliament's) previous position on the appropriateness of the horizontal approach, to regulating only consumer collective redress (above all only regarding infringements of EU law listed in the annex to the Directive).[100] That is, the directive would apply to representative actions brought against infringements by traders of EU law provisions listed in Annex I that harm or may harm the collective interests of consumers (namely, law covered by 59 directives and regulations from various sectors such as financial services, energy, telecommunications, sale of goods, health, environment, travel).[101] It seems that by doing so, the Commission has not realized the potential problems that MS might face when transposing the Directive, in particular those MS that have already adopted general legislation on compensatory collective actions, the principles of which do not correspond fully to those of the Directive (but correspond, for

Collective Actions Act that also applies (after much debate) to cases of mass harm taking place before the entry into force of the act as long as the relevant limitation period has not expired. *See* also the interpretation of CAT in *Gibson*, 1257/7/7/16. *See* Vlahek (2017), *supra* note 2; Galič, Vlahek (2018), *supra* note 3.

[99] Para. 59 of the Recommendation; Explanatory Memorandum, p. 9, states that "[w]hile the Recommendation has a horizontal dimension, given the different areas in which mass harm may occur, the absence of an EU-wide collective redress mechanism is of particular practical relevance to consumer protection, as shown by concrete cases, including the diesel emissions case".

[100] The Explanatory Memorandum of the Proposal states, *e.g.*, that evaluations of EU consumer law demonstrate that the risk of infringements of EU law affecting the collective interests of consumers is increasing due to economic globalisation and digitalisation. It also mentions increasing cross-border trade and EU-wide commercial strategies increasingly also affecting consumers. Otherwise, the Proposal does not offer any reasons for the limited scope of the Directive and even refers to acts favouring horizontal application. The Council's amendments to the text of the Proposal, as set out in the general approach of November 2019, prolonged the list of the annex by adding nine directives and regulations (some of these were adopted after the Proposal of 2018) and deleted five acts from the list.

[101] Art. 2/1 of the Proposal. What is interesting is that the Antitrust Damages Directive (Dir. 2014/104) that omitted regulating collective actions because they were said to be regulated horizontally, is not on this list although in many cases it is consumers who are the victims of antitrust infringements. One of the most attractive areas of law for implementing collective redress will thus not be covered by the directive because obviously only directives and regulations dealing exclusively with consumer protection are listed in the annex. The idea is, however, to supplement the list automatically with novel EU consumer protection legislation (the risk of leaving out general legislation also protecting consumers would remain). Explanatory Memorandum, p. 14.

example, to the 2013 Recommendation[102]). Although the Proposal claims that the Directive does not prevent MS from adopting or maintaining in force provisions designed to grant qualified entities or any other persons concerned other procedural means to bring actions aimed at protecting the collective interests of consumers,[103] it will be interesting to see how the MS will tackle transposition. The collective actions regulation in these MS might have to be drafted anew in order to align the general scheme to the Directive's provisions to avoid having different sets of rules for infringements from different areas of law; existing legislation might on the other hand be merely amended as regards consumer collective actions (which would probably apply not only to infringements of the 59 EU acts listed in the annex to the directive, but generally to all infringements of (EU or national) consumer law). The MS will, however, also have to take due regard to the existing ('first-stage') sectoral directives laying down the rules on collective injunctions as the Proposal does not repeal them.[104]

Another shift in this fourth stage is that from soft-law to hard-law regulation. This was anticipated already because of the Parliament's call in 2017 on the Commission to put forward a legislative proposal. The Proposal states that "[s]imilarly to the Injunctions Directive, the only suitable instrument for addressing procedural law with the above objectives is a Directive",[105] and refers to the findings of the 2018 Report on implementation of the Recommendation which showed that existing national collective compensatory actions regimes vary significantly in terms of their effectiveness and modalities, and that nine MS have still not introduced them.[106] When stressing the increased risk of

---

102 As is the case for Slovenia. *See* Galič, Vlahek (2018), *supra* note 3.
103 The amended Art. 1 of the Proposal now states that MS may adopt or maintain in force their own provisions aimed at protecting the collective interests of consumers at national level, but must ensure that at least one representative action mechanism complies with the directive. *See also* recs. 6a to 6e as drafted by the Council in 2019.
104 It repeals only the general Injunctions Directive: Art. 17 of the Proposal.
105 Explanatory Memorandum, p. 6 ff.
106 According to the 2018 Report (*see supra* note 83 on the accuracy of this data), compensatory collective redress is available in 19 MS (Austria, Belgium, Bulgaria, Germany, Denmark, Finland, France, Greece, Hungary, Italy, Latvia, Malta, the Netherlands, Poland, Portugal, Romania, Spain, Sweden, the UK). In more than half of the MS it is limited to specific sectors, mainly to consumer claims. In some of these MS the sectoral approach is very limited while in some it is broader. Only six MS have taken a horizontal approach (Bulgaria, Denmark, Lithuania, the Netherlands, Portugal, the UK). The Commission has reported that only seven MS have reacted to its Recommendation: Belgium and Lithuania introduced compensatory collective redress for the first time while Slovenia and the Netherlands were about to enact new laws and some further MS were undergoing reforms of their existent legislation (the UK, France and the Netherlands). The majority of these

mass harm situations requiring adoption of the Directive, the Commission does not, however, offer any explanation as to the number and outcome of collective compensatory actions already filed, and the challenges the parties and the courts have faced in the MS that have already introduced such redress mechanisms and which could be taken into account in the process of drafting the Directive's provisions. The European Parliament called on the Commission to assess, when drafting the legislative proposal, existing systems within and outside the EU with a view to identifying best practices in this field and to include them in its legislative proposal.[107] It seems, reading the Proposal and detecting a series of pitfalls and unclarities of the proposed measures, that the Commission has failed to do so. Intense assessment of existing collective actions legislation and practice of the MS and other jurisdictions is a *conditio sine qua non* for regulation of collective redress on the EU level. The Proposal merely mentions the 2013 Recommendation as being taken into account by the Directive, but at the same time stresses that due to the focused application of the Directive and the limited rules it supposedly contains and are to be supplemented by national law, not all the Recommendation's principles could be reproduced.[108] It also mentions a plethora of various studies, reports and other acts which unfortunately mostly stay on the level of general discussion on the need for collective redress but lack detailed assessment of the functioning of the collective actions regime in practice.[109]

Differently from other analysed EU acts on collective redress, the Proposal defines the collective interests of consumers as the "interests of a number of consumers" (or, as amended by the Council, "the general interest of consumers and, in particular for the purpose of redress measures, the interests of a group

---

initiatives have a broad scope (only Belgium has restricted its collective redress to consumer matters only) and several MS enable the opt-out system (*e.g.* Slovenia). In some of the rest of MS, active discussion on future regulation of collective actions is taking place. The Commission also reports that practice shows that, where available, collective redress is mainly used in the area of consumer protection and related areas such as passenger rights or financial services as well as in competition follow-on actions. The relative absence of recourse to collective redress in other fields is in the Commission's view not only a result of the fact that in many MS compensatory or indeed injunctive relief is available only for consumers or in competition law, but it also appears to be linked to other factors such as the complexity and length of the proceedings or restrictive rules on admissibility, often related to legal standing.

107 Para. 59 of the 2013 Recommendation.
108 Explanatory Memorandum, p. 4.
109 Although an EU instrument may not lay down all the details of the procedure as this might be left to the MS, it is nevertheless very important to take into account how EU-level rules would react with national rules and the impact they would have on the general national legal framework.

of consumers"), while a representative action is defined as "an action for the protection of the collective interests of consumers to which the consumers concerned are not parties".[110] It seems that this is the first time the Commission has stressed one of the most important features of collective actions, namely that the victims are not parties to the proceedings and do not enjoy the procedural status of claimant which is – under the directive – reserved for the qualified entity. The Council has, however, deleted this part of the definition so that a representative action is currently defined as "an action for the protection of the collective interests of consumers brought by a qualified entity aiming at an injunction measure or a redress measure, or both". It is, however, clear from other provisions that the EU-model of collective redress offers only representative collective actions, but not US-style class actions.[111] The Council has categorized representative actions into "domestic representative actions" (namely, those brought by a qualified entity in the MS in which they are designated) and "cross-border representative actions" (namely, those brought by a qualified entity in a MS other than that in which it is designated).[112] Consequently, the amended Proposal also differentiates between qualified entities for the purpose of domestic representative actions, and qualified entities for the purpose of cross-border representative actions.

Building on the Injunctions Directive regime, the Proposal of 2018 introduces the term 'qualified entity' as an entity having standing in collective representative actions. It defines qualified entities as entities designated, at their request, by the MS in advance for this purpose and placed in a publicly available list.[113] An entity may be designated as qualified entity if it complies with the following criteria: (a) it is properly constituted according to the law of a MS; (b) it has a legitimate interest in ensuring that the provisions of EU law covered

---

110   Arts. 3/1 (3) and (4) of the Proposal.
111   *See, e.g.*, rec. 13a and Art. 5/4a of the amended Proposal.
112   Arts. 3/1 (4a) and (4b) of the amended Proposal.
113   Art. 4/1 of the Proposal. According to Art. 16 of the Proposal, any qualified entity designated in advance in one MS should be able to apply to the courts or administrative authorities of another MS upon presentation of a publicly available list from its own MS. MS should ensure that where the infringement affects or is likely to affect consumers from different MS an action may be brought to the competent authority of a MS by several qualified entities from different MS acting jointly or represented by a single qualified entity, for the protection of the collective interest of consumers from different MS. The Commission should be informed of the MS lists. Compliance with the Directive's criteria on qualified entities will be monitored and the designation of an entity as qualified revoked where appropriate. Problems arising in the absence of such rules are presented in Tzakas, *supra* note 50, pp. 235 ff, 241.

by the Directive are complied with; (c) it has a non-profit making character.[114] The MS must assess on a regular basis whether a qualified entity continues to comply with these criteria. If it does not, it loses its status.[115] A MS may also designate a qualified entity on an *ad hoc* basis for a particular representative action, at its request, if it complies with the above criteria[116] (this may, however, not be the case with cross-border actions).[117] The Proposal adds that MS must ensure that in particular consumer organisations and independent public bodies[118] are eligible for qualified status and that they may designate as qualified entities consumer organisations that represent members from more than one MS.[119] MS may set out rules specifying which qualified entities may seek all or some of the measures available under the directive.[120] It must be stressed that compliance by a qualified entity with these criteria does not prevent the court or administrative authority from examining whether the purpose of the entity justifies its taking action in a specific case, that is, provided a direct relationship exists between the main objectives of the entity and the rights granted under EU law that are claimed to have been violated in respect of which the action is brought (standing v. representativeness).[121] The presented regime on standing has, however, been modified by Council amendments of November 2019. It retains the categorization of qualified entities as either entities designated in advance or *ad hoc*-designated entities, as well as the categorization of entities being either private organizations or public bodies. It also requires that in cross-border actions, only advance-designated entities have standing. The difference is that the amended Proposal implements different sets of rules on the eligibility criteria depending on whether a representative

---

114 Art. 4/1 of the Proposal.
115 *Ibid.*
116 Art. 4/2 of the Proposal.
117 Art. 16 of the Proposal.
118 The 2013 Recommendation, too, gave explicit standing to public authorities, while public bodies also have standing under the Injunctions Directive regime. Rec. 9b of the Preamble of the amended Proposal reveals that according to national legal traditions, public bodies could also play an active role in ensuring compliance with relevant provisions of EU law by bringing representative actions. Slovenia, which implemented the 2013 Recommendation in 2017, has, *e.g.*, decided to grant this role to higher state attorneys (not, however, in actions against the state). The drafters opined that a public authority is also an appropriate person to initiate collective proceedings, as these are carried out also in the public interest. *See* Galič, Vlahek (2020), *supra* note 82. *Cf.* rec. 39 of the Preamble to the Proposal Directive.
119 Art. 4/3 of the Proposal.
120 Art. 4/4 of the Proposal.
121 Arts. 4/5 and 5/1 of the Proposal.

action to be filed is domestic or cross-border.[122] In the case of domestic actions, the amended proposal states merely that MS are to ensure in particular that consumer organizations, including those representing consumers from more than one MS, are eligible to apply for the status of a qualified entity under national law (whereas it does not – in contrast to the original text of the Proposal of 2018 – set the criteria for their eligibility). Public bodies may also be designated as qualified entities. Information on qualified entities designated in advance must be made available to the public. Entities may also be designated on an *ad hoc* basis. The latter may, however, not be the case in cross-border representative actions as only advance-designated public or private entities may file such actions.[123] Further, the amended Proposal sets out seven specific criteria for the designation of private law organizations as qualified entities in cross-border representative actions (criteria that do not apply – unless national law itself requires them – to domestic representative actions).[124] Detailed rules on drafting, amending and publishing the relevant lists are also laid down.[125] It is not entirely clear why the Commission and additionally the Council have

---

122 Arts. 4, 4a and 4b of the amended Proposal.
123 Art. 4a read together with rec. 11a of the amended Proposal.
124 The criteria set out in Art. 4a/3 are: (a) it is a legal person properly constituted according to the law of the MS of designation 18 months prior to the designation request and can demonstrate 12 months of actual public activity in the protection of consumers' interests; (b) in accordance with its statutory purpose, it has a legitimate interest in protecting consumer interests as provided by EU law covered by the directive; (c) it has a non-profit making character; (ca) it possesses knowledge and skills in the field of its activity necessary for bringing cross-border representative actions in that field; (caa) it is in a sound and stable financial situation; (cb) it is not influenced by persons, other than consumers, who have an economic interest in bringing any representative action, in particular by traders, including in the case of funding by third parties, and it has procedures to prevent such an influence; (cc) it discloses publicly by any appropriate means, in particular on its website, information on the above-listed criteria and information about the source of funding of its activity in general. Art. 4a/3a adds that the MS may set out rules to limit the right of a qualified entity to bring an action in the area of activity of that entity (it may be presumed that in practice, this will anyway be the case). MS may take measures to ensure that the courts or administrative authorities have the competence to examine compliance with the criteria set out in Art. 4a/3 if justified concerns are raised in that regard. The amended Proposal retains the provision empowering the authorities with which representative actions are filed to examine in each specific case whether the statutory purpose of the qualified entity justifies the action. The MS could additionally empower their courts or other authorities to examine whether a qualified entity bringing a cross-border representative action for redress is funded by a third party having an economic interest in the outcome of the action and, if so, reject the legal capacity of the qualified entity for the purpose of that specific action. The amended Proposal then generally adds that the admissibility of specific cross-border actions will be assessed under national law.
125 Art. 4a/3b-6 of the amended Proposal.

decided on these differentiations taking into account that, in practice, collective actions will probably be filed mostly by domestic entities. The reason could lie in the fact that the Injunctions Directive's rules on eligibility of entities already applied only to 'intra-Community infringements' and that the legal basis for adoption of the directives prevents any further harmonization. It will be interesting to see how this dual set of rules on eligibility is implemented in the MS, although it is safe to predict that the MS will for reasons of clarity mostly decide to apply the rules on cross-border actions to domestic representative collective actions as well (meaning that the rules on standing would be more stringent and collective redress as such less available).

According to the Proposal of 2018, qualified entities could seek the following injunctive measures:[126] (a) an injunction order as an interim measure for stopping a practice or, if the practice is imminent, prohibiting the practice (protective or provisional order);[127] (b) an injunction order establishing that the practice constitutes an infringement of law (declaratory redress or, more specifically, an interlocutory declaratory claim),[128] and if necessary, stopping the practice or, if the practice is imminent, prohibiting the practice ((prohibitory) injunction).[129] The Proposal states that in order to seek injunction orders, qualified entities would not have to obtain the mandate of the individual consumers concerned or provide proof of actual loss or damage on the part of the consumers concerned or of intention or negligence on the part of the trader,[130] whereby the substance and purpose of such 'mandate' is unfortunately not explained (but signals that a mandate is required in other cases). The amended Proposal adds that MS may require that injunctive measures be sought only after the qualified entity has attempted to achieve cessation of the infringement in consultation with the trader.[131] Qualified entities would – according to the Proposal of 2018 – also be entitled to seek "measures eliminating the continuing effects of the infringement".[132] The Proposal allows for both

---

126 Art. 5/2 of the Proposal (the amended version now states that *at least* these measures are to be ensured by MS).

127 *See, e.g.*, A. Galič, 'Civil Procedure Slovenia', in Blanpain, Colluci, Taelman, *International Encyclopaedia of Laws – Civil Procedure* (Wolters Kluwer, 2014) para. 415.

128 *Ibid*, paras. 195–196. The amended Proposal uses the term 'definitive measure' – see Art. 5a.

129 *Ibid*, para. 450.

130 Art. 5/2 of the Proposal.

131 If a trader, after receiving a request for consultation, does not cease the infringement within two weeks, the qualified entity may bring a representative action without further delay. *See* Art. 5a/3 of the amended Proposal.

132 Art. 5/3 of the Proposal. The Proposal does not define 'measures eliminating the continuing effects of the infringement'. This notion has been applied in the first sectoral

follow-on and stand-alone representative actions.[133] The Proposal requires MS to ensure that qualified entities are entitled to bring representative actions seeking a redress order, which obligates the trader to provide, *inter alia*, compensation, repair, replacement, price reduction, contract termination or reimbursement of the price paid, as appropriate.[134] Collective compensatory redress is thus also available under the directive and will for the first time be regulated in binding EU law.[135] The Proposal of 2018 adds somewhat ambiguously that a MS may require the mandate of the individual consumers concerned before a declaratory liability decision is made or a redress order is issued.[136] It is not clear what is meant by this but it ensues from Article 6/3 that the MS may require the entities to gather a certain number of mandates (consumers) before filing any representative action.[137] Further, the Proposal

---

injunctions directives, starting with the directive on misleading advertising explaining that a breach which the authorities had instructed the violator to stop could still have negative effects which the authorities must prevent (by, *e.g.*, publishing a cessation order so as to inform consumers of withdrawn advertisements and try to prevent them taking decisions on the basis of these). It is not clear from the normative part of the Directive whether it refers to 'cease and desist' measures or to 'redress orders', or both. The Directive states that qualified entities are able to seek measures eliminating the continuing effects of an infringement together with injunctive measures within a single representative action so they obviously do not cover injunctions. The same conclusion can also be drawn from rec. 16 of the Proposal, the "Detailed explanation of the specific provisions of the proposal" and the Explanatory Memorandum according to which declaratory and redress orders fall under this term. The amended Proposal now omits this ambiguous term.

133   Art. 5/3,4 of the Proposal. According to Art. 10 of the Proposal (now significantly amended by the Council), final decisions taken by a court or an administrative authority within public enforcement procedures, including final injunction decisions issued on the basis of Art. 5/2 of the directive, will have a probative effect in subsequent actions for redress. If a decision establishing an infringement has become final, it should be irrefutable evidence in any subsequent redress action in the same MS. In cross-border cases, such final decisions will, however, provide only for a rebuttable presumption that an infringement of EU law has occurred. In the case of declaratory decisions on a trader's liability towards consumers affected by an infringement (Art. 6/2 of the directive), probative effects are envisaged only within national territory since national rules regarding liability may significantly vary across the EU. Art. 10 now states that the final decision of a court or an administrative authority of any MS establishing an infringement can be used as evidence of the existence of that infringement for the purposes of other actions seeking redress against the same trader for the same infringement, in accordance with national law on evaluation of evidence.

134   Art. 6/1 of the Proposal.

135   It is, however, without prejudice to any additional rights to redress that the consumers concerned may have under EU or national law (Art. 6/4 of the Proposal).

136   Art. 6/1 of the Proposal.

137   Similar grouping is typical of US-style class actions implemented in some of the EU MS where some legislators set a minimal number of victims as class members having

requires the entity to provide the authorities with sufficient information as required under national law to support the action, including a description of the consumers concerned and the questions of fact and law to be resolved.[138] Further, MS could – according to the Proposal of 2018 – empower a court or administrative authority to issue a declaratory decision on the liability of the trader, instead of a redress order.[139] This could be done in duly justified cases where, due to the characteristics of individual harm to the consumers concerned, quantifying individual redress is complex[140] (this would be where the circumstances of each individual case are different and do not enable a common determination of compensation). This rule could not, however, apply (meaning that only a redress order may be sought) if: (a) consumers are individually identifiable and suffered comparable harm caused by the same practice in relation to a period of time or a purchase;[141] in these cases, the 'mandate' is not required;[142] (b) consumers have suffered a small amount of loss and it would be disproportionate[143] to distribute redress to them ('low-value cases'[144]); in such cases, too, the mandate of the individual consumers concerned would not be required, while redress would be directed to a public purpose serving the collective interests of consumers (instead of to the victims

---

    standing (*e.g.*, in existing Polish and Swedish legislation; *see* A. Piszcz, 'Compensatory Collective Redress: Will It Be Part of Private Enforcement of Competition Law in CEE Countries?', 10(15) *Yearbook of Antitrust and Regulatory Studies*, 2017, pp. 226, 234 ff; Komninos, *supra* note 50, p. 234. In representative collective actions, on the other hand, in particular if they are reserved for qualified entities, such prerequisites are not common. As under the Proposal, *ad hoc* entities might also sue, gathering mandates might guarantee the representativeness of the claimant party and aim to prevent abuses of the action. The amended Proposal states in rec. 4b of the Preamble that it should be for the MS to decide on the required degree of similarity of individual claims or the minimum number of consumers affected by an action for redress for the purpose of a case being admitted to be heard as a representative action (i.e. within the certification stage), under the proviso that such national rules do not hamper the effective functioning of representative actions as set out by the Directive.

138   Art. 6/1 of the Proposal.
139   Art. 6/2 of the Proposal.
140   *See also* Explanatory Memorandum of the Proposal, p. 3.
141   The "Detailed explanation of the specific provisions of the proposal" mentions long-term consumer contracts.
142   The reason for such provision (under a) and b)) is not provided (under b), the reason perhaps being that the entity would not be able to find consumers willing to give their mandates if they cannot be compensated).
143   Explanatory Memorandum, p. 3, says 'disproportionate or impracticable'.
144   Explanatory Memorandum, p. 3.

themselves) meaning that a form of *cy-près* would be introduced.[145] The Council has deleted from the Proposal these ambiguous provisions on a declaratory decision on the liability of the trader. Further, in contrast to the Proposal of 2018 – which was entirely silent on the question of opting-in and opting-out and was unclear as to the role of consumers in collective proceedings – the amended Proposal now establishes clear rules as to who is a party to the proceedings and how consumers decide that the effects of representative collective action apply to them or not.[146] The amended Proposal in principle enables both opt-in and opt-out systems, in that it allows individual consumers concerned by the action to explicitly or tacitly express their wish to be or not to be "represented" by a qualified entity within a representative action for redress measures and to be bound by the outcome of the action.[147] In contrast to the original text of the Proposal of 2018 – which did not lay down any rules on how the redress awarded is to be distributed among consumers – the amended version now mentions the different types of redress measures in terms of whether or not the consumers are specified in the award, and requires MS to ensure that the redress measure entitles consumers to seek recovery of damages without the need to bring a separate action, and to lay down or maintain rules on time limits for individual consumers to benefit from the redress measures. The MS may also lay down rules on the destination of any outstanding redress funds that were not recovered within the established time limits.[148] The Proposal also provides for suspension or even interruption of limitation periods applicable to any redress actions.[149]

---

145   Art. 6/3 of the Proposal. The "Detailed explanation of the specific provisions of the proposal" mentions awareness campaigns. It is interesting, on the other hand, that the JURI rapporteur emphasised on 25 March 2019 in its closing remarks in the European Parliament that the objective of the Directive is not to punish anyone, but only to compensate the victims and to have their damage repaired, <http://www.europarl.europa.eu/sides/getDoc.do?pubRef=-//EP//TEXT+CRE+20190325+ITEM-017+DOC+XML+V0//EN&language=EN>, visited on 30 June 2019.
146   *See* Art. 5b of the amended Proposal.
147   Rec.15b of the Preamble to the amended Proposal states that the decision on the opt-in and/or opt-out system is left to the MS to best respond to their legal traditions. Consumers who are not habitually resident in the MS in which the collective action has been brought may only take part on the basis of opt-in. The same solution is provided for in collective proceedings in Slovenia and before CAT. For further details, *see* Vlahek (2017), *supra* note 2. The amended Proposal also states that consumers who have explicitly or tacitly expressed their wish to be represented in a representative action cannot be represented in other representative actions, nor can they bring an individual action with the same cause of action and against the same trader.
148   *See* Art. 5b of the amended Proposal.
149   Art. 11 of the Proposal.

MS would have to ensure that – at the request of a qualified entity that has presented reasonably available facts and evidence sufficient to support the action, and has indicated further evidence which lies in the control of the defendant (or, as per the amended Proposal, a third party) – the court or administrative authority may order, in accordance with national procedural rules, that such evidence be presented by the defendant (or the third party), subject to the applicable EU and national rules on confidentiality (and, as per the amended Proposal, on proportionality).[150] The Proposal requires that the MS ensure procedural expediency.[151] The MS are also required to lay down rules on effective, proportionate and dissuasive penalties for non-compliance with the specific obligations set out in the Directive.[152] They would also be required to ensure that the infringing trader may be obliged, at its own expense, to inform consumers affected about the final decisions and settlements.[153]

While the Proposal of 2018 expressly allows and regulates third party funding (whereby the provisions differ from those of the Recommendation which could have an important impact on funding of collective actions in practice),[154] the amended version of the Proposal has deleted Article 7 on third party funding and has relocated (and partially amended) the provisions on third party funding to the Preamble and to Article 4b regulating the bringing of cross-border representative actions[155] No reasons are given for the shift from the

---

150 Art. 13 of the Proposal. The amended Proposal sets out the same rules for such requests by the defendant.
151 *See* Art. 12 of the Proposal that now, after amendment by the Council, requires an expediency/summary procedure only for injunctive measures.
152 Art. 14 of the Proposal, which was considerably amended by the Council. Different situations in which penalties may be imposed are now listed. The original rule – that when deciding on the allocation of revenues from penalties in the form of fines, MS would have to take into account the collective interests of consumers – is no longer included.
153 Art. 9 of the Proposal. This would have to be performed by means appropriate to the circumstance of the case and within specified time limits, including, where appropriate, through notifying all consumers concerned individually. Such information includes in intelligible language an explanation of the subject-matter of the action, its legal consequences and, if relevant, the subsequent steps to be taken by the consumers concerned.
154 For further details, *see* Djinović, Vlahek (2019), *supra* note 93.
155 Rec. 10 explains that qualified entities should not be influenced by any third party, other than their legal counsel and the consumers concerned, in taking their procedural decisions in the context of the representative action, including on settlements, and that such third parties should not provide financing for a representative action for redress against a defendant who is a competitor of the fund provider, or against a defendant on whom the fund provider is dependent, whereas this should be without prejudice to any public funding. Rec. 11ea and Art. 4b/3/2 state that in order to prevent conflicts of interest, the MS should be able to set out rules enabling their courts or administrative authorities to examine whether a qualified entity bringing a cross-border representative action for redress is

original Proposal (and the Recommendation). The Directive does not affect national rules on recovery of procedural costs or on the 'loser pays' principle.[156] In contrast to the Recommendation, contingency fees are not addressed in the Proposal, although the amended Proposal does state that individual consumers concerned by an action should not bear the costs of the proceedings, neither those of the qualified entity nor the trader, and that the costs of the proceedings should include, for example, any costs resulting from the fact that either party was represented by a lawyer or another legal professional, or any costs arising from service or translation of documents.[157] The amended Proposal of 2019 adds that the consumers concerned by the action may bear the costs of the proceedings only in exceptional circumstances in accordance with national law,[158] and that the MS may set out rules allowing for modest entry fees or similar participation charges.[159] The Proposal also states that procedural costs related to representative actions must not constitute financial obstacles (insurmountable obstacles as per the amended Proposal) for qualified entities preventing them from effectively exercising their right to seek measures under the Directive. It explains that, having regard to the fact that representative actions pursue the public interest by protecting the collective interests of consumers, MS should ensure (as per the amendment, only "maintain or aim to find means for the purpose of ensuring") that qualified entities are not prevented from bringing representative actions due to the costs arising from the procedures. These means could include limiting applicable court or administrative fees, granting qualified entities access to legal aid where necessary or providing them with public funding for bringing representative actions as well as other means of support; at the same time, however, the Council has stressed that the MS should nevertheless not be required to finance representative actions.[160] MS would have to take the necessary measures to ensure that in cases where entities are required to inform consumers about the ongoing representative action (or, as per the amended Proposal, about the final decision) the related cost may be recovered from the trader if the action is

---

   funded by a third party having an economic interest in the outcome of a specific cross-border representative action and, if this is the case, reject the legal capacity of the qualified entity for the purpose of that action.

156 Rec. 13c of the Proposal.
157 *Ibid.*
158 Such as when a consumer deliberately or negligently causes unnecessary legal costs by, *e.g.*, prolonging the proceedings by unlawful conduct, or when it is otherwise exceptionally justified. Rec. 13c of the Preamble.
159 Art. 5/4a and rec. 13c of the amended Proposal.
160 Rec. 39 of the Preamble.

successful. The MS and the Commission should support and facilitate cooperation from qualified entities and exchange of information about best practices and experience as regards resolution of infringements.

Apart from laying down the rules on representative actions, the Proposal also regulates collective redress settlements reached by the qualified entity and the trader during the proceedings by representative action. Such settlements are approved by the court or administrative authority[161] and the consumers concerned may accept or refuse to be bound by them.[162]

4   Conclusion

The analysed acts and EU institutional activities show that, for the last decade, the EU has been struggling rather unsuccessfully to regulate collective redress, in particular compensatory collective redress. In search of its own, non US-style collective redress,[163] the EU has been shifting from (draft) directives regulating collective actions in specific areas of law to a soft law Recommendation having horizontal application, and eventually turned back to drafting a directive in the area of consumer protection. A disorderly amount of different acts drafted by different bodies in different fields of law having different legal effects, and introducing different and at times ambiguous definitions and concepts without enough valuable interpretation and insight into the reasons for choosing them, signals lack of a clear vision of why and how to best regulate collective redress on the EU level.[164] It is thus somewhat difficult to understand

---

161   Art. 8 of the Proposal. It is interesting that collective settlements under the Directive may be reached only after a representative action has been filed.

162   Art. 8/6 of the Proposal. The Directive does not explain what exactly is meant by this and how this would operate in practice, especially having regard to the legal certainty of defendants entering into such settlements. It is not clear whether the Directive gives the MS or the parties freedom to set out an opt-in or opt-out system or whether it is always consumers who eventually decide to be bound by already agreed and confirmed settlements without the option for the parties to decide on an opt-in or opt-out system in the first place.

163   *See, e.g.*, the latest address by Commissioner Jourová and the JURI rapporteur to MEPs on 25 March 2019, <http://www.europarl.europa.eu/sides/getDoc.do?pubRef=-//EP//TEXT+CRE+20190325+ITEM-017+DOC+XML+V0//EN&language=EN>, visited on 30 June 2019.

164   Analysis of (altogether 7 out of 751) MEPs' positions expressed on 25 March 2019 during the debate on the Proposal on the first reading shows that they mostly referred to Dieselgate (which was a special topic on the agenda in the Parliament that day) and pointed to the pitfalls of the US system without going into the details of the Proposal's provisions, <http://www.europarl.europa.eu/sides/getDoc.do?pubRef=-//EP//TEXT+CRE+20190325+ITEM-017+DOC+XML+V0//EN&language=EN>, visited on 30 June 2019.

the haste with which the Commission has drafted the latest directive on collective consumer representative actions.¹⁶⁵ The MS have only started to react to the 2013 Recommendation, and now they are suddenly faced with a novel set of rules. In MS where collective compensatory redress has already been introduced on the basis of the Recommendation or best practices from abroad, transposition of the new directive will represent a challenge and might make national rules on collective redress chaotic and user-unfriendly. It might be wiser if the Commission waited some time for actual compensatory collective redress case-law to evolve throughout the EU, perform an in-depth analysis of the national provisions and their application in practice, detect the focal elements for efficient collective redress, and only then decide to draft uniform rules as appropriate. Pushing forward with poorly thought-through solutions may turn the light twinkling for decades at the end of the tunnel (which is, above all, now planned to be generally reserved only to one group of victims) into a black hole of vague and inefficient rules that cannot guarantee access to justice to the highest possible extent. Having analysed the latest Council amendments addressing many of the pitfalls and unclarities of the Commission Proposal of 2018, it seems that the EU is nevertheless finally moving towards adopting an acceptable piece of legislation on collective redress.

---

165   It is clear from reading the JURI document of November 2018 presenting the amendments proposed by the MEPs that positions on the specific provisions of the Proposal are still very different, <http://www.europarl.europa.eu/sides/getDoc.do?pubRef=-//EP//NONSGML+COMPARL+PE-630.456+01+DOC+PDF+V0//EN&language=EN>, visited on 30 June 2019. The same goes for the positions of the Parliament committees (JURI, TRAN, IMCO) issued in November and December 2018 (AD/2018/627034, AD/2018/627831, A/2018/0447) and the opinion of the European Economic and Social Committee (<https://eur-lex.europa.eu/legal-content/EN/TXT/?uri=celex:52018AE2126>, visited on 30 June 2019).

Consumer Protection in the EU Conflict-of-Laws Framework

*Carlos Llorente**

Abstract

Consumer law nowadays pervades all areas of activity where consumers are present. The EU, along with its Member States, is probably one of the leading actors in promoting consumer protection. Also, in a globalized world, where the fact of being a consumer is a valuable asset (given their purchasing power), the cross-border implications of consumer contracts need to be effectively tackled by legislators. The EU has tried to address global legal concerns concerning consumer contracts by producing conflict-of-law rules such as article 6 of the Rome I Regulation and others contained in specifically-focused directives. This article reviews the scope and application of those rules and offers some insight into the not-so-well construed interaction between them all, keeping in mind that article 6 of the Rome I Regulation should be the centre of rotation of all EU PIL law in this field.

Keywords

contracts – consumers – applicable law – conflict of laws – protection – Rome I – consumer directives

1 Introduction

Nowadays it is a commonplace, both in primary and secondary sources (although not unanimously shared),[1] to affirm without hesitation that consumers merit protection in so-called (virtual and non-virtual) B2C transactions on account of consumers' lack of bargaining power and, more importantly, their lack of the information needed to agree on equal terms with their

---

* PhD (Hons) Universidad de Navarra, LL.M (Harlan Fiske Stone Scholar) Columbia University, Attorney-At-Law (Spain Bar), Co-Chairman (EALG), Visiting Professor (Riga Graduate School of Law).
1 See E. Valpuesta Gastamiza, 'Sujetos que actuan en el Mercado (I). El consumidor', in J.Mª. de la Cuesta Rute (Dir.), *Derecho mercantil I*, 3rd ed. (Huygens, Barcelona 2015) pp. 68–70.

counterparties.[2] And, in truth, much has been done, mostly in developed economies, in order to fulfil this goal since 'Consumer Law' became a feature of the legal landscape during the last third of the 20th century.

At national constitutional level some countries have enshrined consumer protection as a fundamental right of sorts (in my own country, for example, article 51 of the 1978 Spanish Constitution).[3] And the EU boasts a specific consumer protection policy currently grounded on article 169 of the Treaty on the Functioning of the EU (TFEU) (Consolidated version).[4] The EU has, in fact, been extremely (pro-) active in this field during recent decades, along with Member States, as consumer protection is considered a shared competence under article 4.2, (f) TFEU. Whether to consider consumer protection a fundamental right constitutionally enshrined, as in the case of Spain,[5] or something of a different nature, as in the TFEU, might be seen today as a theoretical issue since protection of consumers is one fundamental policy of the EU and its

---

2   *See* in EU case law, C-89/91, *Shearson*, para. 18 ("the concern to protect the consumer as the party deemed to be economically weaker and less experienced in legal matters than the other party to the contract"). *See also* Michael Bogdan, *Concise Introduction to Private International Law*, 2nd ed. (Europa Law Publishing 2012) p. 130.

3   "Article 51. 1. The public authorities shall guarantee the protection of consumers and users and shall, by means of effective measures, safeguard their safety, health and legitimate financial interests. 2. The public authorities shall make means available to inform and educate consumers and users, shall foster their organisations, and shall provide hearings for such organisations on all matters affecting their members, under the terms to be established by law. 3. Within the framework of the provisions of the foregoing clauses, the law shall regulate domestic trade and the system of licensing commercial products".

4   TITLE XV. – CONSUMER PROTECTION. Article 169 (ex Article 153 TEC) "1. In order to promote the interests of consumers and to ensure a high level of consumer protection, the Union shall contribute to protecting the health, safety and economic interests of consumers, as well as to promoting their right to information, education and to organise themselves in order to safeguard their interests. 2. The Union shall contribute to the attainment of the objectives referred to in paragraph 1 through: (a) measures adopted pursuant to Article 114 in the context of the completion of the internal market; (b) measures which support, supplement and monitor the policy pursued by the Member States. 3. The European Parliament and the Council, acting in accordance with the ordinary legislative procedure and after consulting the Economic and Social Committee, shall adopt the measures referred to in paragraph 2(b). 4. Measures adopted pursuant to paragraph 3 shall not prevent any Member State from maintaining or introducing more stringent protective measures. Such measures must be compatible with the Treaties. The Commission shall be notified of them".

5   Under the Spanish Constitution, though, not all fundamental rights (Title I) have an identical hierarchy. Those on top are rights covered in Chapter 2 of Title I (Freedoms and liberties) (articles 14–38). Consumer protection rights (article 51) belong to Chapter 3 (articles 39–52), regulated under the heading of "guiding principles of the social and economic policy". In other words, they are to be considered fundamental rights of a social and economic nature which deserve constitutional protection.

Member States, incorporated into the highest levels of statutory hierarchy both in the EU (TFEU) and in Member States themselves.

Specifically, the EU has adopted two levels of unification/harmonization in this area: one focused on material (substantive) rules and another affecting conflict-of-laws (or, in general, applicable law) rules within the area of Private International Law (PIL).[6]

On the one hand, material harmonization has been basically achieved through directives (with a tendency and evolution from 'minimum' to 'full' harmonization). And, on the other hand, conflict-of-laws (or applicable law) harmonization (or unification) has been developed, primarily in the field of (consumer) contracts, by means of Regulations, and specifically the Rome I Regulation (RR-I) through its article 6 (general rule), but also by means of domestic (national) PIL rules adopted by each Member State in transposition of certain PIL-oriented articles contained in the above-mentioned directives (special rules).

This paper will analyze article 6 RR-I (Section 2 below) in connection with those specific directive-based PIL rules (Section 3 below) in order to determine if consumer protection in the EU is well served by a multiple set of applicable law rules or if a unified and simplified normative approach to this problem is a preferred solution (Section 4 below).

---

6 Within the realm of PIL, consumer protection has also been part of EU legislative efforts in the field of international jurisdiction, as is presently demonstrated by articles 17–19 of Regulation (EU) No 1251/2012 of the European Parliament and of the Council of 12 December 2012, on jurisdiction and the recognition and enforcement of judgments in civil and commercial matters (recast), OJEU No L 351/1, 20 December 2012 (hereinafter RBIBis). RBIBis is the present understanding of EU consumer protection in jurisdictional matters, but this policy dates back to the Brussels Convention of 1968 (articles 13–15) (OJ C 27/1, 26 January 1998) (see A.-L. Calvo Caravaca (ed.), *Comentario al Convenio de Bruselas relativo a la competencia judicial internacional y a la ejecución de resoluciones judiciales en materia civil y mercantil*, Madrid 1994) and to Council Regulation (EC) No 44/2001 (RBI) (articles 15–17) (OJ L 12/1, 16 January 2001). For a brief account of the RBI rules on jurisdiction in consumer contracts, *see* D. Alexandre and A. Huet, *Règlement Bruxelles I (Matières civile et commerciale)*, Rep. internat. Dalloz, juin 2010, pp. 26–29). We will not address consumer international jurisdiction issues in this paper but we will mention decisions issued by the CJEU on the interpretation of those rules, which are also to be taken into account in the field of applicable law. In this respect, *see* Recital (24) of Regulation Rome I on the law applicable to contractual obligations (below), which, in the field of consumer contracts, requires 'consistency' with similar rules on protection of consumers to be found in EU Regulations dealing with jurisdiction. *See also*, about this, although in more general terms, Recital (7) of Regulation Rome I, with support on EU case law: C-585/08 and C-144/09, *Pammer* (exception in C-125/92, *Mulox*).

2 Article 6 of the Rome I Regulation

2.1 Rome I and the Hierarchy of PIL Sources Applicable to Consumer Contracts

Within the scope of application of Rome Regulation I,[7] article 6 RR-I governs consumer contracts.[8] This is the natural (though significantly amended) successor to article 5 of the Rome Convention (RC),[9] which was the first rule to establish uniform conflict-of-law rules applicable to (certain) consumer contracts in the European Economic Community.[10]

---

[7] Regulation (EC) No 593/2008 of the European Parliament and of the Council, of 17 June 2008, on the law applicable to contractual obligations (Rome I) (*OJ L* 177/6, 4 July 2008). The Rome I Regulation is applicable in all EU Member States (with the exception of Denmark: Recital 46 and article 1.4) (geographical scope) to contracts concluded after 17 December 2009 (article 28) (scope of application in time) and, specifically, to contractual obligations in civil and commercial matters in situations involving a conflict of laws (article 1.1, first paragraph) (material scope of application). It applies irrespective of whether or not the law specified by the Regulation is the law of a Member State (article 2) (universal application). For a full theoretical as well as practical detailed analysis of RR-I, *see* Michael McParland, *The Rome I Regulation on the Law Applicable to Contractual Obligations* (Oxford University Press, Oxford, 2015).

[8] In addition to article 6 RR-I, consumer contracts are also governed by article 11.4 RR-I in relation to the law applicable to the formal validity of these contracts, which is the law of the country where the consumer has his habitual residence (except where the consumer contract is a contract the subject matter of which is a right *in rem* in immovable property or a tenancy of an immovable property: *see* paragraph 5). We will not review article 11 RR-I in this paper. In general, on article 11 RR-I, *see* Tim W. Dornis, 'Article 11' in Franco Ferrari (ed.), *Rome I Regulation. Pocket Commentary* (Selp-NYU, Munich, 2015) pp. 389–402.

[9] Convention on the law applicable to contractual obligations, Rome, 19 June 1980 (*OJ L* 266/1, 9 October 1980). Article 24 RR-I provides a rule for the relationship between the Regulation and the Convention where it says that the "(…) Regulation shall replace the Rome Convention in the Member States, except as regards the territories of the Member States which fall within the territorial scope of application of that Convention and to which this Regulation does not apply pursuant to Article 299 of the Treaty". Consequently, the Rome Convention is still applicable to determine the law applicable to contractual (consumer) obligations when the courts having jurisdiction are the courts of Denmark or the courts of any of the (overseas) territories expressly mentioned in article 355 TFEU (which replaced article 299). For an authoritative short explanation of RC, *see* "Report on the Convention on the law applicable to contractual obligations by Mario Giuliano, Professor University of Milan, and Paul Lagarde, University of Paris I" (*OJ C* 282, 31 October 1980, pp.1–50). *See also*, among many others, Tullio Treves (dir.), *Verso una disciplina comunitaria della legge applicabile ai contratti*, Cedam, Padova 1983 and P.M. North (ed.), *Contracts Conflicts. The E.E.C. Convention on the Law Applicable to Contractual Obligations: A comparative Study* (North-Holland, 1982).

[10] For the transition between RC and RR-I, one should look at the Proposal for a Regulation of the European Parliament and of the Council on the law applicable to contractual

Article 6 RR-I is both a *specific* and a *general* conflict-of-laws rule. It is a *specific* rule because it prevails over the general conflict-of-laws rules contained within the Regulation (mainly, articles 3 and 4).[11] In other words, if a situation (consumer contract) falls within the scope of application of article 6 (as we shall see below), the law applicable to the contract is determined by article 6 directly without the need to resort to articles 3 (Freedom of choice)[12] or 4 (Applicable law in the absence of choice), both of which serve to identify the national law applicable to international contractual obligations which are not governed by specific articles of the Regulation.

On the other hand, article 6 RR-I is a *general* conflict-of-laws rule, within the strict realm of the sector of the law applicable (PIL) to consumer contracts, because, as we have proposed earlier, other PIL rules are applicable to specific consumer contracts or consumer-related transactions contained in EU directives implemented in Member States (Section 3 below).

2.1.1 The Role of Article 23 RR-I

Article 23 RR-I (Relationship with other provisions of Community law) says:

> (...) this Regulation shall not prejudice the application of provisions of Community law which, in relation to particular matters, lay down conflict-of-law rules relating to contractual obligations.

Article 23 RR-I therefore gives precedence to other EU provisions over article 6 RR-I (*lex specialis* rule).[13]

---

obligations (Rome I) (COM (2005) 650 final). *See* C. Llorente Gómez de Segura, 'La propuesta comunitaria de Reglamento sobre la ley aplicable a las obligaciones contractuales (Roma I). Una primera aproximación', in M.P. Canedo Arillaga (Coord.), *Diversas implicaciones del Derecho transnacional* (Universidad de Deusto, Bilbao, 2006) pp. 331–365. In the Regulation Proposal, consumer contracts were also regulated in art. 5. *See also* A. Bonomi, 'A Conversion of the Rome Convention on Contracts into an EC Instrument. Some Remarks on the Green Paper of the EC Commission', *Yearb. PIL*, 2003, pp. 53–97

11 This feature is common, although for more or less slightly different reasons, to the situations covered by art. 5 (contracts of carriage), art. 7 (insurance contracts) and art. 8 (individual employment contracts). Specifically, protection of the weaker party is expressly mentioned by Rec. (24) of the Rome I Regulation: "As regards contracts concluded with parties regarded as being weaker, those parties should be protected by conflict-of-law rules that are more favourable to their interests than the general rules".

12 Notwithstanding the above, art. 6.2 RR-I makes specific reference to art. 3 RR-I, which we will address later in the main text.

13 Not everyone, though, shares this otherwise clear outcome of the literal wording of art. 23 RR-I, although for different reasons. *See* Francesca Ragno, 'Article 6' in Ferrari, *supra* note 8, pp. 244–246, in particular footnote 229. For reasons we will explain in the main

A couple of issues need to be reviewed here regarding the relationship between articles 23 and 6 RR-I.

In the first place, article 23 RR-I mentions "(...) provisions of Community law which (...) lay down conflict-of-law rules". These provisions are those that prevail over the rules in RR-I and, specifically, over article 6 RR-I. But, what is the exact meaning of that expression? Naturally, they have to be strictly speaking of 'conflict-of-laws' provisions, and not of any other type of PIL rules even in the field of applicable law. In addition, article 23 RR-I clearly encompasses conflict-of-laws rules contained in EU Regulations, but it also includes conflict-of-laws rules incorporated into EU directives, and finally – and despite the wording of the article (provisions of Community law) – those conflict-of-laws rules to be found in domestic legislation implementing the abovementioned directives in each Member State.[14] Consequently, article 6 RR-I has to give way to particular conflict-of-laws rules contained in all those statutory instruments.

Secondly, in relation to the above description, it is open to discussion whether or not the prevalence of those specific provisions over article 6 RR-I is to be maintained when their respective national implementation is not in line with what the directives established. In this respect, a review of legal literature shows a clear position in favour of not allowing prevalence when this situation occurs.[15] Consequently, article 6 RR-I should be applied when Member States fail to faithfully implement the directives' conflict-of-laws rules.

Thirdly, article 23 RR-I is applicable only when EU law provisions are issued "(...) in relation to particular matters (...)" (*lex specialis*). In fact, article 6 RR-I deals with a particular matter (consumer contracts) in relation to the general scope of the Regulation (civil and commercial contracts). However, in the framework of the relationship between articles 6 and 23 RR-I, it is undeniable that article 23 RR-I also refers to particular matters affecting consumer contracts, such as those falling under the material scope of application of the respective directives. So, we should say, there is a double degree, or double level, of particularity affecting consumer contracts in terms of determining the law applicable to such contracts within the framework of EU PIL. One level is to

---

text, we also share the view that the relationship between arts. 6 and 23, specifically in the field of consumer contracts, need not be one of hierarchy but of cooperation.

14   In this respect, art. 20 Rome Convention was more precise when it referred to "(...) provisions which (...) lay down conflict of law rules (...) and which are or will be contained in acts of the institutions of the European Communities or in national laws harmonized in implementation of such acts".

15   See Ragno, *supra* note 13, pp. 244–246.

be assumed by article 6 RR-I, and the second to be provided by each of the directives (and respective implementing national legislation) containing a conflict-of-laws rule.

Finally, the rule found in article 23 RR-I is somehow in contrast – more than with any other type of contract – with Recital 40 of the Regulation. It is true that, in line with article 23 RR-I, this Recital establishes that Rome I "(...) should not exclude the possibility of inclusion of conflict-of-law rules relating to contractual obligations in provisions of Community law with regard to particular matters". But in the first sentence of the same recital, it is also crystal clear that the legislative mandate of the EU is that "[A] situation where conflict-of-law rules are dispersed among several instruments and where there are differences between those rules should be avoided". This Recital encompasses two situations. First, the 'dispersion' of conflict-of-laws rules among several EU instruments, and, second, the existence of 'differences' among those rules. According to its literal wording ('and'), the recital seems to mandate avoidance of both situations when they occur simultaneously. However, from a logical point of view, it seems more reasonable to understand that the Regulation wants to avoid dispersion as well as differences. It would not be efficient (or logical), on the one side, to have identical rules dispersed in several instruments. Only one rule would suffice and this rule might well be the one included in a general instrument like Rome I (article 6). On the other side, it would be counterproductive to have several and different-in-content rules applicable to the same type of contracts, unless the differences were clearly justified. In relation to consumer contracts the present situation is exactly as described in Recital 40: on the one hand, there are several rules (article 6 RR-I and the conflict-of-laws or applicable law rules contained in each directive and in the respective national legislation implementing the directives) and, on the other hand, all these rules reflect differences with the underlying principles governing article 6 RR-I. In a later section (Section 3) of this paper we will specifically address this particular problem.

2.1.2   International Conventions

A different, although complementary, issue regarding the application of article 6 RR-I is related to the hierarchy of the Rome I Regulation in the context of other potential statutory sources which might regulate the problem of the law applicable to international consumer contracts. Specifically, we discuss the relationship between RR-I and some potentially applicable international conventions. Article 25 RR-I sets the tone here.

This article establishes the prevalence over the Regulation of international conventions containing contractual conflict-of-laws rules which were in force at the time of adoption of the Regulation (17 June 2009)[16] (article 25.1) or, exceptionally, of those international conventions amended or concluded afterwards in compliance with the procedures established by Regulation (EC) No 662/2009.[17] Out of these situations, therefore, no international convention will prevail over the Regulation,[18] except, of course, international conventions concluded by the EU itself.

In this area of law special attention has been paid, with respect to consumer contracts, to the Hague Convention on the Law Applicable to the International Sales of Goods (1955)[19] and to the United Nations Convention on Contracts for Contracts for the International Sales of Goods (1980) (CISG).[20] However, neither of these two conventions should set aside application of the Regulation and, particularly, of its article 6.

The 1995 Hague Convention is indeed potentially applicable to international sales of goods with consumers as its article 1 does not exclude these consumer contracts from its scope of application and it is indeed a Convention that lays down conflict-of-laws rules relating to contractual obligations. However, the Hague Conference on Private International Law declared – in relation to article 5 of the Rome Convention – that special rules on the law applicable to consumer sales prevail over the rules in the 1995 Convention in Contracting States. Clearly, this principle or declaration must also apply nowadays in the realm of article 6 RR-I as successor to article 5 of the Rome Convention.

With respect to the CISG,[21] the analysis is even simpler. Article 2(a) CISG generally excludes consumer sales from its material scope of application, unless the seller, at any time before or at conclusion of the contract, neither knew nor ought to have known that the goods were bought for personal, family or household use. So there might be – although in a very limited scenario – an

---

16 Art. 26 RR-I requires Member States to notify the Commission of the Conventions referred to in article 25.1 (as well as their denunciation), information that will be published in the OJEU for clarification purposes. *See* "Notifications under Article 26(1) of Regulation (EC) No 593/2008 of the European Parliament and of the Council on the law applicable to contractual obligations (Rome I)" (2010/C 343/04).
17 OJ L 200/25, 31 July 2009. *See* Rec. (42) RR-I.
18 Including those international conventions referred to in art. 25.2 RR-I (exclusively inter-Member-State Conventions),
19 Five EU Member States are parties to this Convention: Denmark, Finland, France, Italy and Sweden.
20 All EU Member States are Contracting States of the CISG with the exception of Ireland, Malta, Portugal and the United Kingdom.
21 On the CISG, *see* for all Clayton P. Gillette and Steven D. Walt, *The UN Convention on Contracts for the International sale of Goods* (Cambridge University Press, 2nd ed., New York, 2016).

application of the CISG to consumer sales. However, even in such a situation, a potential clash between article 6 RR-I and the CISG must be discarded since both sources, although applicable law sources as such, operate on different levels. Article 6 RR-I is strictly speaking a conflict-of-laws rule in that it indicates the national law applicable to the contract – an indirect method of regulation – while the CISG is a special material set of rules which, within its scope, gives a direct answer to the problem in need of solution, and is thus a direct method of regulation. Indeed, article 25.1 RR-I only gives precedence to conventions laying down conflict-of-laws rules. Precedence of conventions laying down special material rules is not based on article 25.1 RR-I, but on the universally accepted principle that special material rules prevail over conflict-of-laws rules. In other words, the CISG and RR-I (article 6) may potentially apply to the same consumer sales contract but only when the CISG does not address a particular issue will article 6 RR-I come forward to determine the national law under which the problem will be resolved.[22]

2.2   Scope of Application of Article 6 RR-I
2.2.1   Presentation

Before we move into analysis of how we should determine the law applicable to international consumer contracts under article 6 RR-I (see Section 2.3 below), we need to understand when this article applies (scope or sphere of application), because, despite what its title clearly states (Consumer contracts), not all of such contracts are to be governed by article 6 RR-I, but instead some of them will fall under the scope of application of the general uniform rules contained in the Regulation (basically, articles 3 and 4).

Article 6 RR-I does not make for easy reading. This article mixes issues of scope of application of the article itself with identifying connecting factors and, within the former issues (scope of application), a number of consumer contracts are typologically excluded from its sphere, although these are listed in a disorganized way, and other consumer contracts which are excluded for other different reasons.

So, let us try to put some order into this.

Article 6 RR-I defines its scope of application, in a positive (inclusive) way, in its paragraph 1. It governs contracts:

---

22   In accordance with art. 7.2 CISG, "[Q]uestions concerning matters governed by this Convention which are not expressly settled in it are to be settled in conformity with the general principles on which it is based or, in the absence of such principles, in conformity with the law applicable by virtue of the rules of private international law".

(...) concluded by a natural person for a purpose which can be regarded as being outside his trade or profession (the consumer) with another person acting in the exercise of his trade and profession (the professional) (...) provided that the professional: (a) pursues his commercial or professional activities in the country where the consumer has his habitual residence, or (b) by any means, directs such activities to that country or to several countries including that country, and the contract falls within the scope of such activities.

This is the genuine and essential material (and subjective) scope of application of article 6 RR-I and we shall review it extensively very shortly (see 2.2.3 below). However, before we get to this point, we need to identify those matters or situations (or contracts) that are excluded from its scope (negative sphere of application) and which, consequently, will not be governed by article 6 but, again, by the general uniform rules in the Regulation (article 3 or 4).

2.2.2   Exclusions

Consumer contracts excluded from the scope of application of article 6 RR-I are mentioned in its paragraphs 1, 3 and 4.

2.2.2.1   *Carriage and Insurance Contracts*

In paragraph 1 of article 6 RR-I we read that this article is applicable "[W]ithout prejudice to articles 5 and 7". In other words, it is not applicable to contracts of carriage with consumers (article 5 RR-I)[23] and to contracts of insurance with consumers (article 7 RR-I),[24] which are two types of contracts where consumers are frequent clients of carriers and insurers.[25]

Nothing is said further about insurance consumer contracts in the articles of the Regulation, but, curiously enough, article 6.4 (b) RR-I duplicates, again, the rule that contracts of carriage are excluded from the scope of application of article 6 RR-I, although only when it is "a contract of carriage other than a contract relating to package travel within the meaning of Council Directive

---

[23] Regarding art. 5 RR-I, *see* Carlos Llorente, 'La ley applicable al contrato de transporte internacional segñun el Reglamento Roma I', *Cuadernos de Derecho Transnacional* (Octubre 2009), vol. 1, No 2, pp. 160–178.

[24] *See*, in general, on insurance contracts and art. 7 RR-I, Celia Caamiña and José Manuel Almudí Cid, 'Contrato internacional de seguro', in Mariano Yzquierdo (ed.), *Contratos*, vol. 17 (Thomson Reuters-Aranzadi, Navarra, 2014) pp. 581–635. From a critical perspective, H. Heiss, 'Insurance Contracts in Rome I: Another Recent Failure of the European Legislature', *Yearb PIL*, 2008, pp. 261–283.

[25] Rec. (32) RR-I: "Article 6 should not apply in the context of those particular contracts".

90/314/ECC of 13 June 1990 on package travel, package holidays and package tours".[26] Probably, there was no intention to be redundant here, but simply the purpose was to make clear that 'package' contracts falling within the scope of application of the applicable directive are also covered by article 6 RR-I, even when, as is usual, carriage operations are part of the agreed package. That said, however, the legislative drafting could have been improved here.

The reasons for excluding consumer insurance contracts or consumer carriage contracts from the scope of application of article 6 RR-I are not very clear. Recital (32) RR-I tries to offer an explanation:

> Owing to the particular nature of contracts of carriage and insurance contracts, specific provisions should ensure an adequate level of protection of passengers and policy holders. Therefore, Article 6 should not apply in the context of those particular contracts.

The last sentence of Recital (32) is understandable 'beyond any reasonable doubt': RR-I does not want article 6 to be extended to consumer insurance and carriage contracts. Apparently, this is due to the particular nature of these two contract types, which, again apparently, would need to be addressed by specific provisions ensuring an adequate level of protection to certain persons. Since those 'specific provisions' cannot be other than articles 5 and 7 RR-I, it seems that Recital (32) is simply justifying why special rules (specific provisions) should apply to carriage and insurance contracts, but not why these rules should also apply to those contracts, instead of article 6, when one of the parties is a consumer. The only explanation for this would be – but this should be tested – that for the drafters of RR-I consumer protection in those two contracts is better achieved through the rules in articles 5 and 7 ('adequate level of protection') than through article 6. It is curious, too, that Recital (32) specifically mentions protection of 'passengers' (carriage of persons) but not of 'consignors' and/or 'consignees' (carriage of goods), probably because it is more frequent to find consumers in carriage of persons (passengers) than in carriage of goods, which is typically a commercial activity.[27]

---

26 Directive (EU) 2015/2302 of the European Parliament and of the Council, of 25 November 2015, on package travel and linked travel arrangements (*OJ L* 326/1, 11 December 2015), repealed Directive 90/314/EEC. Regarding these concepts, *see* joined cases C-585/08, *Pammer* and C-144/09, *Hotel Alpenhof*.

27 It should not be forgotten that art. 5 RR-I applies to contracts both of carriage of goods and of passengers and also that Rec. (22), relying on the previous art. 4.4 RC, accepts a broad concept of contract of carriage which includes "single-voyage charter parties and other contracts the main purpose of which is the carriage of goods".

2.2.2.2 Other Types of Contracts Excluded

In addition to contracts of insurance and carriage, as mentioned above, article 6.4 RR-I, excludes the following contracts or legal transactions from its material scope:

1) Contracts for the supply of services where the services are to be supplied to the consumer exclusively in a country other than that in which he has his habitual residence (article 6.4a).[28]

From a typological point of view, contracts for the supply of services[29] are generally included in the scope of application of article 6 RR-I as long as the criteria and requirements established by its paragraph 1 are met (general rule). Only when the services are to be supplied to a consumer in a country other than that in which he has his habitual residence (exception) is article 6 RR-I I left out and the general rules (articles 3 and 4) apply to determine the law applicable, even if all the requirements of article 6.1 RR-I are met.[30] Therefore, the only ground for exclusion from article 6 RR-I (and from its protective scope) is the location of the services provided outside of the consumer's country of habitual residence.[31]

2) Contracts relating to a right *in rem* in immovable property or a tenancy of immovable property other than a contract relating to the right to use immovable property on a timeshare basis within the meaning of Directive 94/47/EC (article 6.4c).[32]

---

[28] This exclusion is exactly the same as contemplated by art. 5.4(b) RC.

[29] Both art. 6.4(a) RR-I and art. 5.4(b) RC use the expression 'supply of services'. Interestingly, when RR-I regulates services in a different article (art. 4.1b), the expression used is that of 'provision of services'. Irrespective of the terminology, though, it is clear that both expressions cover the same type of contracts, 'contracts for services', and that the meaning of this category of contracts must be interpreted independently of domestic categories, as the CJEU has determined in many situations affecting different kinds of services. See Carlos Llorente, *Practicum Daños 2019* (Thomson Reuters, Navarra, 2019) p. 156.

[30] Accordingly the law applicable will be the law chosen by the parties (art. 3 RR-I) or, in the absence of choice, the law of the country of habitual residence of the service provider (the professional) (art. 4.1, letter b RR-I).

[31] This would look initially like a reasonable outcome because, otherwise, a professional offering services to consumers in another country might potentially be subject to many different national laws depending on the country of habitual residence of each consumer (as per article 6.1 RR-I). On the other hand, as there is, nevertheless, a consumer involved (who merits some protection) in this kind of contract, some authors consider that application of the general rules might be inappropriate and would promote the application of the law of the country where the services are provided as a fairer solution.

[32] Dir. 94/47/EC has been replaced by Dir. 2008/122/EC (see below).

This exclusion was not contemplated by article 5 RC. It is usually understood[33] that the reason for leaving these contracts out of the scope of application of article 6 lies in the particularly strong and foreseeable connection, from a legal point of view, between the immovable property and the specific country where the property is located, as article 4.1(c) and (d) RR-I also shows. But again, some sort of protection might be needed when a consumer is a party to these transactions, as we proposed in relation to the situations covered by article 6.4(a) RR-I.

3) Rights and obligations which constitute a financial instrument and rights and obligations constituting the terms and conditions governing the issuance or offer to the public and public take-over bids of transferable securities, and subscription to and redemption of units in collective investment undertakings in so far as these activities do not constitute provision of a financial service (article 6.4 d).[34]

This is another exclusion not contemplated by article 5 RC. Its wording is rather complex – indeed, a recurrent trademark of legal finance terminology nowadays – and should be completed by reference to Recitals (26), (28), (29) and (30) in RR-I and by a direct and unavoidable consultation of the applicable EU financial legislation, in particular Directive 2014/65/EU, which repealed Directive 2004/39/EC.[35] It is important to notice, though, that article 6.4(d) does not exclude from its scope of application contracts for the provision of financial services as such, but only those specific instruments and operations mentioned therein. And the exclusion is basically justified on the need that these operations be governed by one law and not by a myriad of laws corresponding to the habitual residence of each investor.[36]

4) Contracts concluded under the type of system falling within the scope of article 4.1h RR-I (article 6.4e).

Article 4.1(h) deals with contracts:

> (…) concluded within a multilateral system which brings together or facilitates the bringing together of multiple third-party buying and selling interests in financial instruments as defined by article 4(1), point (17) of

---

33 Rec. (27) offers no clue about the background reasons supporting this exclusion.
34 *See* generally F.J. Garcimartín Alférez, 'The Rome I Regulation: Exceptions to the Rule on Consumer Contracts and Financial Instruments', *Yearb. PIL*, 2008, pp. 245–259.
35 Directive 2014/65/EU of the European Parliament and of the Council, of 15 May 2014, on markets in financial instruments and amending Directive 2002/92/EC and Directive 2011/61/EU (recast), *OJ L* 173/349, 12 June 2014.
36 See Rec. (28).

Directive 2004/39/EC, in accordance with non-discretionary rules and governed by a single law.

These contracts were not covered at all by the Rome Convention and their exclusion could be understood as a tribute to their particular legal nature and to their use strictly within professional circles.

2.2.2.3 Contracts Excluded by Article 6.3 RR-I

The above-mentioned exclusions in paragraphs 1 and 4 of article 6 RR-I need to be complemented, finally, with those in paragraph 3, where RR-I also excludes from the scope of application of article 6 consumer contracts that do not fulfil the requirements mentioned in letters (a) and (b) of paragraph 1. This is not a typological exclusion (as those analyzed before), because it affects all types of consumer contracts (except those groups excluded by paragraphs 1 and 4) and is therefore the most relevant of all the exclusions mentioned by article 6 RR-I. Basically, article 6.3 RR-I excludes from the range of protection granted by this article consumer contracts when the contracting consumer may be characterized as an 'active consumer' as opposed to a 'passive' one (referred to in paragraph 1 of article 6, letters a and b). And the best approach to understanding how this exclusion works is through specific analysis of paragraph 1 of article 6 RR-I which, as we mentioned before, sets out the essential, positive, scope of application of this rule.

2.2.3 Positive Scope of Application

Several factors and conditions (both of a subjective and objective nature) need to be found in the particular case to trigger the application of article 6 RR-I.

(1) In the first place, a contract must have been 'concluded' between the parties. Any type of contract, except those types expressly excluded by paragraphs 1 and 4, would make for application of article 6, as long as the parties have already concluded it.[37]

(2) Secondly, the contract must be one entered into between two parties (persons) identified respectively by the rule as 'the consumer' and 'the professional'.[38] Indeed, this is why these contracts are called 'consumer contracts'.

---

37 Art. 5 RC was more limited in scope as it only applied to contracts for the supply of goods and services (paragraph 1).
38 Art. 5 RC did not contain any mention of a professional as the party opposed to the consumer under the contract.

The consumer is defined[39] as a natural person who concludes a contract for a purpose that can be regarded as being outside his trade or profession. A couple of points merit attention here.

First, contrary to the Rome Convention (article 5), which was silent on this particular issue, legal persons are not considered to be consumers for the purpose of application of article 6 RR-I. Only natural or physical persons are.

Second, the legal role of consumer is attributed to a person by taking into account specifically the 'purpose' sought by that person when concluding the contract, which has to be a purpose outside his trade or profession (if he has any, we should say). This requirement might be theoretically understood as being merely subjective, because it apparently relies on the consumer's intention. However, in fact, the purpose required by article 6 RR-I needs to be objectivized and, more importantly, it has to be recognized as such by the other party to the contract (the professional) ('which can be regarded').[40] If a natural person is indeed a consumer but appears in the market as a professional (the so-called 'hidden consumer'), then article 6 RR-I is not applicable to his contractual relationship with a true professional.

Thirdly, a consumer protected under article 6 RR-I does not need to have his habitual residence in the EU.[41]

Fourthly, application of article 6 RR-I requires that the party relying on its application must be the one providing evidence as to participation of a consumer in the contract.

In relation to the definition of the other party to the contract (the 'professional'), RR-I offers a much simpler perspective. This person is identified as any

---

39 As an autonomous definition provided by the Regulation this has to be interpreted independently from the particular approaches to be found in domestic Member-State legislation on this topic.

40 *See*, in particular, in EU case law, C-269/95, *Benincasa* paras. 52–54 (jurisdiction in consumer contracts). In a similar but different context, when the consumer enters into a contract for a purpose that is both outside and inside his trade of profession (mixed purpose), RR-I does not provide an answer as per the application of its art. 6. But again, by extrapolating EU case law on jurisdiction in consumer contracts (Brussels system), we could arguably defend that in these mixed situations art. 6 RR-I must be excluded unless the professional purpose is evidently marginal (C-464/01, *Gruber* para. 39). Under art. 5 RC the position on this issue was expressed by the Giuliano/Lagarde Report: "If such a person acts partially within, partially outside his trade or profession the situation only falls within the scope of article 5 if he acts *primarily* outside his trade or profession" (our emphasis).

41 This is a different approach from that in the Rome I Proposal but it goes in line with art. 2 RR-I (Universal application).

person who acts in the exercise of his trade or profession.[42] As opposed to the consumer, a professional, under article 6 RR-I, may be either a natural or legal person and it is qualified not by a contracting 'purpose' but simply through factual elements that show he is acting objectively within his trade or profession.[43]

(3) For article 6 to apply the consumer must be a so-called 'passive' consumer. This is outlined by article 6.1 when it requires that:

> (...) the professional: (a) pursues his commercial activities in the country where the consumer has his habitual residence, or (b) by any means, directs such activities to that country or to several countries including that country.

In other words, consumer contracts will fall under the protective rule of article 6 RR-I only when the contract is concluded as a result of an activity (actively) pursued or directed by a professional in the country of habitual residence of the consumer. Consequently, as we proposed before, consumer contracts will be left out of article 6 when letters (a) or (b) are not met in the particular situation (contracts with active consumers) (article 6.3 RR-I).

Letters (a) and (b) of article 6.1 RR-I have raised some debate both in legal literature and in case law in relation to the meaning of the expressions 'pursues' and 'directs', mainly the latter. When the rule talks about *pursuing* activities *in the* country of habitual residence of the consumer (letter a), it is clear that this requires that the professional must somehow be 'present' in that country (the 'doing business' rule), although not necessarily in a regular or permanent manner and also not in person but through someone else acting on behalf of the professional (agency, branch, and so on). More open to debate is how to understand the meaning of *directing* activities *to* the country of habitual residence of the consumer (which is of particular importance in the internet era) (the so-called 'stream of commerce' rule). Clearly, 'direct to' must have to mean something different from 'pursue in' (otherwise article 6 would not have made such a distinction). So, on the one hand, it cannot mean to require that the professional has a presence 'in' the country of habitual residence of the consumer, but somewhere else. And, on the other hand, provided the

---

42   This definition is solely for the purpose of application of the Regulation and cannot be construed on the basis of national law.
43   However, according to EU case law when a person is not a professional at the time of concluding a contract but enters into the contract with a future professional purpose, then they must be considered a professional (Case C-190/11, *Mühlleitner*, para. 37).

before mentioned premise is met, it seems that everything should revolve around evidence of the intention of the professional to offer, advertize or solicit business *vis-à-vis* the consumer in their country of residence.[44]

(4) Finally, article 6.1 RR-I requires, as a condition for its application, that the consumer contract fall within the scope of the commercial or professional activities of the so-called 'professional'. By use of the expression 'as a result of', Recital (25) of RR-I has opened up some debate as to whether there a causal connection must exist between the contract and the activities mentioned.[45] In my opinion, Recital (25) has introduced some confusion here because what this Recital expresses is more directly related to the 'targeted activity' principle assumed by letters (a) and (b) of article 6.1 RR-I than to the particular meaning of the expression 'within the scope of such activities'.

2.3   Conflict-of-laws Rules

We have so far identified the (somewhat complex) scope of application of article 6 RR-I. If the contract is not covered by this scope, then the law applicable will be determined by the general rules basically established in articles 3 and 4 RR-I. But if the contract falls within the scope of article 6 RR-I then the law applicable to the consumer contract is determined by the conflict-of-laws rules to be found in its paragraphs 1 and 2. These rules are the following two.

In the first place, the rule in article 6.1 RR-I establishes that the law applicable is the law of the country (not necessarily an EU member State: article 2 RR-I) of habitual residence of the consumer (to be fixed at the time of conclusion of the contract: article 19.3 RR-I).[46] This is a very simple rule that goes in line with other similar rules in the Regulation (such as article 4) and presents only the 'difficulty', more practical than legal, of determining in each particular case what 'habitual residence' means.[47]

The second conflict-of-laws rule provided by article 6 RR-I, now in its paragraph 2, contemplates the role of choice of law in relation to consumer contracts governed by this article. According to this rule, choice of law made in

---

44   See Recital (24) RR-I on the connection between art. 6.1, letter (b) RR-I and distance-selling techniques developed particularly through Internet sites (on-line).
45   This has been decided in the negative by case C-218/12, *Emrek*, in relation to the rule contained in the Brussels I Regulation.
46   Paras. 1 and 2 of art. 19 RR-I offer a definition of 'habitual residence' but it is not applicable to consumers.
47   Guidance on an operative concept of 'habitual residence' is to be taken from CJEU case law where there is an understanding that habitual residence is where a person has his 'centre of interests' measured by time and purpose.

accordance with article 3 RR-I[48] is allowed but only to the extent that such choice does not: "(...) have the result of depriving the consumer of the protection afforded to him by provisions that cannot be derogated from by agreement by virtue of the law, which in the absence of choice would have been applicable on the basis of paragraph 1".

In other words, choice is allowed, but may be limited by the (simple)[49] mandatory rules of the law of habitual residence of the consumer. In practical terms, applying this rule is not easy as it requires not only to identify both the law chosen by the parties and the applicable mandatory rules, if any, of the law of the country of habitual residence of the consumer, but, more importantly, to compare (and evaluate) both sets of rules in order to determine which provides the specific consumer with better protection in the (also) specific situation in conflict. This is a really tough call both for judges and attorneys representing the parties in the dispute, which will have to be resolved under criteria supplied by the *lex fori* (in the absence of any help or guidance from article 6.2 RR-I to this respect).

3 Other EU Rules on the Law Applicable to Consumer Contracts

As we proposed earlier in this paper, the EU has produced a number of consumer-protection directives in different fields whose purpose has been to harmonize consumer law throughout the EU with material rules to be implemented in each Member State. These directives also contain PIL (applicable law) rules also aimed at harmonizing this particular field.

Let us first identify those directives and their specific PIL rules (in chronological order).

1) Directive 93/13/EEC, of the Council, of 5 April 1993, on unfair terms in consumer contracts (in force).[50] Article 6.2 of this Directive reads as follows:

"Member States shall take the necessary measures to ensure that the consumer does not lose the protection granted by this Directive by virtue of the

---

48   Under art. 3 RR-I, choice of law may be made expressly or implicitly, totally or partially applicable to the contract (paragraph 1) and at any time (with the limits expressed by para. 2).

49   Not to be mistaken for/confused with the 'overriding' mandatory provisions governed by art. 9 RR-I, which, nevertheless, may have some scope of application in consumer contracts although at a different level of scrutiny.

50   *OJ L* 95/29, of 21 April 1993. This Directive was later modified by Dir. 2011/83/EU (*see* below). *See* D. Dal Bo, 'La Direttiva Comunitaria del 5 aprile 1993 in material di clausole abusive nei contratti stipulati con I consumatori', *DCI*, 1993, vol. VII, pp. 567–580.

choice of the law of a non-Member country as the law applicable to the contract if the latter has a close connection with the territory of the Member States". This rule sets the tone for rules that will appear in subsequent directives with slightly different wordings.

2) Directive 94/47/EC of the European Parliament and of the Council, of 26 October 1994, on the protection of purchasers in respect of certain aspects of contracts relating to the purchase of the right to use immovable properties on a time sharing basis.[51] Its article 9 is the rule to be considered here. It says that "[t]he Member States shall take the measures necessary to ensure that, whatever the law applicable may be, the purchaser is not deprived of the protection afforded by this Directive, if the immovable property concerned is situated within the territory of a Member State".

3) Directive 97/7//EC, of the European Parliament and of the Council, of 20 May 1997, on the protection of consumers in respect of distance contracts.[52] Article 12.2 of this Directive follows almost literally (or identically) the wording of article 6.2 of Directive 93/13/ECC: "Member States shall take the measures needed to ensure that the consumer does not lose the protection granted by this Directive by virtue of the choice of the law of a non-member country as the law applicable to the contract if the latter has close connection with the territory of one or more Member States".

4) Directive 98/27/EC of the European Parliament and of the Council, of 19 May 1988, on injunctions for the protection of consumers' interests.[53] Article 2.2 of this Directive simply establishes that: "[T]his Directive shall be without prejudice to the rules of private international law, with respect to the applicable law, thus leading normally to the application of either the law of the Member State where the infringement originated or the law of the Member State where the infringement has its effects". Strictly speaking, no PIL rules are contained here though but simply a direct and straightforward remittance to the application of general EU applicable law (conflict-of-laws) rules.

5) Directive 99/44/EC, of the European Parliament and of the Council, of 25 May 1999, on certain aspects of the sale of consumer goods and associated guarantees.[54] Article 7.2 of the Directive follows the path of the previous

---

51   OJ L 280/83, 29 October 1994. This Directive was later repealed by Dir. 2008/122/EC (*see below*).

52   OJ L 144/19, of 4 June 1997. This Directive was later repealed by Dir. 2011/83/EU (*see below*).

53   OJ L 166/51, 11 June 1998. See, Michael Bogdan, 'Some Reflections regarding the New EU Directive on Injunctions for the Protection of Consumers' Interests', [1998] *Consumer L.J.* 69–75.

54   OJ L 171/12, of 7 July 1999. This Directive was amended by Dir. 2011/83/EU (*see below*).

directives: "Member States shall take the necessary measures to ensure that consumers are not deprived of the protection afforded by this Directive as a result of opting for the law of a non-member State as the law applicable to the contract where the contract has a close connection with the territory of the Member States".

6) Directive 2002/65/EC, of the European Parliament and of the Council, of 23 September 2002, concerning the distance marketing of consumer financial services.[55] Its article 12.2 follows again the path of the previous directives: "Member States shall take the measures needed to ensure that the consumer does not lose the protection granted by this Directive by virtue of the choice of the law of a non-member country as the law applicable to the contract, if this contract has a close link with the territory of one or more Member States".

7) Directive 2008/48/EC, of the European Parliament and of the Council, of 23 April 2008, on credit agreements for consumers.[56] Article 22.4 of the Directive, with slight changes, adopts a familiar rule: "Member States shall take the necessary measures to ensure that consumers do not lose the protection granted by this Directive by virtue of the choice of the law of a third country as the law applicable to the credit agreement, if the credit agreement has a close link with the territory of one or more Member States".

8) Directive 2008/122/EC, of the European Parliament and of the Council, of 14 January 2009, on the protection of consumers in respect of certain aspects of timeshare, long-term holiday product, resale and exchange contracts.[57] Its article 12.2 contains the following rule:

> Where the applicable law is that of a third country, consumers shall not be deprived of the protection granted by this Directive, as implemented in the Member State of the forum if: any of the immovable properties concerned is situated within the territory of a Member State or in the case of a contract not directly related to immovable property, the trader pursues commercial or professional activities in a Member State or, by any means, directs such activities to a Member State and the contract falls within the scope of such activities.

9) Directive 2011/83/EU, of the European Parliament and of the Council, of 25 October 2011, on consumer rights.[58] Interestingly, this Directive does not

---

55   *OJ L* 27/16 of 9 October 2002.
56   *OJ L* 133/66, of 22 May 2008. This Directive repealed Dir. 87/102/EEC, of the Council, of 22 December 1986 (*OJ L* 42/48, 12 February 1987), which did not contain PIL rules.
57   *OJ L* 33/10, of 3 February 2009.
58   *OJ L* 304/64, 22 November 2011.

contain any rule like the ones we have identified before in other similar directives but addresses PIL applicable law issues in its Recital (10) which reads: "This Directive should be without prejudice to Regulation (EC) No 593/2008 of the European Parliament and of the Council of 17 June 2008 on the law applicable to contractual obligations (Rome I)".

In the light of the above-indicated rules, some assertions and conclusions may be put forward.

First. With the exception of the rules to be found in the time-sharing related Directives (94/47/EC and 2008/122/EC), and in Directives 98/27 and 2011/83, which have specialties of their own (see immediately below), the wording, and more importantly the purpose, of the rest of them are identical or quite similar. They contemplate a mandate to Member States, when transposing the Directive, so they ensure that when the law applicable to the contract, by virtue of choice of the parties, is the law of a non-Member State (or Country) (or third country), this choice does not deprive consumers of the protection granted by the respective directive when the contract is closely connected (or linked) with the (territory of the) EU (Member States or one or more Member States).

Second. The directives related to timesharing (94/47 and now 2008/122) have a similar purpose to those mentioned above (not to deprive consumers of the protection granted by the directives), although there are some differences. One, these rules apply, apparently, not only when a 'choice' of law is made by the parties but instead whatever the law applicable might be (and, we should imply, irrespective of whether a choice was, or was not, made by the parties). And two, the close connection or link required is directly specified in these rules (property located in a Member State or activities pursued in, or directed to, Member States and contracts falling within the scope of such activities).

Third. Directives 98/27 and 2011/83 also have a similar purpose (to assure consumers are protected by these directives' material rules as implemented at national level). However they do not purport to create any specific PIL rule but merely refer to application of the general conflict-of-laws rules contained in EU Regulations, such as Rome I.

Fourth. The rules found in the majority of directives (irrespective of what the national implemented rules look like) are without any doubt PIL rules in the field of the law applicable to consumer contracts. Their qualification as conflict-of-laws rules, though, might be open to discussion (or may even be denied), as they look more like 'rules of application' of the directives than strictly speaking rules determining the national law applicable to the contract. Not surprisingly, almost all of these rules are contained in articles whose titles or names indicate the 'binding' or 'imperative' nature of the rules of the directives. This is important because, in the context of what we said earlier about article 23 RR-I and the prevalence of special conflict-of-laws rules over the general rule in article 6 RR-I, we might come to the conclusion that if those rules in the directives are not conflict-of-laws rules, they should not prevail over, but complement, article 6 RR-I (or articles 3 and 4 RR-I, when a consumer contract is not covered by article 6 RR-I).

Fifth. Following on what we have just said, it is interesting to notice that all directives (including particularly Directives 98/27 and 2011/83) presuppose that the law applicable to a consumer contract has already been identified by choice of law or otherwise. The PIL rules in the majority of directives say 'choice of law' or 'opt for the law'. Only the timesharing directives are broader in their wording as they refer to "the law applicable" (not necessarily chosen by the parties).[59] But in any case those rules do not aim to determine the law applicable to the contract but to make sure that, irrespective of the law applicable (identified by other sources), especially if it is the law of a non-EU member State, the protective rules in the directives and in implementing national legislation are preserved. This is crystal clear in Directives 98/27 and 2011/83.

Sixth. PIL Rules contained in the directives have not been implemented uniformly in all Member States. Autonomous, and lengthy, research might be dedicated to explore the scope and range of these national differences. Although this is a potential risk common to implementation of directives in general, it might be especially counterproductive in the field of PIL as it goes directly against the goal of uniformity proclaimed by the EU in this sector of law as it is enshrined in article 81 TFEU, which aims to ensure "(...)(c) the compatibility of the rules applicable in the Member States concerning conflict of laws (...)". If compatibility means 'a state in which two things are able to exist or occur together without problems or conflict', this result is not warranted when Member States fail, purposely or not, in implementing the appropriate PIL rules in their legal systems. No wonder that we agree with the idea that PIL should be more for the realm of regulations than of directives. And, as we explained earlier, we also support the idea that when national transposition rules go beyond a directive's mandate, these national rules are not to prevent the application of article 6 RR-I and the directive's rules as they are.

---

59   Even though the use of different expressions (choice, etc.) might be confusing, we understand that the directives' PIL rules should be applied in all situations where the law applicable is the law of a third State (i.e., a non-EU Member State), whether determined by the choice of the parties or objectively through absence-of-choice rules. It is true that protection to consumers is better served in those situations where the law applicable is 'chosen' by the parties in situations where the choice is imposed on the consumer by the professional. But we see no reason to close other doors to consumer protection. And not surprisingly, from a terminological perspective, the expression 'choice of law' is often used as an equivalent to conflict-of-laws (or applicable law).

Seventh. The vast majority of the PIL rules in the directives require a close link or connection of the consumer contract with the EU in order for the directive's rules to apply, even if the law applicable is the law of a third country (non-EU Member State). This raises the issue of defining the meaning of 'close connection' or 'close link'. The CJEU has proclaimed a flexible approach to this problem that leaves in the hands of the courts an evaluation of all data and criteria, which, present in a particular matter, might help conclude on the closeness or not of the connection between the contract and the EU.[60] In the timesharing-related directives (94/47 and now 2008/122), to the contrary, a close connection or link with the EU is provided by the fact of the location of immovable property in a Member State or, when there is no immovable property involved, in situations where the trader's (the 'professional' under article 6RR-I) activities are pursued in, or directed to, a member State and the contract falls within the scope of such activities.

4 Conclusions: Where do we Go from Here?

Consumer protection's pervasive presence in EU law and in EU Member States' national law is projected upon all areas of consumer involvement. Starting from being recognized at the highest statutory hierarchical level (article 169 of the TFEU) (including national Constitutions such as Spain: article 51), this protection, whether to be considered of a constitutional nature or otherwise, has expanded through EU and national law, both intertwined, to cover not just material rules but also conflict-of-laws rules. Article 6 of RR-I is the most important conflict-of laws rule in the EU PIL system of consumer protection, along with some special PIL rules contained in EU Directives transposed into Member State legislation.

Analysis of article 6 RR-I and of these consumer protection directives' rules points to the complexity of EU conflict-of-laws or, in broader terms, of the EU's system of PIL applicable law rules in consumer contracts. This complexity goes against the general principle established in recital (40) of RR-I by the EU which says that, even though exceptions might be allowed, "(...) a situation where conflict-of-law rules are dispersed among several instruments and where there are differences between those rules should be avoided". EU Consumer PIL has several rules, each somehow different from the other. And their 'exceptionality' has not been adequately justified up to date (or, at least, we do not see it). To the contrary, the most recent of the directives dealing with

---

60 Case C-70/03, 9 September 2004, *EC Commission v. Kingdom of Spain*.

consumer protection (Directive 2011/83, on consumer rights) has opted to avoid creating a new PIL applicable law rule and has simply referred applicable law issues, within the scope of application of the Directive, to the Rome I Regulation. This should be the future path to follow in the EU: to centre around RR-I the problem of identifying the law applicable to consumer contracts and to stop incorporating in the domestic legislation of the Member States specific conflict-of laws (or applicable law) rules which are not really necessary (as RR-I itself provides a very satisfactory regime) and sometimes are not a well-executed transposition of the Directives.

In the present situation of dispersion of rules, though, an approach to a correct understanding of how to determine the law (legal rules) applicable to a consumer contract should be based on the following two principles.

The law applicable to consumer contracts should be determined in the first place by the conflict-of-laws rules provided in paragraphs 1 and 2 of article 6 RR-I, when a consumer contract is included within its scope of application. In these situations, the law applicable will be the law of the country (not necessarily an EU Member State) of habitual residence of the consumer (article 6.1) or the law of the country chosen by the parties, unless the latter deprives consumer of the protection granted by the mandatory rules of the law of the country of his habitual residence (article 6.2). On the other hand, the law applicable to consumer contracts not covered by article 6 RR-I should be determined simply by the general rules incorporated in articles 3 (choice) or 4 (absence of choice) RR-I.

If, in accordance with the criteria mentioned above, the law applicable to a consumer contract is the law of a non-EU Member State, the domestic (material) rules of the law of the forum (EU Member State) implementing (correctly) the directives will nevertheless be applicable if they provide better protection to the consumer than the law otherwise applicable to the contract under article 3, 4 or 6 RR-I. This consequence is to be drawn from the special (simple) mandatory nature of the rules implemented in transposition of the directives, which are also PIL applicable law rules (and have to be applied in connection with, but not necessarily in prevalence to, RR-I). But a similar effect could also be obtained, at least partially, through the application of article 3.4 RR-I. In accordance with this article, where all other elements relevant to the situation at the time of the choice are located in one or more Member States (principle of close connection or close link incorporated in the consumer protection directives), the parties' choice of applicable law other than that of a Member State shall not prejudice the application of provisions of EU law, where appropriate as implemented in the Member State of the forum, which cannot be derogated from by agreement (mandatory rules). Clearly, what article 3.4 RR-I mandates is so much in line with what the PIL applicable rules in the consumer protection directives (and in the implemented PIL rules) purport, that we could reasonably wonder if these rules are really necessary (and probably this is the reason explaining the most recent consumer directive does not contain any similar rule). It is true that article 3.4 RR-I only plays this particular role when there is a 'choice' of law and not in those situations where the law applicable is determined through objective connections (articles 6.1 and 4 RR-I). But, on the one hand, the majority of the directives are only applicable, in their own words, when there is a 'choice' of law (at least in a restricted interpretation of this term, which as we mentioned before we do not necessarily share). Therefore, even within this limited framework, the PIL rules in the directives (and in the implemented legislation) would seem to be superfluous in the light of article 3.4 RR-I. And, on the other hand, out of the scope of article 3 (choice), although not everyone is in agreement with this proposition,[61] article 9.2 RR-I could also be called into play if we consider that those implemented (material) consumer protection rules are 'overriding mandatory provisions' and, consequently, must be applied irrespective of the law otherwise applicable to the contract.[62]

---

61   *See* about different positions, Ragno, *supra* note 13, pp.250–253. Interestingly enough, this author also mentions the possibility of recourse to the escape clause in art. 4.3 RR-I if the non-application of article 9.2 should have to be accepted.
62   *See* A. Bonomi, 'Overriding Mandatory Provisions in the Rome I Regulation on the Law Applicable to Contracts', *Yearb. PIL*, 2008, pp. 285–300.

Geo-blocking Regulation: Antitrust or Consumer Protection?

*Klemen Podobnik**

Abstract

The author attempts to show that the seeming absorption[1] of a large-scale, *general*[2] geo-blocking prohibition in the field of competition law (antitrust) is unsystematic, and can negatively influence the further development of European competition law and policy and related goals. The positive implications of the GBR regime in the area of consumer protection law (and for trade regulation as such) are not negated. The author, however, attempts to underscore the fact that, in certain constellations, legislative instruments should be very clearly designated, their nature and scope concisely labelled. Formal oversights, such as omission of clear denominations or even plain wrong designations can – in certain circumstances – lead to functional consequences. For this reason the author stresses the view that the GBR is a legislative instrument of market regulation and consumer protection and has no real appreciable link to antitrust.

Keywords

geo-blocking – European Union – consumer protection – competition law – antitrust – geographic discrimination

1   Introduction

Some while has passed since the date of applicability of Regulation 2018/302,[3] commonly known as the Geo-blocking regulation (hereinafter "the GBR"). The

---

*   PhD (University of Ljubljana), LL.M (Columbia University). Associate Professor at the University of Ljubljana, Faculty of Law.
1   As will be shown in the article, the European Commission tends to characterize the GBR as an instrument of competition law.
2   The term *general* here denotes the character of the GBR, whereby geographic price/non-price discrimination is prohibited *in toto*, i.e. in the total absence of a condition of existence of market power.
3   Regulation (EU) 2018/302 of the European Parliament and of the Council of 28 February 2018 on addressing unjustified geo-blocking and other forms of discrimination based on

fervour and euphoria that prevailed around the time of its adoption have long since subsided. Proponents of the Commission's (uninspired)[4] approach already have new pieces of proposed legislation to shield while critics have slowly ceased their efforts to prove how and where the regulation erred, most probably due to the fact that their pleadings were not listened to in an atmosphere of joy and jubilation over the new regime that was supposed to allow every consumer to buy everything and anything everywhere and anywhere on the Net. Now is clearly the time to be calm and collected and to analyse the measures undertaken by Member States in order to make the regime operational. Have they changed their relevant "material" national legislation (if necessary)? Have they decided on the respective national institutions that are to be entrusted with sanctioning infringements? The most interesting question this analysis should give answers to is undoubtedly: which area of the "law of the market" have the MS identified as the governing or most topically relevant for the issue of geo-blocking (and its prohibition)? These results may also help some lawyers to decide which narrow, delimited, dust-proof dogmatic drawer they should archive the geo-blocking regulation in.

2 Competition Law – Consumer Welfare, Consumer Protection or Public Policies?

The question of the legal nature of the measure analyzed is important not only because the answer can serve as a marker by which the implementing measures of the Member States can be assessed but because – more importantly – it might at least cast a shadow of a doubt over the growing perception that the prohibition of geo-blocking is an antitrust issue.

The author will thus try to convince the reader that the seeming absorption[5] of a large-scale, *general*[6] geo-blocking prohibition into the field of competition law (antitrust) is unsystematic, phenomenologically wrong and can negatively influence the further development of European competition law and policy

---

customers' nationality, place of residence or place of establishment within the internal market and amending Regulations (EC) No 2006/2004 and (EU) 2017/2394 and Directive 2009/22/EC.

4 At least to my mind.
5 As will be shown in the article, the European Commission tends to characterize the GBR as an instrument of competition law.
6 The term *general* here denotes the character of the GBR, whereby geographic price/non-price discrimination is prohibited *in toto*, i.e. even in the total absence of the condition of existence of market power.

and their goals. It must be emphasized that *certain types of* business practices characteristic of different forms of geographic discrimination (be it virtual or real-world) fell under the umbrella of competition even before the introduction and adoption of the GBR. As plainly put by Maduro, Monti and Coelho, "… the prohibitions (…) prohibit the kind of unilateral conduct which is already forbidden when this kind of conduct is part of an agreement between two undertakings, or when the conduct is carried out unilaterally by a dominant undertaking".[7] Consequently, this paper tries to address the question whether the prohibition of geo-blocking (and also the prohibition of refusals to deal based on citizenship or residency) stretching over *non-dominant* single firms really "covers the regulatory gap"[8] and whether the patch used to cover it should be perceived as a competition law instrument. Due to the absence of a set-in-stone perception of competition law in the European Union on the one hand and the importance of its role in the process of European integration on the other, it is extremely difficult to settle for an overarching definition of its goals and objectives. The somewhat sophistic question whether competition and competition law could or should be perceived as goals in themselves or as instruments used to achieve further (more) important goals[9] loses its initial importance if a rational, logical understanding and application of basic economic tenets still remains the first weapon of choice when battling different issues of market failures. Setting aside critique of or praise for the recently fairly popular revival of the so-called populist antitrust (the epithet of the "neo-Brandeis movement"[10] is also widely used, while "hipster antitrust"[11] is perceived more as a slur) in the United States and the more European approach of "competition second, public policies first"[12] (again, a somewhat "populist" perception with a distaste for economic efficiency and welfare

---

[7] M.P. Maduro, G. Monti and G. Coelho, 'The Geo-Blocking Proposal: Internal Market, Competition Law and Regulatory Aspects', IP/A/IMCO/2016-14, 2017, p. 22.

[8] *Id.*

[9] *See e.g.* I. Lianos, 'Some Reflections on the Question of the Goals of EU Competition Law', CLES *Working Paper Series* 3/2013, p. 37.

[10] *Cf.* H.J. Hovenkamp, 'Is Antitrust Consumer Welfare Principle Imperilled?' (2019). *Faculty Scholarship at Penn Law.* 1985.

[11] *Cf.* J.D. Wright, J. Klick, J.M. Rybnicek and E. Dorsey, 'The Dubious Rise and Inevitable Fall of Hipster Antitrust', *Columbia Law School Blog on Corporations and the Capital Markets*, Oct. 2018; *Cf.* J. Wright, A. Portuese, 'Antitrust Populism: Towards a Taxonomy', 25 (1) *Stanford Journal of Law, Business & Finance*, 2020.

[12] *Cf.* A. Witt, 'Public policy goals under EU competition law – now is the time to set the house in order', *University of Leicester School of Law Research Paper* No. 14–0.

standards, largely confrontational especially towards the digital giants[13]), it must be said that there was a timeframe in the history of EU antitrust when – at least declaratorily – the values promoted, standards to be analysed, and goals to be achieved were quite clearly pronounced. After 1999, it was all about consumer welfare; competition and not competitors; freedom of choice; consumer harm as a requirement for anti-competitiveness.[14] If the Commission Guidance Paper on Abusive Exclusionary Conduct seemed to represent the peak of the economic, effects-based approach to antitrust in the EU, the judgment of the Court in *TeliaSonera*[15] could be perceived as signalling the end of that short era.[16] Underscoring yet again that the task of identification of or decision on the ultimate, true, correct standard of competition law is difficult to a fault, a tentative conclusion could be drawn that consumer (and not total) welfare is the most appropriate so far.[17] Regardless of the absence of consensus on the goals and standards of EU competition law, we strongly believe that fundamental economic notions and concepts should be observed and applied. One of those concepts is undoubtedly the absence of any "special responsibility" for non-dominant undertakings as far as their single-firm market behaviour is concerned. We use the term "special responsibility" (or lack thereof), however flawed,[18] to stress the absence of any competition law constraints for

---

13 *Cf.* L. Khan & S. Vaheesan, 'Market power and inequality: The antitrust counterrevolution and its discontents'. 11 *Harv. L. & Pol'y Rev.* (2017) p. 235.
14 *Cf.* N. Kroes, 'Preliminary Thoughts on Policy Review of Article 82': Speech at the Fordham Corporate Law Institute New York, 23rd September 2005;, *Cf.* M. Monti, 'The Future for Competition Policy in the European Union': Address at Merchant Taylor's Hall, London (July 9, 2001) etc.
15 Judgment of the Court of 17 February 2011, *Konkurrensverket* v *TeliaSonera Sverige AB*, C-52/09, EU:C:2011:83.
16 *Cf.* A. Witt, p. 28.
17 This is not to say that we reject the notion of the public policy implications of competition law. As pointed out elsewhere in this paper, the integration process gained momentum and impetus exactly from competition law and policy. We do, however, urge caution in the sense that basic economic tenets must prevail when dealing with questions of restrictive business behaviour. Applying this to the field of merger control, cf. Motta: "… there may well exist instances where public policy considerations could play a role in competition enforcement in general and in merger control in particular, but they should be exceptional, very precisely defined, and taken from a precise set of rules. Above all, they should obey the principle of proportionality – namely, they should achieve the stated objectives and should not go beyond what is necessary to attain them. Allowing anticompetitive mergers are unlikely to pass the test". M. Motta, M. Peitz, 'Competition policy and European firms' competitiveness', <https://voxeu.org/content/competition-policy-and-european-firms-competitiveness>, visited on 10 May 2020.
18 On the consequences of this flawed notion, *see e.g.* Miguel de la Mano, 'The dominance concept: new wine in old bottles', <http://www.justice.gov/atr/public/hearings/single_

non-dominant firms in the ambit of Article 102 TFEU. As will be shown in this paper, the imprudent designation of the GBR as a competition law instrument may result in a dangerous spill-over effect of the spirit of the GBR's prohibition to the field of competition law, thereby dimming the otherwise clear delimitation between firms with and without market power on the one hand, while further limiting the leeway of dominant undertakings on the other. We do not negate the positive implications of the GBR regime for consumers (and for trade regulation as such) but would like to mark the fact that in certain constellations, legislative instruments should be very clearly designated, their nature and scope concisely labelled. Formal oversights, such as omission of clear denominations or even plain wrong designations can – in certain circumstances – lead to functional consequences, which, in the present case might mean a subtle but significant change in the perception of what is and what is not allowed to firms with or without market power especially in the area of discrimination, refusals to deal, and the like. This paper is organized as follows: in the first section, we analyse the atmosphere during the formation and subsequent adoption of the Regulation; the second section briefly outlines the main characteristics of the Regulation; in the third section we outline the implementation methods utilised by the Member States; and in the last section we draw conclusions stemming from the previous sections. The basic idea of the paper is that the perception of the geo-blocking prohibition regulation as an instrument of antitrust (or, better, competition) law can have ambiguous results in certain areas of competition policy in the EU, mainly the issues of price discrimination, refusals to deal (in the ambit of Article 102 TFEU) and vertical restraints in the ambit of Article 101 TFEU.

3 "Today we put an end to unjustified discrimination when shopping online"[19]

And so it came to pass that in November of 2017 the "European Parliament, the Council and the Commission (…) delivered on commitments made during September's Digital Summit in Tallinn"[20] by delivering the European consumer body of the wretched plague called geo-blocking. The decision was firm, as

---

firm/docs/222012.htm>. , visited on 10 May 2020: "Ultimately proof of dominance was almost sufficient to establish an abuse (the special responsibility doctrine)".

19 Vice-President Andrus Ansip, responsible for the Digital Single Market, Brussels, 20 November 2017.

20 <http://europa.eu/rapid/press-release_IP-17-4781_en.htm>, visited on 10 May 2020.

the EU institutions had to stand by their promise that, by Christmas the following year, Europeans would be able to buy "their new furniture online, book hotel rooms or use their credit card across borders, like at home..."[21] The language of public statements was triumphant, yet somewhat military-sounding, which is most excellently illustrated by the example of usage of the promise of "next Christmas", most certainly just a nod to the highest-in-year shopping season but still bearing an unfortunate connotation to many broken promises as to the victorious end of hostilities in the previous century. Despite the declared reasons and goals behind this legislative impetus, one cannot draw a conclusion but that pinpointing the ever-present notion of the single (digital) market is one of its underlying motives. It most probably would not be a mistake to claim that achieving a single digital market is an object in itself and the effort to attain it could therefore result in a disregard of certain (economic) rationales. This also holds true as far as other types of market integration objectives are concerned.[22] The other area of Commission policy most affected by the aforementioned market failures is certainly the one dealing with consumers. It is not surprising, then, that the final report of the Commission's so-called Geo-blocking Study[23] was commissioned by DG Justice and Consumers and that the Directorate-General responsible for the Proposal for the Geo-blocking Regulation[24] was DG Connect. Judging from the contents of the *travaux préparatoires* (chiefly the above mentioned Geoblocking study), the Commission's paramount objective was to achieve consolidation and unification of the digital marketplace. Artificial barriers, set up by traders themselves, non-existent in a "virtual" web world, were to be torn down, and consumers were to be free(d) as to their decision regarding the internet trader (supplier) and website they chose to do business with. It all seemed very similar to the underlying notion of the 2006 Services Directive.[25] The tenet of "thou shalt not discriminate"

---

21 Commissioner Mariya Gabriel, in charge of the Digital Economy and Society, Brussels, 20 November 2017.
22 Think of the treatment of vertical restraints before the reform, and mainly the issue of non-price and price discrimination by firms with market power, and certain other types of exclusionary behaviour.
23 Mystery shopping survey on territorial restrictions and geo-blocking in the European Digital Single Market (Final Report), Brussels 2016 (Prepared for the Commission by GfK Belgium).
24 Proposal for a regulation of the European Parliament and of the Council on addressing geo-blocking and other forms of discrimination based on customers' nationality, place of residence or place of establishment within the internal market and amending Regulation (EC) No 2006/2004 and Directive 2009/22/EC, COM(2016) 289 final.
25 Directive 2006/123/EC of the European Parliament and of the Council of 12 December 2006 on services in the internal market.

on the basis of citizenship or place of residence had to be applied to the non-spatial world of the digital and the internet (where, due to the intrinsic characteristics of the technology, such discrimination was elementary to achieve and, indeed, had much more effect and importance than in the "real" world).[26] Generally, the issue of having to decide whether to (non-price or price) discriminate between one's customers on the basis of their residence or citizenship was practically moot in the in-store, "real-world" retail of small consumer goods or personal services. It was all but unfathomable to envisage a consumer from Slovenia travelling to Denmark to buy a pair of headphones because they were not offered in Ljubljana or because they were 6 EUR cheaper in Copenhagen. This, of course, changed at the exact moment that consumers were able to "travel" to a different geographical market with the help of their smartphone while taking a bus to their graduate consumer protection law class. Bluntly put, the instruments of potential differentiation (or discrimination) between consumers were (and are) the same in both the real and the virtual marketplace, the only difference being that the volume of cross-border transactions in the physical marketplace (especially in the market for small personal consumer goods) was probably too low to allow identification of (almost) general, methodical, pervasive discrimination on the basis of a customer's citizenship or residence. As the issue was much more pressing in the area of cross-border supply of services, the Services Directive was adopted in 2006, aimed at expunging the practice of discrimination on the basis of citizenship (and residence). Stopping just short of enshrining a duty to deal as a tenet of internal market/consumer protection law, Article 20 of the Directive prohibits various types of discriminatory business practices (based on citizenship or residence) by service providers. The Services Directive thus heralded the beginning of the fight against unequal treatment of consumers by *service providers*.[27] Unequal treatment was not deemed illegal if based on objective justifications (justified by objective criteria). Interpretation of the breadth and depth of such justifications was primarily set forth by the legislator itself, providing for a very wide understanding of the standard in Recital 95 of the Directive.[28]

---

26 Especially true as regards the issue of so-called "passive sales".
27 In contrast to the well-established concept of prohibition of discrimination of EU citizens by Member States in Art. 18 of the TFEU.
28 "The principle of non-discrimination within the internal market means that access by a recipient, and especially by a consumer, to a service on offer to the public may not be denied or restricted by application of a criterion, included in general conditions made available to the public, relating to the recipient's nationality or place of residence. It does not follow that it will be unlawful discrimination if provision were made in such general conditions for different tariffs and conditions to apply to the provision of a service, where those tariffs, prices and conditions are justified for objective reasons that can vary from

We want to especially underscore the recognition of market conditions as a potentially objective justification for differentiated treatment of service consumers *even* on the basis of their citizenship or residence. Service providers are therefore allowed unequal treatment when approaching unequal situations caused by market realities (such as seasonality, lower or higher demand, competition, and so on, as non-exhaustively cited by Recital 95).

4 A Measure of Consumer Protection and Market Regulation?

As already pointed out at the outset of this article, digital era technology and ensuing new business models (mainly web commerce) enabled service (and goods) providers to erect artificial barriers between different geographic markets, introduce price differentiation and efficiently prevent arbitrage, thus optimizing their pricing policies throughout the Union. Such business behaviour is certainly not nefarious as such, especially in the absence of market power. But we diverge here into the world of microeconomics and competition (antitrust) law, an area of law and policy not frequently mentioned during the time leading to adoption of the GBR. As pointed out earlier, a brief analysis of the *travaux préparatoires* and also of the public statements issued just before or at adoption of the GBR, shows that the main aim of the legislative effort was to curtail (or extinguish) activities of traders perceived as *unequal treatment* of consumers based on citizenship or place of residence. True, all of the examples of such business practices can also be detected in antitrust law – some of them deemed legal, some not; however, at the outset of the legislative process any particular antitrust issues were obviously off the table. Logically, although such business practices may *prima facie* be seen as restrictive (exclusionary refusals to supply, certain types of price and non-price discrimination, RPM schemes) they cannot be deemed as such if lacking certain anti-competitive characteristics, that is, market power (for single-firm dominance claims) or the existence of an agreement (for vertical restraints). As far as competition law is concerned, unequal treatment of a single firm's consumers may (in specific circumstances) be deemed illegal only if the existence of a firm's market power

country to country, such as additional costs incurred because of the distance involved or the technical characteristics of the provision of the service, *or different market conditions, such as higher or lower demand influenced by seasonality, different vacation periods in the Member States and pricing by different competitors, or extra risks linked to rules differing from those of the Member State of establishment.* Neither does it follow that the non-provision of a service to a consumer for lack of the required intellectual property rights in a particular territory would constitute unlawful discrimination". (Emphasis added by the author.)

is beyond doubt.[29] Looking at the basic economic tenets (of antitrust), one has to underscore that especially the practice of price discrimination is not necessarily always perceived as negative.[30] Risking a firm knee-jerk reaction from hard-line legalists, one might claim that even, under conditions of market power, price and non-price discrimination of a dominant firm's final consumers can never be deemed an abuse of dominance, as Article 102 TFEU contains no provision prohibiting such behaviour. Charging different prices for the same goods and services or "applying dissimilar conditions to similar transactions", in theory better known as second-line discrimination, can be seen as anticompetitive only when a dominant firm discriminates between its trading partners, namely, undertakings which are in competition with one another. Despite some well-founded theoretical opinions opposing such a view,[31] I wholeheartedly concur with those[32] who omit (final) consumers from the ambit of the term "trading parties".

5   GBR – Antitrust Legislation?

During the period between adoption of the Regulation and especially after the start date of its application, it seemed as if the Regulation's legal nature had been modified incrementally. What was clearly a legal instrument of consumer protection law at the outset now began to slowly morph into competition law legislation. This modification came about as a consequence of multiple non-aligned factors. Firstly, there appeared articles on the topic of the single digital market, some focused on the GBR, some merely observing its existence. These articles and notes were usually published by European law firms on their websites. The confusing part of these posts is, above all, the fact that they were unmistakably listed under these website's "competition" sub/page or even as part of the website's competition "newsletter". Furthermore, the published

---

29   The existence of market power tantamount to a *dominant position* is, of course, a prerequisite for all types of violation of Art. 102 TFEU.

30   *Cf.* T.P. Gehrig and R. Stenbacka, 'Price discrimination, competition and antitrust in the Pros and Cons of price discrimination', p. 134, Konkurrensverket 2005, <http://www.konkurrensverket.se/globalassets/english/research/the-pros-and-cons-of-price-discrimination-9356kb.pdf>, visited on 10 May 2020.

31   *Cf.* P. Akman, 'To Abuse, or not to Abuse: Discrimination between Consumers', CCP *Working Paper* 06-18, <http://competitionpolicy.ac.uk/documents/8158338/8256117/CCP+Working+Paper+06-18.pdf>, visited on 10 May 2020.

32   *Cf.* J. Temple Lang, 'Anticompetitive non-pricing abuses under European and national antitrust law', in B. Hawk (ed.), *International Antitrust Law & Policy* (Fordham Corporate Law 2003) p. 245 *et seq.*

material more than hinted at the conclusion of the competition-law nature of the regime set forth by the GBR despite the fact that some of the posts also included short memos of the Commission proceedings against undertakings that would undoubtedly have taken place in the absence of the GBR. A case in point is the reporting on the Commission's procedure against Nike. A prominent European law firm's website includes a report on the Commission's fine of 12.5 million EUR on Nike for restricting cross-border sales of football merchandising products in breach of Article 101 TFEU, confusingly linking it to the GBR and its regime. One should note that this procedure opened with the beginning of a formal investigation into Nike's practices (vertical restraints – restricting cross-border sales by licensees, and the like) in 2017, almost a year before the GBR was even adopted, let alone applicable. It is true that the Commission's procedure was in the ambit of competition law, but had nothing to do with the GBR itself. Similarly wrong was the perception of the Commission's *Guess?* Decision,[33] where there were many reports describing a vanilla-type vertical restraint procedure as if governed by the GBR.

In all fairness one must admit that the Commission's own official press report explicitly links the *Guess?* decision[34] with the GBR despite the fact, already mentioned, that the proceedings began a while before adoption of the regulation and that the text of the decision does not even refer to the GBR. This is comprehensible, as the Commission of course has no jurisdiction in the field of enforcing the GBR regime as this question is left for the Member States to address in the GBR implementation process. Such practices have probably sent (the wrong) signals around the legal community and – especially to those unfamiliar with the intricacies of competition law – made it "clear" that the GBR is to be perceived as an instrument of competition law and policy.

6   Member States See It as It Is

On the flipside, implementation of the regulation regime in the Member States unravelled in a different, more rational way. Although the hazard of an incorrect "antitrust" perception of the GBR was appreciable due to the actions described above, the Member States recognized this piece of secondary EU

---

33   Case AT.40428, Commission Decision of 17. 12. 2018.
34   The Press release (<http://europa.eu/rapid/press-release_IP-18-6844_en.htm>, visited on 10 May 2020) includes Commissioner Vestager's statement explaining the basics of the decision and adding that the case: "complements the geo-blocking rules that entered into force on 3 December – both address the issue of sales restrictions that are at odds with the Single Market".

legislation for what it actually is – a measure of internal market and consumer protection law – and also reacted accordingly. A brief analysis of the implementation measures (as available on the Commission's Geo-blocking website[35]) shows that the Member States implemented the regime of the GBR mostly by either adopting new legislative acts (on rare occasions) or by way of amendments to their pre-existing legislation. The conclusion that the GBR has been recognized as a piece of legislation aimed at consumer protection or market (trade) regulation is thus corroborated by the place and manner of implementation, as only exceptionally was the implementing act from the field of competition law. A very similar pattern can also be observed concerning the question of enforcement. The majority of the Member States entrusted their existing consumer protection authorities with powers to enforce the GBR regime, others decided for a broader approach by appointing generalist regulatory agencies,[36] while only certain Member States resolved to describe their competition authorities[37] as enforcement bodies. This, of course, is good news. The idea that the GBR is to be perceived as a legislative instrument of competition law might have undesirable consequences for the whole field of antitrust in the European Union.

7 Why Should We Be Careful with Designations?

As already explained elsewhere in this article, some of the GBR's conceptual foundations run counter to the basic tenets of competition law. Take the issue of treatment of online operators with no market power and no vertical distribution schemes – should they opt to "price discriminate" or refuse to enter into transactions with individuals on the basis of their citizenship (unilateral action), they will be fined by the national authorities designated as enforcement bodies for the GBR. There most certainly is no dispute with such a result as long as it is clear that in such circumstances (that is, absence of market power) competition law enforcement would not have been triggered. However, if the GBR and its regime are to be perceived as an instrument of competition law, such a conclusion is no longer very apparent. What is therefore really problematic in these circumstances is the issue of potential "spill-over" or "contagion" of competition law by the new GBR regime. Why might this be problematic?

---

35 <https://ec.europa.eu/digital-single-market/en/geo-blocking-digital-single-market>, visited on 10 May 2020.
36 *Cf.* Germany and its Bundesnetzagentur.
37 Italy, Austria, Ireland and the United Kingdom.

Looking (not only) from the American perspective, European antitrust is sometimes perceived as suffering from absence of the application of economic theory and, to an extent, sacrificing true antitrust goals for the attainment of other, political, objectives.[38] The task of achieving even a partial compromise on the absolutely "correct" goals of competition law is in all probability Utopian, and it is therefore difficult to claim that certain antitrust concepts are better than others. It is true, however, that until the late nineties of the previous century, EU competition law successfully resisted the notion of economic theory playing a major role. It was especially in the areas of vertical restraints,[39] dominance (predation and refusal to deal, special responsibility of dominant firms) and also certain general concepts (such as foreclosure, efficiency defence) that economic theory was sorely missed. The twenty-first century initially signalled a new path for EU competition law. What had started in the nineties with the application of economics to the analysis of vertical restraints was to be continued in the area of dominance with the adoption of Guidance on enforcement priorities in applying Article 82 TEC.[40] The Commission was announcing changes in its approach to certain types of previously vilified "restrictive" unilateral behaviour, especially refusals to deal and certain other practices viewed as exclusionary by the Commission and the Court. The Guidance generally promoted the standard of consumer benefit as the only relevant standard for assessment of exclusionary abuses. A new form of assessment of exclusionary practices could be identified in the Communication, one that

---

38   It should be pointed out that the historical origins of US and EU antitrust most certainly differ greatly, which is one of the reasons behind the great divide between the two important competition law jurisdictions.

39   It took European competition law over forty years to adhere to the economic logic stating that certain vertical restraints affecting intra-brand competition intensify inter-brand competition. *Cf.* L. Peeperkorn, 'The Economics of Verticals', Competition Policy Newsletter 1998 – number 2 – June, <http://ec.europa.eu/competition/speeches/text/sp1998_020_en.html>, visited on 10 May 2020. Unfortunately, even after reform of the verticals, some issues remained unresolved or distant from modern economic concepts. When compared to US antitrust, the one area that stands out is the per se illegality of RPM schemes. While in the US the Supreme Court has set aside almost a century-old approach (*Dr. Miles Medical Co.* v. *John D. Park & Sons Co.*, 220 U.S. 373 (1911)) and opted for a rule of reason test of RPM schemes in *Leegin* (*Leegin Creative Leather Products, Inc.* v. *PSKS, Inc.*, 551 U.S. 877 (2007), the Commission, despite declaring that some RPM schemes could fall under the exception of Art. 101/3 TFEU, actually remains steadfast on its course of per se illegality. *Cf.* F. Amato, RPM in the European Union: Any Developments Since Leegin?, *Competition Policy International* 2013.

40   Communication from the Commission – Guidance on the Commission's enforcement priorities in applying Article 82 of the EC Treaty to abusive exclusionary conduct by dominant undertakings, (2009/C 45/02).

actually (at least *prima facie*) fulfilled the commitment to an effects-based approach coupled with economic theory. According to the wording of the Guidance, pricing abuses were only abusive if resulting in consumer harm. In addition, the concept of foreclosure as a constituent element of abuse was also updated so as to include the necessity for consumer harm.[41] It seemed as if the Commission actually moved away from the erroneous syllogistic equation that associated any restriction of access by competitors (actual or potential) to the market with harm to consumers. Unfortunately, the Commission's approach to (and more importantly the Court of Justice's dealing with) the above mentioned types of abuse, namely price predation,[42] refusals to deal[43] and, above all, the "artificial" stand-alone abuse of margin squeeze,[44] speak volumes about the on-going evasion of a real effects-based, economic approach to certain areas of dominance (not to mention the verticals and mergers) of European competition law. Arguably, the most strongly criticised concept is undoubtedly the notion of protecting competitors and their position and/or entry to the market and, as a consequence, procedures and fines against efficient, successful undertakings with a dominant position for business practices that cause no harm to consumers or competition, but are hazardous for their (sometimes also incompetent) competitors.

---

[41] "In this document the term 'anti-competitive foreclosure' is used to describe a situation where effective access of actual or potential competitors to supplies or markets is hampered or eliminated as a result of the conduct of the dominant undertaking whereby the dominant undertaking is likely to be in a position to profitably increase prices to the detriment of consumers"., Guidance, para. 19.

[42] No proof of recoupment by the dominant firm is necessary to allege predation in EU competition law, as we still stick with protecting competitors. This formalistic approach to the issue of predatory pricing can best be seen in the CJEU judgment in the *Wanadoo* case (Judgment of 2 April 2009, Case C 202/07 *France Télécom v Commission*, EU:C:2009:214). *Cf.* A. Emch and G.K. Leonard, 'Predatory Pricing after linkLine and Wanadoo', *Global Competition Policy*, May 2009. One of the latest examples of the EU approach to predation can be observed in the Commission's decision AT.39711 – *Qualcomm*.

[43] Where the concept of "anticompetitive intent" still plays an important role. For an outstanding critical evaluation of such an approach in the United States, see Judge Posner's assessment of "intent" in competition in the *Olympia* case: "We add, what has become an antitrust commonplace, that if conduct is not objectively anticompetitive the fact that it was motivated by hostility to competitors is irrelevant. Such inferences would be possible in antitrust cases if the purpose of antitrust law were to protect the prosperity or solvency (...) of competitors, but it is not". *Olympia Equipment Leasing Company Alfco v. Western Union Telegraph*, 797 F. 2d 370, 1986.

[44] Whereby the Court in *TeliaSonera* adopted an approach foreign to any economic theory of antitrust, as it declared the objective necessity of input was not a prerequisite for a stand-alone abuse of margin squeeze.

In the light of these findings, the already mentioned "spill-over" or "contagion" of European antitrust with the notions included in the GBR would be extremely precarious. If the concept, strongly embedded in the GBR, that undertakings with no market power are prohibited from any real price discrimination (the GBR's regime allowing for price discrimination, but prohibiting the prevention of arbitrage results in price differentiation being *de facto* prohibited) should trickle into EU competition law because of the above-analyzed incorrect perception of the GBR being an antitrust measure, it may further confuse the already murky waters of first-line and secondary-line price (and non-price) discrimination. An even more dangerous proposition that might come to life as a by-product of wrong designation of the GBR would be the idea that, even in the absence of market power, undertakings have a duty to enter into transactions not only with their customers, but perhaps also with their competitors. This could additionally limit companies' freedom to contract and essentially eliminate the possibility for a successful defence of a refusal to deal.

I therefore hope that the GBR regime, however flawed it may be[45] and whatever success it will have, will lead its life independently, separate from EU (and Member States') competition law. We must thus always try to underscore that the GBR is a legislative instrument of market regulation and consumer protection and has no real appreciable link to antitrust. According to analysis of their implementation measures, the Member States predominantly share this view, so the real concern remains with the Commission.

---

45 One could predict that, in certain situations, the reaction of online traders to a *de facto* prohibition of price discrimination will be to adopt a uniform price policy, whereby the price will be the highest they were able to charge before the adoption of GBR. This conclusion follows simple economic logic: if a trader determines that it is better off losing some clients with lower buyer power and serving only high buyer-power clients, the uniform price will be too high for so-called low valuation customers. *Cf.* A. Perot, 'Towards an effects-based approach of price discrimination', *The Pros and Cons of Price Discrimination*, Konkurrensverket, 2005, <http://www.konkurrensverket.se/globalassets/english/research/the-pros-and-cons-of-price-discrimination-9356kb.pdf>, visited on 10 May 2020.

Elements of Practices of the Baltic States in International Law

Republic of Estonia Materials of International Law 2017–2018

*Edited by René Värk**

[*Editorial Notes*[1]

1. Republic of Estonia Materials on International Law 2016 (REMIL 2016) have been classified according to the Recommendation (97)11 of 12 June 1997 of the Committee of Ministers of Council of Europe, as applied by the British Yearbook of International Law from the year 1997, with certain minor amendments.
2. The REMIL mostly concern opinions issued by Estonian institutions and officials. If not expressly stated otherwise, the institutions and officials mentioned in the REMIL are those of Estonia. Often, different officials express views on the same issues. In order to prevent undue repetition, the editor has selected materials from the highest possible level. Some materials are quoted at length due to their importance or because they provide useful insights into relevant aspects of Estonian history, politics and geopolitical concerns, and the like.
3. There were several recurring topics in the speeches given and statements made by officials, for example, cyber issues, human rights, migration, on-line freedom of expression, the conflict in Ukraine, and an unpredictable Russia. In many cases, nothing new was added compared to the speeches and statements of previous years, so the editor has not included them or has limited their inclusion in the materials.
4. The European Court of Human Rights handed down six judgments on the merits against Estonia and found violations in two cases. The violations concerned Articles 6 and 8. Six applications were declared inadmissible or struck out of the list.]

---

* Dr iur; Associate Professor of International Law at the School of Law, University of Tartu, Estonia; Legal Advisor at the Estonian Defence Forces.
1 The editor has compiled the state practice report in a private capacity. Research and writing were supported by the grant PRG969 from the Estonian Research Council.

1   **Index**[2]

Part One: International Law in general
I. Nature, basis, purpose
    A. In general
    B. *Jus cogens*
    C. Soft law
II. History

Part Two: Sources and Codification of International Law

I. Sources of international law
    A. Treaties
    B. Custom
    C. General principles of law
    D. Unilateral acts, including acts and decisions of international organisations and conferences
    E. Judicial decisions
    F. Opinions of writers
    G. Equity
    H. Comity (*comitas gentium*)
II. Codification and progressive development of international law

Part Three: The Law of Treaties

I. Definition, conclusion and entry into force of treaties
    A. Definition
    B. Conclusion, including signature, ratification, and accession
    C. Reservations, declarations, and objections
    D. Provisional application and entry into force
II. Observance, application, and interpretation of treaties
    A. Observance of treaties
    B. Application of treaties
    C. Interpretation of treaties
    D. Treaties and third States
III. Amendment and modification, derogation
IV. Invalidity, termination and suspension of the operation
    A. General rules
    B. Invalidity

---

[2] The Baltic Yearbook provides the Index for State practice reports only in front of the first State report – Ed.

C. Termination and suspension of operation, denunciation, and withdrawal
  D. Procedure
  E. Consequences of invalidity, termination, or suspension of operation
V. State succession in respect of treaties (see Part Five)
VI. Depositaries, notifications, corrections, and registration
VII. Consensual arrangements other than treaties

Part Four: Relationship between International Law and Internal Law

I. In General
II. Application and implementation of international law in internal law
III. Remedies under internal law for violations of international law

Part Five: Subjects of International Law

I. States
  A. Status and powers
    1. Personality
    2. Sovereignty and independence
    3. Non-intervention
    4. Domestic jurisdiction
    5. Equality of States
    6. State immunity
    7. Other powers, including treaty-making power
  B. Recognition
    1. Recognition of States
    2. Recognition of governments
    3. Types of recognition
      (a) *de facto/de jure*
      (b) conditional/unconditional
    4. Acts of recognition
      (a) implied/express
      (b) collective/unilateral
    5. Effects of recognition
    6. Non-recognition (including non-recognition of governments) and its effects
    7. Withdrawal of recognition
  C. Types of States
    1. Unitary states
    2. Personal and real unions
    3. Protected States

D. Formation, identity, continuity, extinction, and succession of States
   1. Conditions for statehood
   2. Formation
   3. Identity and continuity
   4. Extinction
   5. Succession
      (a) Situations of State succession
         (i) Union with or without the demise of the predecessor State
         (ii) Dismemberment
         (iii) Separation
         (iv) Newly independent States
      (b) Effects of State succession
         (i) Territory and other areas under national jurisdiction
         (ii) Nationality
         (iii) Succession in respect of treaties
         (iv) Archives
         (v) Debts
         (vi) Property
         (vii) Responsibility
         (viii) Other rights and obligations

II. International organisations
   A. In general
      1. Status and powers
         (a) Personality
         (b) Privileges and immunities of the organisation
         (c) Powers, including treaty-making power
      2. Participation of States and international organisations in international organisations and in their activities
         (a) Admission
         (b) Suspension, withdrawal, expulsion, and deportation
         (c) Obligations of membership
         (d) Representation of States and international organisations to international organisations, including privileges and immunities
      3. Legal effect of the acts of international organisations
      4. Personnel of international organisations
      5. Responsibility of international organisations (see Part Thirteen)
      6. Succession of international organisations
   B. Particular types
      1. Universal organisations

      2. Regional organisations
      3. Organisations constituting integrated (e.g. economic) communities
      4. Other types
III. The Holy See
IV. Other subjects of international law and other entities or groups
    A. Mandated and trust territories
    B. Dependent territories
    C. Special regimes
    D. Insurgents
    E. Belligerents
    F. Others (indigenous people, minorities, national liberation movements, etc.)

Part Six: The Position of the Individual (including the Corporation) in International Law

I. Nationality
II. Diplomatic and consular protection (see Part Thirteen)
III. Aliens
IV. Members of minorities
V. Stateless persons
VI. Refugees
VII. Immigration and emigration, extradition, expulsion, asylum
    A. Immigration and emigration
    B. Extradition
    C. Expulsion
    D. Asylum
VIII. Human rights and fundamental freedoms
    A. General concept
    B. Under United Nations treaty system
    C. Under the Council of Europe treaty system
    D. Other aspects of human rights and fundamental freedoms
IX. Crimes under international law
X. Responsibility of the individual (see Part Thirteen)

Part Seven: Organs of the State and their Status

I. Heads of State
II. Ministers
III. Other organs of the State

IV. Diplomatic missions and their members
V. Consulates and their members
VI. Special missions
VII. Trade and information offices, trade delegations, etc.
VIII. Armed forces
IX. Protecting powers

Part Eight: Jurisdiction of the State

I. Bases of jurisdiction
    A. Territorial principle
    B. Personal principle
    C. Protective principle
    D. Universality principle
    E. Other bases
II. Types of jurisdiction
    A. Jurisdiction to prescribe
    B. Jurisdiction to adjudicate
    C. Jurisdiction to enforce
III. Extra-territorial exercise of jurisdiction
    A. General
    B. Consular jurisdiction
    C. Jurisdiction over military personnel abroad
    D. Other (artificial islands, *terrae nullius*, etc.)
IV. Limitations upon jurisdiction (servitudes, leases, etc.)
V. Concurrent jurisdiction

Part Nine: State Territory

I. Territory
    A. Elements of territory
        1. Land, internal waters, lakes, rivers, and land-locked seas (see also Parts Ten and Eleven)
        2. Sub-soil
        3. Territorial sea (see Part Eleven)
        4. Airspace (see Part Twelve)
    B. Good neighbourliness
II. Boundaries and frontiers
    A. Delimitation
    B. Demarcation

C. Stability
III. Acquisition and transfer of territory
    A. Acquisition
    B. Transfer

Part Ten: International Watercourses

I. Rivers and lakes
    A. Definition
    B. Navigation
    C. Uses for purposes other than navigation
    D. Protection of the environment
    E. Institutional aspects
II. Groundwaters
III. Canals

Part Eleven: Seas and Vessels

I. Internal waters, including ports and bays
II. Territorial sea
III. Straits
IV. Archipelagic waters
V. Contiguous zone
VI. Exclusive economic zone, exclusive or preferential fisheries zones
VII. Continental shelf
VIII. High seas
    A. Freedoms of the high seas, including overflight
    B. Visit and search
    C. Hot pursuit
    D. Piracy
    E. Conservation of living resources
IX. Islands, rocks and low-tide elevations
X. Enclosed and semi-enclosed seas
XI. International sea bed area
XII. Land-locked and geographically disadvantaged States
XIII. Protection of the marine environment
XIV. Marine scientific research
XV. Cables and pipelines
XVI. Artificial islands, installations, and structures
XVII. Tunnels

XVIII. Vessels
- A. Legal regime
    1. Warships
    2. Public vessels other than warships
    3. Merchant vessels
- B. Nationality
- C. Jurisdiction over vessels
    1. Flag State
    2. Coastal State
    3. Port State
    4. Other exercises of jurisdiction

Part Twelve: Airspace, Outer Space, and Antarctica

I. Airspace
- A. Status
- B. Uses
- C. Legal regime of aircraft

II. Outer space and celestial bodies
- A. Status and limits
- B. Uses
- C. Legal regime of spacecraft

III. Antarctica
- A. Limits and status
- B. Uses
- C. Protection of the environment

Part Thirteen: International Responsibility

I. General concept

II. General issues of international responsibility
- A. The elements of responsibility (such as wrongfulness of the act, imputability)
- B. Factors excluding responsibility (self-defence, necessity, reprisals)
- C. Procedure
    1. Diplomatic protection
        (a) Nationality of claims
        (b) Exhaustion of local remedies
    2. Consular protection
    3. Peaceful settlement of disputes (see Part Fourteen)
- D. Consequences of responsibility (*restitutio in integrum*, damages, satisfaction, guarantees)

III. Responsible entities
- A. States
- B. International organisations
- C. Entities other than States and international organisations
- D. Individuals and groups of individuals (including corporations)

Part Fourteen: Peaceful Settlement of Disputes

I. The concept of an international dispute
II. Means of settlement
- A. Negotiations and consultations
- B. Good offices
- C. Enquiry (fact-finding)
- D. Mediation
- E. Conciliation
- F. Arbitration
    1. Arbitral tribunals and commissions
    2. Permanent Court of Arbitration
- G. Judicial settlement
    1. International Court of Justice
    2. Other courts and tribunals
- H. Settlement within international organisations
    1. United Nations
    2. Other organisations

I. Other means of settlement

Part Fifteen: Coercive Measures Short of the Use of Force

I. Unilateral measures
- A. Retorsion
- B. Counter-measures
- C. Pacific blockade
- D. Intervention (see also Part Five)
- E. Other unilateral measures

II. Collective measures
- A. United Nations
- B. Outside the United Nations

Part Sixteen: Use of Force

I. Prohibition of the use of force
II. Legitimate use of force

A. Self-defence
B. Collective measures
    1. United Nations
    2. Outside the United Nations
C. Others
III. Use of disarmament and arms control

Part Seventeen: The Law of Armed Conflict and International Humanitarian Law

I. International armed conflict
    A. Definition
    B. The law of international armed conflict
        1. Sources
        2. The commencement of international armed conflict and its effects (e.g. diplomatic and consular relations, treaties, private property, nationality, trading with the enemy, *locus standi personae in judicio*)
        3. Land warfare
        4. Sea warfare
        5. Air warfare
        6. Distinction between combatants and non-combatants
        7. International humanitarian law
        8. Belligerent occupation
        9. Conventional, nuclear, bacteriological, and chemical weapons
        10. Treaty relations between combatants (cartels, armistices, etc.)
        11. Termination of international armed conflict, treaties of peace
II. Non-international armed conflict

Part Eighteen: Neutrality and Non-Belligerency

I. The laws of neutrality
    A. Land warfare
    B. Sea warfare
    C. Air warfare
II. Permanent neutrality
III. Neutrality in the light of the United Nations Charter
IV. Policy of neutrality and non-alignment
V. Non-belligerency

Part Nineteen: Legal Aspects of International Relations and Co-operation in Particular Matters

I. General economic and financial matters
    A. Trade
    B. Loans
    C. Investments
    D. Taxes
    E. Monetary matters
    F. Development
II. Transport and communications
III. Environment
IV. Natural resources
V. Technology
VI. Social and health matters
VII. Cultural matters
VIII. Legal matters (e.g. judicial assistance, crime control, etc.)
IX. Military and security matters

Part Five: I.D. 3. Subjects of International Law – States – Formation, identity, continuity, extinction, and succession of States – Identity and continuity

5/1

On 22 August 2018, the Ministry of Foreign Affairs celebrated its 100th anniversary. The Ministry has been active without recess for 100 years and is the only government institution that did not cease to exist during the Soviet occupation. After 1940 some Estonian foreign representations continued to operate in countries that refused to recognize the occupation by annexation of Estonia by the Soviet Union. The Consulate General in New York remained open under the helm of Johannes Kaiv and later Ernst Jaakson until Estonia restored its independence in 1991. One notable instance from this period was the Apollo lunar landing in summer 1969 – together with messages from other countries, the spacecraft carried a statement by Jaakson on behalf of the Republic of Estonia. The Estonian Embassy in London remained active until 1989 and was reopened after Estonia restored its independence.

(Available at the website of the Ministry of Foreign Affairs, <https://vm.ee/en/news/foreign-minister-mikser-100th-anniversary-ministry-foreign-affairs-estonias-diplomats-are-0>, visited on 31 December 2019)

Part Five: IV. F. Subjects of International Law – Other subjects of international law and other entities or groups – Others (indigenous people, minorities, national liberation movements, etc.)

5/2
On 2 October 2017, Foreign Minister Sven Mikser took a position on the issue of Catalonia in connection with the independence referendum.

> The European Union is undoubtedly keeping a watchful eye on developments. Both Estonia and the European Union support the territorial integrity of Spain. It is critical that all political processes take place in a democratic and peaceful manner. The Catalonian referendum constitutes Spain's internal matter, and as such it must be resolved on the basis of Spanish law.
>
> We expect that Spain's constitutional order be maintained without violence. The current situation is certainly a cause for concern, and the Spanish authorities must do their part to consider what kinds of measures are necessary to ensure order. I hope that the parties will find an opportunity for dialogue in the coming days.

(Available at the website of the Ministry of Foreign Affairs, <https://vm.ee/en/news/position-foreign-minister-sven-mikser-issue-catalonia>, visited on 31 December 2019)

5/3
On 24 October 2017, the *Riigikogu* (the Parliament) issued a statement on the Iraqi Kurdistan Independence Referendum of 25 September 2017.

> Recalling that:
>
> - the right of self-determination of peoples' upon which the Republic of Estonia was founded in 1918, is a cardinal principle of international law that continues to be in force through the Charter of the United Nations;
> - the Republic of Estonia respects the principle of territorial integrity;
> - the borders of states can only be changed peacefully, through democratic, free and fair expression of will of people;
> - in 1920 the participant countries in World War I signed the Treaty of Sèvres under which they recognized the right of the Kurdish people to a self-determination referendum.

- that the Republic of Estonia, represented by General Johan Laidoner, Chairman of the League of Nations Committee, participated in determining the existing state border of Iraq;
- the Republic of Estonia has suffered 20 casualties as killed or wounded in defending the democracy of Iraq since 2003;
- the Republic of Estonia always strives for peaceful resolution of conflicts;

the *Riigikogu*, the Parliament of the Republic of Estonia:

1. Affirms that it respects the territorial integrity of the Republic of Iraq, as long as preserving it will not bring along violent suppression of the human and political rights of the Kurdish minority in Iraq;
2. Understands the legitimate aspirations of the Kurdish people in exercising their right to national self-determination;
3. Invites all parties to maintain a peaceful, transparent, democratic and mutually respectful attitude after the Iraqi Kurdistan independence referendum;
4. Calls upon all countries of the region not to interfere with the internal affairs of the Republic of Iraq;
5. Calls upon the Government of the Republic of Iraq and the Government of the Kurdish Autonomous Region, in the post-referendum situation, to solve the question of the status of Iraqi Kurdistan through negotiations
6. Expresses hope that the Iraqi Kurdistan independence referendum of 25 September will be a step in nonviolent resolution of the status of the Kurdish minority in Iraq by reconciling the right to self-determination and the principle of territorial integrity.

(Available at the website of the *Riigikogu*, <https://www.riigikogu.ee/wpcms/wp-content/uploads/2017/10/Statement-of-the-Riigikogu-On-Iraqi-Kurdistan-Independence-Referendum-PDF-76-kB.pdf>, visited on 31 December 2019)

Part Six: VII. A. The Position of the Individual (including the Corporation) in International Law – Immigration and emigration, extradition, expulsion, asylum – Immigration and emigration

6/1
On 26 November 2018, the *Riigikogu* (the Parliament) issued a statement on the United Nations Global Compact for Safe, Orderly and Regular Migration which had resulted in divergent debates in the society and in the *Riigikogu*.

The statement contained several legally relevant conclusions. First, all states have a sovereign right to shape their national migration policy in conformity with international law. Second, the global compact is not legally binding and does not create legal concepts. Third, immigrants are entitled to human rights and fundamental freedoms, but immigration is not a human right.

(Available in the Official Journal in Estonian, <https://www.riigiteataja.ee/akt/328112018004>, visited on 31 December 2019)

6/2

On 27 November 2018, the prime minister issued a statement on the United Nations Global Compact for Safe, Orderly and Regular Migration which had resulted in divergent debates in the society and had caused a rift within the government.

> The UN Global Compact for Migration is a non-legally binding document. This statement is clearly expressed in clause 7 of the migration pact and complies with the conclusion of the Estonian Chancellor of Justice. The document also unequivocally supports every nation's own sovereign right to establish their migration policy. We will continue to make independent decisions on whether to allow migrants in our country, who and how many people are allowed to enter, and how we protect our borders.
>
> The UN Global Compact for Migration fights against illegal migration and supports sending back people who have entered a country illegally. The Compact stresses the importance of an efficient border guard in ensuring security. It helps to improve international cooperation on migration. The Compact also puts a lot of focus on fighting against human trafficking and smuggling and protecting first and foremost the rights of women and children. The Compact will also help to protect the rights of Estonian people abroad. With this agreement, we are expressing our preparedness to find solutions along with other nations of the world.
>
> The UN is founded on cooperation and solutions, not problems and obligations. The Compact will not put any much-feared obligations on neither us nor any of the more than 180 countries who are planning to approve the compact.

(Available at the website of the Government, <https://www.valitsus.ee/en/news/statement-prime-minister-juri-ratas-after-parliament-voted-statement-about-un-global-compact>, visited on 31 December 2019)

6/3

On 19 December 2018, the United Nations General Assembly adopted the Global Compact for Safe, Orderly and Regular Migration. A total of 154 countries, including Estonia, supported the compact. Ambassador Sven Jürgenson read out Estonia's position based on the statement issued by the *Riigikogu* (the Parliament). Ambassador Jürgenson reaffirmed Estonia's position that the compact does not seek to establish customary international law or a human right to migrate.

> Migration is a global phenomenon that requires cooperation of all countries and therefore, we appreciate the active engagement of all actors in this inclusive and transparent process.
>
> The Global Compact on Migration will provide an opportunity to improve international cooperation on migration, by preventing irregular migration and combating trafficking and smuggling of persons. However, our international cooperation is built on national sovereignty.
>
> I would like to take this opportunity to emphasize Estonia's position on following:
>
> The Global Compact on Migration is not a legally-binding framework and it does not create any legal obligations for States, nor does it seek to establish international customary law.
>
> All states enjoy their sovereign right to shape and decide their national migration policy and legislation in conformity with international law. Effective border management is key to ensuring the security of states. By supporting the Global Compact for Migration, states do not assume any obligation to broaden the legal channels of migration.
>
> The Global Compact on Migration recognizes that universal fundamental rights and freedoms apply to all persons, including migrants. However, it does not establish a human right to migrate.
>
> Ensuring the possibility of return is a significant part of the Compact. It clearly recognizes the existing obligation of all States to duly receive and readmit all their own nationals.
>
> Global Compact for Migration also emphasizes the need to deal with the root causes behind irregular migration, and to make efforts to achieve the UN Sustainable Development Goals by 2030.

Estonia hopes that the objectives set out in the Global Compact for Migration contribute to combating and reducing irregular migration, among other things, by mitigating the negative consequences for the victims.

(Available at the website of the Ministry of Foreign Affairs, <https://vm.ee/en/news/global-compact-safe-orderly-and-regular-migration-explanation-vote-estonia-after-vote>, visited on 31 December 2019)

Part Six: VIII. C. The Position of the Individual (including the Corporation) in International Law – Human rights and fundamental freedoms – Under Council of Europe treaty system

6/4

On 12 September 2017, the European Court of Human Rights issued a judgment in the case of *Rõigas* v. *Estonia*, where the applicant complained of lack of effective investigation into her son's maltreatment and subsequent death in a hospital as a result of alleged medical negligence (Articles 2 and 3), that various medicines were administered without her son's consent or the consent of the applicant herself (Article 8), and about the medical procedures of intubation and tracheotomy performed on her son and the use of physical restraints to attach her son's hands to the bed against his will as well as that of the applicant (Article 3). The Chamber held that there was no violation of Article 2 and declared the remainder of the application inadmissible.

(*Rõigas* v. *Estonia*, app. no. 49045/13, 12 September 2017, Judgment of the Chamber)

6/5

On 7 November 2017, the European Court of Human Rights issued a judgment in the case of *Leuska and Others* v. *Estonia*, where the applicants complained that they had not been heard by a court and that the courts had not adjudicated on their claim for reimbursement of their legal costs (Article 6 § 1). The Chamber held that there was a partial violation of Article 6 § 1.

(*Leuska and Others* v. *Estonia*, app. no. 64734/11, 7 November 2017, Judgment of the Chamber)

6/6

On 23 October 2018, the European Court of Human Rights issued a judgment in the case of *M.T.* v. *Estonia*, where the applicant complained of a lack of objectivity, independence and thoroughness by the medical committee, whose opinions the domestic courts relied on when refusing to alter or terminate her son's treatment (Article 5 § 1), and of the impossibility for her son to challenge the lawfulness of his detention (Article 5 § 4). The Chamber held that there was no violation of Article 5 § 4 and declared the remainder of the application inadmissible.

(*M.T.* v. *Estonia*, app. no. 75378/13, 23 October 2018, Judgment of the Chamber)

6/7

On 30 October 2018, the European Court of Human Rights issued a judgment in the case of *Jatsõšõn* v. *Estonia*, where the applicant complained about the transport conditions provided for his prison leave to attend his grandmother's funeral, namely a small compartment without a seat belt or handles (Article 3). The Chamber held that there was no violation of Article 3 and declared the remainder of the application inadmissible.

(*Jatsõšõn* v. *Estonia*, app. no. 27603/15, 30 October 2018, Judgment of the Chamber)

6/8

On 13 November 2018, the European Court of Human Rights issued a judgment in the case of *A.T.* v. *Estonia*, where the applicant complained about the conditions resulting from the security requirements of his hospital visits (Articles 3 and 8), about the circumstances of his visit to a hospital to see his seriously ill daughter (Article 8), and that the latter had not been addressed by the domestic courts (Article 6 § 1). The Chamber held that there was no violation of Article 3 and 8, but there was a partial violation of Article 6 § 1.

(*A.T.* v. *Estonia*, app. no. 23183/15, 13 November 2018, Judgment of the Chamber)

6/9

On 13 November 2018, the European Court of Human Rights issued a judgment in the case of *A.T.* v. *Estonia (No. 2)*, where the applicant complained that the conditions of his detention under additional security measures, in particular the use of handcuffs on him at all times when he was outside of his cell and his being banned from using the prison's sports facilities and exercising, restriction on his movement and communication with others and a ban on participating in social and family events, had amounted to inhuman and degrading treatment (Article 3). The Chamber held that there was no violation of Article 3.

(*A.T.* v. *Estonia (No. 2)*, app. no. 70465/14), 13 November 2018, Judgment of the Chamber)

Part Six: VIII. D. The Position of the Individual (including the Corporation) in International Law – Human rights and fundamental freedoms – Other aspects of human rights and fundamental freedoms

6/10

On 22 September 2017, Foreign Minister Sven Mikser stated at a discussion on indigenous rights at the United Nations, organised by Estonia and the European Commission, that countries must contribute more to defending indigenous people.

> The UN Declaration on the Rights of Indigenous Peoples adopted ten years ago by the UN General Assembly has not demonstrated the desired progress. There continue to be gaps in the protection of indigenous rights. In many countries, the economic, social and cultural rights of indigenous people are not respected. In many parts of the world, the situation of indigenous rights defenders has also deteriorated.

The Foreign Minister called on countries to fully implement the Declaration on the Rights of Indigenous Peoples.

(Available at the website of the Ministry of Foreign Affairs, <https://vm.ee/en/news/mikser-un-states-must-contribute-more-defending-indigenous-people>, visited on 31 December 2019)

6/11

On 29 March 2018, the Government decided to approve the Foreign Minister's proposal to impose restrictive measures under the International Sanctions Act against individuals involved in grave human rights violations, including the death of Sergei Magnitsky. Under the proposal, 49 individuals on the so-called Magnitsky List are denied entry to Estonia. Foreign Minister Sven Mikser explained:

> The government's unity and decisiveness on this matter demonstrates our desire to draw attention to the rising number of violations of international law committed in Russia. ... We cannot fail to respond to violations of human rights.

The Foreign Minister said that Estonia supports enforcement of the rule of law by implementing such measures.

> Estonia takes human rights very seriously and we would also like to send this message to our allies. All of us must respond to attempts to

undermine the rules-based world order and thereby contribute to our security.

(Available at the website of the Ministry of Foreign Affairs, <https://vm.ee/en/news/government-approves-foreign-ministers-proposal-refuse-individuals-magnitsky-list-entry-estonia>, visited on 31 December 2019)

Part Seven: IV. Organs of the State and their Status – Diplomatic missions and their members

7/1

On 25 January 2018, at the African Union Summit, Foreign Minister Sven Mikser and the Foreign Minister of Sudan, Ibrahim Ghandour, established diplomatic relations between Estonia and Sudan.

(Available at the website of the Ministry of Foreign Affairs, <https://vm.ee/en/news/estonia-and-sudan-establish-diplomatic-relations>, visited on 31 December 2019)

7/2

On 26 March, Foreign Minister Sven Mikser announced that Estonia had decided to expel a Russian diplomat in connection with the Salisbury attack directed at Sergei and Yulia Skripal.

> As the activities of the employee of the Russian Embassy are not compatible with the diplomatic status agreed in the Vienna Convention, we have decided to expel the diplomat. We informed the Ambassador of the Russian Federation today of the diplomat's expulsion from Estonia. … Estonia's decision is part of a coordinated response of the EU leaders 23 March decision against Russia's activities and its unwillingness to fully cooperate with the UK on identifying those responsible for the Salisbury attack. … Salisbury attack is not only a dispute between the UK and Russia, it threatens international security and undermines international law.

The Foreign Minister emphasised that a nerve agent attack is a serious crime and Estonia has condemned it. He affirmed that the European Union agrees with the United Kingdom's assessment that it is highly likely that Russia was behind the attack.

> We continue to urge Russia to cooperate with the UK and the international community to identify the individuals responsible for this crime.

(Available at the website of the Ministry of Foreign Affairs, <https://vm.ee/en/news/foreign-minister-mikser-salisbury-attack-not-only-dispute-between-uk-and-russia>, visited on 31 December 2019)

7/3
On 6 July 2018, at the United Nations, Ambassador Sven Jürgenson and the Ambassador of the Democratic Republic of the Congo, Ignace Gata Mavita, established diplomatic relations between Estonia and the Democratic Republic of the Congo.

(Available at the website of the Ministry of Foreign Affairs, <https://vm.ee/en/news/estonia-and-democratic-republic-congo-establish-diplomatic-relations>, visited on 31 December 2019)

7/4
On 28 September 2018, at the United Nations, Foreign Minister Sven Mikser and Foreign Minister of Chad, Mahamat Zene Cherif, established diplomatic relations between Estonia and Chad.

(Available at the website of the Ministry of Foreign Affairs, <https://vm.ee/en/news/estonia-and-chad-establish-diplomatic-relations>, visited on 31 December 2019)

7/5
On 25 October 2018, in Wellington, New Zealand, the Ambassador to Australia, Andres Unga, and the High Commissioner for the Cook Islands to New Zealand, Karkopaerangi Ngatoko, established diplomatic relations between Estonia and the Cook Islands.

(Available at the website of the Ministry of Foreign Affairs, <https://vm.ee/en/news/estonia-and-cook-islands-establish-diplomatic-relations>, visited on 31 December 2019)

Part Sixteen: 1. Use of Force – Prohibition of the use of force

16/1
On 16 March 2018, Foreign Minister Sven Mikser issued a statement on the occasion of the upcoming anniversary of the Crimea annexation.

> Four years ago today, 16 March, the Russian Federation stage-managed a farce on Ukrainian soil that was billed as a referendum. Two days later, on 18 March, Crimea was illegally annexed by Russia. We condemn the

unlawful annexation perpetrated by the Russian Federation four years ago, which ignored the Ukrainian constitution, the will of the Ukrainian people and internationally agreed rules. Crimea is, and will remain part of Ukraine.

Estonia also denounces the serious breaches of international law committed by Russia as an occupying power since the annexation: forced conscript of locals into the Russian armed forces; imposed adoption of Russian citizenship; seizure of property; and restriction of freedom of speech and religion. The situation of the residents of the peninsula has worsened in the last four years, and almost 40,000 locals have fled the region as a result of both psychological and physical intimidation. The occupying power continues to breach human rights and fundamental freedoms: Ukrainian citizens have been unlawfully detained; there have been reports of torture and mistreatment; and the situation of the indigenous people of Crimean Tartars is particularly deplorable. Annexation has also made it more difficult to keep relations with Crimean Estonians as close as before.

Russia continues to integrate Crimea into its political and economic space. Significant efforts are also being taken to militarise the peninsula, threatening security in the Black Sea region as a whole. Estonia denounces the construction of the Kerch Strait Bridge, which has not been authorised by Ukraine and which will not only have a negative impact on security but also restrict the access of cargo vessels to Ukrainian port cities.

Breaches of international law must have consequences. Estonia continues to support the sovereignty and territorial integrity of Ukraine. We shall continue to raise the issue of Crimea in the international arena. We strongly support the continuation and updating the non-recognition policy of the illegal annexation of Crimea, including sanctions, and call for the release of those illegally imprisoned. It is of utmost importance that international organisations would be given access to Crimea.

Estonia condemns the holding of elections by the Russian Federation in Crimea and Sevastopol and does not recognise their results.

(Available at the website of the Ministry of Foreign Affairs, <https://vm.ee/en/news/foreign-minister-sven-mikser-crimea-ukraine>, visited on 31 December 2019)

16/2

On 25 November 2018, Foreign Minister Sven Mikser condemned Russia's activities on the Sea of Azov.

> Estonia condemns Russia's attack on Ukraine's naval forces in the Kerch Strait, and calls on Russia to immediately stop this attack, to release the ships and allow them to move unobstructedly to Ukrainian ports. It is a conscious step by Russia towards escalating the tension. These actions violate both international law and Ukraine's sovereignty and territorial integrity.

(Available at the website of the Ministry of Foreign Affairs, <https://vm.ee/en/news/foreign-minister-mikser-condemns-russias-activities-azov-sea>, visited on 31 December 2019)

16/3

On 28 November, the Ministry of Foreign Affairs of Estonia summoned Russia's Ambassador to Estonia Aleksandr Petrov after Russia used military force against Ukrainian soldiers and vessels in the Kerch Strait. Foreign Minister Sven Mikser publicly condemned Russia's attack in the Kerch Strait.

> The attack was a deliberate escalation of tensions, a grave violation of international law and an act of aggression against Ukraine's sovereignty and territorial integrity.

At the meeting with the Ambassador, the Ministry of Foreign Affairs called on Russia to immediately return the vessels and release the crew members. The Ministry of Foreign Affairs also emphasised that under international law, Russia must ensure that vessels from Ukraine and other countries can pass through the Kerch Strait and sail in the Sea of Azov unhindered.

Estonia does not recognize the illegal annexation of Crimea and reaffirms its support for Ukraine's sovereignty and territorial integrity.

(Available at the website of the Ministry of Foreign Affairs, <https://vm.ee/en/news/ministry-foreign-affairs-estonia-summons-russian-ambassador>, visited on 31 December 2019)

16/4

On 3 December 2018, the *Riigikogu* (the Parliament) issued a statement in support of the sovereignty and territorial integrity of Ukraine in connection with the aggression in the Kerch Strait.

The *Riigikogu* condemns the attack on Ukrainian ships and the wounding and detention of Ukrainian seamen perpetrated by the Russian Federation in the Kerch Strait.

The *Riigikogu* emphasises that Russia must immediately release the Ukrainian ships and seamen, and allow them unhindered passage to Ukrainian ports.

The *Riigikogu* calls for the restoration of unimpeded maritime traffic in the Kerch Strait and the Sea of Azov.

The *Riigikogu* urges all nations to support Ukraine in defending its territorial integrity, and to heed the call of the *Riigikogu* to condemn Russia's aggression against sovereign Ukraine, and to not recognise the unlawful annexation of Crimea.

The *Riigikogu* supports the calls by the European Union and NATO to de-escalate the situation and ease the tensions.

The *Riigikogu* maintains that, under the current situation, sanctions against Russia must be upheld and expanded.

The *Riigikogu* firmly believes that the only way to achieve lasting peace is to put an end to Russia's aggression against Ukraine.

(Available at the website of the *Riigikogu*, <https://www.riigikogu.ee/wpcms/wp-content/uploads/2018/12/UKRAINA-avaldus-inglise-k.pdf>, visited on 31 December 2019)

Part Sixteen: II. C. Use of Force – Legitimate use of force – Others

16/5

On 7 April 2017, the Minister of Foreign Affairs issued a statement on the situation in Syria in connection with the missile strike by the United States against the Shayrat airbase.

The crisis in Syria has gone on for too long and efforts to solve the situation have not been successful. Humanitarian disaster caused by the civil war has grown to enormous proportions.

> The United States' reaction to the use of weapons of mass destruction against Syrian civilians was necessary. We deem the resoluteness of our ally, the United States, important. The United States and the European Union should play a much more active role in the peace process.
>
> Russia has blocked all opportunities to use mechanisms of the United Nations to solve this crisis and ease the suffering of the civilian population. Chemical attack in Idlib showed that Russia's initiative to eliminate all chemical weapons from Syria has failed. It is clear that a stronger involvement of the international community is needed. Political transition must be reached to end this civil war.

(Available at the website of the Ministry of Foreign Affairs, <https://vm.ee/en/news/statement-minister-foreign-affairs-estonia-situation-syria>, visited on 31 December 2019)

Part Sixteen: III. Use of Force – Use of disarmament and arms control

16/6

On 4 September 2017, Foreign Minister Sven Mikser denounced North Korea's testing of a claimed hydrogen bomb.

> It is unacceptable for a country to violate the international obligations it has taken and to threaten the world's peace and security. ... While the international community cannot accept this, above all we need peaceful solutions. ... The European Union must remain united in its policy toward North Korea and, if necessary, toughen sanctions to prevent North Korea from continuing nuclear weapons development.

(Available at the website of the Ministry of Foreign Affairs, <https://vm.ee/en/news/foreign-minister-mikser-condemns-north-korean-nuclear-test>, visited on 31 December 2019)

16/7

On 14 April 2018, the Ministry of Foreign Affairs issued a statement regarding action in Syria.

> The Ministry of Foreign Affairs reiterates its firm condemnation of the use of chemical weapons in any circumstance. There is no justification of committing such acts.
>
> Estonia strongly condemns the use of chemical weapons by the Syrian regime, most recently in Douma on April 7, 2018 and calls for those responsible to be brought to justice.
>
> We regret that the United Nations Security Council has so far not been able to agree on how to stop the use of chemical weapons in Syria.
>
> The action taken by the United States, the United Kingdom and France on April 14, 2018 was a proper and proportionate response to the repeated use of chemical weapons by the Syrian regime against the Syrian people. The international community should be determined to act in unity in order to stop the use of such weapons.
>
> The Ministry of Foreign Affairs reaffirms Estonia's support for UN-led efforts to achieve a lasting political resolution to the Syrian conflict, consistent with UNSCR 2254 (2015) and the Geneva Communique (2012) and calls on all members of the UN Security Council to uphold their responsibilities in this regard.

(Available at the website of the Ministry of Foreign Affairs, <https://vm.ee/en/news/statement-regarding-action-syria>, visited on 31 December 2019)

Part Seventeen: 1. B. 8. The Law of Armed Conflict and International Humanitarian Law – International armed conflict – The law of international armed conflict – Belligerent occupation

17/1

On 10 April 2017, the Ministry of Foreign Affairs issued a statement on the so-called elections and referendum in Georgia's occupied region South Ossetia

> Estonia condemns the so-called Presidential elections and referendum on amending the name of the Georgian occupied region South Ossetia that took place on April 9.
>
> Estonia finds these actions illegal and does not recognize the outcome of the elections. So-called elections and referendum undermine efforts to

> find a peaceful resolution to the conflict and therefore damage security and stability in the region.
>
> Estonia reaffirms its resolute support for the sovereignty and territorial integrity of Georgia within its internationally recognized borders. South-Ossetia and Abkhazia are integral parts of Georgia.

(Available at the website of the Ministry of Foreign Affairs, <https://vm.ee/en/news/statement-ministry-foreign-affairs-estonia-so-called-elections-and-referendum-georgias-occupied>, visited on 31 December 2019)

17/2

On 8 November, Foreign Minister Sven Mikser issued a statement on the announcement of illegal elections in Donbas on 11 November 2018.

> We condemn the announcement by the so-called Donetsk and Luhansk People's Republics to hold "elections" on 11 November. This illegal action under full control and supervision by Russia is in sharp contradiction with the spirit and the letter of the Minsk agreements and undermines efforts to achieve long-awaited peace to the conflict in eastern Ukraine.
>
> The Minsk agreements provide for local elections to be held in accordance with Ukrainian law and OSCE standards. Thus, the holding and the results of these "elections" are to be considered null and void.
>
> We call on Russia to start fulfilling its Minsk commitments, stop hostilities and withdraw its armed formations from eastern Ukraine. Russia should do everything possible to cancel the announced "elections" in parts of eastern Ukraine under its control.
>
> Estonia supports the efforts of France and Germany in the Normandy format to advance implementation of the Minsk agreements and find a peaceful solution to the conflict.
>
> We reiterate our strong support for the independence, sovereignty and territorial integrity of Ukraine within its internationally recognised borders.

(Available at the website of the Ministry of Foreign Affairs, <https://vm.ee/en/news/statement-foreign-minister-estonia-sven-mikser-announcement-illegal-elections-donbas-11>, visited on 31 December 2019)

Part Nineteen: IX. Legal Aspects of International Relations and Co-operation in Particular Matters – Military and security matters

19/1

On 15 February 2018, Foreign Minister Sven Mikser condemned Russia for the destructive NotPetya cyber-attack against Ukraine, and called on Russia to act responsibly and in accordance with international law in cyberspace.

> The NotPetya cyber-attack which targeted Ukraine's financial, energy and government sectors and undermined the sectors' resilience, demonstrated disrespect for Ukrainian sovereignty and caused significant economic losses in other countries too. It is very important for Estonia to maintain an open, stable and secure cyber space and for that, countries have to act responsibly and follow the rules of international cooperation and the norms of international law that apply in cyber space just like everywhere else.

(Available at the website of the Ministry of Foreign Affairs, <https://vm.ee/en/news/foreign-minister-mikser-condemns-russia-notpetya-attacks-against-ukraine>, visited on 31 December 2019)

19/2

On 7 March 2018, Foreign Minister Sven Mikser and his Baltic counterparts met with House of Representatives Foreign Affairs Chairman Edward Royce and other committee members today to discuss the security situation and Russia's activities in Europe. The Foreign Minister highlighted that Russia is now waging its information war on a significantly broader front.

> Russia's breaching of the accepted principles of international law and ignoring its obligations demands the reinforcement of deterrence measures not only in the Baltic States but in NATO as a whole. ... We've always agreed with the United States that allies in Europe also need to boost their defence spending, which is something we'll definitely be discussing at the NATO summit in Brussels in July.

The Foreign Minister says that both the European Union and the United States must be prepared to prevent threats emerging from Russia.

> Hybrid threats and hostile propaganda are nothing we haven't seen before in the Baltic States, but Russia's now waging its information war on a significantly broader front. ... It's important that society as a

whole is aware of these threats and knows how to identify misleading information.

He added that people need to be aware of Russian activities designed to create divisions in society and generate distrust in democratic institutions, referring to Russian interference in European and American elections.

(Available at the website of the Ministry of Foreign Affairs, <https://vm.ee/en/news/foreign-minister-mikser-usa-russia-now-waging-its-information-war-significantly-broader-front>, visited on 31 December 2019)

19/3
On 13 March 2018, Foreign Minister Sven Mikser issued a statement on the use of chemical weaponry in Salisbury.

> Estonia is deeply concerned and disturbed by the reported use of chemical nerve agent in the United Kingdom on March 4 that has severely poisoned Sergei and Yulia Skripal and endangered the lives of hundreds of others.
>
> The Salisbury attack was the first use of a chemical weapon in Europe since World War II. We are shocked that we may still be confronted with the use of such weapons in Europe. This attack is a brutal violation of international law and order and demonstrates complete disregard for human life and suffering.
>
> We have every confidence in the UK investigation in this matter. Perpetrators of this heinous crime must be held accountable. We call for the full cooperation of the international community in this regard.
>
> We call on Russia to reassure the international community of its declaration of full destruction of its chemical weapons stockpile in October 2017 and that the integrity and effectiveness of non-proliferation regimes will be upheld.
>
> We offer our utmost support to our ally and friend the UK in its efforts to resolve the issue.

(Available at the website of the Ministry of Foreign Affairs, <https://vm.ee/en/news/statement-foreign-minister-sven-mikser-use-chemical-weapon-salisbury>, visited on 31 December 2019)

ANNEX I.A Agreements signed by Estonia before 2017 but entered into force in regard to Estonia in 2017–2018 – Bi- and multilateral agreements

Title	Conclusion	Entry into Force
Protocol Amending the Agreement between the Government of the Republic of Estonia and the Government of the Republic of Italy on Mutual Protection of Classified Information	21.10.2016	06.01.2017
Agreement between the Republic of Estonia and the Republic of India on the transfer of sentenced persons	15.11.2016	01.03.2017
Protocol to the North Atlantic Treaty on the Accession of Montenegro	19.05.2016	01.06.2017
Protocol Amending the Protocol between the Government of the Republic of Estonia, the Government of the Republic of Latvia and the Government of the Republic of Lithuania Concerning the Status of the Baltic Defence College and Its Personnel	14.06.2016	11.06.2017
Agreement between the Government of the Kingdom of Denmark and the Government of the Republic of Estonia on the Amendment to the Agreement between the Government of the Kingdom of Denmark and the Government of Republic of Estonia for the Promotion and Reciprocal Protection of Investments, signed on 6 November 1991 in Tallinn and on the Termination thereof	25.07.2016	16.08.2017
Agreement between the Republic of Estonia and Hungary on the Exchange and Mutual Protection of Classified Information	08.12.2016	01.09.2017
Agreement between the Republic of Estonia and Australia on Social Security	14.09.2015	01.01.2018
Convention between the Government of the Republic of Estonia and the Council of Ministers of the Republic of Albania for the Avoidance of Double Taxation and the Prevention of Fiscal Evasion with Respect to Taxes on Income	05.04.2010	01.01.2018

ANNEX I.B Agreements signed by Estonia before 2017 but entered into force in regard to Estonia in 2017–2018 – Conventions

Title	Conclusion	Entry into Force
Amendments to the Annex of the International Convention for the Prevention of Pollution from Ships, 1973, as Modified by the Protocol of 1978 relating thereto (Amendments to Regulation 12 of MARPOL Annex I)	15.05.2015	01.01.2017
Amendments to the Annex of the Protocol of 1978 relating to the International Convention for the Prevention of Pollution from Ships, 1973 (Amendments to MARPOL Annexes I, II, IV and V)	15.05.2015	01.01.2017
Amendments to the International Convention on Standards of Training, Certification and Watchkeeping for Seafarers (STCW), 1978, as Amended	11.06.2015	01.01.2017
Amendments to Part A of the Seafarers' Training, Certification and Watchkeeping (STCW) Code	11.06.2015	01.01.2017
Amendments to the Protocol of 1988 relating to the International Convention for the Safety of Life at Sea, 1974	11.06.2015	01.01.2017
European Agreement Concerning the International Carriage of Dangerous Goods by Road	30.09.1957	01.01.2017
Amendments to the International Convention on Tonnage Measurement of Ships	04.12.2013	28.02.2017
Maritime Labour Convention	23.02.2006	05.05.2017
Amendments to the Annex of the International Convention for the Prevention of Pollution from Ships, 1973, as Modified by the Protocol of 1978 relating thereto (Amendments to MARPOL Annex II)	22.04.2016	01.09.2017

ANNEX I.B Agreements signed by Estonia before 2017 but entered into force in regard to Estonia in 2017–2018 – Conventions (*cont.*)

Title	Conclusion	Entry into Force
Amendments to the Annex of the International Convention for the Prevention of Pollution from Ships, 1973, as Modified by the Protocol of 1978 relating thereto (Amendments to MARPOL Annex IV)	22.04.2016	01.09.2017
Amendments to the Annex of the Protocol of 1997 to Amend the International Convention for the Prevention of Pollution from Ships, 1973, as Modified by the Protocol of 1978 relating thereto (Amendments to Regulation 13 of MARPOL Annex VI)	22.04.2016	01.09.2017
Work in Fishing Convention	14.06.2007	16.11.2017
Amendments to the Annex to the Convention on Facilitation of International Maritime Traffic, 1965	08.04.2016	01.01.2018
Universal Postal Convention	06.10.2016	01.01.2018
First Additional Protocol to the General Regulations of the Universal Postal Union	06.10.2016	01.01.2018
Ninth Additional Protocol to the Constitution of the Universal Postal Union	06.10.2016	01.01.2018
Amendments to the Annex of the Protocol of 1997 to Amend the International Convention for the Prevention of Pollution from Ships, 1973, as Modified by the Protocol of 1978 relating thereto (Amendments to MARPOL Annex VI)	28.10.2016	01.03.2018
Amendments to the Annex of the International Convention for the Prevention of Pollution from Ships, 1973, as Modified by the Protocol of 1978 relating thereto (Amendments to MARPOL Annex I)	28.10.2016	01.03.2018

ANNEX I.B Agreements signed by Estonia before 2017 but entered into force in regard to Estonia in 2017–2018 – Conventions (*cont.*)

Title	Conclusion	Entry into Force
Amendments to the Annex of the International Convention for the Prevention of Pollution from Ships, 1973, as Modified by the Protocol of 1978 relating thereto (Amendments to MARPOL Annex V)	28.10.2016	01.03.2018
Amendments to the International Convention on Standards of Training, Certification and Watchkeeping for Seafarers (STCW), 1978, as Amended	25.11.2016	01.07.2018
Amendments to Part A of the Seafarers' Training, Certification and Watchkeeping (STCW) Code	25.11.2016	01.07.2018

ANNEX II.A Agreements signed by Estonia in 2017–2018 – Bi- and multilateral agreements

Title	Conclusion	Entry into Force
Agreement on Defense Cooperation between the Government of the United States of America and the Government of the Republic of Estonia	17.01.2017	06.07.2017
Agreement between the Government of the Republic of Estonia, the Government of the Republic of Latvia and the Government of the Republic of Lithuania on the Development of the Rail Baltic/Rail Baltica Railway Connection	31.01.2017	24.10.2017
Agreement the Government of the Republic of Estonia and the Government of the Republic of Kyrgyz for the Avoidance of Double Taxation and the Prevention of Fiscal Evasion with Respect to Taxes on Income	10.04.2017	07.02.2018

ANNEX II. A Agreements signed by Estonia in 2017–2018 – Bi- and multilateral agreements (*cont.*)

Title	Conclusion	Entry into Force
Memorandum of Understanding on the Implementation of the EEA Financial Mechanism 2014–2021 between the Republic of Estonia, and Iceland, the Principality of Lichtenstein and the Kingdom of Norway	09.05.2017	10.05.2017
Memorandum of Understanding on the Implementation of the Norwegian Financial Mechanism 2014–2021 between the Republic of Estonia and the Kingdom of Norway	09.05.2017	10.05.2017
Agreement between the Republic of Estonia and the Grand Duchy of Luxembourg on the hosting of data and information systems	20.06.2017	16.05.2018
Agreement between the Republic of Estonia and the Kingdom of Norway on Schengen Visa Representation	29.06.2017	01.07.2017
Convention between the Republic of Estonia and Japan for the Elimination of Double Taxation with respect to Taxes on Income and the Prevention of Tax Evasion and Avoidance	30.08.2017	29.09.2018
Agreement Concerning the Mutual Protection of Military Classified Information between the Government of the Republic of Estonia and the Government of the Kingdom of Denmark	26.09.2017	20.12.2017
Agreement between the Republic of Estonia andthe Grand Duchy of Luxembourg on the Establishment of a Framework for the Statistical Transfer of Energy from Renewable Sources for Target Compliance Purposes under Directive 2009/28/EC	07.11.2017	01.04.2018
Agreement between the Government of the Republic of Estonia and the Swiss Federal Council concerning the Exchange of Classified Information	14.11.2017	01.02.2018

ANNEX II. A Agreements signed by Estonia in 2017–2018 – Bi- and multilateral agreements (*cont.*)

Title	Conclusion	Entry into Force
Agreement between the Government of the Republic of Estonia and the Government of the Socialist Republic of Vietnam on Educational and Scientific Cooperation	22.11.2017	22.11.2017
Agreement between the Government of the Republic of Estonia, the Government of the Republic of Latvia and the Government of the Republic of Lithuania on Mutual Assistance and Cooperation in the Field of Disaster Prevention, Preparedness and Response	23.11.2017	24.12.2017
Agreement between the Republic of Poland and the Republic of Estonia on the Amendment and Termination of the Agreement between the Republic of Poland and the Republic of Estonia on the Reciprocal Promotion and Protection of Investments	19.03.2018	07.03.2019
Agreement between the Republic of Estonia and the Portuguese Republic on Co-operation in Defence Matters	01.06.2018	30.09.2019
Agreement among the Government of the Republic of Estonia, the Government of the Republic of Latvia and the Government of the Republic of Lithuania on the Automatic Academic Recognition of Qualifications Concerning Higher Education	08.06.2018	07.01.2019
Agreement between the Government of the Republic of Estonia and the Government of the Republic of Mali on the Status of the Contingent of the Republic of Estonia in the Territory of the Republic of Mali	14.06.2018	25.06.2018
Agreement between the Government of the Republic of Estonia ant the Government of the Republic of Latvia on the Exchange of Data from the Population Register	21.08.2018	17.01.2019

ANNEX II. A Agreements signed by Estonia in 2017–2018 – Bi- and multilateral agreements (*cont.*)

Title	Conclusion	Entry into Force
Agreement between the Government of the Republic of Estonia and the Government of the United Arab Emirates for Air Services Between and Beyond Their Respective Territories	28.09.2018	13.01.2019
Agreement between the Government of the Republic of Estonia and the Government of the Republic of Poland on the Mutual Protection of Classified Information	27.11.2018	01.09.2019

ANNEX II. B Agreements signed by Estonia in 2017–2018 – Conventions

Title	Conclusion	Entry into Force
Additional Protocol to the Convention on the Contract for the International Carriage of Goods by Road (CMR) Concerning the Electronic Consignment Note	20.02.2008	31.01.2017
Convention on the Protection of Children against Sexual Exploitation and Sexual Abuse	25.10.2007	01.03.2017
Convention on Preventing and Combating Violence against Women and Domestic Violence	11.05.2011	01.02.2018
Implementing Agreement for a Programme of Research, Development and Demonstration on Bioenergy	13.04.1978	26.02.2018
European Landscape Convention	20.10.2000	01.06.2018
International Convention for the Control and Management of Ships' Ballast Water and Sediments	13.02.2004	17.07.2018
Protocol No. 16 to the Convention for the Protection of Human Rights and Fundamental Freedoms	02.10.2013	01.08.2018
Convention on the European Forest Institute	28.08.2003	26.08.2018

Republic of Latvia Materials on International Law 2017–2018

Edited by Kristaps Tamužs*

[*Editorial Notes:*

1. Republic of Latvia Materials on International Law 2017–2018 (RLMIL 2017–2018) have been classified according to Recommendation (97)11 of 12 June 1997 of the Committee of Ministers of the Council of Europe, as applied by the British Yearbook of International Law from the year 1997, with certain minor amendments.
2. The RLMIL mostly concern opinions of the institutions and officials of Latvia. Often, different officials expressed views on the same issues. In order to prevent unnecessary repetition, the editor has selected materials from the highest possible level. The statements of officials and in particular the decisions of the courts have been occasionally edited in order to ensure brevity, focus and consistency.
3. Several recurring topics appeared in the speeches given and statements made by officials; for example, the unlawful annexation of Crimea by the Russian Federation and human rights abuses in Crimea subsequent to the annexation. Representatives of Latvia continued to express support for reform of the United Nations Security Council.
4. On 24 August 2018 Latvia was approved as the next presiding country of the Arms Trade Treaty. In November of 2018, the Latvian Ambassador to the UN chaired the Annual Conference of the Member States to the Convention on Certain Conventional Weapons in Geneva. In the light of its leading role in the two international mechanisms, Latvia's representatives made frequent statements concerning nuclear non-proliferation as well as effective control of trade and use of conventional and chemical weapons.
5. In 2017–2018 the European Court of Human Rights (ECtHR) communicated 16 cases to the Latvian Government and handed down judgments with respect to twelve applications by a seven-judge chamber and judgments with respect to eleven applications by a three-judge committee. A further three applications were declared inadmissible by a decision of a chamber and six by a decision of a committee. The ECtHR in committee

---

* LL.M.; Legal Advisor, Constitutional Court of the Republic of Latvia; Visiting Lecturer, Riga Graduate School of Law.

formation also decided to strike three cases out of the Court's list of cases. Finally, 486 cases were either declared inadmissible or struck out of the ECtHR's list of cases by unpublished decisions of either a single-judge formation or a three-judge committee.]

Part Four: 11. Relationship between International Law and Internal Law – Application and implementation of international law in internal law

The Constitutional Court of the Republic of Latvia continued to demonstrate its commitment to the doctrine of the Latvian legal system's openness to international law by extensively invoking the provisions of various instruments of international law, including in particular the European Convention on Human Rights. During the reference period the Constitutional Court for the first time in its history referred for a preliminary ruling to the Court of Justice of the European Union (CJEU) and subsequently adopted a judgment on the basis of the interpretation of EU law contained in the judgment of the CJEU. The Supreme Court of the Republic of Latvia continued to address issues related to the role in the Latvian legal system of decisions of various international dispute-settlement mechanisms.

4/1

In its judgment of 10 February 2017 in case no. 2016-06-01 the Constitutional Court was called upon to decide on the compatibility of several aspects of the Latvian system governing clearances for access to official secrets. Similar issues had already been assessed by the Court in 2003. However, first, more than ten years had elapsed since that judgment which had been adopted "at the time when in the Latvian legal system transformation was on-going from the Soviet law to law compatible with a democratic state governed by the rule of law, the core value of which is ensuring of human rights" (para. 17.8 of the judgment) and, second, in the meantime the ECtHR had adopted two rulings (judgment of 29 April 2014 in *Ternovskis* v. *Latvia*, application no. 33637/02, and decision of 18 November 2014 in *Spūlis and Vaškevičs* v. *Latvia*, applications no. 2631/10 and no. 12253/10) which concerned a disputed legal regulation. With regard to the interplay between the Constitution of the Republic of Latvia and the Convention the Court indicated as follows:

> 29. Article 89 of the [Constitution] provides that the state recognises and protects fundamental human rights in accordance with the [Constitution], laws, and international treaties binding upon Latvia. A finding

has been enshrined in the case law of the Constitutional Court that the State's obligation to take into consideration international commitments in the field of human rights follows from this article of the [Constitution]. The aim of the constitutional legislator has been to harmonise norms of human rights included in the [Constitution] with international human rights provisions ...

29.1. The Constitutional Court has found that the first sentence of Article 92 of the [Constitution] must be interpreted, first and foremost, in interconnection with Article 6 of the Convention. ... ECHR has recognised that the right to access to court as one of the elements of the right to a fair trial means the possibility for a person to initiate proceedings for the protection of civil rights and obligations in an institution that should be considered as being " a court" within the meaning of the Convention ...

However, the right of access to a court ... does not mean that the possibility to turn to court with regard to any issue should be ensured to a person. The concept of "determination of civil rights and obligations" used in this provision makes it applicable only in cases, the outcome of which is decisive with respect to a person's civil rights and obligations ... ECHR has also recognised that a person's right of access to a court in cases with respect to employment in the public service may be restricted in view of the special relationship between the state and a civil servant which is characterised by the obligation of loyalty and duty of discretion (see ... "*Spūlis and Vaškevičs v. Latvia*" ..., paras. 41 and 42). However, if a person's civil rights are affected, then the state has the obligation to prove the existence of "objective grounds in the state's interests" for denying a person access to a court...

29.2. Article 53 of the Convention provides: "Nothing in this Convention shall be construed as limiting or derogating from any of the human rights and fundamental freedoms which may be ensured under the laws of any High Contracting Party or under any other agreement to which it is a Party". Thus, if it follows from norms of the Convention and their interpretation in the case law of ECHR that certain fundamental rights enshrined in the Convention encompass the specific situation, then it usually also falls within the scope of the respective fundamental rights enshrined in the [Constitution]. Whereas if human rights enshrined in the Convention do not encompass the particular situation, it does not mean that this situation would not fall within the scope of fundamental rights enshrined in the [Constitution]. In such a case the Constitutional

Court must verify whether no circumstances exist that would indicate that a higher level of fundamental rights protection is envisaged in the [Constitution].Thus, the Convention envisages the minimum standard of protection of human rights and fundamental freedoms; however, the state may guarantee a broader scope of these rights and higher standards of protection in its laws, first of all – in the constitution of the state. In interpreting [the Constitution], the Constitutional Court must take into consideration the Convention and the case law of ECHR; however, this does not prohibit the Constitutional Court from arriving at the conclusion that the [Constitution] provides for a higher level of protection of fundamental rights than the Convention ...

30. The Constitutional Court has already concluded that annulment of a special permit results in restriction upon a person's fundamental right ... to freely choose and retain workplace ...

ECHR, in turn, has established that annulment of a special permit had a decisive impact upon the applicant's personal situation – without the required access he could not continue to working in the position in which he had served for seven years, which undeniably had clear pecuniary repercussions for him. The link between the decision not to grant the applicant security clearance and his loss of income was certainly more than tenuous or remote (see ... "*Ternovskis* v. *Latvia*", ... para. 44). ...

Thus, in legal reality annulment of a special permit may restrict a person's fundamental rights. The Constitutional Court holds that in the case where a person's rights enshrined in the first sentence of Article 106 of [the Constitution (right to choose one's employment and workplace)] are restricted he should have the possibility to defend his rights in the way that complies with the first sentence of Article 92 of the [Constitution (right to a fair trial)] ...

32. ... The Constitutional Court holds that the reference to the procedure for appealing against a decision on annulling a special permit included in the judgment of the ECHR is important. Although the ECHR in this case did not directly review this procedure, it concluded that the procedure in which the Prosecutor General adopted a decision with respect to the applicant's special permit did not comply with the adversarial principle and the principle of equality. The ECHR also concluded that the applicant had no possibility to respond to evidence against him and, this, he was

in an unequal position, compared to the other party (see ... "*Ternovskis* v. *Latvia*", ... para. 72) ...

(Available at the website of the Constitutional Court, <http://www.satv.tiesa.gov.lv/web/viewer.html?file=/wp-content/uploads/2016/04/2016-06-01_Judgment_ENG.pdf>, visited on 22 November 2019)

4/2

The judgment of the Constitutional Court of 15 June 2017 in case no. 2016-11-01 pertained to one aspect of the heritage of the Soviet legal system in the Republic of Latvia. The case concerned the right to early retirement for persons who had taken care of their children with a disability. The child in question had an amputated forearm. This condition was not grounds for recognising a child as a person with a disability under Soviet law (because disability was linked to loss of the ability to work). Therefore the child was officially recognised as a person with a disability only after Latvia's independence was restored in 1990 and consequently it was considered that their parent had taken care of a child with a disability for less than eight years – the length of time necessary to become entitled to early retirement. The Constitutional Court examined the compatibility of the respective legal regulation with the principle of equality before law (Article 91 of the Constitution) and the right to social security (Article 109 of the Constitution). The interplay between the Latvian legal system and international law was addressed by the Constitutional Court when it was assessing whether the legitimate aim of the unequal treatment (ensuring the effectiveness and predictability of the social security system) could not have been achieved by means that are less restrictive of fundamental rights. The Court held as follows:

> 21.2. ... Prior to 13 December 1979 in the USSR it was legally impossible to officially recognise the disability of children. [After 1979 it became possible to recognise the disability of children on the basis of a limited list of medical indicators].
>
> The Constitutional Court indicates that already the Declaration of the Rights of the Child which was adopted by the United Nations on 20 November 1959 contained several principles according to which a child should receive special protection under any circumstances. Principle 4 of the Declaration of the Rights of the Child emphasises the right of a child to specific social security, as well as the right to grow and develop in health. On the other hand, the Declaration on the Rights of Disabled

Persons of 9 December 1975, which is based, *inter alia*, on the principles contained in the Declaration of the Rights of the Child, provides for the enjoyment of the rights of persons with a disability on the basis of equality as well as the special role of families of such persons. These human rights documents placed on an international scale the principles of protection of rights of persons with disabilities and the best interests of children.

On the basis of the aforementioned principles the Convention on the Rights of the Child of 20 November 1989 and the Convention on the Rights of Persons with Disabilities of 13 December 2006 were drafted. Article 7 of the Convention on the Rights of Persons with Disabilities provides that States Parties shall take all necessary measures to ensure the full enjoyment by children with disabilities of all human rights and fundamental freedoms on an equal basis with other children and that in all actions concerning children with disabilities, the best interests of the child shall be a primary consideration. On the other hand, pursuant to Article 23(1) of the Convention on the Rights of the Child a disabled child should enjoy a full and decent life, in conditions which ensure dignity, promote self-reliance and facilitate the child's active participation in the community. Paragraph 2 of the same article provides that States Parties recognize the right of the disabled child to special care. States ought to encourage and ensure the extension, subject to available resources, to the eligible child and those responsible for his or her care, of assistance for which application is made and which is appropriate to the child's condition and to the circumstances of the parents or others caring for the child. ...

The impugned norm contains a reference to the USSR legal regulation which was obviously insufficient with regard to the aforementioned general [principles] of protection of children with disabilities and their family members. The Latvian legislator when adopting the impugned norm had to take into account the principle of priority of best interests of the child and the need to ensure special protection of children with disability and their family members at the stage of development and on the basis of equality.

21.3. ... The legal regulation of another state, namely the USSR, with respect to the criteria to be taken into account when granting a disability status to children is noticeably different from the international law principles of protection of the rights of children with disabilities and their family members previously indicated by the Constitutional Court and the legal regulation adopted by a democratic state based on the rule of law, namely – Latvia. The Constitutional Court emphasises that such criteria established by a totalitarian state may not be the basis for denying to a person the rights that are granted to another person who is in the same and comparable circumstances. ...

Hence the application of the legal acts adopted after the restoration of Latvia's independence and the criteria for granting disability status contained therein with respect to the care for a child during the time prior to the restoration of independence ought to be considered to be one of the possible alternative means that would interfere with the fundamental rights guaranteed by the Constitution to a lesser extent. ..."

(Available, only in Latvian, at the website of the Constitutional Court, <https://www.satv.tiesa.gov.lv/web/viewer.html?file=/wp-content/uploads/2016/07/2016-11-01_Spriedums-1.pdf>, visited on 23 November 2019)

4/3

In its judgment of 19 December 2017 in case no. 2017-02-03 the Constitutional Court dealt with the issue of the interplay between environmental law and human rights in the context of noise pollution. The Court examined the constitutionality of legal provisions regulating the permitted noise levels emanating from racing tracks. International law proved to be useful in particular when examining the precautionary principle. The Constitutional Court held as follows:

19.2. The Constitutional Court has acknowledged that the precautionary principle is one of the principles of environmental law. ...

The European Court of Human Rights has pointed out that the precautionary principle is applicable, *inter alia*, in order to ensure the highest attainable standard of human health and environmental safety. The precautionary principle provides that the state may not avoid adopting effective and proportionate measures that are necessary in order to eliminate the risk that human health and environment might be subjected to grave or irreversible damage only for the reason that the technical and scientific information at the particular time could not provide a definite answer about the level of such a risk. If the health and welfare of complainants are subjected to a significant and serious risk, the state has a positive obligation to take reasonable and appropriate measures in order to protect human rights and generally promote environmental health and protection already at the stage when no negative consequences have arisen. This means that the decision-making process ought to commence with due research that would allow to make a preliminary assessment of the consequences that certain actions might have on the environment and individual rights, to prevent negative consequences and to ensure a fair balance between the various competing interests (see the judgment of 27 January 2009 of the European Court of Human Rights in *Tătar* v. *Romania*, application no. 67021/01, paras. [88, 107 and 120]).

On the other hand, the European Court of Justice considers the precautionary principle to be one of the cornerstones of the policy of the European Union that is directed towards a heightened level of environmental protection; it applies it, *inter alia*, in cases that are related to the protection of the right to healthcare (see, for instance, the judgments of the European Court of Justice of 5 May 1998 in cases C-180/96 and C-157/96). ...

In a democratic state based on the rule of law the precautionary principle requires that the state does not have to wait until a real and existing harm has been done to human health; it is sufficient for there to be reasonable suspicion that such harm is possible for the state to have to implement timely, effective and proportionate measures in order to prevent such harm. A proper assessment of the possibility of harm is inextricably linked with, *inter alia*, the obligation of the state to carry out due research and to do everything possible to effectively prevent such harm or to restrict it as much as is possible even before it has occurred. ...

(Available, only in Latvian, at the website of the Constitutional Court, <https://www.satv.tiesa.gov.lv/web/viewer.html?file=/wp-content/uploads/2017/01/2017-02-03_Spriedums.pdf>, visited on 24 November 2019)

4/4

The first of three judgments that demonstrates the role that the law of the European Union plays in the decision-making of the Constitutional Court was adopted on 11 April 2018 in case no. 2017-12-01. The case concerned the procedure for refunding excessive payments of VAT. With regard to the EU law the Constitutional Court held:

> 13. Upon ratifying the treaty on Latvia's accession to the European Union the law of the European Union has become an inextricable part of the Latvian legal system. Hence the legal acts of the European Union and

their interpretation in the jurisprudence of the CJEU ought to be taken into account when interpreting and applying national legal acts ... It follows that when the legislator is adopting legal norms, in particular – legal norms by which the requirements of directives of the European Union are implemented in the national legal system, it has to comply with general principles of law and other provisions of the Constitution as well as principles of the law of the European Union. ...

[The] impugned norms were adopted when implementing the requirements of ... Directive 2006/112/EC. ...

Therefore the compliance of the impugned norms with ... Article 105 of the Constitution [the right to own property] shall be assessed by taking into account the principles deriving from Article 183 of Directive 2006/112/EC.

14. ...Article 183 of Directive 2006/112/EC contains the rules pertaining to Member States' actions with respect to excess VAT. The CJEU has emphasised on several occasions that, although pursuant to Article 183 of Directive 2006/112/EC the procedure for refunding excess VAT in principle falls within the scope of the procedural autonomy of Member States, this procedure may not endanger the principle of VAT neutrality by shifting all or part of the burden of this tax to the taxpayer (compare with the judgment of the Court of Justice of European Union of 28 February 2018 in case C-387/16, paras. 21–24). ...

22. In order to assess whether the benefit for society from restriction of the fundamental rights provided for by the impugned norms exceeds the harm done to the taxpayer, the Constitutional Court must, by taking into account the conclusions from the case law of the CJEU concerning the contents of the principle of VAT neutrality, determine whether the impugned norms do not create a financial burden for the taxpayer. ...

On several occasions the CJEU has assessed the reasonability of the period of refunding excess VAT provided for by national legal provisions. After assessing the factual and legal circumstances of the respective cases, the CJEU has found that a period of three months is a reasonable time for refunding excess VAT (see the judgment of the CJEU of 12 May 2011 in case C-107/10, para. 49). ... The CJEU has found that a three-month period is not reasonable and does not comply with the principle of VAT neutrality (see the judgment of the ECJ of 10 July 2008 in case C-25/07, para. 27, and the judgment of the CJEU of 21 October 2015 in case C-120/15, paras. 25 and 26). ...

According to the impugned norms the period within which excess VAT is returned to the taxpayer may be within the range of approximately one month to one year or even longer. This means that pursuant to the impugned norms excess VAT might be returned to the taxpayer after the expiry of time which may be considered to be reasonable ..."

(Available, only in Latvian, at the website of the Constitutional Court, <https://www.satv.tiesa.gov.lv/web/viewer.html?file=/wp-content/uploads/2017/04/2017-12-01_Spriedums.pdf>, visited on 25 November 2019)

4/5

The second of three judgments regarding the law of the European Union was adopted by the Constitutional Court on 29 June 2018 in case no. 2017-28-0306. This was the first case in the history of the Constitutional Court in which the Court assessed the compliance of national legal provisions with the Treaty on Functioning of the European Union (TFEU). The case concerned the rates of real estate tax in Riga that were different, depending on the nationality of the persons residing in the residential real estate. The Court held as follows:

> 8. ... The impugned provision establishes the order for application of reduced real estate taxes due from a payer of a real estate tax ... if real estate has been declared as a place of residence of a foreign national. The provision concerns foreigners with various legal statuses and different grounds for residence in the Republic of Latvia. Articles 18(1) and 21(1) TFEU [invoked by the petitioner] pertain only to one part of persons concerned by the impugned provision. On the other hand, Article 91 of the Constitution [(equality before the law)] guarantees the existence of a united legal order and an impact of law that includes all persons in Latvia ...

> 10. ... Pursuant to Article 89 of the Constitution the state recognises and protects fundamental human rights in accordance with the Constitution, laws, and international treaties binding upon Latvia. International human rights provisions and their practical application serve, at the level of constitutional law, as a means of interpretation, in order to determine the scope and contents of certain fundamental rights and other general

principles of law, insofar as this does not lead to curtailment or restriction of the fundamental rights enshrined in the Constitution ...The Constitutional Court has held that when determining the content of Article 91 of the Constitution, it is necessary to be guided by, *inter alia*, international human rights documents ...

On the other hand, pursuant to Article 68 of the Constitution after Latvia's accession to the European Union, the law of the European Union has become an inextricable part of the legal system of Latvia ... Latvia must comply with the obligations that derive from its membership in the European Union ...

Legal acts of Latvia ought to be interpreted in a manner that would avoid contradictions with Latvia's obligations towards the European Union, unless this pertains to the fundamental principles included in the Constitution ... The legal acts of the European Union and their interpretation in the jurisprudence of the CJEU must be taken into account when determining the contents of national legal acts and applying them ... In the jurisprudence of the CJEU it has been established that all situations involving the exercise of the fundamental freedoms guaranteed by the EU Treaties, in particular those involving the freedom to move and reside within the territory of the Member States, fall within the scope of application of the law of the European Union (see, for instance, judgment of the ECJ of 29 April 2004 in case C-224/02, para. 17).

In interpreting the provisions of the Constitution, international human rights documents and the TFEU, a solution ought to be sought that ensures their mutual harmony. Hence the interpretation of Article 91 is affected by the provisions and their application of international human rights documents and, in certain situations, also of the TFEU.

10.1 Article 26 of the International Covenant on Civil and Political Rights (hereafter – the Covenant) provides that all persons are equal before the law and are entitled without any discrimination to the equal protection of the law. In this respect, the law shall prohibit any discrimination and guarantee to all persons equal and effective protection against discrimination on any ground such as race, colour, sex, language, religion, political or other opinion, national or social origin, property, birth or other status.

Even though this article does not *expressis verbis* mention citizenship, it should be taken into account that the list of the criteria included in the Covenant is not an exhaustive one. In the practice of the Human Rights Committee in certain cases, for instance, in situations concerning confiscated property or the right to receive a pension, citizenship has been found to be "other status", on the grounds of which discrimination is prohibited (see, for example, decision of the Human Rights Committee of 3 April 1989 in *Ibrahima Gueye et al.* v. *France*, communication no. 196/1985, para. 9.4, and decision of 30 October 2001 in *Des Fours Walderode and Kammerlande* v. *Czech Republic*, communication no. 747/1997, para. 8.4). In a case that concerned a difference in pensions paid to former citizens of the Netherlands residing abroad the Human Rights Committee, after taking into account the circumstances of the specific case, pointed out that different treatment which has reasonable and objective grounds is not to be considered to be discrimination within the meaning of Article 26 of the Covenant (see decision of the Human Rights Committee of 23 July 1997 in *Van Oord* v. *Netherlands*, communication no. 658/1995, para. 8.5).

Pursuant to Article 14 of the European Convention for the Protection of Human Rights and Fundamental Freedoms (hereafter – the Convention), the enjoyment of the rights and freedoms set forth in the Convention shall be secured without discrimination on any ground such as sex, race, colour, language, religion, political or other opinion, national or social origin, association with a national minority, property, birth or other status. It has to be taken into account that Article 14 of the Convention is engaged only in conjunction with the rights guaranteed by the Convention.

Similarly to Article 26 of the Covenant, Article 14 of the Convention does not directly contain citizenship as a [forbidden] criterion. However, pursuant to the case law of the European Court of Human Rights (hereafter – the ECtHR) in certain situations permanent residence (domicile) abroad or citizenship are to be considered to be "other status" indicated in Article 14 of the Convention on the basis of which discrimination is prohibited (see, for instance, judgment of the ECtHR of 30 September 2003 in *Koua Poirrez* v. *France*, application no. 40892/98, para. 49, and judgment of the Grand Chamber of the ECtHR of 16 March 2010 in *Carson and Others* v. *the United Kingdom*, application no. 42184/05, paras. 66 and 70). The ECtHR has also held that contracting states enjoy a certain margin of appreciation in assessing whether and to what extent differences in otherwise similar situations justify a difference in treatment (see, for instance, judgment of the Grand Chamber of the ECtHR of 7 November 2013 in *Vallianatos and Others* v. *Greece*, application nos. 29831/09 and 32684/09, para. 76). The scope of the margin of appreciation will vary according to the circumstances, the subject matter and its background (see, for example, judgment of the ECtHR of 8 April 2014 in *Dhahbi* v. *Italy*, application no. 17120/09, para. 46). For instance, a wide margin is usually allowed to the contracting states when it comes to general measures of economic or social strategy (see, for example, judgment of the Grand Chamber of the ECtHR of 7 July 2011 in *Stummer* v. *Austria*, application no. 37542/02, para. 89). Nevertheless, the ECtHR has concluded that a contracting state would have to put forward very weighty reasons in order to regard a difference of treatment based exclusively on the ground of nationality as compatible with the Convention (see, for example, judgment of the ECtHR of 16 September 1996 in *Gaygusuz* v. *Austria*, application no. 17371/90, para. 42).

Thus from norms of international human rights law binding on Latvia it follows that citizenship is to be regarded as one of the criteria, discrimination on the grounds of which is forbidden. However, differences in treatment on the basis of this criterion are not absolutely prohibited – in certain situations the use of this criterion may be justified.

10.2 Article 20(1) TFEU establishes citizenship of the European Union which means that every person holding the nationality of a Member State is a citizen of the European Union. EU citizenship is additional to and does not replace national citizenship. One of the aims of the institute of EU citizenship is ensuring proper legal protection of persons moving within the EU (see Krūma K. "EU Citizenship, Nationality and Migrant Status. An Ongoing Challenge". Leiden: Nijhoff, 2014, p. 120). European Union citizenship is a fundamental status of citizens that ensures to persons the rights guaranteed by the EU Treaties as well as other privileges (see, for example, judgment of the European Court of Justice of 20 September 2001 in case C-184/99, para. 31).

One of the most significant rights that directly derive from the status of a citizen of the European Union is the right to free movement and residence included in Article 21(1) TFEU. According to this provision every citizen of the European Union has the right to move and reside freely within the Member States. Article 21(1) TFEU grants subjective rights to every EU citizen and it has direct effect in the Member States of the EU (see, for example, judgment of the European Court of Justice of 19 October 2004 in case C-200/02, para. 26). At the same time, the first paragraph of Article 18 TFEU provides that within the scope of application of the Treaties, and without prejudice to any special provisions contained therein, any discrimination on grounds of nationality is prohibited.

Article 21(1) TFEU in conjunction with the first paragraph of Article 18 TFEU provides each EU citizen with the right to an equal treatment in the host Member State, namely the right to treatment that is the same as with regard to the citizens of that Member State. The right to a free movement of citizens of the European Union mean not only the right to physically move and reside in another EU Member State but also the right not to be discriminated in another Member State for the sole reason that he is not a citizen of that Member State. In addition, the right to free movement protects citizens of the EU from such measures of Member States that might prevent them from using the aforementioned rights or place them in a less beneficial situation only due to the fact that they have exercised their right to freedom of movement. ...

Hence from the obligations that Latvia has undertaken in conjunction with its membership in the European Union it follows that citizenship is a criterion on the basis of which discrimination is forbidden.

Therefore citizenship is one of the criteria falling within the scope of Article 91 of the Constitution.

...

15.4.1 The Constitutional Court in this judgment has already pointed out that citizens of the European Union have the right to free movement and residence in other Member States of the EU, and it has also indicated the contents of the principle of non-discrimination under the EU law. ...

Pursuant to the jurisprudence of the CJEU in the legal space of the European Union, different treatment on the basis of citizenship may be justified only if it is based on objective considerations independent of the nationality of the persons concerned (see judgment of the European Court of Justice of 16 December 2008 in case C-524/06, para. 75, and judgment of 20 January 2011 in case C-155/09, para. 69). ..."

(Available, only in Latvian, at the website of the Constitutional Court, <https://www.satv.tiesa.gov.lv/web/viewer.html?file=/wp-content/uploads/2017/11/2017-28-0306_Spriedums.pdf>, visited on 1 December 2019)

4/6

The third judgment of the Constitutional Court that is related to EU law was adopted on 18 December 2018 in case no. 2016-04-03. This judgment is notable because it was adopted after the Constitutional Court – for the first time in its history – referred to the Court of Justice of the European Union several questions for preliminary ruling. The case concerned the issue of whether early retirement support that is paid to elderly farmers who decide to stop farming may be inherited after the death of those farmers. On 28 February 2017 the Constitutional Court decided to suspend the proceedings in the case and to refer three questions to the Court of Justice which provided its answers in a judgment of 7 August 2018 in case C-120/17. The CJEU explained that inheriting early retirement support is precluded by Council Regulation (EC) No 1257/1999 of 17 May 1999, yet the fact that the Cabinet of Ministers of the Republic of Latvia had granted such a right of inheritance had created legitimate expectations for the heirs of retired farmers. The Constitutional Court held as follows:

> 18.4 After joining the European Union Latvia has become bound to comply with its obligations that follow from the treaty on the accession to the European Union. That means that upon ratifying the treaty on Latvia's accession to the European Union the law of European Union has become an inextricable part of the Latvian law. Pursuant to this treaty Latvia is bound by the legal acts adopted by the institutions of the European Union. The interpretation of these acts in the jurisprudence of the CJEU is binding when interpreting and applying national legal acts, in order to eliminate the possible contradictions between the legal norms of Latvia and the European Union. ...
>
> 19.1 ... The Court of Justice of the European Union has held that Articles 10 to 12 of Regulation No 1257/1999 cannot be deemed to be norms of the law of the European Union that are sufficiently clear for persons to have been able to understand that the Member States are precluded from making it possible to inherit the early retirement support. ...
>
> 19.2 ... the Constitutional Court concludes that when concluding an agreement on [early retirement] support ... persons (the transferees of

agricultural holdings as well as their heirs) could rely on the transfer of the [support] payments to the [heirs]. Hence in the specific circumstances the right of the heirs ... to receive early retirement support payments after the death of the transferee of the agricultural holding may be considered an object of property rights. By adopting the impugned norm, the Cabinet of Ministers has restricted the aforementioned right by denying the heirs ... further [support] payments ...

21.2 A significant component of the principle of a democratic state governed by the rule of law is the unity of the legal system. The legal norms existing in a state must be mutually concordant and they should operate harmoniously within the framework of a unified legal system. The same applies also to the compliance of legal norms of Latvia, a Member State of the European Union, with the law of the European Union which is a component of Latvian law. The Constitutional Court has previously held that legal norms of the European Union are compatible only with national legal systems that comply with the requirements for a democratic state governed by the rule of law ...

Within the context of the present case the Court of Justice of the European Union has held that when Member States are implementing the law of the European Union they have discretion to decide upon amendments to the [national legal acts] pursuant to which persons are entitled to inherit the early retirement support. ...

The principle of a democratic state governed by the rule of law obliges the state to ensure that early retirement support would be paid lawfully, in accordance with the provisions of the law of the European Union. The restriction of fundamental rights contained in the impugned provision has been imposed with the aim to eliminate the contradiction between the [regulation of the Cabinet of Ministers] and the provisions of Regulation No 1257/1999. Hence the restriction of fundamental rights contained in the impugned provision has a legitimate aim – the protection of the democratic structure of the state. ...

24. Taking into account the answer given in the Judgment of the Court of Justice of the European Union to the first preliminary question asked by the Constitutional Court, namely, that Articles 10 to 12 of Regulation No 1257/1999 preclude Member States from adopting measures making it possible inherit support ..., the contradiction between the respective

provision of the [previously valid regulation of the Cabinet of Ministers] and Articles 10 to 12 of Regulation No 1257/1999 could only be eliminated by adopting the impugned provision. Therefore the Constitutional Court agrees with the argument of the Cabinet of Ministers that in the specific case it was not possible to achieve the legitimate aims by other means; the only option was ceasing the support payments to the heirs of the [initial] recipient of [those payments].

Therefore there are no less restrictive means that would permit achieving the legitimate aims of the restriction of fundamental rights in at least the same quality.

...

25.2 It follows from the drafting materials of the impugned provision, as well as from the written reply of the Cabinet of Ministers that the impugned provision had been adopted in order to eliminate the contradiction between national legal acts and the legal acts of the European Union. If the European Commission were to conclude that the support payments ... do not comply with the requirements of Regulation No 1257[1999], it could request from the Member State repayment of improperly made support payments as well as impose a surcharge ... The Court of Justice of the European Union has held that economic operators are not justified in having an expectation that national authorities, when implementing EU law, will not amend national legal regulation pursuant to which persons may inherit early retirement support (see the [j]udgment of the Court of Justice [of 7 August 2018 in case C-120/17], para. 66, and the judgment of 22 October 2009 in case C-449/08 *Elbertsen*, ... para. 45) ...

(Available, only in Latvian, at the website of the Constitutional Court, <https://www.satv.tiesa.gov.lv/web/viewer.html?file=/wp-content/uploads/2016/02/2016-04-03_Spriedums.pdf>, visited on 27 November 2019)

4/7

The judgment of the Constitutional Court of 15 March 2018 in case no. 2017-16-01 is an example of a situation where the Court has held that the level of human rights protection guaranteed by the Constitution exceeds that of the European Convention on Human Rights. The case pertained to the procedural guarantees applicable in court proceedings concerning administrative violations, more specifically – with regard to proceedings in an appeal court. One of the central issues to be resolved was the extent to which Article 92 (right to a fair trial) applied with respect to such proceedings. With respect to the interaction of domestic and international law in this respect the Court indicated as follows:

> 9.1 When establishing the contents of the fundamental rights enshrined in the Constitution, it is necessary to take into account Latvia's international obligations in the field of human rights. The obligation of the state to comply with international obligations in the field of human rights is contained in, *inter alia*, Article 89 of the Constitution which provides that the state recognises and protects fundamental human rights in accordance with the Constitution, laws, and international treaties binding upon Latvia. The aim of the constitutional legislator has been to harmonise norms of human rights included in the Constitution with international human rights provisions ...
>
> In the current case the first sentence of Article 92 of the Constitution is to be assessed in conjunction with Article 6 of the Convention ... In interpreting the provisions of the Constitution and the Convention, a solution ought to be sought that ensures their mutual harmony ...
>
> 9.2. The petitioners consider that cases of administrative violations may be compared to criminal cases within the meaning of Article 6 of the Convention and therefore the guarantees deriving from the right to a fair trial with respect to criminal cases are equally applicable with respect to cases of administrative violations ...
>
> The Constitutional Court has already held that in cases where the penalty that may be imposed for an administrative violation may be compared to a criminal law sanction, the criminal law aspect of Article 6(1) of the Convention is applicable ...
>
> However, the Code [of Administrative Violations] also describes administrative violations which, if committed, are punishable by a penalty that by its nature and severity may not be considered comparable to a criminal law sanction. For instance, a warning may be issued in case if an administrative violation has been committed. Furthermore, according to ... the Code a monetary penalty may be imposed in a minimal amount of two euros.

If the particular case may be equated to a criminal case within the meaning of Article 6 of the Convention, Article 2 of Protocol No. 7 to the Convention is also applicable in that respect. It provides that everyone convicted of a criminal offence by a tribunal has the right to have his conviction or sentence reviewed by a higher tribunal. The same article provides that this right may be subject to exceptions, for instance, with regard to offences of a minor character.

Hence the minimum standard of Article 2 of Protocol No. 7 to the Convention provides for an obligation of the state to ensure the right to an appeal in the cases that may be equated to criminal cases within the meaning of Article 6 of the Convention, unless the state has chosen to implement a different procedure in respect of, for instance, offences of a minor character.

However, the legislator is entitled to implement a higher level of protection of fundamental rights than that provided for by the Convention and to apply the rights and procedural guarantees that derive from Article 6(1) of the Convention also towards cases of administrative violations. The legislator in … the Code has provided for a right to appeal against all decisions adopted in cases of administrative violations and has not provided for an exception even with respect to offences of a minor character. Hence the legislator has applied the guarantees of the right to a fair trial that derive from the first sentence of Article 92 of the Constitution also to all cases of administrative violations.

Therefore the state is obliged to create a procedure for examining cases of administrative violations that would ensure to persons the guarantees of the right to a fair trial that derive from the first sentence of Article 92 of the Constitution in the same manner as in criminal cases.…

(Available, only in Latvian, at the website of the Constitutional Court, <https://www.satv.tiesa.gov.lv/web/viewer.html?file=/wp-content/uploads/2017/05/2017-16-01_Spriedums.pdf>, visited on 29 November 2019)

4/8

In the judgment that the Constitutional Court adopted on 14 June 2018 in case no. 2017-23-01 it addressed the different roles played by the Constitutional Court and the European Court of Human Rights. The case concerned the issue of motivation of decisions of a cassation instance court in criminal proceedings, an issue which has been repeatedly analysed in the case law of the ECtHR. In this regard the Constitutional Court pointed out:

> 14. The persons invited to give an opinion in the case in their opinions refer to the judgment of the [European Court of Human Rights of 13 October 2016] in *Talmane* v. *Latvia* [, application no. 47938/07], and suggest that the ECtHR has found the existing practice of the cassation instance court in criminal cases to be compatible with the Convention. The Constitutional Court points out that in that case the ECtHR assessed the cassation complaint that had been submitted by the applicant and held: "given the nature of the applicant's appeal on points of law, the [ECtHR] considers it sufficiently proved that the Senate had ruled out the existence of circumstances warranting the initiation of cassation proceedings. In all her appeals the applicant raised several complaints concerning the procedure followed in establishing the evidence in her criminal case. These complaints were duly examined by two court instances with full jurisdiction, and in their judgments the lower courts provided proper reasoning. It was not for the Senate to re-examine the existing evidence or to obtain new evidence, as requested by the applicant. Furthermore, as showed by the documents submitted to the [ECtHR], the Senate had considered the applicant's arguments, had given the reason for rejecting the complaint and had explained to the applicant its competence in relation to the re-examination of evidence ... In these circumstances the ECtHR is satisfied that the Senate has duly examined the grounds of the applicant's appeal on points of law, and that the cassation court's reasoning in this case has been sufficient" (...*Talmane* v. *Latvia*, ... para. 32).
>
> It follows that in the judgment in *Talmane* v. *Latvia* the ECtHR exercised its principal function – it assessed whether the fundamental rights of the applicant had been violated in the circumstances of the specific case. The ECtHR assessed the actions of the Senate of the Supreme Court after receiving the applicant's cassation complaint, and not the legal regulation of examining cassation complaints.
>
> On the other hand, the task of the Constitutional Court is, within the limits of its competence, to ensure the existence of a legal system that to the broadest possible extent would prevent the existence of legal regulation that is contrary to the Constitution or other legal norms (acts)

with a higher legal force, as well as to state its position with regard to constitutionally significant issues. ... The task of the Constitutional Court is to prevent the existence of legal regulation that, even if it were to be applied correctly, might lead to a violation of fundamental rights.

Thus the functions and tasks of the Constitutional Court are broader than the functions and tasks of the ECtHR. If valid legal regulation at all allows for a situation in which its application might lead to a violation of fundamental rights enshrined in the Constitution, then the Constitutional Court must find such a regulation to be contrary to the Constitution and invalid. A proper legal regulation that complies with the Constitution will always contain guarantees that, in the case of proper and systemic application of the regulation, will completely exclude the possibility of a violation of fundamental rights.

Article 53 of the Convention does not prevent Member States providing more extensive guarantees of fundamental rights according to their constitutional traditions. The Constitutional Court assesses the procedure for initiating cassation proceedings in criminal cases that has been established in accordance with the impugned provisions, taking into account the legal system of Latvia as a democratic state governed by the rule of law. It derives from the case law of the Constitutional Court that the right to be heard is implemented by using several different means, including the right to expect that the decision of the court will be reasoned on the basis of the arguments submitted by the parties ... In the case law of the ECtHR it has been established that how detailed reasoning has to be indicated in decisions of the court may vary according to the nature of the decision and in the light of the circumstances of the case that are to be assessed individually in each particular case (see the judgment of 9 December 2004 of the European Court of Human Rights in *Ruiz Torija* v. *Spain*, application no. 18390/91, para. 29). In addition, the obligation to give reasons for decisions cannot be understood as a general requirement to give a detailed answer to every argument (see the judgment of 21 January 1999 of the Grand Chamber of the European Court of Human Rights in *García Ruiz* v. *Spain*, application no. 30544/96, para. 26) ...

(Available, only in Latvian, at the website of the Constitutional Court, <https://www.satv.tiesa.gov.lv/web/viewer.html?file=/wp-content/uploads/2017/09/2017-23-01_Spriedums.pdf>, visited on 30 November 2019)

4/9

In its judgment of 29 June 2018 in case no. 2017-25-01 the Constitutional Court continued to address an issue that has been topical for decades, namely, the restrictions of passive election rights for persons who, around the time when the Republic of Latvia regained its independence in 1990–1991, had been active in a number of organisations whose activities were directed against the independence of Latvia. This issue has been addressed by the European Court of Human Rights (judgment of the Grand Chamber of 16 March 2006 in *Ždanoka v. Latvia*, application no. 58278/00, and judgment of 24 June 2008 in *Ādamsons v. Latvia*, application no. 3669/03) as well as by the Constitutional Court itself (judgment of 30 August 2000 in case no. 2000-03-01 and judgment of 15 June 2006 in case no. 2005-13-0106). With regard to the international-law aspects of the case the Court held as follows:

> **14** ... The European Court of Human Rights has ... pointed to the increasing level of stability of the Latvian democracy, which has been facilitated by Latvia's full integration in Europe, and has urged Latvia to regularly review the restriction included in the contested norm (see ... "*Ždanoka v. Latvia*", ... para. 135) ...
>
> **17.1** ... In the case under review, Articles 1 and 9 of the *Satversme* must be reviewed in interconnection with Article 3 of the First Protocol to the Convention, as well as the case-law of the European Court of Human Rights regarding its application ...
>
> Article 3 of the First Protocol to the Convention provides that Member States of the Convention commit themselves to holding free elections at reasonable intervals by secret ballot, under conditions, which will ensure the free expression of the opinion of the electorate in the choice of legislature.
>
> The European Court of Human Rights has recognised that Article 3 of the First Protocol to the Convention indirectly envisages a person's rights, inter alia, the right to vote and the right to stand for election. However, in view of the fact that the historical and political conditions differ in each country, the states enjoy broad discretion in setting the rules with respect to the status of a member of the parliament, inter alia, to define the criteria, due to incompatibility with which persons may not be elected. Moreover, the state may set additional criteria for exercising a person's right to stand for election (see the judgment of the European Court of Human

Rights of 2 March 1987 in the case *"Mathieu-Mohin and Clerfagt* v. *Belgium"*, application no. 9267/81, para. 54, and the judgment of 9 April 2002 in the case *"Podkolzina* v. *Latvia"*, application no. 46726/99, para. 34). ...

23 ... The Constitutional Court has already concluded that the procedure of elections is closely linked to the historical development, political situation and a number of other factors in each country .... The European Court of Human Rights has recognised that the restriction included in the contested norm should be examined by taking into account the State's broad discretion in establishing such restrictions (see ... *"Ždanoka* v. *Latvia"*, ... para. 115). Therefore the Constitutional Court in considering whether no more lenient measures exist for reaching the legitimate aim must take into account that the state enjoys broad discretion in organising its system of elections. ...

24.1 The Constitutional Court has already recognised that the restriction on fundamental rights included in the contested norm may exist only for a definite period of time; therefore the legislator, by regularly assessing the political situation in the state, must decide on the necessity and justification of this restriction ... The Constitutional Court has pointed to the need to review this restriction within as short period of time as possible also in its judgment in the case no. 2005-13-0106 ... Likewise, the European Court of Human Rights ... has noted that the Latvian parliament must keep the restriction included in the contested norm under constant review, with a view to bring it to an early end (see ... *"Ždanoka* v. *Latvia"*, ... para. 135). It has been recognised in the case-law of the European Court of Human Rights that, in assessing the proportionality of a restriction, the existence of a time-limit and the possibility to review it are essential (see the judgment of the Grand Chamber of the European Court of Human Rights of 6 January 2011 in the case *"Paksas* v. *Lithuania"*, application no. 34932/04, para. 109). ...

24.3 The contested norm is not directed against the pluralism of ideas in Latvia or the political views of a certain person but rather against persons who by their actions imperilled and continue to imperil the national independence of Latvia and the principles of democratic state governed by the rule of law (see, for example, the judgment of the European Court of Human Rights of 1 June 2015 in the case *"Petropavlovskis* v. *Latvia"*, application no. 44230/06, paras. 69–70). Also, it should be taken into account that the contested norm does not prohibit person to whom the prohibition included therein applies from being actively engaged in political parties and public organisations....

(Available at the website of the Constitutional Court, <http://www.satv.tiesa.gov.lv/web/viewer.html?file=/wp-content/uploads/2017/10/2017-25-01_Judgment_ENG.pdf>, visited on 30 November 2019)

4/10

In a decision of 6 July 2018 in case no. SKA-130/2018 the Administrative Cases Department of the Supreme Court addressed an issue concerning the prohibition of torture and inhumane or degrading treatment that has previously not been expanded upon in international law. Namely, the case concerned a situation where the applicant, who at the relevant time had been in prison, had been placed in a metal "cage" during his meetings with his lawyer. The Court held as follows:

[5] No identical cases have been found in the practice of the European Court of Human Rights. However, the European Court of Human Rights has found a violation of the prohibition of inhumane and degrading treatment in several cases where a person has been held in a dock encircled by bars (a metal cage) during court hearings.

The European Court of Human Rights held that the employment of measures of restraint does not normally cause a violation [of the Convention] where they have been imposed in connection with lawful arrest or detention and do not entail the use of force, or public exposure, exceeding what is reasonably considered necessary in the circumstances. In such cases it is important to assess whether there is reason to believe that the person concerned would try to abscond or cause injury or damage or suppress evidence (judgment of [the Grand Chamber of] the European Court of Human Rights of 17 July 2014 in *Svinarenko and Slyadnev v. Russia*, application nos. 32541/08 and 43441/08, para. 117).

However, the Court also found no convincing arguments to the effect that, in present-day circumstances, holding a defendant in a cage during trial is a necessary means of restraining him, preventing his escape, dealing with disorderly or aggressive behaviour, or protecting him against aggression from outside. Therefore such practice is only a means of degrading and humiliating the caged person (*ibid.*, para. 135). The European Court of Human Rights found that holding a person in a metal cage during a trial constitutes – having regard to its objectively degrading nature which is incompatible with the standards of civilised behaviour that are the hallmark of a democratic society – an affront to human dignity and a breach of the prohibition of inhumane and degrading treatment (*ibid.*, para. 138).

The European Court of Human Rights also found a violation of the prohibition of inhumane and degrading treatment in a case where a prisoner had been placed in a metal cage at the time when he took part in a court hearing by means of a video link and hence was physically located in prison and not the courtroom. The [respondent] Government considered that there had been no violation because in the specific case the element of publicity had been missing. However, the Court rejected this argument by holding that a violation can also be found in a case where the specific actions have not been public; it is sufficient that the person is humiliated in his own eyes, even if not in the eyes of others (judgment of the European Court of Human Rights of 17 April 2018 in *Karachentsev v. Russia*, application no. 23229/11, paras. 46 and 52).

The European Committee for Prevention of Torture and Inhuman or Degrading Treatment or Punishment has indicated that metal bars as an instrument of delimitation may be unacceptable in a place of imprisonment. The Committee in its report on a visit to Latvia in 2009 mentioned that life-sentenced prisoners often undergo medical interventions and consultations while separated from a doctor by metal bars. The report found such practice to be highly questionable from the standpoint of human dignity (*Report to the Latvian Government on the visit to Latvia carried out by the European Committee for the Prevention of Torture and Inhuman or Degrading Treatment or Punishment (CPT) of 3 to 8 December 2009, para 34; https://rm.coe.int/1680697312*).

Taking into account the above, it may be concluded that the prohibition of inhumane and degrading treatment may be violated if a prisoner is placed in a metal cage while on the premises of prison.

[6] However, ... the employment of measures of restraint in prison may also be justified if it is done on objective grounds. This also derives from other cases examined by the European Court of Human Rights that the application of various means of separation in prisons is not completely

forbidden. For instance, in a case where the dispute pertained to a [possible] violation of the right of [inviolability] of private and family life, the European Court of Human Rights held that physical separation of a detainee from his visitors may be justified by security considerations. However, such a measure cannot be considered necessary in the absence of any concrete security risk (judgment of the European Court of Human Rights of 9 October 2008 in *Moiseyev* v. *Russia*, application no. 62936/00, para. 258). Meanwhile in another case the European Court of Human Rights criticised the automatic application in respect of all life-sentenced prisoners of such measures of restraint as handcuffing and the use of dogs for escorting prisoners in the territory of the prison (judgment of the European Court of Human Rights of 27 November 2012 in *Savičs* v. *Latvia*, application no. 17892/03, para. 140). ...

Therefore it may be concluded that the placement of a prisoner in a unit with metal bars during his meetings with his lawyer may comply with the prohibition of inhuman and degrading treatment only in a situation where concrete security risks have been established as a result of an individual assessment of the prisoner.

(Available, only in Latvian, at the website of the Supreme Court, <http://at.gov.lv/downloadlawfile/5556>, visited on 20 December 2019)

4/11

In a decision adopted in 2017 (the date of the decision and the identification number of the case are not disclosed to the public) the Civil Cases Department of the Supreme Court of the Republic of Latvia applied the Convention of 25 October 1980 on the Civil Aspects of International Child Abduction (the Hague Convention), as interpreted by the European Court of Human Rights, and Council Regulation (EC) No 2201/2003 of 27 November 2003 concerning jurisdiction and the recognition and enforcement of judgments in matrimonial matters and matters of parental responsibility in a case concerning a requested return of an unlawfully removed child. The lower courts had rejected the child's mother's request to reopen the proceedings which had ended in a decision that the child had to be returned to his father. The mother had brought evidence that the child might have been subjected to sexual violence by the father but the lower courts had considered that this was not a "newly discovered circumstance" that would warrant reopening the original return proceedings. The Supreme Court held:

[12.2] ...The application of grounds for not returning a child contained in the Hague Convention is significant from the point of view that when such grounds are established, they allow to retain the child in a state to which he has been brought unlawfully or where he has been unlawfully detained or abducted and prevent the return of the child. These exceptions clearly derive from a consideration of the interests of the child, to which the Hague Convention gives a definite content. Thus, the interest of the child in not being removed from his or her habitual residence without sufficient guarantees of stability in the new environment gives way before the primary interest of the child in not being exposed to physical or psychological danger or being placed in an intolerable situation. Lastly, there is no obligation to return a child when, in terms of Article 20 of the Hague Convention, his or her return "would not be permitted by the fundamental principles of the requested State relating to the protection of human rights and fundamental freedoms" (compare with the judgment of the Grand Chamber of the European Court of Human Rights of 26 November 2013 in *X* v. *Latvia*, application no. 27853/09, para. 35).

The ECtHR has repeatedly stated that according to the established case law of courts in the area of international child abduction the obligations imposed by Article 8 [of the Convention] on the Contracting States must be interpreted in the light of the requirements of the Hague Convention and the Convention on the Rights of the Child of 20 November 1989 (see, for example, the judgment of the ECtHR of 25 January 2000 in *Ignaccolo-Zenide* v. *Romania*, application no. 31679/96, judgment of 29 April 2003 in *Iglesias Gil and A.U.I.* v. *Spain*, application no. 56673/00, judgment of 6 December 2007 in *Maumousseau and Washington* v. *France*, application no. 39388/05, judgment of the Grand Chamber of the ECtHR of 6 July 2010 in *Neulinger and Shuruk* v. *Switzerland*, application no. 41615/07, etc.). The decisive point is to strike a fair balance between the competing interests at stake – those of the child, of the two parents, and of public order, within the margin of appreciation afforded to states in such matters, taking into account, however, that the best interests of the child must be of primary consideration and that the objective of immediate return corresponds to the specific conception of "the best interests of the child". As the ECtHR has held in the cases cited above, the same idea is inherent in the Hague Convention, which associates this interest with restoration of the *status quo*, while taking account of the fact that non-return may sometimes prove justified for objective reasons that correspond to the child's interests, thus explaining the existence of exceptions, specifically in the event of a grave risk that his or her return would expose the child to physical or psychological harm or otherwise place the child in an intolerable situation (Article 13, first paragraph, (b)). It follows from Article 8 of the Convention and also from Articles 12, 13 and 20 of the Hague Convention, that the child's prompt return cannot be ordered "automatically or mechanically", particularly where exceptional factors are raised by one of the parties to the proceedings. Then the court must make a decision that is sufficiently reasoned on this point that would allow to verify that those questions have been effectively examined. ...

In the present case ... an assessment of the additional circumstances indicated by the applicant – possible sexual violence by the child's father against the child and the child's ability to formulate an opinion ... may have an impact on the outcome of the adjudication of the case.

[12.3] ... As has been established by the ECtHR, the refusal to take into account an allegation of the applicant that is based on a certificate issued by a professional, which could disclose the possible existence of a grave risk within the meaning of Article 13, first paragraph, (b) of the Hague Convention, is contrary to the requirements of Article 8 of the Convention (see ... "*X* v. *Latvia*" ..., para. 117).

(Available, only in Latvian, at the website of the Supreme Court, <http://www.at.gov.lv/downloadlawfile/5162>, visited on 23 November 2019)

Part Four: III. Relationship between International Law and Internal Law – Remedies under internal law for violations of international law

4/12

In a decision of 4 October 2017 in case no. SKA-424/2017 the Administrative Cases Department of the Supreme Court had to examine the question of restarting administrative proceedings after the Human Rights Committee on 30 November 2010 had adopted its views with regard to communication No. 1621/2007. The case concerned the spelling of the applicant's name. The applicant is a Latvian national belonging to the Jewish and Russian-speaking minorities. His name in his official documents was spelled according to the rules of Latvian grammar. The applicant considered that the refusal of Latvian authorities to inscribe his name and surname in official documents according to their spelling in the Russian language constituted a violation of his right to privacy because the spelling in Latvian "look[s] and sound[s] odd" and creates difficulties in his daily life. The Human Rights Committee found a violation of Article 17 of the International Covenant on Civil and Political Rights "with respect to the unilateral change of the author's name by the State party". The applicant subsequently requested that administrative proceedings with respect to the spelling of his name in official documents be restarted in the light of the views adopted by the Human Rights Committee. The administrative authorities refused to do so, and the issue eventually reached the Supreme Court.

With regard to the interaction between national law and views adopted by the Human Rights Committee the Supreme Court ruled as follows:

> [7] The main issue to be decided in this case is related to the impact of the views of the Human Rights Committee in the [*Raihman*] case on the decision in the specific case....
>
> [12] The Constitutional Court has indicated that the views of the Human Rights Committee cannot be considered to be *res judicata*, namely, they are not legally binding on states ...; however, the views of the Committee are to be considered an authoritative opinion that explains the contents of the provisions of the Covenant that are to be assessed by the national authorities ...
>
> The Supreme Court has previously held that, albeit the views of the Human Rights Committee are not directly legally binding, they disclose the scope of the human rights provisions included in the Covenant. The human rights provisions included in the Covenant (as interpreted by the Committee) are binding on Latvia as norms of international law.
>
> In this respect the Supreme Court repeatedly emphasises that it fully agrees with the views adopted by the Human Rights Committee in the [*Raihman*] case with regard to the scope of the right to privacy deriving from Article 17 of the Covenant. At the same time, after carefully examining the ... factual circumstances, the Supreme Court cannot agree to the assessment of the factual circumstances by the Human Rights Committee in the specific case and to the related conclusion that proportionality has been violated in the specific case.
>
> States have to consider the views of the Human Rights Committee in good faith; on the other hand, they are not debarred from dismissing them, after careful consideration, as not reflecting the true legal position

with regard to the case concerned (European Commission for Democracy through Law (Venice Commission) *"Report on the implementation of international human rights treaties in domestic law and the role of courts".* Strasbourg, 8 December 2014, Study No 690/2012, para. 78).

(Available, only in Latvian, at the website of the Supreme Court, <http://www.at.gov.lv/downloadlawfile/5586>, visited on 10 December 2019)

4/13

In its decision of 8 December 2017 in case No. SKK-J-637/2017 the Criminal Cases Department of the Supreme Court of the Republic of Latvia decided upon the recurrent issue of the need to reopen criminal proceedings after a violation of the right to a fair trial has been established by the European Court of Human Rights. The case came before the Supreme Court in the aftermath of the judgment of the ECtHR of 2 December 2014 in *Taraneks* v. *Latvia*, application no. 3082/06 in which it was established, *inter alia*, that the applicant's conviction had originated in unlawful police incitement. Insofar as is relevant, the Supreme Court held as follows:

> [17] Recommendation No. R (2000) 2 of the Committee of Ministers of the Council of Europe "On the re-examination or reopening of certain cases at domestic level following judgments of the European Court of Human Rights" (hereinafter – recommendation) provides for situations in which re-examination of cases would be desirable.
>
> [17.1] It follows from the text of the recommendation that the principal criterion for reopening proceedings or re-examining cases is related to the possibility to ensure the restitution of the initial situation (*restitutio in integrum*), namely, if in exceptional circumstances re-examination of a case or reopening of proceedings is the most efficient or the only means of achieving restitution of the initial situation (paragraph 6 of the preamble of the recommendation). Re-examination of the case or reopening proceedings is recommended in instances where the injured party continues to suffer very serious negative consequences, which are not adequately remedied by just satisfaction and cannot be rectified except by re-examination or reopening, and if there have been violations of the Convention in the domestic decision or the procedure (para. 11 of the recommendation). Thus the national court, when examining the question of re-examining the case, is guided by the criterion of whether re-examination of a case might lead to restitution of the initial situation and reverse the negative consequences, which are not adequately remedied

by just satisfaction and cannot be rectified except by re- examination of the case.

[17.2] The European Court of Human Rights has repeatedly pointed out situations in which, in order for a violation to be rectified, it is exactly an obligation to re-examine the case that is imposed. In *Oleksandr Volkov* v. *Ukraine* the European Court of Human Rights has indicated that in situations where it considers that the most appropriate individual remedy would be re-examination of a case, it specifies this measure in the judgment (see judgment of the European Court of Human Rights of 9 January 2013 in *Oleksandr Volkov* v. *Ukraine*, application no. 21722/11, para. 206, as well as judgment of 8 January 2013 in *Baltiņš* v. *Latvia*, application no. 25282/07, para. 73).

[18] In the current case the European Court of Human Rights in its judgment has not directly specified that the most appropriate remedy would be re-opening of the criminal proceedings. At the same time, the Supreme Court considers that it follows from the substance of the violations found [by the ECtHR] that the criminal proceedings ought to be reopened.

The Supreme Court finds that the judgment of the European Court of Human Rights in *Taraneks* v. *Latvia* is to be recognised as a newly discovered circumstance that could sufficiently affect the outcome of the case …

(Available, only in Latvian, at the website of the Supreme Court, <http://www.at.gov.lv/downloadlawfile/5325>, visited on 17 December 2019)

Part Five: I. B. 6. Subjects of International Law – States – Recognition – Non-recognition (including non-recognition of governments) and its effects

5/1

On 18 March 2018 the Ministry of Foreign Affairs issued a statement to mark four years that had passed since the illegal annexation of Crimea:

> Four years will have passed on 18 March 2014 since the violations of Ukraine's sovereignty and territorial integrity committed by the Russian Federation, which illegally annexed the Crimean Peninsula and launched

military aggression in the east of Ukraine. By its actions, the Russian Federation has violated international law and basic principles of relations between countries.

The Ministry of Foreign Affairs reiterates Latvia's principled position on the issues of sovereignty and territorial integrity of Ukraine:

Latvia does not recognise the illegal annexation of Crimea by the Russian Federation;

Latvia condemns the Russian Federation's aggression in the east of Ukraine and stands up for maintaining EU sanctions till the full implementation of the Minsk agreements.

In line with the policy of non-recognition of the annexation of Crimea, Latvia does not recognise the holding of the Russian presidential election in Crimea and Sevastopol on 18 March.

(Available at the website of the Ministry of Foreign Affairs, <https://www.mfa.gov.lv/en/news/latest-news/59472-latvia-s-position-on-the-illegally-annexed-crimea>, visited on 3 November 2019)

5/2

The Ministry of Foreign Affairs has consistently argued in favour of the territorial integrity of Georgia and condemned all attempts at legitimation of separatism in the Georgian regions of Abkhazia and South Ossetia:

Developments in Georgia's regions of Abkhazia and South Ossetia are a matter of concern, including the closure of border crossing points along the Administrative Boundary Line of the region of Abkhazia. These actions go against commitments to work towards enhanced security and improved living conditions for the conflict-affected population, as well as having a negative effect on the human rights situation and stability in the region.

The Ministry of Foreign Affairs reiterates that it does not recognise the so-called parliamentary elections illegitimately held in the Georgian region of Abkhazia in March 2017, and the so-called presidential elections and a referendum held in the Georgian region of South Ossetia in April 2017. The actions of this kind by separatist regimes do not contribute to a peaceful resolution of the conflict.

(Available at the website of the Ministry of Foreign Affairs, <https://www.mfa.gov.lv/en/news/latest-news/60846-statement-by-the-ministry-of-foreign-affairs-on-marking-ten-years-since-russia-s-aggression-against-georgia>, visited on 4 November 2019)

> **Part Five: II. A. 2. (d) Subjects of International Law – International organisations – In general – Participation of States and international organisations in international organisations and in their activities – Representation of States and international organisations to international organisations, including privileges and immunities**
>
> *5/3*

During the 72nd session of the United Nations General Assembly in New York on 22 September 2017 the Minister of Foreign Affairs Mr. Edgars Rinkēvičs spoke about the ineffectiveness of the United Nations Security Council in certain situations:

> Edgars Rinkēvičs highlighted the UN Security Council's responsibility for preserving peace and security across the globe. He expressed regret that in many cases the permanent members of the Security Council misuse their veto powers thereby paralysing the Council's work.
>
> The frequent inability of the UN Security Council to take effective action to prevent and bring an end to genocide, crimes against humanity and war crimes, which are the most serious crimes under the provisions of international law, is a challenge to all UN member states, said Foreign Minister Rinkēvičs.
>
> He noted that Latvia firmly supports two mutually complementary and reinforcing initiatives aimed at making the Security Council's responsibility more effective: a proposal by France and Mexico about the permanent members of the Security Council refraining voluntarily from the use of their veto powers in the case of mass atrocities; and the Security Council's Code of Conduct proposed by the informal Accountability, Coherence and Transparency group, urging all members of the Security Council not to vote against SC resolutions in such situations.
>
> Edgars Rinkēvičs expressed Latvia's support for the work of the International Criminal Court and stressed the need for the UN Security Council

to address the International Criminal Court when there is evidence of a crime being committed in a country, while the country itself does not cooperate with the Court and does not hold the perpetrators accountable. Where a country does not intend to bring perpetrators to the International Criminal Court, the Council itself should consider referring the case to the ICC, the Minister emphasised.

At the same time, he said, the Council should consistently encourage the countries to honour their commitments and fight impunity in regard to the most serious crimes defined by international law.

By timely engagement and preventive diplomacy, the Security Council can urge governments to address problems and reduce risks to in order to forestall mass atrocities, said Minister Rinkēvičs in conclusion.

(Available at the website of the Ministry of Foreign Affairs, <https://www.mfa.gov.lv/en/news/latest-news/57897-foreign-minister-rinkevics-un-security-council-s-work-not-effective-in-preventing-mass-crime>, visited on 6 November 2019)

5/4
The need to reform the UN Security Council was invoked by the Permanent Representative of the Republic of Latvia to the United Nations Mr. Andrejs Pildegovičs in his statement at the United Nations General Assembly plenary debate on the question of equitable representation on and increase in the membership of the Security Council and other matters related to the Security Council on 20 November 2018:

> In our view, all regions must be adequately represented on the Council to ensure its legitimacy. The reform should ensure equitable geographic distribution of both permanent and non-permanent seats in the Council, including allocation of at least one additional non-permanent seat to the Eastern European Group. We also believe that during the nomination and election of non-permanent members of the Council due consideration should be given to adequate representation of small and medium size member states.
>
> The question of the veto, no doubt, is a very important part of the reform. Discussions on the use of this special power in certain circumstances should be continued. Yet some things should be beyond debate. Blocking the work of the Council in matters related to mass atrocities is

unacceptable. Council's permanent members should refrain from using their veto in situations of mass atrocity crimes. We support the French-Mexican initiative in this regard.

Latvia has signed the *Code of Conduct regarding Security Council action against genocide, crimes against humanity and war crimes.* We are satisfied to see that so far 118 UN Member States have joined this important initiative.

We also support improvement of the Security Council working methods to increase transparency, inclusiveness and representativeness of its work. Certain positive efforts in the transparency direction, demonstrated by the members of the Council in recent years, can be noted. We believe such approach enhances Council's legitimacy and facilitate implementation of its decisions.

To conclude, Latvia believes that the United Nations' capacity to address the current global challenges largely depends on the political will to move forward the Security Council reform. We look forward to work with the Co-Chairs of the Intergovernmental Negotiations and with other Member States in order to produce progress on the reform at this GA session.

(Available at the website of the Ministry of Foreign Affairs, <https://www.mfa.gov.lv/en/newyork/latvia-in-the-un/other-statements-at-the-general-assembly/61983-statement-by-h-e-mr-andrejs-pildegovics-permanent-representative-of-the-republic-of-latvia-general-assembly-plenary-debate-on-the-question-of-equitable-representation-on-and-increase-in-the-membership-of-the-security-council-and-other-matters-related-to-the-security-council-new-york-20-november-2018>, visited on 14 November 2019)

Part Six: VIII. D. Human rights and fundamental freedoms – Other aspects of human rights and fundamental freedoms

6/1

On 11 January 2017 during a meeting with the United Nations Secretary-General, António Guterres the Minister of Foreign Affairs of Latvia, Mr. Edgars Rinkēvičs expressed concern over the situation of the Crimean Tatars and called on the UN to actively engage in resolving that situation.

(Available at the website of the Ministry of Foreign Affairs, <https://www.mfa.gov.lv/en/news/latest-news/55805-edgars-rinkevics-expresses-support-for-the-priorities-of-the-new-un-secretary-general>, visited on 5 November 2019)

Part Sixteen: II. C. Use of force – Legitimate use of force – Others

16/1

The Ministry of Foreign Affairs of Latvia released a statement concerning missile strikes launched by the United States on the Al-Shayrat air base in Syria on 7 April 2017:

> The Latvian Ministry of Foreign Affairs believes that the missile strikes launched by the United States on the Al-Shayrat air base in Syria are an adequate response to prevent a repeated use of chemical weapons against Syria's civilians. This is a clear signal that the proliferation and use of chemical weapons is not to be tolerated.
>
> On 5 April, the Ministry of Foreign Affairs condemned the chemical attack on civilians in the Syrian province of Idlib and called for an immediate investigation into the circumstances, urging that those responsible for such crimes must be held accountable.
>
> At the same time, the Foreign Ministry hopes that the members of the UN Security Council will still be able to agree a resolution that would condemn the chemical weapons attack and make it possible to investigate the circumstances.
>
> The chemical weapons attack by the Syrian government is a gross violation of international norms and law, including the Convention on Convention on the Prohibition of the Development, Production, Stockpiling and Use of Chemical Weapons and on their Destruction. As a State Party to the Convention, Syrian government is responsible for compliance with obligations laid down in the Convention.

(Available at the website of the Ministry of Foreign Affairs, <https://www.mfa.gov.lv/en/news/latest-news/56528-us-missile-strikes-on-syria-is-adequ

ate-response-to-prevent-the-use-of-chemical-weapons>, visited on 5 November 2019)

16/2

On 14 April 2018 the Ministry of Foreign Affairs of Latvia released a statement supporting missile strikes against Syrian military infrastructure. In its statement Latvia highlighted the failure of the system of authorisation of use of force by the UN Security Council in the specific instance:

> The Ministry of Foreign Affairs of Latvia believes that missile strikes by the United States, France and the United Kingdom targeting Syrian military infrastructure is appropriate action to prevent any further use of chemical weapons against Syrian civilians. The use of chemical weapons is a flagrant breach of international law, a serious crime that is not and cannot be justified.
>
> We express regret at Russia's decision on 10 April to exercise its right of veto at the United Nations Security Council thereby stopping a draft resolution on the establishment of a new independent mechanism for investigations into chemical attacks in Syria. This is now the sixth time that Russia is using its veto right over the use of chemical weapons in Syria. Actions of this kind have a negative impact on the diplomatic capacity of the international community to prevent the use of chemical weapons.
>
> Russia's behaviour in subsequent sessions of the Security Council clearly demonstrated what had already been obvious for several years since Russia's military engagement in the Syrian conflict. Russia protects the official regime of Syria by covering up and supporting its criminal conduct.
>
> Thus, over this week, possibilities were exhausted for achieving a diplomatic solution to the investigation into the chemical attack on the town of Douma on 7 April.

(Available at the website of the Ministry of Foreign Affairs, <https://www.mfa.gov.lv/en/news/latest-news/59766-latvia-supports-the-efforts-by-the-u-s-france-and-the-u-k-seeking-to-stop-and-prevent-syria-s-war-crimes>, visited on 11 November 2019)

Part Seventeen: 1. 9. The Law of Armed Conflict and International Humanitarian Law – International armed conflict – Conventional, nuclear, bacteriological, and chemical weapons

17/1

On 3 May 2017 at the first Preparatory Committee for the 2020 NPT Review Conference of the Parties to the Nuclear Non-Proliferation Treaty the Head of the Arms Control Division at the Ministry of Foreign Affairs outlined Latvia's position with regard to non-proliferation:

> Referring to the unwavering long term goal of achieving a world free of nuclear weapons, her speech expressed support for an approach that envisages incremental and well-thought-out actions on the way toward nuclear disarmament, while preserving strategic balance in the world.
>
> Latvia emphasised that the NPT is the most vital treaty on the non-proliferation of nuclear weapons and disarmament, and therefore, the implementation of decisions made at the previous Review Conferences, especially the Action Plan approved in 2010, should be continued.
>
> In its statement Latvia welcomed international efforts in the field of non-proliferation, especially achievements with restrictions on Iran's nuclear programme. At the same time, North Korea's aggressive rhetoric, recurrent nuclear tests and launches of ballistic missiles were strongly condemned as posing increasing threats to stability and security in the region and across the globe.
>
> Latvia repeated its deep concern about the violation of core provisions of the Budapest Memorandum on security assurances to Ukraine. Non-compliance with international commitments erodes the level of trust and undermines non-proliferation measures.

(Available at the website of the Ministry of Foreign Affairs, < https://www.mfa.gov.lv/en/news/latest-news/49415-latvia-welcomes-iran-s-direction-on-its-nuclear-programme>, visited on 4 November 2019)

17/2

The President of Latvia, Mr. Raimonds Vējonis, during his speech at the 72nd session of the United Nations General Assembly referred to the progress made with respect to the nuclear program of Iran but at the same time expressed concern with the nuclear activities carried out by North Korea:

> Today security is truly a global issue. In particular, Latvia is deeply worried about the proliferation of weapons of mass destruction and the threat of the use of nuclear weapons.
>
> North Korea's actions have increased global insecurity. Latvia strongly condemns all nuclear tests and launches of ballistic missiles conducted by North Korea, and its continuous provocative rhetoric. We call on North Korea to return to a credible and meaningful dialogue with the international community and to refrain from any further action that would increase regional tensions.
>
> It is a priority to find a peaceful and diplomatic solution to this situation. In the meantime, all States must fully implement relevant UN Security Council resolutions.
>
> The use of chemical weapons in Syria, which blatantly disregards Syria's obligations as a party to the Chemical Weapons Convention, is a deplorable crime which must be fully investigated, and the perpetrators must be held accountable.
>
> Latvia has constantly called for accountability regarding these attacks, an accountability which is closely linked to the credibility of the whole international system. For this reason, Latvia has supported the International, Impartial and Independent Mechanism to assist the investigation and prosecution of serious crimes committed in Syria. We will continue to support the Syrian people and the UN-led political process towards a political resolution of this bloody conflict which has lasted far too long.

(Available at the website of the Ministry of Foreign Affairs, <https://www.mfa.gov.lv/en/newyork/latvia-in-the-un/statements-at-the-general-assembly-general-debate/58129-statement-by-h-e-mr-raimonds-vejonis-president-of-the-republic-of-latvia-at-the-72nd-session-of-the-united-nations-general-assembly>, visited on 4 November 2019)

17/3

The Ministry of Foreign Affairs consistently condemned the testing of nuclear weapons in North Korea:

Latvia condemns in the strongest terms North Korea's irresponsible, aggressive and provocative actions in holding ballistic missile launches and nuclear tests, which increase instability and pose threat to peace and security not only on the Korean Peninsula but also on a global scale. These exercises are in blatant disregard of the resolutions of the United Nations Security Council, which impose obligations on North Korea to abandon its current ballistic missile and nuclear programmes.

North Korea's aggressive move on 3 September is a reminder that the international community should be strong and united to achieve a peaceful resolution of the situation. Latvia supports and welcomes international efforts to date and calls on the region's countries, China in particular, to continue exerting pressure that would urge Korea to resume a dialogue with the international community.

Latvia also supports the efforts of the United Nations Security Council and calls on all countries to implement, strictly and without exception, the sanctions imposed on North Korea by the UNSC.

North Korea must without further delay and unconditionally resume fulfilment of its international obligations: fully comply with the United Nations Security Council's resolutions; restart participation in the Non-Proliferation Treaty and reassume its obligations under the International Atomic Energy Agency safeguards programme; as well as acceding to the Comprehensive Nuclear-Test-Ban Treaty.

(Available at the website of the Ministry of Foreign Affairs, < https://www.mfa.gov.lv/en/news/latest-news/57667-statement-of-the-foreign-ministry-on-north-korea-s-nuclear-test>, visited on 4 November 2019)

Part Seventeen: I. 10. The Law of Armed Conflict and International Humanitarian Law – International armed conflict – Treaty relations between combatants (cartels, armistices, etc.)

17/3
The importance of the Minsk agreements for ceasing conflicts in Ukraine was repeatedly stressed by representatives of Latvia in various fora. The Minister of Foreign Affairs of Latvia, Mr. Edgars Rinkēvičs, emphasised this in his remarks

in the 25th Ministerial Council of the Organisation for Security and Cooperation in Europe on 6 December 2018:

> Despite our efforts, despite the Minsk agreements and despite repeated calls for Russia to abide by the principles and commitments enshrined in Helsinki and Paris, no progress has been achieved so far. Even worse. Recent illegitimate "elections" in the so-called "Donetsk and Luhansk people's republics" further violate international and Ukrainian law, as well as the Minsk agreements. The recent provocation by Russia, which illegally opened fire and seized three Ukrainian navy vessels near the Kerch Strait, is the latest demonstration of that.

(Available at the website of the Ministry of Foreign Affairs, <https://www.mfa.gov.lv/en/belgium?catid=0&id=62073>, visited on 4 November 2019)

17/4

The Minsk agreements assumed a central role in a statement by the Ministry of Foreign Affairs of Latvia with regard to so-called elections that were held in Eastern Ukraine in 2018:

> Latvia condemns the organizing of illegitimate "elections" in the so-called "Donetsk and Luhansk People's Republics" on 11 November, as they are a clear violation of the Minsk agreements and thus have the potential to aggravate the situation in eastern Ukraine. Latvia will not recognize the results of these illegal "elections", which were supported by Russia.
>
> Latvia strongly supports the sovereignty and territorial integrity of Ukraine and insists that the full implementation of the Minsk agreements is the only way to secure a peaceful settlement of the conflict in eastern Ukraine.

(Available at the website of the Ministry of Foreign Affairs, < https://www.mfa.gov.lv/en/moscow/dvustoronnie-otnosheniya/ekonomicheskoe-sotrudnichestvo/372-latest-news/61750-latvia-condemns-the-holding-of-so-called-elections-in-donbass>, visited on 14 November 2019)

ANNEX I. A Agreements signed by Latvia before 2017 but entered into force in regard to Latvia in 2017 or 2018 – Bi- and multilateral agreements

Title	Conclusion	Entry into Force
Agreement between the Government of the Republic of Latvia and the Governments of the BENELUX States on Readmission of Persons whose Entry and Residence is Illegal	09.06.1999	01.12.2017
Agreement between the Government of the Republic of Latvia and the Government of the Republic of Kazakhstan on Cooperation in Combating Terrorism, Illicit Trafficking in Narcotic Drugs and Psychotropic Substances and Organized Crime	08.10.2004	13.08.2018
Association Agreement between the European Union and the European Atomic Energy Community and their Member States, of the one part, and Ukraine, of the other part	21.03.2014	01.09.2017
Agreement between the Government of the Republic of Latvia and the Government of the Republic of Poland on Bilateral Defence Co-operation	13.06.2014	20.02.2018
Minamata Convention on Mercury	24.09.2014	18.09.2017
Council of Europe Convention against Trafficking in Human Organs	25.03.2015	01.03.2018
Agreement between the Government of the Republic of Latvia and the Government of the Republic of Cyprus on Mutual Protection of Classified Information	22.06.2015	01.03.2017
Additional Protocol to the Council of Europe Convention on the Prevention of Terrorism	22.10.2015	01.11.2017
Agreement between the Government of the Republic of Latvia and the Government of the Hong Kong Special Administrative Region of the People's Republic of China for the Avoidance of Double Taxation and the Prevention of Fiscal Evasion with respect to Taxes on Income	13.04.2016	24.11.2017
Paris Agreement	22.04.2016	15.04.2017

ANNEX I.A Agreements signed by Latvia before 2017 but entered into force in regard to Latvia in 2017 or 2018 – Bi- and multilateral agreements (*cont.*)

Title	Conclusion	Entry into Force
Agreement on Economic Co-operation between the Government of the Republic of Latvia and the Government of the United Arab Emirates	08.05.2016	07.05.2018
Protocol Amending the Protocol between the Government of the Republic of Estonia, the Government of the Republic of Latvia and the Government of the Republic of Lithuania Concerning the Status of the Baltic Defence College and its Personnel	28.06.2016	11.06.2017
Postal Payment Services Agreement	06.10.2016	01.01.2018
Universal Postal Convention	06.10.2016	01.01.2018
Agreement between the Government of the Republic of Latvia and the Government of the Kyrgyz Republic on Co-operation in the Field of Education and Science	17.10.2016	20.06.2017
Comprehensive Economic and Trade Agreement (CETA) between Canada, of the one part, and the European Union and its Member States, of the other part	28.10.2016	21.09.2017
Protocol between the Government of the Republic of Latvia and the Swiss Federal Council Amending the Convention of 31 January 2002 between the Government of the Republic of Latvia and the Swiss Federal Council for the Avoidance of Double Taxation with respect to Taxes on Income and on Capital	02.11.2016	03.09.2018
Convention on the International Protection of Adults	15.12.2016	09.11.2017

ANNEX II Agreements signed by Latvia in 2017–2018 – Bi- and multilateral agreements

Title	Conclusion	Entry into Force
Agreement on Defense Co-operation between the Government of the Republic of Latvia and the Government of the United States of America	12.01.2017	05.04.2017
Convention between the Republic of Latvia and Japan for the Elimination of Double Taxation with respect to Taxes on Income and the Prevention of Tax Evasion and Avoidance	18.01.2017	05.07.2017
Council of Europe Convention on Cinematographic Co-production (revised)	30.01.2017	01.10.2017
Agreement between the Government of the Republic of Estonia, the Government of the Republic of Latvia and the Government of the Republic of Lithuania on the Development of the Rail Baltic / Rail Baltica Railway Connection	31.01.2017	24.10.2017
Agreement between the Government of the Republic of Latvia and the Government of the Republic of France on Cooperation in the Field of Defence	07.02.2017	01.07.2017
Agreement between the Government of the Republic of Finland, the Government of the Republic of Latvia, the Government of the Kingdom of Norway, the Government of the Republic of Poland, the Government of the Russian Federation, the Government of the Kingdom of Sweden on the Establishment of the Secretariat of the Northern Dimension Partnership on Culture	07.02.2017	29.12.2019
Agreement between the Government of the Republic of Latvia and the Government of the Republic of Azerbaijan on Visa Exemption for Holders of Service Passports	13.02.2017	05.07.2017
Cooperation Agreement on Partnership and Development between the European Union and its Member States, of the one part, and the Islamic Republic of Afghanistan	18.02.2017	

ANNEX II   Agreements signed by Latvia in 2017–2018 – Bi- and multilateral agreements (*cont.*)

Title	Conclusion	Entry into Force
Reciprocal Defence Procurement Agreement between the Government of the United States of America and the Government of the Republic of Latvia	10.04.2017	10.04.2017
Second Protocol Amending the Agreement between the Government of the Republic of Latvia and the Government of the Republic of Singapore for the Avoidance of Double Taxation and the Prevention of Fiscal Evasion with Respect to Taxes on Income	20.04.2017	03.08.2018
Agreement between the Government of the Republic of Latvia and the Government of the Republic of India on Exemption from Visa Requirements for Holders of Diplomatic Passports	23.05.2017	08.09.2017
Multilateral Convention to Implement Tax Treaty Related Measures to Prevent Base Erosion and Profit Shifting	07.06.2017	
Protocol amending the Treaty concerning a European Vehicle and Driving Licence Information System (EUCARIS)	08.06.2017	01.03.2018
Agreement between the Government of the Republic of Latvia and the Government of the Republic of Azerbaijan on Cooperation in the Field of Education	17.07.2017	15.11.2017
Framework Agreement between the European Union and its Member States, of the one part, and Australia, of the other part	07.08.2017	
Agreement between the Government of the Republic of Latvia and the Government of the People's Republic of China on Cooperation in the Field of Culture	22.09.2017	22.09.2017
Agreement between the Government of the Republic of Latvia and the Government of the State of Kuwait on the Waiver of Visa Requirements for Holders of Diplomatic, Special and Service Passports	11.10.2017	28.02.2018

ANNEX II Agreements signed by Latvia in 2017–2018 – Bi- and multilateral agreements (*cont.*)

Title	Conclusion	Entry into Force
Agreement between the Government of the Republic of Latvia and the Government of the State of Kuwait for the Economic and Technical Co-operation	11.10.2017	15.05.2018
Agreement between the Government of the Republic of Latvia and the Government of the Socialist Republic of Viet Nam for the Avoidance of Double Taxation and the Prevention of Fiscal Evasion with respect to Taxes on Income	19.10.2017	06.08.2018
Agreement between the Government of the Republic of Latvia and the Government of the Republic of Moldova on Cooperation in the Fields of Education, Culture, Science, Youth and Sports	06.11.2017	27.12.2017
Agreement on the Amendments to the Agreement between the Government of the Republic of Latvia and the Government of the Russian Federation of 20 December 2010 on the Simplification of Mutual Travels of Inhabitants in the Territories of the Border Area of the Republic of Latvia and the Russian Federation	14.11.2017	16.12.2018
Agreement between the Government of the Republic of Latvia and the Government of the People's Republic of China on Co-operation in the Field of Education	22.11.2017	04.03.2018
Agreement between the Government of the Republic of Latvia, the Government of the Republic of Estonia and the Government of the Republic of Lithuania on Mutual Assistance and Cooperation in the Field of Disaster Prevention, Preparedness and Response	23.11.2017	24.12.2018
Agreement between the Government of the Republic of Latvia and the Government of the Republic of Belarus on Co-operation in Civil Aviation Aircraft Search and Rescue	07.02.2018	06.07.2018

ANNEX II   Agreements signed by Latvia in 2017–2018 – Bi- and multilateral agreements (*cont.*)

Title	Conclusion	Entry into Force
Agreement between the Government of the Republic of Latvia and the Government of the Republic of Belarus on Early Notification of Nuclear Accidents, Exchange of Information and Co-operation in the Field of Nuclear Safety and Radiation Protection	07.02.2018	03.09.2018
Agreement between the Government of the Federal Republic of Germany and the Government of the Republic of Latvia on the Mutual Protection of Classified Information	16.02.2018	16.02.2018
Agreement between the Government of the Republic of Latvia and the Government of the Kingdom of Thailand on Exemption of Visa Requirements for Holders of Diplomatic, Service and Official Passports	13.06.2018	11.12.2018
Strategic Partnership Agreement between the European Union and its Member States, of the one part, and Japan, of the other part	17.07.2018	01.02.2019
Additional Protocol to the Universal Postal Convention	07.09.2018	
Second Additional Protocol to the General Regulations of the Universal Postal Union	07.09.2018	
Tenth Additional Protocol to the Constitution of the Universal Postal Union	07.09.2018	
Free Trade Agreement between the European Union and the Republic of Singapore	07.09.2018	
Agreement between the Government of the Republic of Latvia and the Government of the Republic of Belarus on International Railway Traffic	02.10.2018	30.05.2019
Agreement between the Government of the Republic of Latvia and the Government of the People's Republic of China on Cooperation in the Field of Science and Technology	15.10.2018	15.10.2018

Republic of Lithuania Materials on International Law 2018

Edited by Andrius Bambalas* and Saulius Katuoka**

[*Editorial Notes:*

1. Republic of Lithuania Materials on International Law 2018 (RLMIL2018) are drafted and classified pursuant to Recommendation (97)11 of 12 June 1997 of the Committee of Ministers of the Council of Europe.
2. For ease of reading a number of abbreviations are used in RLMIL 2018, namely ECHR – Convention for the Protection of Human Rights and Fundamental Freedoms, 1950; ECtHR – European Court of Human Rights; *Seimas* – Parliament of the Republic of Lithuania; Government – Government of the Republic of Lithuania. Unless explicitly provided for otherwise, references to cases or decisions in RLMIL2018 are references to acts of national courts and institutions. Cases decided by national courts referred to herein are available in Lithuanian free of charge at the following website: https://eteismai.lt/paieska. The case law of the Constitutional Court of the Republic of Lithuania is available in Lithuanian on its website https://www.lrkt.lt/lt/. Case law of the European Court of Human Rights is available through the website http://www.echr.coe.int/echr/. Information on treaties of Lithuania is available at the following website: https://www.urm.lt/default/en/foreign-policy/treaties/bilateral. Universal and regional international instruments mentioned in RLMIL2018 do not bear any reference to their source, as these may be easily accessed from various pages on the internet. Due to limited scope, RLMIL2018 does not reproduce entire texts, therefore certain information is omitted and marked as [...].
3. RLMIL2018 consists mainly of translations of texts made by the authors; therefore, translations should not be regarded as official and should be used for information purposes only. Documents of which translations are provided by national institutions and are available in English on the internet are attached with a particular link.
4. A rather technical remark should be made in regard to ratifications by the *Seimas* and approvals by the Government, noted in the Appendix hereto,

---

* Attorney-at-law, PhD student at the Mykolas Romeris University (Vilnius).
** Professor at the Mykolas Romeris University (Vilnius).

meaning expression of consent to be bound under natioal law, rather than meaning an international act attributed to the notion "ratification" in Article 2 part 1(b) of the Vienna Convention on the Law of Treaties, 1969.]

Part Four: 11. Relationship between international law and internal law – Application and implementation of international law in domestic law

4/1

In case No. EA-3-822/2018 of 24 January 2018, the Supreme Administrative Court of Lithuania assessed international protection of the right to personal data protection. The relevant extract from the case is reproduced below:

> The right to the protection of personal data enshrined in Article 8 of the Charter of Fundamental Rights of the European Union is a separate fundamental right. It has no equivalent in the European Convention for the Protection of Human Rights and Fundamental Freedoms. Judgments of the Court of Justice of the European Union in the field of personal data protection are rich in content and significant in their effect in ensuring the right of every natural person to adequate protection of his or her data.
>
> Such conclusion can be drawn by considering only several fundamental judgments of the CJEU in this area, such as *Google Spain and Google* (Judgment of 13 May 2014, C-131/12, EU: C: 2014: 317), *Digital Rights Ireland and Seitlinger et al.* (Judgment of 8 April 2014, Joined Cases C-293/12 and C-594/12, EU: C: 2014: 238) and *Schrems* (Judgment of 6 October 2015, C: C 362/14, EU: C: 2015: 650). Pursuant to Articles 7 and 8 of the Charter of Fundamental Rights of the European Union the CJEU established pillars in these judgments that form the basis of a modern legal framework for the protection of personal data in the European Union. In principle, in these judgments, the CJEU established guidelines which are binding on private and public entities to ensure compliance with the standard of protection of personal data under the Union's legal order. Individuals have the opportunity to defend the right to protection of personal data through both administrative and judicial means at both national and European Union level.

4/2

In its judgment of 13 June 2018 in case No. A-205-756/2018, the Supreme Administrative Court of Lithuania interpreted the UN Convention on Psychotropic

Substances of 1971 and state power to adopt more stringent control measures than those provided in the convention. Relevant extracts from the case are reproduced below:

> In the current proceedings, the applicant asks the Ministry of Health to classify controlled substances into categories – mild, severe and severe narcotic substances, according to their type and harm to human health.
>
> Under order No. V 239 of the Minister of Health of the Republic of Lithuania dated 23 April 2003 'Recommendations for the determination of small, large and very large quantities of narcotic drugs and psychotropic substances' (the order has been amended several times) substances are divided into three lists: List I – narcotic drugs and psychotropic substances prohibited for medical purposes (drawn up in accordance with Lists I and IV of the General Convention of 1961 and Lists I-IV of 1971 Convention); List II – narcotic drugs and psychotropic substances authorized for medical purposes (drawn up in accordance with List I of the 1961 General Convention and List II of the 1971 Convention); List III – psychotropic substances authorized for medical purposes (drawn up in accordance with Lists III and IV of the 1971 Convention). [...]
>
> Thus, the legislator has instructed the Ministry of Health to compile lists of narcotic drugs and psychotropic substances, taking into account the provisions of international agreements. It should be noted that the United Nations Convention on Psychotropic Substances of 1972 also does not preclude the application of more stringent control measures than those provided for in the Convention if it considers such measures to be desirable or necessary for the protection of the health and well-being of the population (Article 23).

4/3

In its judgment of 29 June 2018 in case No. EA-3505-858/2018, the Supreme Administrative Court of Lithuania decided to interpret the concept of 'political opinion' in the Convention Relating to the Status of Refugees broadly and in accordance with criteria for 'political opinion' provided in Article 10(1)€ of the Qualification Directive. Relevant extracts from the case are reproduced below:

> The Law on the Legal Status of Aliens, legal provisions of legal acts implementing this law, as well as international and European Union legal acts

are applicable to the factual circumstances of the case. First of all, the United Nations Convention relating to the Status of Refugees of 28 July 1951, to which the Republic of Lithuania is a party (ratified by Law No. VIII 85 of the Seimas of the Republic of Lithuania of 21 January 1997) (hereinafter – the Geneva Convention, Convention). Article 1(A)(2) of the Convention among other things establishes that the term "refugee" shall apply to any person who, owing to a well-founded fear of being persecuted for reasons of political opinion, is outside the country of his nationality and is unable or, owing to such fear, is unwilling to avail himself of the protection of that country. Meanwhile Article 33(1) of the Convention provides that no Contracting State shall expel or return a refugee in any manner whatsoever to the frontiers of territories where his life or freedom would be threatened on account of his race, religion, nationality, membership of a particular social group or political opinion.

In regard to EU law, first of all the provisions of Article 18 of the Charter of Fundamental Rights of the European Union should be mentioned, which states that the right to asylum is guaranteed by the Geneva Convention and the Protocol of 31 January 1967 relating to the status of refugees and the Treaty on European Union and the Treaty on the Functioning of the European Union. Thus, from the point of view of EU law, the right to asylum is a fundamental right of the individual.

The provisions of Directive 2011/95/EU of the European Parliament and of the Council of 13 December 2011 on standards for the qualification of third-country nationals or stateless persons as beneficiaries of international protection, for a uniform status for refugees or for persons eligible for subsidiary protection, and for the content of the protection granted (hereinafter – the Qualification Directive) are also relevant to this case. The main objective of this Directive is to ensure that Member States apply common criteria for the identification of persons genuinely in need of international protection, and to ensure that a minimum level of benefits is available for those persons in all Member States (recital 12 of the Qualification Directive).

Article 2(d) of the Qualification Directive provides that 'refugee' means a third-country national who, owing to a well-founded fear of being persecuted for reasons of race, religion, nationality, political opinion or membership of a particular social group, is outside the country of nationality and is unable or, owing to such fear, is unwilling to avail himself or herself of the protection of that country, or a stateless person, who, being outside of the country of former habitual residence for the same reasons as mentioned above, is unable or, owing to such fear, unwilling to return to it, and to whom Article 12 does not apply. Meanwhile Article 2(f) of the Qualification Directive provides that 'person eligible for subsidiary protection' means a third-country national or a stateless person who does not qualify as a refugee but in respect of whom substantial grounds have been shown for believing that the person concerned, if returned to his or her country of origin, or in the case of a stateless person, to his or her country of former habitual residence, would face a real risk of suffering serious harm as defined in Article 15, and to whom Article 17(1) and (2) does not apply, and is unable, or, owing to such risk, unwilling to avail himself or herself of the protection of that country

As regards the definition of acts of persecution in the State of origin, Article 9(1) of the Qualification Directive (acts of persecution) provides that in order to be regarded as an act of persecution within the meaning of Article 1(A) of the Geneva Convention, an act must (a) be sufficiently serious by its nature or repetition as to constitute a severe violation of basic human rights, in particular rights from which derogation cannot be made under Article 15(2) of the European Convention for the Protection of Human Rights and Fundamental Freedoms; or (b) be an accumulation of various measures, including violations of human rights, which is sufficiently severe as to affect an individual in a similar manner as mentioned in point (a).

[...]

Article 9(2) of the Qualification Directive prescribes that acts of persecution qualified in paragraph 1 can, *inter alia*, take the form of: (a) acts of physical or mental violence, including acts of sexual violence; (b) legal, administrative, police, and/or judicial measures which are in themselves discriminatory or which are implemented in a discriminatory manner; (c) prosecution or punishment which is disproportionate or discriminatory; (d) denial of judicial redress resulting in a disproportionate or discriminatory punishment; (e) prosecution or punishment for refusal to perform military service in a conflict, where performing military service would include crimes or acts falling within the scope of the grounds for exclusion as set out in Article 12(2); (f) acts of a gender-specific or child-specific nature. Under Article 9(3) of the Qualification Directive in accordance with point (d) of Article 2, there must be a connection between the reasons mentioned in Article 10 and the acts of persecution as qualified in paragraph 1 of this Article or the absence of protection against such acts.

Point (e) paragraph 1 of Article 10 of the Qualification Directive provides that Member States shall take the following elements into account when assessing the reasons for persecution: the concept of political opinion, which, in particular, shall include the holding of an opinion, thought or belief on a matter related to the potential actors of persecution mentioned in Article 6 and to their policies or methods, whether or not that opinion, thought or belief has been acted upon by the applicant. Paragraph 2 of Article 10 of the Qualification Directive prescribes that when assessing if an applicant has a well-founded fear of being persecuted it is immaterial whether the applicant actually possesses the racial, religious, national, social or political characteristic which attracts the persecution, provided that such a characteristic is attributed to the applicant by the actor of persecution.

In regard to adoption of a decision on whether an applicant has a well-founded fear of being persecuted or is at real risk, under paragraph 2 of Article 2 of the Qualification Directive, in examining whether an applicant has a well-founded fear of being persecuted or is at real risk of suffering serious harm, or has access to protection against persecution or serious harm in a part of the country of origin in accordance with paragraph 1, Member States shall at the time of taking the decision on the application have regard to the general circumstances prevailing in that part of the country and to the personal circumstances of the applicant in accordance with Article 4. To that end, Member States shall ensure that precise and up-to-date information is obtained from relevant sources, such as the United Nations High Commissioner for Refugees and the European Asylum Support Office.

The panel of judges also notes that paragraph 5 of Article 4 of the Qualification Directive provides that when Member States apply the principle according to which it is the duty of the applicant to substantiate the application for international protection and where aspects of the applicant's statements are not supported by documentary or other evidence, those aspects shall not need confirmation when the following conditions are met: (a) the applicant has made a genuine effort to substantiate his application; (b) all relevant elements at the applicant's disposal have been submitted, and a satisfactory explanation has been given regarding any lack of other relevant elements; (c) the applicant's statements are found to be coherent and plausible and do not run counter to available specific and general information relevant to the applicant's case; (d) the applicant has applied for international protection at the earliest possible time, unless the applicant can demonstrate good reason for not having done so; and (e) the general credibility of the applicant has been established.

[...]

First of all the panel of judges notes that insofar as concerns establishment of a well-founded fear, the Court of Justice of the European Union (hereinafter – the EU:C) has ruled that this ""assessment" takes place in two different stages. The first stage concerns the establishment of factual circumstances which may constitute evidence that supports the application, while the second stage relates to the legal appraisal of that evidence, which entails deciding whether, in the light of the specific facts of a given case, the substantive conditions laid down by Articles 9 and 10 or Article 15 of Directive 2004/83 for the grant of international protection are met" (see judgment of 22 October 2012 in *M* v. *Minister for Justice, Equality and Law Reform, Ireland, Attorney General*, C-277/11, EU:C:2012:744, paragraph 64)).

Therefore, from the above interpretation it follows that the establishment of a well-founded fear is closely linked to the assessment of the evidence and its reliability, as defined in Article 4 of the Qualification Directive.

[...]

According to the panel of judges, the circumstances alleged by the applicant, in view of the impending deprivation of liberty, thereby restricting one of the fundamental rights, could be regarded as constituting acts of persecution within the meaning of Article 9 of the Qualification Directive. Furthermore, criminal prosecution for the purpose of compelling a person to give false evidence in criminal proceedings must be regarded as discriminatory within the meaning of Article 9 (2) of the Qualification Directive: since such prosecution would not be based on legal regulation, criminal law provisions would be applied selectively without a legal basis.

As regards the legal assessment of such persecution in determining whether it was committed on political grounds, it should be noted that the Geneva Convention does not define the concept of 'political opinion'. As mentioned above, Article 10 (1) (e) of the Qualification Directive states that Member States shall take into account the following factors when assessing the grounds for persecution: the concept of political opinion shall, in particular, include the holding of an opinion, thought or belief on a matter related to the potential actors of persecution mentioned in Article 6 and to their policies or methods, whether or not that opinion, thought or belief has been acted upon by the applicant. Such a definition of the concept of political opinion suggests that it should be interpreted broadly; a broad interpretation of this concept is also supported by legal doctrine and case law of other EU Member States (see e.g. Qualification for International Protection (Directive 2011/95/EU). Judicial Analysis. International Association of Refugee Law Judges. European Chapter (IARLJ-Europe). December 2016, p. 53–55: <https://www.easo.europa.eu/sites/default/files/QIP%20-%20JA.pdf>). The panel of the judges is of the opinion that in this respect there is no reason to distinguish between punishment for unfavourable political convictions referred to in the respondent's Opinion and the desire to influence a person's behaviour in order to commit a criminal offence.

4/4

In its judgment of 26 November 2018 in case No. EI-29-415/2018, the Supreme Administrative Court of Lithuania assessed the limits of freedom of speech of a politician under the ECHR and the Framework Convention for the Protection of National Minorities. The basis of the case was public statements by a local politician that disparaged a Lithuanian partisan commander and his memory and spread knowingly incorrect information about him. The court decided that the right of expression of persons belonging to national minorities does not differ in any way from the general grounds established in the Constitution and the Convention. Relevant extracts from the case are reproduced below:

> Regarding the provisions of the Convention on restrictions on freedom of expression

55. Article 10 of the European Convention for the Protection of Human Rights and Fundamental Freedoms provides, insofar as it is related to the present case, that everyone has the right to freedom of expression. This right includes freedom to hold opinions and to receive and impart information and ideas without interference by public authority and regardless of frontiers <...> (paragraph 1); the exercise of these freedoms, since it carries with it duties and responsibilities, may be subject to such formalities, conditions, restrictions or penalties as are prescribed by law and are necessary in a democratic society, in the interests of national security, territorial integrity or public safety, for the prevention of disorder or crime, for the protection of health or morals, for the protection of the reputation or rights of others <...> (paragraph 2).

56. The European Court of Human Rights (the ECtHR) considers freedom of expression to be one of the fundamental foundations of a democratic society and one of the most important conditions for its progress and the development of each individual; its decisions emphasize that this freedom applies not only to information or ideas that are welcomed, considered offensive or unworthy, but also to those that offend, shock or disturb. Such are the demands of pluralism, tolerance and liberalism, without which there is no democratic society. Like most conventional guarantees, freedom of expression is not absolute, and those who exercise it (both journalists and others) must act fairly towards the addressee of the information, strive to provide accurate and reliable information, and adhere to ethical standards. At the same time, the ECtHR emphasizes that the exceptions to freedom of expression enshrined in Article 10 § 2 of the Convention must be interpreted strictly, and that the need for restrictions must be established convincingly. The application of the criterion of 'necessary in a democratic society' to the restriction of freedom of expression must determine whether the restriction of a person's freedom met a 'pressing social need'. States have certain limits on their discretion in deciding whether there is such a need, but may not infringe the standards and principles of freedom of expression guaranteed by Article 10 of the Convention (see judgment of 25 August 1998 in *Hertel* v. *Switzerland* (application no 25181/94), § 46; judgment of 15 February 2005 in *Steel and Morris* v. *United Kingdom* (application no 68416/01), § 87).

57. According to the case law of the ECtHR, the adjective 'necessary' within the meaning of Article 10 § 2 of the Convention means the existence of a "pressing social need". According to the ECtHR, in deciding

whether such a need exists, the Contracting States have a certain margin of appreciation in assessing whether such a need exists, but it goes hand in hand with European supervision, embracing both the legislation and the decisions applying it, even those given by an independent court. Therefore the ECtHR is empowered to issue a final ruling on whether a "restriction" or "penalty" is reconcilable with freedom of expression as protected by Article 10 (see judgment of 8 July 1986 in *Lingens* v. *Austria* (application no 9815/82), § 39 and judgment of 21 January 1999 in *Janowski* v. *Poland* (application no 25716/94), § 30). In exercising its supervisory jurisdiction, the ECtHR looks at the impugned interference in the light of the case as a whole, including the content of the remarks held against the applicant and the context in which she made them. In particular, the ECtHR determines whether the interference in issue was "proportionate to the legitimate aims pursued" and whether the reasons adduced by the national authorities to justify it were "relevant and sufficient". In doing so, the Court has to satisfy itself that the national authorities applied standards which were in conformity with the principles embodied in Article 10 and, moreover, that they based themselves on an acceptable assessment of the relevant facts (judgment of 4 November 2008 in *Balsytė-Lideikienė* v. *Lithuania* (application no 72596/01), §§ 75–77).

58. The ECtHR has noted that while freedom of expression is important for everybody, it is especially so for an elected representative of the people, who represents the electorate, draws attention to their preoccupations and defends their interests. Accordingly, interference with freedom of expression by an opposition member of parliament, like the applicant, calls for the closest scrutiny on the part of the court (judgment of 27 February 2001 in *Jerusalem* v. *Austria* (application no 26958/95), § 36, judgment of 23 April 1991 in *Castells* v. *Spain* (application no 11798/85), § 42).

59. The ECtHR also considers that the freedom of political debate is undoubtedly not absolute in nature (*Castells* v. *Spain*, § 46). However there is little scope under Article 10 para. 2 of the Convention (art. 10-2) for restrictions on political speech or on debate over questions of public interest (judgment of 25 November 1996 in *Wingrove* v. *United Kingdom* (application no 17419/90), § 58). The dominant position which the government occupies makes it necessary for it to display restraint in resorting to criminal proceedings, particularly where other means are available for replying to the unjustified attacks and criticisms of its adversaries. Nevertheless it remains open to the competent State authorities to adopt, in their

capacity as guarantors of public order, measures, even of a criminal – law nature, intended to react appropriately and without excess to such remarks (judgment of 9 June 1998 in *Incal v. Turkey* [...], § 54).

60. From the ECtHR's point of view, in order to classify certain statements into a specific category (statement of facts) or value statements (opinion), it is necessary to take into account the full context of the circumstances of the case: the wording of the statements, the circumstances in which they were made, the form and manner in which they were provided, whether there was an assessment of the real situation or statement of opinion without any factual basis, whether there was a lively discussion, a public action where a higher degree of hyperbole and exaggeration is expected, or whether information was provided, e.g. in a scientific article, etc. Unlike factual statements, evaluations (opinions) cannot be proved, but they must also not be without factual basis. By engaging in a public debate on a sensitive issue of general interest, a person can expect a certain level of exaggeration, hyperbolization, or provocation that should inevitably be tolerated in a democratic society (judgment of 15 February 2005 in *Steel and Morris v. United Kingdom* (application no 68416/01), § 90). Even where a statement amounts to a value judgment, there must exist a sufficient factual basis to support it (judgment of 22 October 2007 in *Lindon and others v. France* (application no 21279/02, 36448/02), § 55).

61. The ECtHR has repeatedly been confronted with application of Article 10 of the Convention in cases concerning historical debates, stressing that the pursuit of historical truth is an integral part of freedom of expression (judgment of 15 October 2015 in *Perincek v. Switzerland* (application no 27510/08), §§ 213–223; judgment of 22 April 2010 in *Fatullayev v. Azerbaijan* (application no 40984/07), § 87). In such cases the ECtHR has clearly reiterated that it does not consider and settle issues of historical truth (judgment of 21 September 2006 in *Monnat v. Switzerland* (application no 73604/01), § 57). However, in determining whether interference with the right of authors or publishers to exercise their freedom of expression in statements relating to historical matters was necessary in a democratic society, the court takes into account a number of factors. One is the manner in which the contested statements were expressed and the manner in which they may be interpreted (judgment of 2 October 2001 in *Stankov and the United Macedonian Organisation Ilinden* (application no 29221/95 ir 29225/95), §§ 102–106; judgment of 15 January 2009 in *Orban*

and Others v. *France* (application no 20985/05), §§ 46–51). Another factor is the specific interest or right that has been affected by the statements. For example in the of *Stankov and the United Macedonian Organization Ilinden*, these were Bulgarian national symbols; in the judgment of 30 March 2004 in *Radio France and Others* (application no. 53984/00); and judgment of 29 June 2004 in *Chauvy and Others* (application no. 64915/01) it was the reputation of living persons which was affected by serious allegations of abuse; in *Monnat*, the statements were not directly directed against those who complained or against the reputation or personal rights of the Swiss people, but against the country's leaders during World War II; in its judgment of 15 January 2009 in *Association of Citizens Radko and Paunkovski* v. *Former Yugoslav Republic of Macedonia* (application no. 74651/01), the statements affected the national and ethnic identity of all Macedonians; in *Orban and others*, the statements could have revived painful memories of the victims of torture. According to the case law of the ECtHR a relevant factor is the effect of statements. For example in *Stankov and the United Macedonian Organization Ilinden* the ECtHR took into account that the group making statements did not have a serious impact, not even locally, and their gatherings were unlikely to become a platform for promoting violence and intolerance; on the contrary, in *Radio France and Others* the ECtHR noted that statements alleging serious defamatory allegations against a living person had been broadcast on national radio sixty-two times. Finally, the ECtHR takes into account the period that has elapsed since the historical events to which the statements were made.

62. The above-mentioned case law of the ECtHR presupposes that the ECtHR's assessment of the need to limit statements relating to historical events should be made on a case-by-case basis and depends on the nature and potential impact of such a statement and the context in which it was made.

63. Thus, under Article 10 of the Convention, there are certain exceptions to freedom of expression. Restrictions on freedom of expression in the context of the current proceedings, in particular the process of applying responsibility, is considered by the extended panel of judges as a measure restricting freedom of expression, the application of which should be carefully examined and the grounds for restriction should be established convincingly.

64. When respondent claims that under Articles 7, 8, 9 of the Framework Convention for the Protection of National Minorities, he has the right to freedom of expression, thought, conscience, beliefs and opinions, even if they do not coincide with the official position of the State, attention should be drawn to the fact that the same convention stipulates that in the exercise of the rights and freedoms flowing from the principles enshrined in the framework Convention, any person belonging to a national minority shall respect national legislation and the rights of others, in particular those of persons belonging to the majority or to other national minorities (Article 20). Thus, the Framework Convention for the Protection of National Minorities not only guarantees national minorities the right to freedom of expression, but also lays down obligations to respect national law and the rights of others in the exercise of freedom of expression. Failure to comply with this obligation, i.e. disregard for national acts and the rights of others, may constitute a reasonable restriction on freedom of expression. The right of expression of persons belonging to national minorities and the grounds for their restriction do not differ in any way from the general grounds established in the Constitution and the Convention.

4/5

In its judgment of 18 May 2018, in civil case No. E3K-3-188-403/2018, the Supreme Court of Lithuania assessed the right to a home under Article 8 of the Convention and guarantees under Article 1 of Protocol No. 1 of the Convention to be given to individuals who have to be evicted from a dwelling after a long term tenancy. Relevant extracts from the case are reproduced below:

The panel of judges, considering the significance of the provisions of Article 8 of the Convention for the Protection of Human Rights and Fundamental Freedoms (right to respect for the inviolability of the home), recalls that Article 8 does not in terms recognise a right to be provided with a particular dwelling (it does not grant the right to be provided with housing (a home)) (see e.g. judgment of 18 January 2001 in *Chapman v. United Kingdom*, application no 27238/95, § 99; judgment of 18 January 2001 in *Jane Smith v. United Kingdom*, application no 25154/94, § 106; etc.).

[...]

Pursuant to the standards formulated in the case law of the European Court of Human Rights (ECtHR) pertaining to loss of housing, it is first necessary to determine whether a person has a right to respect for his home in general and whether there was interference with the enjoyment of such right.

Article 8 of the Convention establishes an autonomous concept of home, which is related to the existence of a sufficient and continuous connection with a particular place, which does not depend on classification under domestic law and is not limited to those which are lawfully occupied or which have been lawfully established but also includes an actual residence, depending on the factual circumstances, namely, the existence of sufficient and continuous links with a specific place (e.g. judgment of 25 September 1996 in *Buckley v. United Kingdom*; judgment of 24 November 1986 in *Gillow v. United Kingdom*; judgment of 8 February 1978 in *Wiggins v. United Kingdom*).

Furthermore, the concept of home is not limited to legally established or occupied housing or housing owned or rented by applicants, but may also be relied on by a person living in an apartment whose lease has not been concluded on his behalf (see e.g. judgment of 18 November 2004 in *Prokopovich v. Russia*, application no 58255/00, § 36; judgment of 17 October 2013 in *Winterstein and others v. France*, application no 27013/07, § 141). Such concept can also encompass living for significant periods in premises owned by a relative (see Grand Chamber judgment of 28 November 1997 in *Mentes and others v. Turkey*, application no 23186/94, § 73).

[...]

In the light of the above criteria for the concept of home, the panel of judges decides that the disputed premises are to be regarded as home within the meaning of Article 8 of the Convention.

[...]

Regarding Grounds for terminating the lease of the disputed premises and eviction

[...]

The case law of the ECtHR has pointed out that conservation of the cultural heritage and, where appropriate, its sustainable use, have as their aim, in addition to the maintenance of a certain quality of life, the preservation of the historical, cultural and artistic roots of a region and its inhabitants. As such, they are an essential value, the protection and promotion of which are incumbent on the public authorities (see judgment of 29 March 2007 in *Debelianovi v Bulgaria*, application no 61951/00, § 54; judgment of 19 February 2009 in *Kozacioğlu v. Turkey*, application no 2334/03, § 54; judgment of 29 March 2011 in *Potomska and Potomski v. Poland*, application no 33949/05, § 64).

After assessing the situation in the light of national law and international standards, the panel of judges decides that there are grounds for terminating the tenancy. It should also be noted that the defendants agree that the lease should be terminated, and they should be evicted, the dispute is only about eviction with or without the provision of other accommodation.

Regarding the inviolability of the right to a home, the conditions for eviction and fair compensation

[...]

The cassation claim argues that the defendants' right to a home is protected as a possession under Article 1 of Protocol No. 1 to the Convention.

[...]

The panel of judges notes that the Convention provides an autonomous concept of possessions, independent of national legal traditions. The autonomy of the concept of possessions under the Convention is linked to a broader understanding of the protected rights. The Convention may protect the right in question as a possession, even if it is not recognized as such under the domestic law of the contracting state. The ECtHR takes a selective ad hoc approach and describes possessions through their attributes without providing a specific definition of the concept of possessions, as it considers that the concept of possessions cannot be separated from the dynamic and evolving nature of the Convention itself and that the definition of possessions.... Thus, by choosing a dynamic concept of possessions defined by features, it is not possible to provide an exhaustive list of objects that could be qualified as objects of possession in the context of Article 1 of Protocol No. 1. The ECtHR takes the position that "possession within the meaning of Article 1 of Protocol No. 1 can be either "existing possessions" or assets, including claims, in respect of which the applicant can argue that he or she has at least a "legitimate expectation" of obtaining effective enjoyment of a property right" (e.g. judgment of 7 January 2003 in *Kopecky v Slovakia*, application no 44912/98; judgment of 24 June 2003 in *Stretch* v. *United Kingdom*, application no 42527/98, etc.). A "legitimate expectation" is based on a reasonably justified reliance on a legal act which has a sound legal basis and which bears on property rights (e.g. Grand Chamber judgment of 7 January 2003 in *Kopecky* v. *Slovakia*, application no 44912/98, § 47; judgment of 12 November 2013 in *Pyrantienė* v. *Lithuania*, application no 45092/07, § 67). In each case the issue that needs to be examined is whether the circumstances of the case, considered as a whole, confer on the applicant title to a substantive interest protected by Article 1 of Protocol No. 1 (e.g. Grand Chamber judgment of 29 March 2010 in *Depalle* v. *France*, application no 34044/02, § 62; judgment of 30 November 2004 in *Öneryildiz* v. *Turkey*, application no 48939/99, § 124). Thus, the rights of tenants and the legitimate expectations arising from a tenancy relationship can be protected as property by the provisions of Article 1 of Protocol No. 1 to the Convention, but for this the right of tenants to a substantive interest has to be established.

Since the defendants are to be evicted from premises in a building of special public value and intended to meet the needs of society, in the present case it is necessary to determine how to ensure the right of individuals to a home on the one hand and access by society to a cultural heritage complex of special value, where the building, part of which the defendants are entitled to use as a home, is located, on the other. [...]

The panel of judges decides that in the present case a fair balance of interests must be ensured by applying the mechanism of compensation for loss of possessions. The case law of the ECtHR recognises that compensation terms under the relevant legislation are material to the assessment of whether the contested measure respects the requisite fair balance and, notably, whether it does not impose a disproportionate burden on the applicant. The taking of property without payment of an amount reasonably related to its value will normally constitute a disproportionate interference and a total lack of compensation can be considered justifiable under Article 1 of Protocol No. 1 only in exceptional circumstances (see e.g. judgment of 19 January 2017 in *Werra Naturstein GmbH & Co KG v. Germany*, application no 32377/12, § 45; judgment of 9 December 1994 in *Holy Monasteries v. Greece*, application nos 13092/87, 13984/88, § 71).

The panel of judges notes that the issue of compensation cannot be resolved without identifying the occupants who use premises as their home within the meaning of the Convention, as only the eviction of such persons constitutes a loss of their right to a home and the property aspects of such right are protected by Article 1 of Protocol No. 1 to the Convention.

[...]

The criteria for determining a person's place of residence are also established in Article 2.17(1) of the Civil Code, whereas a person's declared place of residence is only one of the criteria for determining such factual circumstances. ECtHR case law also follows this practice. The Court observed that when the protection of Article 8 of the Convention is invoked in respect of premises in which the applicant has never or almost never lived, or where he no longer resides for a significant period, his connection with such premises may be weakened and no longer an issue under Article 8 of the Convention (see e.g. judgment of 22 September 2009 in *Andreou Papi v. Turkey*, application no 16094/90, § 54). The Court have considered that the sole fact that the applicant remained registered as living in the flat of his former wife (i.e. not the one for which he requested to apply protection under Article 8 of the Convention) is not sufficient to conclude that he had established his home there. The Court considered that by factually living in other premises, the applicant had developed sufficient and continuous links with such premises for them to be considered his "home" for the purposes of Article 8 of the Convention (see judgment of 14 March 2017 in *Yevgeniy Zakharov v. Russia*, application no 66610/10, § 32).

[...]

The panel of judges notes that in assessing whether the allocation and sale of land on preferential terms to [...] constitutes fair compensation for loss of the right to a home, the assessment of both the land as (in)adequate compensation and its allocation without undue delay is of relevance. As the ECtHR has reiterated, the aspect of determining the amount of compensation is inevitably linked to the question of the method of calculating it. In such case, it is very important to respect the principle of fair balance of interests, which reveals the urgency for a more sensitive approach to the issues of property value, and determination of fair remuneration, since delays exist in the process of taking property. As regards the amount of compensation, the ECtHR has emphasized that it should normally be calculated on the basis of the value of the property at the date of the loss of ownership (see Grand Chamber judgment of 22 December 2009 in *Guiso-Gallisay* v. *Italy*, application no 58858/00, § 103). The Court has also reiterated that the adequacy of compensation would be diminished if it were to be paid without reference to various circumstances liable to reduce its value, such as unreasonable delay. Abnormally lengthy delays in the payment of compensation for expropriation lead to increased financial loss for the person whose land has been expropriated, putting him in a position of uncertainty (see e.g. judgment of 29 March 2006 in *Vassallo* v. *Malta*, application no 57862/09, § 39.). The same applies to abnormally lengthy delays in administrative or judicial proceedings in which such compensation is determined, especially when people whose land has been expropriated are obliged to resort to such proceedings in order to obtain the compensation to which they are entitled.

[...]

The panel of judges notes that general statements on eviction of persons living in the Užutrakis manor homestead complex indicated in the legal acts and letters of state authorized institutions express the general position of the state to evict persons and adapt the complex to meet public needs, but do not decide or say about each person's right to a home. In this context, it must be concluded that in each instance it must be assessed individually whether the dwelling is the home of that person within the meaning of the Convention, and to what extent legitimate expectations for such eviction should be compensated, if at all. Therefore, the panel of judges decides that the fact that other evicted persons have been provided with other accommodation does not per se (automatically) constitute discrimination against the defendants or violate their rights.

4/6

In its judgment of 21 November 2018, criminal case No. 2K-321-303/2018, the Supreme Court of Lithuania reviewed recent practice of the ECtHR and the

CJEU in regard to application of the *non bis in idem* principle in tax and criminal cases. The Court assessed the prohibition of *non bis in idem* principle provided in Protocol 7 Article 4(1) of the ECHR and decided that criminal investigations concerning submission of false VAT returns against a company which prior to such criminal investigation and on the basis of previous tax investigations in relation to such VAT returns had made an agreement with the tax authorities concerning VAT payments, fines and tax penalties to be paid to the tax authorities, constitute a violation of the *non bis in idem* principle. Relevant extracts from the case are reproduced below:

> No one can be punished twice for the same crime (Paragraph 5 Article 31 of the Constitution of the Republic of Lithuania, Paragraph 6 Article 2 of Criminal Code). The prohibition on being punished twice for the same offence for which someone has already been finally acquitted or convicted in accordance with the law and penal procedure of the State is enshrined in Paragraph 1 of Article of the Protocol No. 7 of the ECHR. Such provisions establish the principle of *non bis in idem* (prohibition on being charged and punished twice for the same offence).
>
> [...]
>
> In the case law of the ECtHR this principle must be interpreted as prohibiting the prosecution or trial of a second 'offence' after the final judgment in the case in so far as it arises from identical facts or facts which are substantially the same and inextricably linked together in time and space (Grand Chamber judgment of 10 February 2009 in *Sergey Zolotukhin v. Russia*, application no. 14939/03; judgment of 16 June 2009 in *Ruotsalainen v. Finland*, application no. 13079/03; judgment of Grand Chamber of 15 November 2016 in *A and B v Norway*, application no. 24130/11 and 29758/11).
>
> [...]
>
> Administrative sanctions and criminal liability for VAT offences are intended to ensure the collection of this tax and to combat fraud, thus also implementing European Union law (Article 2 and 273 of Council Directive 2006/112/EC of 28 November 2006 on the common system of value added tax, Article 325 of the Treaty on the Functioning of the European Union). Therefore, the requirements of the Charter of Fundamental Rights of the European Union ('the Charter'), Article 50 of which also

enshrines the principle of *non bis in idem*, as interpreted in the case law of the CJEU, are also applicable in the present criminal proceedings (e.g. CJEU decision of 20 March 2018 in *Mensi*, C-524/15, § § 18–24 and case law indicated herein).

[...]

According to the practice of the ECtHR, when evaluating whether in a particular case an offence is considered as 'criminal', three criteria should be applied: the legal classification of the offence under national law, the nature of the offence, and the severity of sanctions which can be imposed against the offender. It should be noted that in the ECtHR's practice of application of such criteria, violations of tax law, which attract tax fines, are considered as 'criminal' within the meaning of the Convention (judgment of 23 July 2002 in *Janosevic* v. *Sweden*, application no. 34619/97; judgment of 23 November 2006 in *Jussila* v. *Finland*, application no. 73053/01; judgment of 5 January 2010 in *Impar LtD.* v. *Lithuania*, application no. 13102/04; judgment of 17 April 2012 in *Steininger* v. *Austria*, application no. 21539/07; judgment of Grand Chamber of 15 November 2016 in *A and B* v. *Norway*). [...]

[...] It should be noted that, in accordance with the criteria set out in the case law of the ECtHR, such penalties and the administrative offences for which they are imposed are generally also considered 'criminal' within the meaning of the Convention (e.g. decisions of the cassation court in criminal cases Nos. 322/2003, 2K-686/2007, 2K-102/2008; judgment of 4 November 2008 in *Balsytė-Lideikienė* v. *Lithuania*, application no. 72596/01; judgment of 13 June 2017 in *Šimkus* v. *Lithuania*, application no 41788/11). [...]

[...]

Neither Article 4 Paragraph 1 of Protocol No. 7 of the Convention, nor the national law of the Republic of Lithuania prohibits execution of two processes regarding the same offence; however, repeated prosecution or trial is prohibited. Assessment of whether in a particular case the principle of *non bis in idem* is violated has to be based on the following circumstances: 1) whether the sanction imposed against a person is a criminal charge; 2) whether the person was punished for the identical or essentially the same legally significant facts (same conduct); 3) whether the person was punished repeatedly; 4) whether the same person was punished repeatedly (same person). These criteria cannot be applied formally: violation of the said principle can be determined only after examination of all the significant factual circumstances of the case.

[...]

It should be noted that in order to establish an infringement of the *non bis in idem* principle, it is not necessary for the legally relevant facts in both cases to coincide completely: it is sufficient for a person to be prosecuted a second time regarding certain factual circumstances for which he or she has already been finally acquitted or convicted, the circumstances of the same event established in both proceedings may differ slightly, provided that such differences are not substantial; in one of the proceedings, the relevant circumstances may constitute only one of the elements of the composition of the infringement, or the period of the act imputed to a person in both proceedings may coincide only in part (judgment of 18 October 2011 in *Tomasovic* v. *Croatia*, application no 53785/09; judgment of 29 May 2001 in *Franz Fischer* v. *Austria*, application no 37950/97; *mutatis mutandis* decision on admissibility of 27 January 2005 in *Smolickis* v. *Latvia*, application no 73453/01).

The panel of judges notes that the Grand Chamber of the ECtHR in judgment of 15 November 2016 in *A and B* v. *Norway* (application no 24130/11 and 29758/11), considering *inter alia* a widespread practice among European states, recognised a wide margin or appreciation for the States, in accordance with the requirements of legality, to decide on what complementary legal measures to take in response to social misconduct (such as tax evasion). Such should be able legitimately to choose complementary legal responses to socially offensive conduct through different procedures forming a coherent whole so as to address different aspects of the social problem involved, provided that the accumulated legal responses do not represent an excessive burden for the individual concerned (judgment of the Grand Chamber in *A and B* v. *Norway*, § 121). Nonetheless Article 4 of Protocol No. 7 of the Convention does not exclude the conduct of dual proceedings, provided that certain conditions are fulfilled. In particular, to be satisfied that there is no duplication of trial or punishment (bis) as proscribed by Article 4 of Protocol No. 7, it has to be demonstrated convincingly that the dual proceedings in question are sufficiently closely connected in substance and in time. In other words, the purposes pursued and the means used to achieve them should in essence be complementary and linked in time, but also that the possible consequences of organising the legal treatment of the conduct concerned in such a manner should be proportionate and foreseeable for the persons affected (judgment of the Grand Chamber in *A and B v. Norway*, § 130). Material factors for determining whether there is a sufficiently close connection in substance include: (1) whether the different proceedings pursue complementary purposes and thus address different aspects of the social misconduct involved; (2) whether the duality of proceedings concerned is a foreseeable consequence, both in law and in practice, of the same impugned conduct (idem); (3) whether the relevant sets of proceedings are conducted in such a manner as to avoid as far as possible any duplication in the collection as well as the assessment of the evidence, notably through adequate interaction between the various competent authorities to bring about that the establishment of facts in one set is also used in the other set; (4) and, above all, whether the sanction imposed in the proceedings which become final first is taken into account in those which become final last, so as to prevent the individual concerned being in the end made to bear an excessive burden, this latter risk being least likely to be present where there is in place an offsetting mechanism designed to ensure that the overall amount of any penalties imposed is proportionate (judgment of the Grand Chamber in *A and B v. Norway*, § 132). Moreover, combined proceedings will more likely meet the criteria of complementarity and coherence if the sanctions to be imposed in proceedings not formally classified as 'criminal' are specific for the conduct in question and thus differ from "the hard core of criminal law" (judgment of the Grand Chamber in *A and B v. Norway*, § 133). Moreover the requirement of a connection in time nonetheless remains and must be satisfied. This does not mean, however, that the two sets of proceedings have to be conducted simultaneously from beginning to end, but still connection in time must be sufficiently close to protect the individual from being subjected to uncertainty and delay and from proceedings becoming protracted over time (judgment of the Grand Chamber in *A and B v. Norway*, § 134).

The cassation claim correctly points out that a substantially similar position has developed in the recent case law of the Court of Justice (decision of 20 March 2018 in *Menci*, C-524/15; decision of 20 March 2018 in *Di Puma*, C-596/16 and C-597/16; decision of 20 March 2018 in *Garlsson R and Others*, C-537/16).

Decisions of the CJEU state, *inter alia*, that a restriction on the principle of *non bis in idem* enshrined in Article 50 of the Charter may be justified on the basis of Article 52 (1) of the Charter, according to which such a restriction has to be provided for by law and respect the essence of those rights and freedoms; subject to the principle of proportionality, limitations may be made only if they are necessary and genuinely meet objectives of general interest recognised by the Union or the need to protect the rights and freedoms of others. The CJEU has clarified that Article 50 of the Charter does not preclude the application of national legislation which may lead to the prosecution of a person who has not paid VAT on time, even though that person has already been the subject of a final administrative sanction, if such legislation: (1) pursues an objective of general interest which may justify such cumulative application of prosecution and sanctions, i.e. the fight against VAT offences, but those prosecutions and sanctions must have additional objectives; (2) rules are laid down to ensure the cumulative application of proceedings so that the additional burden on the persons concerned does not exceed what is strictly necessary; and (3) to ensure that the severity of any sanctions imposed is limited to what is strictly necessary in relation to the seriousness of the offence.

The panel notes that as can be seen from the content of the principles set out in relatively recent case law, firstly formulated by the Grand Chamber of the ECtHR in s *A and B* v. *Norway*, and their application in currently still limited case law of the ECtHR and the CJEU, the possibility of two legal proceedings of a criminal nature on the same facts is essentially linked to the State's discretion in regulating liability for, *inter alia*, tax evasion. In order to prevent violation of the *non bis in idem* principle, such discretion by the State should be executed only in accordance with the conditions set out above. On the other hand, the ECtHR Grand Chamber in *A and B* v. *Norway*, after reviewing the case law of the ECtHR, also stated that in relation to matters subject to repression under both criminal and administrative law, the surest manner of ensuring compliance with Article 4 of Protocol No. 7 is the provision, at some appropriate stage, of a single-track procedure enabling the parallel strands of legal regulation of the activity concerned to be brought together, so that the different needs of society in responding to the offence can be addressed within the framework of a single process (§ 130).

4/7

In its judgment of 19 October 2018 in civil case No. 3K-3-368-687/2018, the Supreme Court of Lithuania interpreted and applied the Lugano Convention on Jurisdiction and the Recognition and Enforcement of Judgments in Civil and Commercial Matters, in particular the validity and extent of an agreement on the competent court (Article 23) and how to determine the place where a harmful event occurred (Article 5(3)). Relevant extracts from the case are reproduced below:

> Regarding the rules applicable to determine jurisdiction
>
> The case raises the question of the jurisdiction of the courts to hear a dispute following a joint and several action for damages against three defendants. The dispute has a foreign element, as the defendant Bank is domiciled in Switzerland, whereas the defendants – individuals – are domiciled in the Republic of Lithuania.
>
> [...]
>
> All matters of jurisdiction and the recognition and enforcement of judgments in civil and commercial matters between the Member States of the European Union (except Denmark) and the European Free Trade Association (EFTA) – the Kingdom of Norway, the Republic of Iceland and the Swiss Confederation, as well as the Kingdom of Denmark – are regulated by the Lugano Convention on Jurisdiction and the Recognition and Enforcement of Judgments in Civil and Commercial Matters of 30 October 2007, which replaced the 1988 Lugano Convention. This Convention entered into force for Switzerland on 1 January 2011.
>
> The Lugano Convention is in force for Lithuania as a member state of the European Union; therefore the courts, when determining the jurisdiction of the courts of a particular state (Switzerland or Lithuania) in the civil case in question, must follow the rules established in that convention
>
> The panel of judges notes that the Lugano Convention essentially expands application of Council Regulation (EC) No 44/2001 of 22 December 2000 on jurisdiction and the recognition and enforcement of judgments in civil and commercial matters (hereinafter – Brussels I) and Regulation (EU) No 1215/2012 of the European Parliament and of the Council of 12 December 2012 on jurisdiction and the recognition and

enforcement of judgments in civil and commercial matters (hereinafter – Brussels I bis) which repealed Brussels I, to EFTA member states.

The structure of the Lugano Convention is based on the principles of the Brussels I Regulation and reproduces most of its provisions. Pursuant to the Second Protocol to the Lugano Convention, the Contracting Parties also undertook to follow the case law and doctrine of the Court of Justice in interpreting the Brussels I Regulation (now Brussels I bis). Thus, the interpretation and application of the provisions of the Lugano Convention must be based on the rulings of the CJEU in cases in which the Brussels I Regulation (Brussels I bis) has been interpreted and applied, in so far as the provisions of that legislation can be regarded as equivalent.

The provisions on agreed jurisdiction (prorogation of jurisdiction) in Article 23 (1) of the Lugano Convention and Article 25 (1) of the Brussels I (bis) Regulation are essentially identical, i.e., they confer exclusive jurisdiction on a particular court to settle disputes which have arisen or may arise between the parties.

The provisions of Article 5 (3) of the Lugano Convention governing the jurisdiction of claims arising out of tort / delict and Article 7 (2) of the Brussels I bis are also identical. They stipulate that in cases of tort, delict or quasi-delict, in addition to the court of the defendant's domicile, the courts of the place where the harmful event occurred or may occur also have jurisdiction.

The rule of concentration of jurisdictions enshrined in Article 6 (1) of the Lugano Convention in the case of multiple defendants, when related actions are brought against several defendants, is in line with Article 8 (1) of Brussels I (bis).

In the present case in determining the jurisdiction of a dispute, questions concerning the interpretation and application of Articles 5 (3), 6 (1) and 23 (1) of the Lugano Convention are raised. Considering the identical regulation discussed above, the panel of judges will assess the appealed decisions in the context of the respective provisions of the Lugano Convention, while also interpreting the relevant provisions of the Convention based on relevant CJEU case law.

[...]

Regarding the scope of the parties' agreement on jurisdiction (Article 23 of the Lugano Convention)

The general rule of jurisdiction under which actions must be brought in the defendant's State of domicile is set out in Article 2 (1) of the Lugano Convention. With the exception of the provisions on exclusive jurisdiction under Article 22 of the Lugano Convention, which do not apply in the present case, the general rule of jurisdiction may be derogated from in cases of special jurisdiction.

Special jurisdiction is divided into jurisdiction prescribed by law and jurisdiction prescribed by agreement. The panel of judges notes that contractual jurisdiction takes precedence over jurisdiction under the law. [...]

[...] agreements on international jurisdiction are governed by Article 23 of the Lugano Convention. Under paragraph 1 of this Article if the parties, one or more of whom is domiciled in a State bound by this Convention, have agreed that a court or the courts of a State bound by this Convention are to have jurisdiction to settle any disputes which have arisen or which may arise in connection with a particular legal relationship, that court or those courts shall have jurisdiction. Such jurisdiction shall be exclusive unless the parties have agreed otherwise. For an agreement conferring jurisdiction to be valid under the Lugano Convention, it has to be made in writing or evidenced in writing, or in a form which accords with practices which the parties have established between themselves or in international trade or commerce (Article 23(1) of the Lugano Convention, see also CJEU judgment of 7 July 2016 in *Hőszig*, C-222/15:, EU:C:2016:525, § 35).

Such an agreement between the parties, provided that it complies with the formal requirements imposed on it and is not void as to its content, is binding not only on the parties themselves but also on the court (s) of a State which is a contracting party to the Lugano Convention and whose jurisdiction to resolves dispute has been selected by the parties.

[...]

CJEU case law has explained that it is for the national court to interpret the clause conferring jurisdiction invoked before it in order to determine which disputes fall within its scope (CJEU judgment of 10 March 1992 in *Powell Duffryn*, C 214/89, EU:C:1992:115, § 37).

According to the case law of the CJEU the court before which a matter is brought has the duty of examining, *in limine litis* (at the beginning of the proceedings), whether the jurisdiction clause was in fact the subject of consensus between the parties, which must be clearly and precisely demonstrated; the purpose of the requirements as to form is to ensure that consensus between the parties is in fact established (see CJEU judgment of 28 June 2017 in *Leventis and Vafeias*, C 436/16, EU:C:2017:497, § 37 and case law indicated therein). In other words, the existence of an agreement can be established on the basis of the fact that the formal requirements laid down in Article 23 (1) of the Lugano Convention have been met.

In the present case, the agreement on jurisdiction concluded between the parties in regard to the form satisfies the requirements of Article 23 (1) of the Lugano Convention and the criteria laid down in the case law of the Court of Justice (the agreement on jurisdiction is in writing, its content is clear and precise: on this issue see CJEU judgment of 7 July 2016 in *Hőszig*, C-222/15, EU:C:2016:525, § 37 and case law indicated herein). There is no dispute regarding this. However, the defendant Bank challenges the finding of the appellate court as to the scope of the choice of court agreement concluded between it and the plaintiff. The issue that is being considered in this case is whether the plaintiff's demands indicated in the claim fall within the scope of the choice of court provision. Thus, in the present case, the courts were required to determine whether the jurisdiction clause covered the applicant's claim for damages.

The panel of judges notes that, in addition to the above formal requirements, Article 23 (1) of the Lugano Convention contains a requirement as to the content of the jurisdiction clause, i.e. that the agreement must cover disputes which have arisen or which may arise in connection with a specific legal relationship.

With regard to that criterion, the Court of Justice has clarified that an agreement conferring jurisdiction may relate only to disputes which have arisen or may arise as a result of a specific legal relationship, limiting the scope of an agreement conferring jurisdiction solely to disputes which arise from the legal relationship in connection with which the agreement was entered into. Its purpose is to avoid a party being taken by surprise by the assignment of jurisdiction to a given forum as regards all disputes which may arise out of its relationship with the other party to the contract and stem from a relationship other than that in connection with which the agreement conferring jurisdiction was made (see on this issue the above mentioned judgment in *Powell Duffryn*, C-214/89, EU:C:1992:115, § 31).

Thus, an agreement conferring jurisdiction covers all disputes relating to a contract which arise between the parties to the agreement and which relate to a specific legal relationship between the parties. The requirement of a connection between the condition relied on and a defined legal relationship is necessary in order to ensure that jurisdiction can be established.

[…]

It is clear from the wording of the choice of court agreement that, at the time of that agreement, the parties agreed on the exclusive jurisdiction of the courts of the defendant Bank in Geneva (Switzerland), covering all legal relations between the defendant Bank and the applicant and all legal proceedings. The agreement on jurisdiction concluded by the parties does not provide for any exceptions (it is not stated that this provision applies exclusively to contractual or exclusively non-contractual relations).

[…]

In order to determine whether a particular dispute falls within the scope of an agreement conferring jurisdiction, it is necessary to assess whether there is a link between the tort and the contract. According to the case law of the CJEU when the purpose of the claims brought by the applicant in the case is to seek damages, the legal basis for which can reasonably be regarded as a breach of the rights and obligations set out in the contract which binds the parties in the main proceedings, which would make its taking into account indispensable in deciding the action, such claims concern 'matters relating to a contract' (CJEU judgment of 13 March 2014 in *Powell Duffryn, Brogsitter*, C-548/12, ECLI:EU:C:2014:148, §§ 26, 27).

The courts have determined that the defendant Bank and the plaintiff were bound by a contractual relationship. There is no dispute about that in the case. Although the plaintiff claims non-contractual liability against the defendants, which is not directly linked to the plaintiff's bank account agreement with the defendant Bank, the panel of judges is of the opinion that the dispute between the parties arose regarding damages related to a legal banking relationship between the parties.

[...]

The plaintiff 's claims are based, in essence, on the argument that the defendant Bank infringed the standard of care by making a transfer of funds to the personal accounts of the plaintiff's shareholders and their companies. When transfers were made from the plaintiff's accounts at German and Austrian banks to the plaintiff's shareholders' accounts with the defendant's bank, the plaintiff was generally aware only of the existence of account No. 1981. Thus, from the point of view of the applicant at the time, the transfer of funds which, according to the plaintiff itself, caused it damage, related to account No. 1981 and the banking relationship between the plaintiff and the defendant Bank, since, in the absence of any agreement between the parties, there would have been no basis for transferring the funds to the accounts at the defendant Bank. In the absence of a legal relationship regarding account No. 1981 the misappropriation of the funds would not have been possible, since the precondition for the fraud had to be that the plaintiff had accounted the misappropriated funds as being held in account No. 1981. Had the account not been opened, the plaintiff's managers and employees would not have been able to falsely claim that the funds had been credited to the plaintiff's account opened at the defendant's Bank.

In the light of the foregoing considerations, the panel of judges concludes that the jurisdiction clause in the present case includes the plaintiff's claim for damages, since that right derives from the contractual relationship between the parties. For that reason, the plaintiff could have foreseen that the choice of court provision would apply to the plaintiff's claims against the defendant Bank for damages.

Regarding the place where the event giving rise to the harm occurred (Article 5 (3) of the Lugano Convention)

[...]

Article 5 (3) of the Lugano Convention provides that in matters relating to tort, delict or quasi-delict, a person domiciled in a State bound by the Lugano Convention may, in another State bound by that Convention, be sued in the courts for the place where the harmful event occurred or may occur.

According to settled case law of the Court of Justice, the said rule of special jurisdiction is based on the existence of a particularly close linking factor between the dispute and the courts of the place where the harmful event occurred or may occur, which justifies the attribution of jurisdiction to those courts for reasons relating to the sound administration of justice and the efficacious conduct of proceedings (CJEU judgment of 5 June 2014 in *Coty Germany*, C-360/12, EU:C:2014:1318, § 47; judgment of 10 September 2015 in *Holterman Ferho Exploitatie and others*, C-47/14, EU:C:2015:574, § 73 and case law indicated herein).

This rule is based on the fact that in matters relating to tort and delict and quasi-delict, the courts for the place where the harmful event occurred or may occur are usually the most appropriate for deciding the case, in particular on the grounds of proximity and ease of taking evidence (judgment of 21 May 2015 in *CDC Hydrogen Peroxide*, C352/13, EU:C:2015:335, paragraph 40; judgment of 10 September 2015 in *Holterman Ferho Exploitatie and others*, C 47/14, EU:C:2015:574, paragraph 74).

It is settled case law of the Court of Justice that the expression 'place where the harmful event occurred' is intended to cover both the place where the damage occurred and the place of the event giving rise to it; therefore the claim against the defendant by the plaintiff's choice can be brought before either of such courts (judgment of 25 October 2011 in *eDate Advertising and others*, C-509/09 and C-161/10, EU:C:2011:685, paragraph 41 and case law provided herein).

As regards the place where the event giving rise to the damage occurred, the appellate court held that the plaintiff had not substantiated or demonstrated which of the defendants' actions had caused the damage or when it had been decided to execute the appropriation scheme by joint action of the defendants. For this reason, the appellate court correctly concluded that there was no factual and legal basis for considering the place of the events giving rise to the damage to a single State.

This conclusion is not called into question by the case law of the CJEU which takes the view that the special jurisdiction rule in matters of tort, delict or quasi-delict is inoperative when the place where the harmful event allegedly occurred cannot be determined, by virtue of the fact that the infringement on which the action is based consists of actions notable for the multiplicity of places where they were agreed and/or performed, with the result that it is not possible to determine clearly and usefully which court has a particularly close link with the dispute as a whole (CJEU judgment of 21 May 2015 in *Cartel Damage Claims (CDC) Hydrogen Peroxide SA*, C-352/13, ECLI:EU:C:2015:335, paragraph 45, see also paragraph 52 of the Opinion of Advocate General in this case).

However, the defendant challenges the findings of the appellate court as to determination of the place where the damage occurred. The panel of judges notes that in deciding this issue, the appellate court relied on the case law of the CJEU, which clarified that the place where the damage occurred is the place where the damage manifests itself (CJEU judgment of 16 July 2009 in *Zuid Chemie*, C-189/08, EU:C:2009:475, paragraph 27).

The term "place where the harmful event occurred" cannot be construed so extensively as to encompass any place where the adverse consequences can be felt of an event which has already caused damage actually arising elsewhere (CJEU judgment of 19 September 1995 in *Marinari*, C-364/93, EU:C:1995:289, paragraph 14).

The Court of Justice also indicated that the said expression does not refer to the place where the claimant is domiciled or where 'his assets are concentrated' by reason only of the fact that he has suffered financial damage there resulting from the loss of part of his assets which arose and was incurred in another Contracting State (CJEU judgment of 10 June 2004 in *Kronhofer*, C-168/02, EU:C:2004:364, paragraph 21).

Purely financial damage which occurs directly in the applicant's bank account cannot, in itself, be qualified as a 'relevant connecting factor', pursuant to Article 5(3) of Regulation No 44/2001 (Article 5(3) of the Lugano Convention accordingly). It is only where the other circumstances specific to the case also contribute to attributing jurisdiction to the courts for the place where purely financial damage occurred, that such damage could, justifiably, entitle the applicant to bring the proceedings before the courts for that place (CJEU judgment of 16 June 2016 in *Universal*

Music International Holding BV, C 12/15, ECLI:EU:C:2016:449, paragraphs 38, 39).

[...]

According to the case law of the CJEU, the place where the damage occurred is not the place where the claimant resides or the principal place of residence of his property, if he suffered there only financial damage resulting from the loss of property in another country. The place where the damage occurred is only the place where the original, direct damage occurred. [...]

The panel of judges agrees with the arguments of the cassation claim that the place where the funds were credited to the accounts of third parties in Switzerland is the place where the direct damage occurred. Accordingly, if the damage were found to have occurred outside Switzerland, that place would be Austria or Germany, i.e., the countries from which the funds were transferred. [...]

The panel of judges also notes that according to the case law of the Court of Justice the jurisdiction of a court or the courts of a Member State, agreed by the contracting parties in an agreement conferring jurisdiction is, in principle, exclusive (CJEU judgment of 21 May 2015 in *El Majdoub*, C-322/14, EU:C:2015:334, paragraph 24).

Therefore under the provisions of Article 23 of the Lugano Convention the parties making an agreement on jurisdiction can exclude both the general jurisdiction determined by the defendant's place of domicile laid down in Article 2 of the Lugano Convention and the special jurisdictions provided for in Articles 5 and 6 of the Lugano Convention (CJEU judgment 14 December 1976 in *Estasis Salotti di Colzani Aimo e Gianmario Colzani s.n.c.*, C-24/76, paragraph 7; and the above mentioned judgment in *Cartel Damage Claims (CDC) Hydrogen Peroxide SA*, C-352/13, paragraphs 59, 61).

Following the finding in that order that the parties had concluded a valid agreement conferring jurisdiction and conferring exclusive jurisdiction on the Swiss courts, the ground for jurisdiction laid down in Article 5 (3) of the Lugano Convention is no longer relevant. It is eliminated by an agreement on jurisdiction.

Regarding concentration of jurisdictions with multiple defendants (Article 6 (1) of the Lugano Convention

One of the arguments by the plaintiff for submitting this claim before the courts of the Republic of Lithuania is based on the fact that there are three defendants in the case, the Bank and two natural persons; therefore, in accordance with Article 6(1) of the Lugano Convention, the dispute is subject to the jurisdiction of the courts of the Republic of Lithuania according to the place of residence of the two defendants. Under Article 6(1) of the Lugano Convention a person domiciled in a State bound by this Convention may also be sued: where he is one of a number of defendants, in the courts for the place where any one of them is domiciled, provided the claims are so closely connected that it is expedient to hear and determine them together to avoid the risk of irreconcilable judgments resulting from separate proceedings.

It is not disputed in the case that the defendant's Bank is domiciled in Switzerland and the defendants N.S. and R.B. are domiciled in the Republic of Lithuania. In the present case, the question is whether the plaintiff's claim satisfies the requirements for the application of the special jurisdiction rule laid down in Article 6 (1) of the Lugano Convention.

In accordance with the case law of the CJEU, this rule of jurisdiction derogates from the general rule of jurisdiction of the court of the habitual residence of each defendant and must therefore be interpreted strictly (CJEU judgment of 22 May 2008 in *Glaxosmithkline and Laboratoires Glaxosmithkline*, C-462/06, EU:C:2008:299, paragraph 28; judgment of 7 March 2013 in *Painer*, C-145/10, EU:C:2011:798, paragraph 74).

The purpose of Article 6(1) of the Lugano Convention is to facilitate the sound administration of justice, to minimise the possibility of concurrent proceedings and thus to avoid irreconcilable outcomes if cases are decided separately (the said judgment in *Painer*, C-145/10, EU:C:2011:798, paragraph 77).

As stated [...] above, in concluding an agreement conferring jurisdiction under Article 23 (1) of the Lugano Convention, the parties are entitled to derogate not only from the general rule of jurisdiction laid down in Article 2 but also from the rules on special jurisdiction laid down in Articles 5 and 6 thereof.

Therefore, the court seized of a matter is bound by a jurisdiction clause derogating from the rules of jurisdiction laid down in Articles 5 and 6 of Regulation which was concluded by agreement between the parties under Article 23(1) (on this issue see the CJEU judgment in *CDC Hydrogen Peroxide*, C-352/13, EU:C:2015:335, paragraphs 59 and 61).

[...]

Although the condition laid down in Article 6 (1) of the Lugano Convention does not expressly provide for the need to establish separately that the action is brought solely in order to exclude it from the jurisdiction of the competent court (the above mentioned judgment in *Freeport*, paragraph 51; judgment of 21 May 2015 in *CDC Hydrogen Peroxide*, C-352/13, EU:C:2015:335, paragraph 28), in accordance with the consistent case law of the CJEU where claims brought against various defendants are connected within the meaning of Article 6(1) the rule of jurisdiction laid down in that provision is applicable without there being any further need to establish separately that the claims were not brought with the sole object of ousting the jurisdiction of the courts of the Member State where one of the defendants is domiciled (see e.g. CJEU judgment in *CDC Hydrogen Peroxide*, paragraph 27; judgment in *Reisch Montage*, paragraph 32; judgment in *Painer*, paragraph 78). The Court agrees with the argument of the cassation claim that in the present case the plaintiff, by submitting a claim for damages not only to the defendant Bank, but also to two other natural persons, seeks to artificially create the desired jurisdiction of the case in the courts of the Republic of Lithuania.

4/8

The Constitutional Court of the Republic of Lithuania in ruling No. KT20-N11/2018, case No. 17/2017, on the provision of state-guaranteed legal aid in criminal cases, dated 11 October 2018, reiterated the importance of the ECHR and the jurisprudence of the ECtHR concerning the issue of the right to a fair trial. The relevant paragraphs read:

> 24. The provisions of the Convention on Protection of Human Rights and Fundamental Freedoms of 1950 (hereinafter – the Convention) related *inter alia* to the right to trial and access to a court are important in the context of this case.

25. Article 6 of the Convention 'right to fair trial' provides for a right to a court (paragraph 1) examining issues on the civil rights and obligations of a person or a criminal charge against him, which includes a person's right to address the court (in English 'access to a court') and establishes the principles of a fair trial (in English 'fair trial'). Paragraph 3 of this article, which provides guarantees in criminal proceedings, among others prescribes: 'Everyone charged with a criminal offence has the following minimum rights: [...] (c) to defend himself in person or through legal assistance of his own choosing or, if he has not sufficient means to pay for legal assistance, to be given it free when the interests of justice so require [...]".

25.1. The requirements of paragraph 3 of Article 6 of the Convention, which *inter alia* guarantee in criminal proceedings, including the right of the personal charged with a criminal offence to free legal assistance, as provided for in its section c, are specific aspects of the general concept of a fair trial set forth in paragraph 1. Nonetheless, for the purposes of the principle of fair trial under Article 6 Paragraph 1 of the Convention complaints under paragraphs 1 and 3 of Article 6 should be taken together (European Human of Rights Court (ECtHR), Grand Chamber judgment of 2 November 2010 in *Sakhnovskiy* v. *Russia*, no 21272/03, paragraphs 94; ECtHR Grand Chamber judgment of 4 April 2018 in *Correia de Matos* v. *Portugal*, no 56402/12, paragraph 119; ECtHR Grand Chamber judgment of 26 July 2002 in *Meftah and others* v. *France*, nos 32911/96, 35237/97 and 34595/97, paragraph 40)

The guarantees under paragraph 3 Article 6 of the Convention ensure the requirement of fairness of criminal proceedings, considered as a whole, which according to the ECtHR is a primary obligation under paragraph 1 Article 6 of the Convention (ECtHR Grand Chamber judgment of 12 May 2017 in *Simeonovi* v. *Bulgaria*, no 21980/04, paragraph 113).

25.2. It should also be noted that under the case law of the ECtHR the defendant's wishes as to his or her choice of legal counsel, which *expressis verbis* is enshrined in section c paragraph 3 of Article 6 of the Convention is not absolute and subject to certain limitations where free legal aid is concerned and also where it is for the courts to decide whether the interests of justice require that the accused be defended by counsel appointed by them (ECtHR Grand Chamber judgment of 20 October 2015 in *Dvorski* v. *Croatia*, no 25703/11, paragraph 79).

Moreover, 'the right to defend himself in person or to be represented by a lawyer of his own choosing' does not necessarily give the accused the right to decide himself in what manner his defence should be assured (*Correia de Matos* v. *Portugal*, paragraph 122). The decision as to which of the two alternatives should be chosen, namely the applicant's right to defend himself in person or to be represented by a lawyer of his own choosing, depends upon the applicable legislation or rules of court (*Sakhnovskiy* v. *Russia*, paragraph 95). The requirement of compulsory representation by a registered lawyer is a measure taken in the interests of the accused, and national courts are therefore entitled to appoint a lawyer, even against the accused's wishes (*Correia de Matos*, paragraph 124).

25.3. Paragraph 3 of Article 6 of the Convention does not specify the manner in which states have to exercise the said guarantees in criminal proceedings, including a right to free legal aid from counsel. States are free to choose the means of ensuring that it is secured in their judicial systems. It is important only to ascertain whether the method they have chosen is consistent with the requirements of a fair trial (ECtHR judgment of 19 July 2011 in *Jeclovas* v. *Lithuania*, no 16913/04, paragraph 119).

In this respect, it must be remembered that the Convention is designed to "guarantee not rights that are theoretical or illusory but rights that are practical and effective" and that assigning counsel does not in itself ensure the effectiveness of the assistance he may afford an accused In that connection it must be borne in mind that the process against the accused will not be fair if the interests of the defence are not represented in the case (ECtHR judgment of 25 April 1983 in *Pakelli* v. *Germany*, no 8398/78) and the person charged with the offence must be protected at all stages of the proceedings (ECtHR judgment of 24 November 1993 in *Imbrioscia* v. *Switzerland*, no 13972/88).

25.4. As mentioned above, in criminal cases, free legal representation may be subject to certain conditions: first, such legal representation is granted to the accused free of charge only if that person does not have sufficient means to reimburse a lawyer, and second, the need for such legal representation is necessary in the interests of justice (*Dvorski* v. *Croatia*, paragraph 79). The ECtHR has noted that all the circumstances must be taken into account when assessing whether the financial situation of the accused is such that legal representation is necessary; the accused must show that he lacks the funds to pay for it (ECtHR judgment of 21 September 2004 in *Santambrogio v. Italy*, no 61945/00).

Whether the provision of legal representation in a criminal case is necessary in the interests of justice shall also be assessed in the light of all the circumstances of the case. Legal representation is usually provided free of charge where deprivation of liberty of the suspect or accused of the crime (or misdemeanour) is at stake (ECtHR Grand Chamber judgment of 10 June 1996 in *Bentham v. United Kingdom* Grand Chamber, no 19380/92, paragraph 61).

Legal aid must also be provided to those who are unable to defend themselves; in making such assessment, the ECtHR takes into account the complexity of the case and the applicant's education, social situation, personality and other circumstances (judgment of 24 May 1991 in *Quaranta v. Switzerland*, application no 12744/87, paragraph 35). Whether free legal assistance is necessary to protect the interests of justice must be assessed at each stage of the proceedings (judgment of 28 March 1990 in *Granger v. United Kingdom*, application no 11932/86, paragraphs 43–48). If the case is considered complex, effective legal aid must also be provided in the cassation process, *inter alia* to draft the cassation appeal (judgment of 19 July 2011 in *Jeclovas v. Lithuania*, application no 16913/04, paragraphs 118–126).

25.5. In this context it should be noted that under the case law of the ECtHR the Court reiterates that although Article 6 § 1 does not *expressis verbis* provide for free legal aid, in certain cases it has to be granted *inter alia* in courts in civil matters. The ECtHR has emphasised that the Convention is intended to guarantee not theoretical or illusory rights – this is particularly important with regard to the guarantees under Article 6 of the Convention – but rights that are practical and effective (ECtHR Grand Chamber judgment of 12 July 2001 in *Prince Hans-Adam II of Liechtenstein v. Germany*, no 42527/98, paragraphs 45). However, this may not be possible if a person is not entitled to free legal assistance. In *Airey v. Ireland* the ECtHR stressed that an effective right of access to a court may also mean that the state has a duty to grant a person the right to free legal aid in certain civil cases, but not in all cases (ECtHR judgment of 9 October 1979 in *Airey v. Ireland*, no 6289/73, paragraphs 24–28). The ECtHR has also emphasized that the right to a fair trial includes the right of an individual to present his or her case effectively in court and to enjoy the principles of equality of arms and adversarial proceedings (judgment of 28 November 2008 in *Švenčionienė v. Lithuania*, no 37259/04).

The question whether the provision of legal aid is necessary for a fair hearing must be determined on the basis of the specific facts and circumstances of each case and will depend, *inter alia*, on the importance of what is at stake for the applicant in the proceedings, the complexity of the relevant law and procedure and the applicant's capacity to represent him or herself effectively (see mentioned case *Steel and Morris v. United Kingdom* paragraphs 59–61, judgment of 8 November 2016 in *Urbšienė and Urbšys v. Lithuania*, application no 16580/09). As mentioned above, the right of access to a court is not absolute, it may be limited, but the restrictions must be proportionate and pursue legitimate aims (judgment of 4 December 1995 in *Bellet v. France*, application no 23805/94, paragraph 31). Therefore, certain conditions as to the provision of free legal aid may be justified, including possible restrictions related to the applicant's financial situation or the prospects for success in court (see mentioned case *Steel and Morris v. United Kingdom* paragraph 65, judgment of 10 March 2009 in *Anakomba Yula v. Belgium*, application no 45413/07, paragraphs 31–32).

26. Summarizing the provisions of Article 6 §§ 1 and 3 of the Convention and the jurisprudence of the ECtHR in interpreting and applying those provisions in the relevant aspect of the constitutional justice case under consideration, it should be noted that under them, every person suspected or accused of having committed a crime is entitled to free legal aid.

This right is not absolute and may be subject to conditions laid down in domestic law; it is important that those conditions (restrictions imposed) do not infringe the principle of fair trial enshrined in Article 6 § 1 of the Convention as a whole. Such free legal aid in criminal matters may be granted to the accused under two conditions: firstly, if he does not have sufficient funds to pay for the services of a lawyer and secondly, if the interests of justice so require, such as the complexity of the case, the seriousness of the offence or the severity of the possible sentence; this right must be guaranteed throughout the criminal proceedings.

It should also be noted that the special guarantees provided for in Article 6 § 3 of the Convention applicable in criminal proceedings should be considered in conjunction with the principle of fair trial as a whole enshrined in Article 6 § 1 of the Convention.

On the other hand, in order for a person to be able to exercise his right to a court and / or to exercise his right to a fair trial under Article 6 § 1 of the Convention effectively, in certain cases and *inter alia* in civil matters the State has a positive obligation to provide free legal aid considering *inter alia* the applicants' interests in the case, their financial position, the prospects for civil disputes in the courts, the complexity of national law (*Airey v. Ireland*, paragraph 26).

(Available, only in Lithuanian, at the website of the Constitutional Court of the Republic of Lithuania, <https://www.lrkt.lt/lt/teismo-aktai/paieska/135/ta1869/content>, translated by the editor)

4/9

In case No. E3K-7-471-403/2018 of 12 December 2018, the Supreme Court of Lithuania analysed the right of a legal person to institute court proceedings in defence of its business reputation against the State Security Department of Lithuania concerning publicly disclosed information provided to the National Security and Defence Committee of the Seimas of the Republic of Lithuania (Parliament). The claimant sought to recognise that information indicated in a publicly disclosed report that the applicant had committed unlawful acts (including bribery, blackmail) which systematically sought to unlawfully influence state institutions, politicians and political processes, to unlawfully influence law enforcement or other controlling institutions, does not correspond to reality and damage the claimant's business reputation. The lower courts did not accept the claim, but the Supreme Court of Lithuania reversed those decisions in part in accordance with Article 6 of the Convention and found that intelligence agencies do not have immunity from actions protecting the business reputation of a legal person. The relevant paragraphs read:

> The Court of cassation has clarified that a person's right to judicial protection in the material sense is a subjective right, which depends on the facts of a material legal nature. It is possible to determine whether an individual possesses this right only after establishing all the circumstances of the case, examining and evaluating the evidence in the case, and determining the applicable legal norm. The court answers this question by making a decision. The law prohibits refusal to accept or dismissal of a case on substantive legal grounds (for example, it is not possible to

refuse to accept an action on the ground of lack of a right of claim or that the action is time-barred). This is important for the right of claim but not for the procedural right to bring a claim. Such legal regulation is related to the principles of access to a court and universality of judicial protection enshrined in Article 30 (1) of the Constitution of the Republic of Lithuania and Article 6 (1) of the Convention for the Protection of Human Rights and Fundamental Freedoms (the Convention).

A situation where a person loses the opportunity to seek judicial protection of his civil rights before the court can amount to a denial of justice which impairs the very essence of the applicant's right of access to a court, as secured by Article 6 § 1 of the Convention (see e.g. ECtHR judgment of 28 February 2008 in Tserkva Sela *Sosulivka* v. *Ukraine*, application no 16580/09; judgment of 21 June 2011 in *Zylkov* v. *Russia*, application no 5613/04 [...]).

[...]

According to the case law of the ECtHR for the right of access to be effective, an individual must have a clear, practical opportunity to challenge an act that is an interference with his rights (ECtHR judgment of 4 December 1995 in *Bellet* v. *France*, application no 23805/94). This is applicable not only to proceedings which have already been started, because this provision "may be invoked by any person who considers that the restriction of one of his (civil) rights is unlawful and complains about the inability to bring an action (claim) before a court that meets requirements of Article 6 (1) of the Convention" (ECtHR judgment of 23 June 1981 in Le Compte, Van Leuven and *De Meyere* v. *Belgium*, application nos 6878/75 and 7238/75).

Moreover, the case law of the ECtHR consistently reiterates that the right of access to a court is not absolute but may be subject to limitations. Nevertheless, the limitations applied must not restrict the access left to the individual in such a way or to such an extent that the very essence of the right is impaired. A limitation will not be compatible with Article 6 § 1 if it does not pursue a legitimate aim and if there is not a reasonable relationship of proportionality between the means employed and the aim sought to be achieved (ECtHR judgment of 21 May 2015 in *Zavodnik* v. *Slovenia*, application no 53723/13; judgment of 16 February 2017 in *Karakutsya* v. *Ukraine*, application no 18986/06).

The ECtHR has also indicated that the Convention guarantees "practical and effective rights, but not theoretical and illusory ones", and therefore Article 6 § 1 of the Convention obliges States to ensure that every person has an effective right of access to a court (ECtHR judgment of 9 October 1979 in *Airey* v. *Ireland*, application no 6289/73). The degree of "access" to a court afforded under national legislation should be sufficient to secure the individual's "right to a court", having regard to the rule of law in a democratic society (ECtHR judgment of 28 May 1985 in *Ashingdane* v. *United Kingdom*, application no 8225/78). Factual or legal restrictions of the right can be recognised as incompatible with the Convention if they impede the effectiveness of the applicant's right of access to a court.

[...]

According to the indicated legal norms, the Seimas Committee or the Seimas Ombudsman does not have the competence to adopt a decision which could grant to the complainant some positive consequences that could be enforced as mandatory and enabling him to defend his violated rights and legitimate interests (in this case – business reputation). Hence, the effective and efficient protection of individual's rights, which is available to a person while defending his or her rights in court, is not ensured. The right of access to a court [...] is absolute (with the exception of certain procedural restrictions that do not infringe the very essence of this right) and cannot therefore be denied or artificially restricted (limited) [...]. The extended panel of judges, interpreting the Law on Intelligence in the context of the provisions of the Constitution and the Convention, decides that the measures provided for in the Law on Intelligence (parliamentary control and recourse to the Seimas Ombudsman) do not constitute grounds for restricting the right to judicial protection. Accordingly, intelligence agencies do not have immunity from actions protecting the business reputation of a legal person.

Part Four: III. Relationship between International Law and Internal law – Remedies under domestic law for violations of international law

4/10

In case No. 3K-3-324-684/2018of 4 October 2018, the Supreme Court of Lithuania decided on how to rectify a violation of Article 1 of Protocol No. 1 of the

Convention as established by the judgment of the ECtHR. The relevant paragraphs read:

> The ECtHR in judgment of 9 January 2018 in *T* v. *Lithuania*, application no 25545/14, decided that the Republic of Lithuania violated Article 1 of Protocol No. 1 to the Convention for the Protection of Human Rights and Fundamental Freedoms (protection of property), which enshrines that every natural or legal person is entitled to the peaceful enjoyment of his possessions. No one shall be deprived of his possessions except in the public interest and subject to the conditions provided for by law and by the general principles of international law. The preceding provisions do not, however, in any way impair the right of a State to enforce such laws as it deems necessary to control the use of property in accordance with the general interest or to secure the payment of taxes or other contributions or penalties.

> In paragraph 72 the ECtHR reiterated that Article 1 of Protocol No. 1 comprises three distinct rules. The first rule, set out in the first sentence of the first paragraph, is of a general nature and enunciates the principle of the peaceful enjoyment of property. The second rule, contained in the second sentence of the same paragraph, covers deprivation of possessions and makes it subject to certain conditions. The third rule, stated in the second paragraph, recognises that Contracting States are entitled, amongst other things, to control the use of property in accordance with the general interest. The three rules are not distinct in the sense of being unconnected: the second and third rules are concerned with particular instances of interference with the right to peaceful enjoyment of property. They should therefore be construed in the light of the general principle enunciated in the first rule. These rules should also be taken into account when dealing with the values of private property and forest protection. In the above mentioned paragraph the ECtHR agreed that States should enjoy a wide margin of appreciation in order to implement their forest-protection policies. Nevertheless, the Court cannot fail to exercise its power of review and must determine whether the requisite balance was maintained in a manner consonant with the applicants' right of property (see Grand Chamber judgment of 25 October 2012 in *Vistiņš and Perepjolkins* v. *Latvia*, no. 71243/01, § 109).

> In its judgment, the ECtHR directly found that the demolition order in respect of buildings of the applicants D. and R.T. had a legal basis in domestic law. Nothing showed that the provisions of domestic law had

been interpreted or applied by the domestic courts in an arbitrary manner. The interference was therefore lawful for the purposes of Article 1 of Protocol No. 1 to the Convention (§ 74 of the judgment). The Court also accepted that the interference pursued a legitimate aim that was in the general interest: to protect the environment, namely forests, the importance of which has been clearly established (§ 75 of the judgment).

In view of the above, the panel of judges of the Supreme Court of Lithuania considers that in the present case the obligation to demolish the applicants' buildings (upon revocation of the building permit) had a legal basis under Lithuanian national law and was thus lawful and not reviewable in the present case; the panel of judges does not see any new circumstances that would provide a legal basis for the reopening of the proceedings in the case to review the obligation to demolish structures built on forest land providing a legal basis for the reopening of the demolition obligation following the reopening of the proceedings (§§ 80, 81 of the judgment).

[...]

The ECtHR established in its judgment that the actions of public authorities significantly contributed to the applicants' situation and that the applicants under the court decisions had to bear the same, if not a stricter burden as the authorities, i.e. T.D. was obliged to demolish the building at the expense of the guilty parties (public authorities and applicants R. and T.D.) (§ 80 of the judgment). The ECtHR did not share the Government's argument that the applicants should have suspected that the building permission had been "precarious"; there were no indications that the applicants somehow contributed to the adoption of the unlawful decisions (to issue a building permit, to register the building); the Court could not see that the house was knowingly built in flagrant breach by the applicants of the domestic building regulations (§ 78 of the judgment). The ECtHR considered that the applicants had legitimate expectations that they would not be ordered to demolish their summer house, the construction of which was started in accordance with the required building permission issued by the authorities, at their sole or partial expense. The authorities did not consider minimising the burden the decision to demolish the buildings imposed on the applicants. The domestic courts did not look into the degree of responsibility of the applicants as opposed to that of several public authorities, including the Centre of Registers which registered the summer house as 97 % finished, and this registration was not challenged for four years by any authority (§§ 79, 80 of the judgment).

Considering [...] circumstances which were established in the judgment of the ECtHR, there is a legal basis for re-examining the issue of remedying the effects of construction under an illegally issued building permit.

[...] Public authorities must correct errors, even those caused by their own negligence, without imposing a disproportionate burden on individuals. The obligation on the builder to recover the funds used for the demolition of illegal construction through another legal action before the court involving even greater time and other costs is not in line with the principles of economy and concentration, reasonableness and fairness. Moreover, the burden of the error is shifted to those individuals who may not be involved in the illegal issuance of the building permit.

[...]

[...] As noted in the ECtHR judgment, there are no circumstances in the case confirming a certain degree of guilt on the part of D. and R.T. in obtaining a building permit and exercising the builder's rights after the construction of the buildings (see paragraph 43 of the judgment). [...] Consequently, in the case of revocation of a building permit and application of legal consequences, the persons guilty of illegal issuance of building permit must be determined, whose illegal actions also determined the illegality of construction and constituted the basis for demolition of such structures. Should the court determine that actions (omissions) of several persons were illegal, the court should analyse the degree of liability of those persons and decide on the proportionate distribution of the burden of eliminating the consequences of construction. When deciding on the fault and liability of the institutions, the State Enterprise Center of Registers, which registered the buildings in accordance with a construction permit that has been voided, should be included in the case as a defendant (ECtHR judgment, paragraph 80).

Another aspect of revocation of a building permit and elimination of the consequences of construction is compensation of the applicants for demolition of their buildings constructed under an illegally issued building permit. Paragraph 61 of the ECtHR notes that the ECtHR is not persuaded by the Government's argument that the applicants should have started new court proceedings for damages, which, in the Court's view, would only have delayed the outcome of the main proceedings without necessarily bringing any tangible result; under paragraph 77 of the judgment, the risk arising from any mistake made by a State authority must be borne by the State itself, and errors must not be remedied at the expense of the individuals concerned. Thus, the ECtHR stated, in essence, that the applicants were not required to bring a new action for damages and that the matter should therefore be dealt with in the same case concerning revocation of a building permit and the remediation of illegal construction. In the present case, the courts did not decide on the applicants' damages by ordering them to demolish the buildings erected by the applicants. No claim for damages has been made in the case, but even in the absence of such a claim, the court should propose to the builder to formulate a claim for damages, determine the amount of damages, taking into account, *inter alia*, explanations provided by the parties, and other evidence of damages. The applicants stated to the ECtHR that they did not refuse to claim damages for demolition of the buildings but did not claim compensation for them until the buildings had been demolished.

The panel of judges finds that the obligation of the builder to recover the funds used for the demolition of illegal constructions, as well as to indemnity for the demolition of buildings and to initiate other court proceedings, incurring even more time and other costs, would be inconsistent with economy and concentration, as well as fairness and reasonableness, and the burden of error on public authorities would be shifted to those who may not have been involved in the illegal issuance of a building permit. Therefore, when possible, the issue of damages should be decided by a court in the same case concerning revocation of a building permit and elimination of the consequences of construction.

Part Five: II.A.2. (a). Subjects of International Law – International organisations – In general – Participation of States and international organisations in international organisations and in their activities – Admission

5/1

On 5 July 2018 Lithuania finalised the accession process to the Organisation for Economic Co-operation and Development. The Ministry of Foreign Affairs indicated the importance of joining the OECD:

"Lithuania's membership of the OECD is the most significant achievement in the field of Lithuania's integration into the Euro-Atlantic structures after our accession to NATO and the European Union. All inhabitants of Lithuanian will feel positive results of the OECD membership", said the Minister Linkevičius. Lithuania has implemented a number of reforms during the accession period and it will continue to strive to tap into the potential for boosting the country's economy, financial sector, education, social and employment policies, as well as increasing the effectiveness of the fight against corruption, the efficiency of public administration and policies for better regulation.

At the same time, Lithuania's OECD membership will qualitatively contribute to the work of the organization, because the OECD acknowledges that our country has gained a lot of unique experience. Lithuania will also actively contribute to the OECD's ambition to develop better policies for better lives.

(Available in English at the Internet site of the Ministry of Foreign Affairs, <https://www.urm.lt/default/en/news/oecd-accession-agreement-with-lithuania-signed>)

Part Five: II.A.2. (d). Subjects of International Law – International organisations – In general – Participation of States and international organisations in international organisations and in their activities – Representation of States and international organisations to international organisations, including privileges and immunities

5/2

On 5 June 2018 Lithuania's representative elected as Chairperson of the Coordination Committee of Special Procedures of the UNHRC:

On 5 June, Professor Dainius Pūras, United Nations Special Rapporteur on the right of everyone to the enjoyment of the highest attainable standard of health was elected as Chairperson of the Coordination Committee of Special Procedures of the United Nations Human Rights Council. He will coordinate the work of about 80 independent UN experts, who implement the organization's mandates in the field of human rights.

In 2001, Lithuania issued a standing invitation to all special procedures to evaluate human rights situation in Lithuania in 2001. In order to contribute to strengthening international human rights standards, Lithuania has announced its candidature to the Human Rights Council for the term 2022–2024.

Professor Dainius Pūras, who is actively contributing to the consolidation of international health standards in Lithuania, has served as the United Nations Special Rapporteur on the right of everyone to the enjoyment of the highest attainable standard of health since 2014. Between 2007 and 2011, Professor D. Pūras served as a member of the UN Committee on the Rights of the Child.

(Available in English at the Internet site of the Ministry of Foreign Affairs, <http://www.urm.lt/default/en/news/lithuanias-representative-elected-as-chairperson-of-the-coordination-committee-of-special-procedures-of-the-unhrc-for-the-first-time>)

5/3
On 12 July 2018 a Lithuanian representative was elected to the UN Committee on the Rights of Persons with Disabilities:

On 12 June at the United Nations Headquarters in New York, the Lithuanian representative, Professor Jonas Ruškus was re-elected to serve a second term on the Committee on the Rights of Persons with Disabilities (CRPD). Having won the largest number of electoral votes, Lithuania's candidate was elected in the first round.

As many as 22 candidates competed against each other in the election, 9 independent experts were elected for the 2019–2022 term. Besides J. Ruškus, experts from Nigeria, Australia, Switzerland, the Republic of Korea, Ghana, Brazil, Mexico and Indonesia were elected to the Committee.

In 2014, Professor J. Ruškus was the first Lithuanian representative to be elected to the UN Committee on the Rights of Persons with Disabilities. J. Ruškus is a Professor at Social Work Department and Dean of the Faculty of Social Sciences at Vytautas Magnus University in Kaunas. He has authored scientific monographs, research studies, and international publications, as well as become a recognized expert in the area of disability. Professor J. Ruškus has dedicated his career and personal life to working with the disabled, promoting their rights, and reducing social exclusion.

(Available in English at the Internet site of the Ministry of Foreign Affairs, <http://www.urm.lt/default/en/news/lithuanian-representative-elected-to-un-committee-on-the-rights-of-persons-with-disabilities->)

Part Five: I.B.6. Subjects of International Law – States – Recognition – On recognition (including non-recognition of Governments) and its effects

5/4

On 21 February 2018, the Ministry of Foreign Affairs released a statement on the 4th anniversary of the occupation of Crimea:

> On the 4th anniversary of the illegal occupation of Crimea, the Ministry of Foreign Affairs of Lithuania condemns the Russian Federation's military aggression against Ukraine that began four years ago in Ukraine's Autonomous Republic of Crimea and is currently continuing in eastern Ukraine. This has been a serious violation of international law, including the Charter of the United Nations, the Helsinki Final Act, and also the 1994 Budapest Memorandum.
>
> Such actions have not only undermined bilateral and multilateral agreements on ensuring the sovereignty and territorial integrity of Ukraine, but also pose a threat to security and stability in entire Europe. In response to this, the United Nations General Assembly adopted a resolution 68/262 on 27 March 2014. The resolution affirmed the General Assembly's commitment to the territorial integrity of Ukraine within its internationally recognized borders, condemned Russia's actions that were in violation of international law, backed Ukraine's territorial integrity and declared the Crimean 'referendum' invalid.
>
> Lithuania strongly supports the sovereignty, independence, and territorial integrity of Ukraine, consistently pursues the non-recognition policy of illegal occupation and annexation of Crimea, condemns systemic constraints on fundamental human rights by the Russian occupation regime, breaches of the freedoms of the media, peaceful assembly, religion and belief, as well as the persecution of Crimean Tatars. We will continue to strive to maintain the EU and other international sanctions against the Russian Federation in response to the illegal occupation of the peninsula until Russia withdraws from the illegally occupied territory of Ukraine.

(Available in English at the Internet site of the Ministry of Foreign Affairs, <http://www.urm.lt/default/en/news/foreign-ministrys-statement-on-the-4th-anniversary-of-the-occupation-of-crimea>)

5/5
On 30 May 2018, the Ministry of Foreign Affairs released a statement concerning Syria's decision to recognise Russian-occupied regions of Georgia as "independent states":

> Lithuania firmly supports the sovereignty and territorial integrity of Georgia within the borders recognised by the international community and condemns Syria's decision to recognise the Georgian regions of Abkhazia and Tskhinvali (South Ossetia) as "independent states". This is a grave violation of Georgia's sovereignty and territorial integrity and international law. We call upon the Government of Syria to carry out a policy underpinned by norms of international law rather than succumb to pressure from third countries and to repeal the decision without delay.

(Available in English at the Internet site of the Ministry of Foreign Affairs, <http://www.urm.lt/default/en/news/mfas-statement-concerning-syrias-decision-to-recognise-russian-occupied-regions-of-georgia-as-independent-states>)

5/6
On 11 November 2018, the Ministry of Foreign Affairs released a statement on illegitimate "elections" in Donetsk Oblast and Luhansk Oblast, parts of the Ukrainian territory:

> The Ministry of Foreign Affairs of Lithuania strongly condemns illegitimate "voting" conducted by the so-called "Donetsk People's Republic" and "Luhansk People's Republic" on 11 November that is contrary to norms of international law.
>
> Such "elections" gravely violate the Minsk agreements as well as Ukrainian laws and do not create conditions for free expression of political will in the Ukrainian regions mentioned above. Further invasion of the Russian army into the Ukrainian territory, continuing violations of ceasefire, and the escalation of the situation in and militarisation of the Azov Sea are of particular concern. Such illegal actions grossly violate the territorial integrity of Ukraine and international agreements and will seriously affect future relations between the international community and Russia.

> Lithuania firmly supports the territorial integrity and sovereignty of Ukraine. We underline once again that the Constitution of Ukraine and Ukrainian laws are the only legal basis for municipal elections on the Ukrainian territory.
>
> We reiterate our condemnation of the continuing military aggression by the Russian Federation against Ukraine, the on-going escalation of the situation and militarisation of the Azov Sea, and we call on Russia to comply with its commitments, undertaken in Minsk, to withdraw its armed forces from the Ukrainian territory, to terminate any support to illegal armed formations in Donbas, and to restore control on the Russian-Ukrainian border. We underscore the importance of sanctions on Russia which should continue until the Minsk agreements are fully implemented and the territorial integrity of Ukraine is restored.

(Available in English at the Internet site of the Ministry of Foreign Affairs, <http://www.urm.lt/default/en/news/statement-of-the-lithuanian-mfa-on-illegitimate-elections-in-donetsk-oblast-and-luhansk-oblast-parts-of-the-ukrainian-territory>)

Part Six: IX. The individual (including the corporation) in international law – Responsibility of the individual

6/1

On 26 September 2018 in New York, the U.S.A., the Minister of Foreign Affairs of Lithuania Linas Linkevičius took part in a discussion on the Syrian conflict. The minister indicated that the perpetrators of crimes committed against civilians in Syria must be brought to justice:

> We will not find a lasting solution to end the Syrian conflict if the perpetrators of brutal crimes against civilians are not be brought to justice", said Lithuania's Foreign Minister in his statement. L. Linkevičius confirmed Lithuania's support for the International, Impartial and Independent Mechanism to assist in the investigation and prosecution of persons responsible for the most serious crimes under International Law committed in the Syrian Arab Republic since March 2011. He also reiterated that the seven-and-a-half year-long Syrian conflict needed to be resolved peacefully.

(Available in English at the Internet site of the Ministry of Foreign Affairs, <http://www.urm.lt/default/en/news/l-linkevicius-perpetrators-of-crimes-committed-against-civilians-in-syria-must-be-brought-to-justice>)

Part Six: VIII. C. Human Rights and Fundamental Freedoms – Under the Council of Europe Treaty System

From the 17 judgments adopted in cases against Lithuania in 2018 by the ECtHR, the Court found violations in 11 of them and no violation of the Convention in six cases. Several ECtHR cases concerned various and important aspects of the rights guaranteed under the Convention, such as various violations of the Convention due to the existence of a CIA secret prison in Lithuania, interaction between the right to freedom of speech in advertisements and religious sensitivities, as well as requirements to protect privacy and freedom of religion of the individual in a mental hospital.

6/2

On 30 January 2018 in *Sekmadienis Ltd.* v. *Lithuania*, application no. 69317/14 the ECtHR found a violation of Article 10 of the ECHR, considering that there had been an interference with the applicant's right to freedom of expression, contrary to Article 10 of the Convention, on account of the fact that the applicant had been fined for publishing advertisements (which contained images of people resembling religious figures and Lithuanian expressions: "Jesus, what trousers", "Dear Mary, what a dress!", "Jesus [and] Mary, what are you wearing?") that had been deemed to be contrary to public morals. The ECtHR reasoned a violation of Article 10 of the ECHR, as follows:

> 75. Turning to the circumstances of the present case, the Court firstly observes that in its submissions the applicant company did not dispute that the persons depicted in the advertisements resembled religious figures (contrast to its position before the domestic authorities in paragraphs 14, 17 and 20 above). The Court is likewise of the view that all the visual elements of the advertisements taken together (see paragraphs 7–9 above) created an unmistakable resemblance between the persons depicted therein and religious figures.
>
> 76. It further observes that the advertisements had a commercial purpose – to advertise a clothing line – and were not intended to

contribute to any public debate concerning religion or any other matters of general interest (see paragraphs 6, 14, 17, 20, 29 and 55 above). Accordingly, the margin of appreciation accorded to the national authorities in the present case is broader (see paragraph 73 above). Nonetheless, such margin is not unlimited and the Court has to assess whether the national authorities did not overstep it.

77. Having viewed the advertisements for itself, the Court considers that at the outset they do not appear to be gratuitously offensive or profane, nor do they incite hatred on the grounds of religious belief or attack a religion in an unwarranted or abusive manner (see paragraphs 7–9 above; compare and contrast *Müller and Others*, cited above, § 36; *Otto-Preminger-Institut*, cited above, § 56; *Wingrove*, cited above, § 57; *İ.A.* v. *Turkey*, cited above, § 29; *Klein*, cited above, § 49; and *Balsytė-Lideikienė* v. *Lithuania*, no. 72596/01, § 79, 4 November 2008; see also *Aydın Tatlav* v. *Turkey*, no. 50692/99, § 28, 2 May 2006). The domestic courts and other authorities which examined the applicant company's case did not make any explicit findings to the contrary.

78. The Court has previously held that it is not to be excluded that an expression, which is not on its face offensive, could have an offensive impact in certain circumstances (see *Murphy*, cited above, § 72). It was therefore for the domestic courts to provide relevant and sufficient reasons why the advertisements, which, in the Court's view, were not on their face offensive, were nonetheless contrary to public morals (see, *mutatis mutandis*, *VgT Verein gegen Tierfabriken* v. *Switzerland*, no. 24699/94, §§ 75–76, ECHR 2001-VI). The Court also notes that, as submitted by the Government, not every use of religious symbols in advertising would violate Article 4 § 2 (1) of the Law on Advertising (see paragraph 53 above), which means that at least some explanation as to why the particular form of expression chosen by the applicant company was contrary to public morals was required by domestic law as well.

79. However, the Court cannot accept the reasons provided by the domestic courts and other authorities as relevant and sufficient. The authorities considered that the advertisements were contrary to public morals because they had used religious symbols "for superficial purposes", had "distort[ed] [their] main purpose" and had been "inappropriate" (see paragraphs 13, 23 and 25 above). In the Court's view, such statements were declarative and vague, and did not sufficiently explain why the

reference to religious symbols in the advertisements was offensive, other than for the very fact that it had been done for non-religious purposes (see, *mutatis mutandis, Giniewski*, cited above, §§ 52–53, and *Terentyev* v. *Russia*, no. 25147/09, § 22, 26 January 2017; compare and contrast *Balsytė-Lideikienė*, cited above, § 80). It also observes that none of the authorities addressed the applicant company's argument that the names of Jesus and Mary in the advertisements had been used not as religious references but as emotional interjections common in spoken Lithuanian, thereby creating a comic effect (see paragraphs 14, 17, 20 and 24 above; see also, *mutatis mutandis, Vereinigung Bildender Künstler* v. *Austria*, no. 68354/01, § 33, 25 January 2007), although it appears that those emotional interjections must have been known to them.

80. The Court takes particular issue with the reasoning provided in the decision of the SCRPA, which was subsequently upheld by the domestic courts in its entirety. The SCRPA held that the advertisements "promot[ed] a lifestyle which [was] incompatible with the principles of a religious person" (see paragraph 18 above), without explaining what that lifestyle was and how the advertisements were promoting it, nor why a lifestyle which is "incompatible with the principles of a religious person" would necessarily be incompatible with public morals. The Court observes that even though all the domestic decisions referred to "religious people", the only religious group which had been consulted in the domestic proceedings had been the Roman Catholic Church (see paragraph 16 above), despite the presence of various other Christian and non-Christian religious communities in Lithuania (see paragraphs 38, 39 and 56 above). In this connection, the Court notes that the Constitutional Court of Lithuania has held that "no views or ideology may be declared mandatory and thrust on an individual" and that the State "does not have any right to establish a mandatory system of views" (see paragraph 45 above). It also draws attention to the position of the United Nations Human Rights Committee that limitations of rights for the purpose of protecting morals must be based on principles not deriving exclusively from a single tradition (see paragraph 48 above).

81. The Court further observes that some of the authorities gave significant weight to the fact that approximately one hundred individuals had complained about the advertisements (see paragraphs 18 and 25 above). It has no reason to doubt that those individuals must have been genuinely offended. However, the Court reiterates that freedom of expression

also extends to ideas which offend, shock or disturb (see the references provided in paragraph 70 above). It also reiterates that in a pluralist democratic society those who choose to exercise the freedom to manifest their religion cannot reasonably expect to be exempt from all criticism. They must tolerate and accept the denial by others of their religious beliefs and even the propagation by others of doctrines hostile to their faith (see *Otto-Preminger-Institut*, § 47, and *İ.A. v. Turkey*, § 28, both cited above; see also the position of the Venice Commission in paragraph 49 above). In the Court's view, even though the advertisements had a commercial purpose and cannot be said to constitute "criticism" of religious ideas (see paragraph 76 above), the applicable principles are nonetheless similar (in this connection see in particular the findings of the domestic authorities that the advertisements "encourage[d] a frivolous attitude towards the ethical values of the Christian faith" in paragraph 18 above).

82. The Government in their observations argued that the advertisements must have also been considered offensive by the majority of the Lithuanian population who shared the Christian faith (see paragraph 56 above), whereas the applicant company contended that one hundred individuals could not be considered representative of such a majority (see paragraph 61 above). In the Court's view, it cannot be assumed that everyone who has indicated that he or she belongs to the Christian faith would necessarily consider the advertisements offensive, and the Government have not provided any evidence to the contrary. Nonetheless, even assuming that the majority of the Lithuanian population were indeed to find the advertisements offensive, the Court reiterates that it would be incompatible with the underlying values of the Convention if the exercise of Convention rights by a minority group were made conditional on its being accepted by the majority. Were this so, a minority group's rights to, *inter alia*, freedom of expression would become merely theoretical rather than practical and effective as required by the Convention (see, *mutatis mutandis, Barankevich v. Russia*, no. 10519/03, § 31, 26 July 2007; *Alekseyev v. Russia*, nos. 4916/07 and 2 others, § 81, 21 October 2010; and *Bayev and Others*, cited above, § 70).

83. Accordingly, the Court concludes that the domestic authorities failed to strike a fair balance between, on the one hand, the protection of public morals and the rights of religious people, and, on the other hand, the applicant company's right to freedom of expression. The wording of their

decisions – such as "in this case the game has gone too far" (see paragraph 11 above), "the basic respect for spirituality is disappearing" (see paragraph 15 above), "inappropriate use [of religious symbols] demeans them [and] is contrary to universally accepted moral and ethical norms" (see paragraph 25 above) and "religious people react very sensitively to any use of religious symbols or religious persons in advertising" (see paragraphs 11, 13, 15 and 18 above) – demonstrate that the authorities gave absolute primacy to protecting the feelings of religious people, without adequately taking into account the applicant company's right to freedom of expression.

84. There has therefore been a violation of Article 10 of the Convention.

In a concurring opinion judge De Gaetano reasoned:

1. While I agree that in this case there has been a violation of Article 10 of the Convention, it is pertinent to underscore the very narrow ground on which this violation is based. It should be clear from paragraphs 79 to 83 of the judgment that the problem in this case was the insufficiency of the reasons provided by the domestic courts in their considerations upholding the SCRPA's decision. This judgment does not give carte blanche to the use of religious symbols, whatever the medium, context or message intended or tending to be conveyed, whether directly or otherwise. As was stated in § 26 of *İ.A. v. Turkey* (no. 42571/98, § 26, ECHR 2005-VIII), a "State may ... legitimately consider it necessary to take measures aimed at repressing certain form of conduct, including the imparting of information and ideas, judged incompatible with respect for the freedom of thought, conscience and religion of others...". In the instant case, however, there was nothing in the three adverts in question (which, incidentally, can still be viewed online) which could, by any stretch of the imagination, be considered as either offensive, much less as amounting to any form of vilification of religion or religious symbols, and which could be construed as justifying an interference "for the protection of ... the rights of others". The fact that the head of the male figure bore some resemblance to the way in which the image of Christ is depicted in classical art, and the use of the words "Jesus" and "Mary" (see paragraphs 7–9 of the judgment) cannot conceivably, by or of themselves, or in combination, be regarded as violating "public morals". Moreover, the very fact that both the male and the female figure in the adverts displayed tattoos should have been indicative that those figures could not be considered as representations of the historical Jesus Christ or the Virgin Mary – see Leviticus

19:28. This point does not appear to have been given appropriate weight by anyone.

2. In short, this is a case which should not even have been brought to the attention of the SCRPA. What is even more surprising is that the "warning", as it were, by the President of the Supreme Administrative Court (see paragraph 26) was dismissed for reasons which appear to be totally detached from reality (see paragraphs 28 and 29).

3. Finally, if the adverts were considered as somehow inappropriate, one wonders whether it would have been more effective to advise the faithful to boycott the firm using the adverts, rather than to provoke court litigation which twice ended up before the Supreme Administrative Court.

6/3

In a judgment of 27 February 2018 in *Mockutė* v. *Lithuania*, application no. 66490/09 the ECtHR found a violation of Article 8 of the ECHR, considering that a psychiatric hospital had revealed information about her private life to journalists and to her mother, as well as a violation of Article 9 of the ECHR by preventing the applicant from practising her religion-meditation practices in the Lithuanian branch of the Osho religious movement. The ECtHR reasoned a violation of Articles 8 and 9 of the ECHR, as follows:

> 96. The Court firstly notes that the applicant's grievance directly relates only to the actions of Vilnius Psychiatric Hospital and the psychiatrist doctor D.Š. in particular, whom the applicant saw as primarily responsible for the breach of her privacy and against whom she pursued court proceedings for damages at the domestic level (see paragraphs 24, 43 and 81 above). That being so, the Court considers that it is only required to examine the actions of those two actors as that was the main element underlying the applicant's complaint under Article 8 of the Convention. Although in their observations to the Court the Government laid much emphasis on the Srovės broadcast of 17 June 2003 (see paragraph 20 above), the Court will have regard to that programme and the journalists' actions only in so far as they provide the context for the aforementioned conduct by the hospital and its personnel. For the same reason, the Court also does not find the question of whether the applicant could have been recognised by viewers of the Srovės programme to be of critical importance, given that it is the matter of the hospital disclosing private information about the applicant to the journalists and her mother which is at the heart of the applicant's complaint.

97. Although some of the circumstances of this case are not entirely clear, it transpires from the record of the Vilnius Regional Court's hearing that after the applicant had been admitted to Vilnius Psychiatric Hospital without her consent on 7 May 2003, her mother contacted the Srovės journalists and told them where the applicant was being held, but that she did not know her daughter's diagnosis (see paragraph 33 above). For her part, the psychiatrist, doctor D.Š., testified at the hearing that when the journalists had come to that hospital, she had been asked by the hospital's administration to meet them and told that the "talk would be about Mockutė" (see paragraph 34 above), an aspect of the case which the Court finds particularly disturbing. Even though doctor D.Š. denied to the Vilnius Regional Court that she had talked with the Srovės journalists about the applicant's health, that was overruled by that court, which held that the psychiatrist, without obtaining the applicant's consent, had revealed information to the journalists about her diagnosis, acute psychosis, the fact that she was being treated at that psychiatric hospital, and that she had studied in the United States (see paragraph 35 above). That conclusion does not appear to have been overruled by the Court of Appeal, which only disagreed about the fact that the excerpts of the psychiatrist's interview shown during the broadcast had been sufficient to identify the applicant (see paragraph 47 above). The Court further observes that in one of those excerpts the psychiatrist used such statements as "it does not appear that this young woman would participate in orgies" and that "she is not hypersexual" (see paragraph 20 above). In this context it recalls the State's obligation to protect information about a person's sexual life and moral integrity (see the case-law in paragraph 94 above). In deciding whether there was interference with the applicant's right to respect for her privacy, the Court also notes that under the United Nations Convention on the Rights of Persons with Disabilities, which was adopted in 2007, the States' have a duty to protect persons with disabilities from unlawful attacks on their honour and reputation (see Article 22 of the CRDP, cited in paragraph 73 above). Examining further, the Court observes that the psychiatrist also discussed the applicant as manifesting secretive behaviour, which was a trait of those belonging to sects (see paragraph 20 above). At this juncture the Court is also mindful of the applicant's argument that she experienced emotional insecurity because she was afraid of which of the additional facts the psychiatrist had forced out of her might have been revealed to the journalists (see paragraph 87 in fine above; also see *Surikov*, cited above, § 75).

98. Lastly, the Court would add that it has not been contested that Vilnius Psychiatric Hospital is a public hospital and that the acts and omissions of its administration and medical staff were capable of engaging the responsibility of the respondent State under the Convention (see paragraph 11 in fine above, also see *Glass v. the United Kingdom*, no. 61827/00, § 71, ECHR 2004-II; *I. v. Finland*, cited above, § 35, and *Avilkina and Others*, cited above, § 31).

99. Having regard to those considerations, the Court finds that the disclosure by Vilnius Psychiatric Hospital psychiatrist doctor D.Š. to the Srovės journalists of highly personal and sensitive confidential information about the applicant, obtained during her involuntary hospitalisation and treatment at that hospital, entailed an interference with the applicant's right to respect for her private life guaranteed by paragraph 1 of Article 8.

100. Lastly, the Court turns to the applicant's complaint that Vilnius Psychiatric Hospital revealed information about her state of health to her mother. Although the Government disputed that such a disclosure had taken place, the Court notes that the Court of Appeal did not deny such a fact, but instead stated that Vilnius Psychiatric Hospital had been entitled to act in that way (see paragraph 48 above). Given the applicant's statements about her tense relationship with her mother (see paragraphs 21 and 89 above), the Court is also ready to concede that disclosure by Vilnius Psychiatric Hospital of information about the applicant's health to her mother, whichever form it might have taken, also amounted to an interference with the applicant's right to respect for her private life.

101. The above-mentioned interference contravened Article 8 of the Convention unless it was "in accordance with the law" and pursued one or more of the legitimate aims referred to in paragraph 2 of that Article. The Court will examine each of these criteria in turn.

102. The Court notes that Lithuanian legislation provides for stringent obligations to ensure protection of patient privacy (see paragraphs 58–62 above). In particular, Article 14 of the Law on Mental Health Care at the material time stipulated that patients had a right to confidentiality with regard to information concerning their health, an obligation which extended to the doctors in charge of someone's treatment and to hospital administrations (see paragraph 59 above). In fact, Article 52 of the Law on the Health System explicitly forbade health-care specialists from

violating the rules of confidentiality of information about a person's health which they had acquired in the course of their professional activity (see paragraph 60 above). Furthermore, under Articles 2 and 11 of the Law on the Legal Protection of Personal Data, information about a person's religious beliefs, health or sexual life was attributed particular protection, and it could only be released provided that the person had undisputably agreed to such disclosure (see paragraph 61 above). The duties to protect the confidentiality of all personal data relating to a person with disability, as well as to protect such persons from attacks on their honour or dignity, have been underlined within the framework of the United Nations and by Council of Europe institutions (see Article 22 of the CRPD, cited in paragraph 73 above, point 7.4.c of the Parliamentary Assembly Recommendation 1235(1994), cited in paragraph 75 above, and Article 13 of the Committee of Ministers Recommendation Rec(2004)10, cited in paragraph 76 above).

103. In the present case, the Court finds it clear that the applicant did not give her consent to doctor D.Š. or the Vilnius Psychiatric Hospital to discuss her state of health, her sexual life or her beliefs, either with the Srovės journalists, or with her mother. Furthermore, the Court fails to see what were the legal grounds justifying the release of such information, whether under Lithuanian law or under Article 8 § 2 of the Convention. In fact, the Court notes that all the relevant domestic and international law cited above expressly prohibits the disclosure of such information to the point that it even constitutes a criminal offence (see paragraph 62 above). Even if there were exceptions to the rule of non-disclosure, none of those have been argued by the Government, which instead pleaded a legitimate aim of informing society about new religious movements. The interference with the applicant's right to respect for her private life was therefore not "in accordance with the law" within the meaning of Article 8 § 2 of the Convention.

104. Lastly, as to the legal basis for disclosing information related to the applicant's health to her mother, the Court observes that the Court of Appeal focused its analysis on the proportionality of the interference, in particular, on the fact that the applicant's mother had known of her history of mental troubles, without citing any legal basis for such a disclosure (see paragraph 48 above). The Government, asked explicitly by the Court to identify such a legal basis, did not specify one either (see *Radu*, cited above, § 29). That being so, and since no legal basis had been cited

by the domestic courts, the Court cannot but hold that Vilnius Psychiatric Hospital's release of information about the applicant's health to her mother, whichever form it might have taken, was likewise not "in accordance with the law" within the meaning of Article 8 of the Convention.

105. As that is the case, the Court is not required to determine whether the interference pursued a legitimate aim and, if so, whether it was proportionate to the aim pursued (see *Y.Y. v. Russia*, no. 40378/06, § 59, 23 February 2016).

106. There has therefore been a violation of Article 8 of the Convention.

[...]

121. The Court firstly notes that the Government did acknowledge that the right to practise one's religion in accordance with the Osho teaching fell within the scope of Article 9 of the Convention (see paragraph 113 above). The Court has no reason to hold otherwise, all the more so since pursuant to the Supreme Administrative Court's decision the Ojas Meditation Center had been registered as a religious community (see paragraph 56 above; also see Grand Chamber judgment in case *İzzettin Doğan and Others v. Turkey* [GC], no. 62649/10, § 68, ECHR 2016). Indeed, and although a State actor – Vilnius Psychiatric Hospital – during the domestic court proceedings in the applicant's case prayed in aid that the lack of recognition of the Osho movement as religion in Lithuania in 2003 deprived individual adherents of that religion of the protection of Article 9, the Court cannot share such a suggestion (see paragraphs 25, 42 and 98 above). To hold so would mean that the State could exclude certain beliefs by withholding recognition. The Court has already held that punishing those who manifest religious beliefs which have not been recognised by the State constitutes a violation of Article 9 (see *Masaev v. Moldova*, no. 6303/05, § 26, 12 May 2009).

122. The Court has regard to the applicant's claims about interference with her right to practise Osho teaching whilst being held at Vilnius Psychiatric Hospital, those allegations having been supported by the first instance court's findings (see paragraph 37 above). The applicant's claims were however contested by the Government, which, in turn, relied on the conclusions by the Court of Appeal and asserted that the applicant had been able to practise her religion during her stay at that institution (see

paragraph 50 above). The Court therefore finds that it has been presented with diverging accounts of the applicant's factual situation in Vilnius Psychiatric Hospital. The Court points out that in principle it is not its task to substitute its own assessment of the facts for that of the domestic courts (see *Kyriacou Tsiakkourmas and Others v. Turkey*, no. 13320/02, § 165, 2 June 2015, and *Kudrevičius and Others v. Lithuania* [GC], no. 37553/05, § 169, ECHR 2015). Even so, the Court has already held that, in a situation like this, it remains free to itself evaluate the facts in the light of all the material at its disposal (see, *mutatis mutandis*, *Ribitsch v. Austria*, 4 December 1995, § 32, Series A no. 336, and *Alexandridis*, cited above, § 34; also see *Klimov v. Russia*, no. 54436/14, § 64, 4 October 2016; *Idalov v. Russia* (no. 2), no. 41858/08, § 99 *in fine*, 13 December 2016). It has also held that the position of inferiority and powerlessness which is typical of patients confined in psychiatric hospitals calls for increased vigilance in reviewing whether the Convention has been complied with (see *Herczegfalvy*, cited above, § 82).

123. Examining further, the Court turns to the applicant's twofold argument that at Vilnius Psychiatric Hospital she had been prevented from practicing her religion, firstly, because of restrictive regime therein, and, secondly, because of the doctors' unsympathetic views towards her beliefs. The Court notes that, after the applicant was placed in Vilnius Psychiatric Hospital, she was forcibly administered drugs, physically restrained, and various restrictive treatment regimes were applied to her during the fifty-two days of her stay at that institution (see paragraphs 12 and 14–18 above; on the issue of the consent to treatment, or lack of it in the applicant's case, also see paragraphs 38 and 51 above; also see point 101 of the CPT report, cited in paragraph 77 above). The Government have not suggested that the applicant could have left the hospital to practise her religion with the circle of people with whom she shared it, even though she had clearly indicated to the psychiatrists that attending the Ojas Meditation Center "brought her peace" (see paragraphs 15, 23 and 57 above; also see *Kokkinakis*, cited above, § 31 and *Sinan Işık*, cited above, § 38). In fact, the Vilnius Regional Court, which also relied on the CPT standards, had clearly ruled out any possibility for the applicant to leave the hospital for 52 days of her stay therein (see paragraphs 30 and 31 above). This view also appears to be corroborated by the CPT, which, having reviewed the situation at Vilnius Psychiatric Hospital in general, noted that although only few patients therein were formally considered as involuntary, in reality even "voluntary" patients were not free to leave

(see point 100 of the CPT report, cited in paragraph 77 above). It is also plain from the applicant's statements in her open letter (see paragraph 22 above) and in those made to the domestic court (see paragraph 43 above), to this Court (see paragraph 109 above), as well as from her medical records and other documents (see paragraphs 15, 17, 37, 42 and 50 above), that in Vilnius Psychiatric Hospital she had to submit and subordinate her wishes to unyielding authority of the psychiatrists who were trying to "correct" the applicant so that she abandoned her "fictitious" religion, and whom she felt constrained to obey, even on pain of receiving a diagnosis which would make her unemployable (on the issue of undue influence and freedom of religion see *Larissis and Others* v. *Greece*, 24 February 1998, §§ 38 and 45, 51–53, Reports 1998-I; also see the extracts from the Lithuanian Constitutional Court's ruling in paragraph 65 above). The applicant therefore has demonstrated that pressure was exerted on her to change her religious beliefs and prevent her from manifesting them (see, *mutatis mutandis*, *Bayatyan*, cited above, §§ 36 and 112).

[...] That being so, the Court finds that the circumstances examined in the instant case, which concerns the applicant who was an individual with a history of mental troubles, and in a particularly vulnerable situation under effective control of the psychiatrists who worked on her with the view that she became critical towards her religion, were therefore more grim than those examined in *Leela Förderkreis e.V. and Others* where the applicants were a group of religious associations or meditation associations, and thus all the more so amounted to an interference with the applicant's rights under Article 9 of the Convention.

126. In the light of the foregoing, the Court holds that there has been an interference with the applicant's right to respect for her religion.

127. The above-mentioned interference contravened Article 9 of the Convention unless it was "prescribed by law", pursued one or more of the legitimate aims referred to in paragraph 2 of that Article and was "necessary in a democratic society" for achieving such aim or aims.

128. In the present case, however, it is sufficient to note that, except for the first day of her involuntary hospitalisation, the applicant was held at Vilnius Psychiatric Hospital unlawfully (see paragraphs 29–32 and 45 above). Given that the applicant's psycho-correction treatment lasted longer than 7–8 May 2003 (see paragraph 29 above) and, in fact, continued

throughout her stay at that institution, the Court finds that the interference was not "prescribed by law". In the context of the lawfulness of involuntary psychiatric detention, the Court also notes the CPT report which details numerous drawbacks related to the authorisation for holding a person in a psychiatric hospital, including the Vilnius Psychiatric Hospital where the applicant had been held, including the lack of appropriate judicial involvement (see points 96, 98 and 99 of the CPT report, cited in paragraph 77 above). The need for judicial approval for compulsory admission and continued placement at the psychiatric institution has also been underlined by the Parliamentary Assembly of the Council of Europe (see point 7.1.b of the Recommendation 1235(1994), cited in paragraph 75 above; also see the extract from United Nations Special Rapporteur Mr D. Pūras' report in paragraph 74 above, regarding the practice of deprivation of liberty in closed psychiatric institutions). In this particular case, the Vilnius Regional Court and the Court of Appeal both concluded that domestic legal procedures for the applicant's forced hospitalisation and treatment had not only been breached, but outright disregarded (see paragraphs 32 and 45 above).

129. The Court also attaches weight to the fact that, under the Lithuanian Constitution and the Constitutional Court's case-law, freedom of religion becomes a matter of legal regulation only to the extent that an individual expresses his or her thoughts or religion by actions, and that, as long as a person has a religion or faith, it falls within the inviolable sphere of private life and may not be limited in any way (see paragraphs 64 and 65 above). Regarding the situation of the applicant in the instant case, the Court is prepared to accept that the needs of psychiatric treatment might necessitate discussing various matters, including religion, with a patient, when he or she is being treated by a psychiatrist. That being so, it does not transpire from Lithuanian law that such discussions might also take the form of psychiatrists prying into the patients' beliefs in order to "correct" them when there is no clear and imminent risk that such beliefs will manifest in actions dangerous to the patient or others (in this context see, *mutatis mutandis*, *Biblical Centre of the Chuvash Republic v. Russia*, no. 33203/08, § 57, 12 June 2014). On this last point, the Court refers to its earlier finding that the applicant's behaviour did not require her hospitalisation after 8 May 2003 (see paragraph 128 in limine above). The Court further reiterates the principle of the States' limited margin of appreciation to justify interference with the freedom of individual conscience (see paragraph 118 above). Notwithstanding that limited margin

of appreciation which is applicable to manifestation of religious beliefs, the Court has also emphasised the primary importance of the right to freedom of thought, conscience and religion and the fact that a State cannot dictate what a person believes or take coercive steps to make him change his beliefs (see *Ivanova*, cited above, § 79 *in fine*; also see paragraph 119 above). Lastly, the Court has never held in its case-law that the scope of the States' margin of appreciation could be broader or narrower depending on the nature of the religious beliefs.

130. Where it has been shown that an interference was not in accordance with the law, it is not necessary to investigate whether it also pursued a "legitimate aim" or was "necessary in a democratic society" (see *Church of Scientology of St Petersburg and Others* v. *Russia*, no. 47191/06, § 47, 2 October 2014).

131. The foregoing considerations are sufficient to enable the Court to conclude that there has been a violation of Article 9 of the Convention.

6/4

In a unanimous judgment of 31 May 2018 in *Zubyadah* v. *Lithuania*, application no. 46454/11 the ECtHR assessed various items of evidence provided for the Court and determined that the CIA 'black site" codenamed "Detention Site Violet" operated in Lithuania from 17 or 18 February 2005 until March 2006. The Court found that Lithuania violated Articles 3, 5, 8 and 13 of the ECHR and awarded the applicant EUR 100,000 in respect of non-pecuniary damages. The Court held that there had been a violation of Article 3 in its procedure in conjunction with Article 13 of the Convention on account of Lithuania's failure to carry out an effective investigation into the applicant's allegations of serious violations of the Convention, including inhuman treatment and undisclosed detention. Moreover, the Court held that there had been a violation of Article 3 of the Convention in its substantive aspect, on account of Lithuania's complicity in the CIA's High-Value Detainee Programme, in that it had enabled the US authorities to subject the applicant to inhuman treatment on Lithuanian territory and to transfer him from its territory, in spite of a real risk that he would be subjected to treatment contrary to Article 3. Furthermore, the Court held that there had been a violation of Article 5 of the Convention on account of the applicant's undisclosed detention on Lithuanian territory and the fact that Lithuania had enabled the US authorities to transfer the applicant from its territory, in spite of a real risk that he would be subjected to further undisclosed detention. Finally, the Court also held that there had been a violation of Article 8 of the Convention. As a substantial part of the matter was in regard to the existence of certain facts the ECtHR reasoned the violations of the ECHR, as follows:

> 16. It is to be noted that in the present case involving, as the applicant's previous application before the Court, complaints of secret detention and torture to which the applicant was allegedly subjected during the extraordinary rendition operations by the United States authorities (see paragraphs 19–88 below) the Court is deprived of the possibility of obtaining any form of direct account of the events complained of from the applicant (see *Husayn (Abu Zubaydah) v. Poland*, cited above, § 397; and *Al Nashiri v. Poland*, cited above, § 397; see also paragraph 90 below).
>
> As in *Husayn (Abu Zubaydah) v. Poland* and *Al Nashiri v. Poland* (both cited above), in the present case the facts as adduced by the applicant were to a considerable extent a reconstruction of dates and other elements relevant to his rendition, detention and treatment in the US authorities' custody, based on various publicly available sources of information. The applicant's version of the facts as stated in his initial application of 14 July 2011 evolved and partly changed during the proceedings before the Court (see paragraphs 111–117 below).
>
> The respondent Government contested the applicant's version of the facts on all accounts, maintaining that there was no evidence demonstrating that they had occurred in Lithuania (see paragraphs 398–405 and 423–446 below).
>
> 17. In consequence, the facts of the case as rendered below (see paragraphs 90–211 below) are based on the applicant's account supplemented by various items of evidence in the Court's possession.
>
> [...]
>
> *As regards the establishment of the facts and assessment of evidence relevant to the applicant's allegations concerning his rendition by the CIA to Lithuania, secret detention in Lithuania and transfer by the CIA out of Lithuania (17 or 18 February 2005 to 25 March 2006)*

(a) Whether a CIA secret detention facility existed in Lithuania at the time alleged by the applicant (17 or 18 February 2005 to 25 March 2006)

498. It is alleged that a CIA secret detention facility, codenamed "Detention Site Violet" operated in Lithuania from 17 or 18 February 2005, the dates on which either or both CIA rendition planes N724CL and N787WH brought CIA detainees to Lithuania, to 25 March 2006, when it was closed following the detainees' transfer out of Lithuania on board the rendition plane N733MA (see paragraphs 111–117 and 449–459 above). The Government denied that a CIA detention facility had ever existed in Lithuania (see paragraphs 423–446 above).

499. The Court notes at the outset that although the Government have contested the applicant's version of events on all accounts, they have not disputed the following facts, which were also established in the Seimas inquiry and confirmed in the course of the pre-trial investigation conducted in 2010–2011 (see paragraphs 174, 199, 307–349, and 367–370 above):

(a) In 2002–2005 the CIA-related aircraft repeatedly crossed Lithuania's airspace; according to the CNSD Findings [Findings of the parliamentary investigation by the Seimas Committee on National Security and Defence concerning the alleged transportation and confinement of persons detained by the Central Intelligence Agency of the United States of America on the territory of the Republic of Lithuania], on at least twenty-nine occasions.

(b) In the period from 17 February 2005 to 25 March 2006 four CIA-related aircraft landed in Lithuania:

– planes N724CL and N787WH landed at Vilnius International Airport on, respectively, 17 February 2005 and 6 October 2005;

– planes N787WH and N733MA landed at Palanga International Airport on, respectively, 18 February 2005 and 25 March 2006.

(d) On three occasions the SSD [State Security Department] officers received the CIA aircraft and "escorted what was brought by them" with the knowledge of the heads of the SSD:

– on 18 February 2005 N787WH, which landed at Palanga airport with five US passengers on board, without any thorough customs inspection of the plane being carried out; according to the CNSD Findings, "no cargo was unloaded from it or onto it";

– on 6 October 2005 N787WH, which landed at Vilnius airport, where a certain R.R., the SBGS officer, was prevented from inspecting the aircraft and no customs inspection of the plane was carried out; and

– on 25 March 2006 N733MA, which landed at Palanga airport, but the SBGS documents contained no records of the landing and inspection of the plane, and no customs inspection was carried out.

(e) In connection with the landing of N787WH in Vilnius on 6 October 2005 and of N733MA in Palanga on 25 March 2006 the SSD issued classified letters to the SBGS, but the letter regarding the landing on 6 October 2005 was delivered *ex post facto*, and before that event the SSD had never issued such letters.

(f) The SSD high-ranking officers provided the US officers with unrestricted access to the aircraft at least on two occasions, including on 6 October 2005.

(g) In 2002–2006 the SSD and the CIA were in "partnership cooperation", which involved the "equipment of certain tailored facilities", i.e. Project No. 1 and Project No. 2.

(h) The facilities of Project No. 1 were installed in 2002.

(i) The SSD started the implementation of Project No. 2 in cooperation with the CIA at the beginning of 2004; this involved assisting the CIA in the acquisition of the land and building in Antaviliai and carrying out construction work in order to equip the facility; the work was carried out by contractors brought by the CIA to Lithuania; the materials and equipment for the facility were brought to Lithuania by the CIA in containers.

(j) Project No. 1 and Project No. 2 were fully financed by the CIA.

(k) Witnesses A and B2, politicians questioned in the criminal investigation, were addressed in connection with "the temporary possibility of holding persons suspected of terrorism" and "as regards the transportation and holding [of] people in Lithuania".

[...]

501. The Government have contested the evidential value of the above publications and, in general terms, expressed reservations as to the evidential value of media and other reports in the public domain (see paragraphs 423–424 above).

However, at the material time the Lithuanian authorities apparently considered the August 2009 ABC News disclosure sufficiently credible, given that the report prompted the joint meeting of the CNSD and Committee on Foreign Affairs on 9 September 2009 and the further parliamentary inquiry, which was opened on 5 November 2009. In the course of the inquiry the CNSD interviewed fifty-five persons, including the highest authorities of the State, and obtained various evidence, including classified information (see paragraphs 167–176 above).

The CNSD, made the following findings:

(a) In 2002–2005 the aircraft that had been linked in official investigations to the transportation of CIA detainees had crossed Lithuania's airspace on repeated occasions.

(b) It had not been established whether CIA detainees had been transported through Lithuania; however, conditions for such transportation had existed.

(c) The SSD had received a request from the CIA to equip facilities suitable for holding detainees.

(d) The SSD, in Project No. 1, had created conditions for holding detainees in Lithuania; "facilities suitable for holding detainees [had been] equipped, taking account of the requests and conditions set out by the partners"; however, according to evidence in the CNSD's possession the premises had not been used for that purpose.

(e) While persons who had given evidence to the CNSD had denied that there existed any preconditions for holding and interrogating detainees at Project No. 2, the layout of the building, its enclosed nature and protection of the perimeter, as well as the fragmented presence of the SSD staff at the premises allowed the CIA officers to carry out activities without the SSD's control and to use the infrastructure at their discretion.

The above Findings were endorsed by the Seimas in its Resolution of 19 January 2010 (see paragraph 174 above).

502. The Government submitted that the CNSD Findings had been subsequently verified in the pre-trial investigation conducted in 2010–2011. According to the Government, the investigation, based on the testimony of witnesses who had been directly involved in the implementation of Project No. 1 and Project No. 2, and in the landing and departure procedures for CIA flights, had conclusively established that there had been no CIA secret detention centre in Lithuania, that the facilities of Project No. 1 and Project No. 2 had not been, and could not have been, used for holding detainees and that there had been no evidence of CIA detainees ever being held in the country. The sole purpose of the CIA planes landing was, in the Government's words, the delivery of a "special cargo", described as a "connection" or "communication" equipment providing the SSD and the CIA "with technical services in order to implement their joint project". The Government also attached importance to the fact that Lithuania had not been the object of any international inquiries conducted into the European countries' collusion in the CIA HVD Programme (see paragraphs 426–446 above).

503. As regards the latter argument, the Court observes that it is true that, on account of the fact that the allegations of the CIA secret prison being run in Lithuania emerged only in August 2009 (see paragraphs 258 and 500 above), Lithuania had not been included in any of the inquiries carried out by the Council of Europe and the European Parliament in 2005–2007 (see paragraphs 269–286 above). Nor were any international investigations of a scale comparable to the Marty Inquiry and the Fava Inquiry subsequently conducted into the allegations concerning Lithuania.

504. However, the investigative work of the experts involved in the 2010 UN Joint Study encompassed Lithuania's possible involvement in the CIA scheme of secret prisons. According to the UN experts, research for the study, including data strings relating to the country, appear to confirm

that it was integrated into the CIA extraordinary rendition programme in 2004 (see paragraph 303 above).

505. The CPT delegation visit to Lithuania on 14–18 June 2010 and the 2011 CPT Report involved the issue of alleged CIA secret prisons. While the central focus for the delegation was to try to assess the effectiveness of the pre-trial investigation which was at that time pending, the CPT considered it important to visit the "two tailored facilities" identified in the CNSD Findings as Project No. 1 and Project No. 2. The 2011 CPT Report, referring to Project No. 2, described the facilities as "far larger than" Project No. 1" and consisting of "two buildings ... connected and divided into four distinct sectors". In one of the buildings, "the layout of premises resembled a large metal container enclosed with a surrounding external structure". The CPT refrained from providing a more detailed description of the facilities but concluded that even though when visited by the delegation the premises did not contain anything that was "highly suggestive of a context of detention", both Project No. 1 and Project No. 2 could be adapted for detention purposes "with relatively little effort" (see paragraphs 350–352 above).

506. It is also to be noted that since at least early 2012, the European Parliament, through the LIBE Committee, has conducted an inquiry into allegations concerning Lithuania's complicity in the CIA extraordinary rendition scheme. As part of the inquiry, the LIBE delegation visited Lithuania and carried out an inspection of Project No. 2 which, in the words of the LIBE Rapporteur, Ms Flautre, was described as a "kind of building within the building, a double-shell structure" equipped with an "enormous air-conditioning system and a water-pumping system, the purpose of which [was] not evident" (see paragraph 289 above). That visit gave rise to concerns subsequently expressed in the 2012 EP Resolution, which stated that "the layout [of Project No. 2] and installations inside appear[ed] to be compatible with the detention of prisoners" (see paragraph 290 above).

507. Furthermore, the conclusions of the pre-trial investigation relied on by the Government and the Government's explanation of the purpose of the CIA planes landing seem to have been contradicted by other evidence in the Court's possession, including material available in the public domain and the experts' testimony.

To begin with, as regards the purpose of the CIA-linked planes landing in Lithuania at the material time, the extensive flight data produced by the applicant, including the data in the 2015 Reprieve Briefing, and expert evidence show that in respect of three out of four planes that landed in and departed from Vilnius and Palanga airports during the period from 17 February 2005 to 25 March 2006 the CIA used its methodology of "dummy" flight planning, that is to say, a deliberate disguise of their true destinations by declaring in the flight plans the route that the planes did not, nor even intended to, fly (see paragraphs 123–125 and 130–133 above). According to expert evidence obtained by the Court in *Al Nashiri v. Poland* and *Husayn (Abu Zubaydah) v. Poland*, as well as in the present case, the methodology of disguising flight planning pertained primarily to those renditions which dropped detainees off at the destination – in other words, at the airport connected with the CIA secret detention facility (see *Al Nashiri v. Poland*, cited above, §§ 316–318; and *Husayn (Abu Zubaydah) v. Poland*, cited above, § 310–312; see also paragraph 127 above).

(a) Significantly, the N787WH's circuit executed on 15–19 February 2005 included two disguised – undeclared – destinations on the plane's route from Rabat to Palanga. The first disguised destination was Bucharest, whereas the flight plan was filed for Constanţa; the second one was Palanga, whereas the flight plan was filed for Gothenburg (see paragraph 123 above).

(b) The N787WH's circuit on 1–7 October 2005 was disguised by both the "dummy" flight planning and switching aircraft in the course of the rendition operation, also called a "double-plane switch" – that is to say, another CIA method of disguising its prisoner-transfers, which was designed, according to expert J.G.S., to avoid the eventuality of the same aircraft appearing at the site of two different places of secret detention (see paragraph 129 above; see also *Al Nashiri v. Romania*, cited above, § 135).

The experts testified that the "double-plane switch" operation had been executed on 5–6 October 2005 in Tirana by two planes – N308AB, which arrived there from Bucharest after collecting detainees from the CIA "black site" in Romania, and N787WH. The CIA detainees "switched" planes in Tirana and they were transferred from N308AB onto N787WH for the rendition flight. On its departure from Tirana, N787WH filed a false plan to Tallinn in order to enable the flight to enter Lithuanian airspace, but its true destination was Vilnius, where it landed on 6 October 2005 in the early hours (see paragraphs 114, 130–131 and 140 above).

In relation to this flight it is also noteworthy that the flight data submitted by the Lithuanian aviation authorities to the CNSD in the course of the Seimas inquiry indicated that N787WH had arrived from Antalya, Turkey (see paragraph 174 above). Witnesses questioned in the pre-trial investigation gave inconsistent indications as to where the plane arrived from. For instance, Witness B3 spoke of an "unplanned aircraft from Antalya" (see paragraph 315 above). Witness B4 ("person B") said that it had "arrived from Tallinn without passengers" and that it had "arrived in Tallinn from Antalya" (see paragraph 316 above). The Administration of Civil Aviation, for its part, informed the prosecutor that "they could [have] confuse[d] the code of Antalya and Tirana due to their similarity" (see paragraph 183 above).

(c) According to the experts, a combination of "dummy" flight planning and aircraft switching methodologies was likewise used in connection with the N733MA flight on 25 March 2006 (see paragraphs 134 and 140 above). The Palanga airport records indicated that on that date the plane had arrived in Palanga from Porto and that it had left for Porto on the same day (see paragraphs 125 and 174 above). However, as stated in the 2015 Reprieve Briefing and confirmed by the experts at the fact-finding hearing, a false plan was filed for Porto, whereas the plane flew to Cairo where it made connection with N740EH, another CIA rendition plane. The 2015 Reprieve Briefing also states that the documents relating to the planning of these two trips showed complex attempts to disguise the fact that the purpose of the trips was to provide a connection between Lithuania and Afghanistan (see paragraph 125 above).

In the Court's view, the CIA's above repeated, deliberate recourse to the complex flight-disguising methodologies typical of rendition flights transporting detainees to "black sites" does not appear to be consistent with the stated purpose of the CIA-linked planes landing in Lithuania, which according to the Government had been merely the delivery of "special cargo", described as "communication" or "connection" equipment", in the context of the routine intelligence cooperation (see paragraphs 427–432 above).

508. The Court further observes that in respect of the above planes the authorities applied a distinct practice, which resembles the special procedure for landings of CIA aircraft in Szymany airport followed by the Polish authorities in December 2002 – September 2003 and found by the Court to have been one of the elements indicative of the State's complicity in the CIA HVD Programme (see *Al Nashiri v. Poland*, cited above, §§ 418 and 442; and *Husayn (Abu Zubaydah) v. Poland*, cited above, §§ 420 and 444).

In particular, as in Poland, the planes were not subject to any customs or the border guard control. On 6 October 2005 the SBGS [State Border Guard Service at the Ministry of the Interior] officer R.R. was prevented from carrying out the N787WH plane inspection (see paragraphs 174 and 366 above). In connection with the arrivals of the "partners'" and the SSD officers at the airports, classified letters asking for access to the aircraft were issued to the SBGS at least on two occasions – one *ex post facto*, following the above incident with the SBGS officer on 6 October 2005 and one in connection with the N733MA landing in Palanga on 25 March 2006. Also, the rendition planes landing involved special security procedures organised by the CIA's counterpart in Lithuania. As confirmed by the SSD officers questioned in the course of the pre-trial investigation, they used to escort "the partners", that is to say, the CIA teams to and from Vilnius and Palanga airports. In that connection, the CIA asked the SSD to make security arrangements. In the airport, the CIA vehicles approached the aircraft, whereas the SSD's escorting vehicles remained at some distance (see paragraphs 174, 184, 315, 329, 337, 346, 366, 370–371 above).

[...]

513. In that context the Court would also note that, as shown by the evidence referred to above, the 17–18 February 2005 flights were followed by the landing on 6 October 2005 of the plane N787WH, which, according to the experts, transferred CIA detainees, via a "double-plane switch" operation in Tirana, from the CIA facility codenamed "Detention Site Black" in the 2014 US Senate Committee Report and located in Bucharest. Mr Black added that Khalid Sheikh Mohammed had been transferred from Romania to Detention Site Violet in Lithuania on that plane (see paragraphs 130–131 and 143–144 above).

514. The experts were not in complete agreement as to which date – 17 or 18 February 2005 – was the one definitely marking the opening of the CIA "black site" in Lithuania.

[...]

However, the Court does not find it indispensable to rule on which specific date the CIA site in Lithuania opened given that, according to the evidence before it, there were only these two, closely situated, dates on which it could have happened.

[...]

518. The Court observes that the 2014 US Senate Committee Report includes several references to Detention Site Violet. It clearly refers to two detention facilities in the country hosting that site: one completed but, "by mid-2003", still unused and considered by the CIA as insufficient "given the growing number of CIA detainees in the program and the CIA's interest in interrogating multiple detainees at the same detention site" and one "expanded" which the CIA "sought to build". In that connection, the CIA offered some redacted sum of USD million "to 'show appreciation' ... for the ... support" for the CIA HVD Programme (see paragraph 147 above). That information is consistent with evidence from witnesses M, N, O and P, who were questioned in the criminal investigation. They confirmed that in 2003 N and O had been assigned to assist their CIA partners in finding suitable premises for a joint project – an "intelligence support centre"– in respect of which the partners had "used to cover all expenses". According to Witness P, in 2002–2003 the "partners" had come and proposed to organise a joint operation, "to establish the premises in Lithuania for the protection of secret collaborators". Witness O said that the CIA partners had chosen the premises which had then become Project No. 2 and that they had started to come in Spring 2004, had carried out the work themselves and had brought material and the equipment in the containers (see paragraphs 333–337 above).

519. The 2014 US Senate Report further states that Detention Site Violet "opened in early 2005" (see paragraph 148 above). This element corresponds to the dates of the landings of the rendition planes N724CL and N787WH-17 and 18 February 2005. It also corresponds to the statement of

Witness S, who testified that Project No. 2 had been "established at the beginning of 2005" (see paragraph 341 above).

The closure of Detention Site Violet is mentioned in the report in a specific context and chronology, namely "press stories", in particular the *Washington Post* publication of 2 November 2005 that led to the closure of Detention Site Black and "the CIA's inability to provide emergency medical care" due to the refusal of the country hosting Detention Site Violet to admit Mustafa al-Hawsawi, one of the CIA detainees, to a local hospital. This refusal, according to the report, resulted in the CIA's having sought assistance from third-party countries in providing medical care to him and "four other CIA detainees with acute ailments". In relation to the *Washington Post* publication, the report gives a fairly specific time-frame for the closure of Detention Site Black, which occurred "shortly thereafter". However, Detention Site Violet still operated in "early January 2006". At that time "the CIA was holding twenty-eight detainees in its two remaining facilities, Detention Site Violet ... and Detention Site Orange". Detention Site Violet was closed in 2006, in the month whose name comprised five characters which were redacted in the report (see paragraph 149 above). As noted in the 2015 Reprieve Briefing, there are only two possibilities: the relevant month could be either "March" or "April" 2006.

520. Considering the material referred to above as whole, the Court is satisfied that there is *prima facie* evidence in favour of the applicant's allegation that the CIA secret detention site operated in Lithuania between 17 or 18 February 2005 and 25 March 2006. Accordingly, the burden of proof should shift to the respondent Government (see *El-Masri*, cited above, §§ 154–165 and paragraph 482 above).

521. However, the Government have failed to demonstrate why the evidence referred to above cannot serve to corroborate the applicant's allegations. Apart from their reliance on the conclusions of the criminal investigation of 2010–2011 and, in particular, the testimony of witnesses who, as the Government underlined, had all consistently denied that any transfers of CIA detainees had taken place or that a CIA had run a secret detention facility in Lithuania, they have not offered convincing reasons for the series and purpose of the CIA-associated aircraft landings at Vilnius and Palanga between 17 February 2005 and 25 March 2006, the special procedures followed by the authorities in that connection and the

actual purpose served by Project No. 2 at the material time (see paragraphs 424–443 above).

522. The witness testimony obtained in the criminal investigation is the key evidence adduced by the Government in support of their arguments (see paragraphs 307–349 above). The Court has not had the possibility of having access to full versions of the testimony since the relevant material was and still is classified. It has nevertheless been able to assess that evidence on the basis of a summary description produced by the Government (see paragraphs 304–306 above).

Having considered the material submitted, the Court finds a number of elements that do not appear to be consistent with the version of events presented by the Government.

523. First, the Government asserted that both Project No. 1 and No. 2 were found to have been completely unsuitable for secret detention (see paragraphs 433–442 above).

The Court does not find it necessary to analyse in detail the purposes actually served by Project No. 1 or determine whether or not that facility was used, as the Government argued at the oral hearing, for "extraction" or "exfiltration" of secret agents or otherwise, since in the present case it is not claimed that CIA detainees were held in that facility. It thus suffices for the Court to take note of the CNSD's conclusion that in Project No. 1 "conditions were created for holding detainees in Lithuania" (see paragraph 174 above).

524. Secondly, as regards Project No. 2, the Government submitted that while the exact purpose served by the premises at the material time could not be revealed since it was classified, the witnesses had unequivocally confirmed that no premises suitable for detainees had been located there. Moreover, access to the premises had been under the permanent surveillance of the SSD and there had been no secret zones inaccessible to the SSD officers in the building. This excluded any possibility of unauthorised access or holding detainees in the premises (see paragraphs 436–441 above).

However, the Court notes that Witnesses N and O, the SSD officers assigned to assist the CIA partners, who escorted them to and from the airports and who were also responsible for supervision of the premises, said that they had not visited all the rooms. Witness N said that he had not had access to the "administration area". O was not given access to all the premises. Moreover, the building was apparently not used for the purpose of the declared "joint operation" of an intelligence support centre. The only Lithuanian intelligence personnel present in the building were the three SSD officers M, N and O, who supervised the building on changing shifts even if nobody was there. Witness O stated that he had not known who had arrived at the premises or "with what they had been occupied with". Witness N "was not aware of the contents of the operations" that were carried out in Project No. 2. Witnesses N and O "actively supervised" the building until the second half of 2005 but then the number of the CIA partners' visits decreased (see paragraphs 333–337 above).

525. As regards the Government's explanation that the premises were acquired for the SSD's needs and used for "short-term meetings" with "their guests" (see paragraph 439 above), the layout of one of the buildings at Project No. 2, depicted by the CPT as "a large metal container enclosed within a surrounding external structure" and by the LIBE delegation as "a kind of building within the building" (see paragraphs 289 and 352 above) does not strike the Court as being a structure typical for the declared purpose. Also, no convincing explanation has been provided as to why Project No. 2, claimed to have been designated for an "intelligence support centre" and reconstructed with evidently considerable effort and expense on the part of the CIA had – according to the witnesses – been virtually unused by the SSD or their partners throughout 2005 (see paragraphs 333–338 and 341 above).

526. The Government further argued that in the light of abundant evidence it had been established in the criminal investigation that the purpose of two CIA-linked flights into Palanga, alleged to have transported the applicant to and out of Lithuania, namely N787WH and N733MA, which had taken place on, respectively, 18 February 2005 and 25 March 2006 had been the delivery of a "special cargo". The object of the delivery was "special equipment for a special investigation department" in a number of boxes, which had all been of the same size, one metre long (see paragraphs 427–432 above).

527. However, the witness statements relied on are not only partly inconsistent with each other but they also do not fully support the Government's

account. Furthermore, the Government's account is at variance with evidence collected in the course of the parliamentary inquiry. In this regard, the Court would refer to testimony given by the SSD officers involved in escorting "cargo" and the CIA partners to and from the Lithuanian airports and to the CNSD Findings.

[...]

530. Having regard to the inconsistency of the Government's version with the witness statements and the factual findings made by the Lithuanian Parliament and in the light of the documentary and expert evidence analysed in detail above, the Government's explanations as to the purposes served by the CIA rendition flights landing in Lithuania between 17 February 2005 and 25 March 2006 and the facility Project No. 2 cannot be regarded as convincing.

531. In view of the foregoing and taking into account all the elements analysed in detail above, the Court concludes that the Government have not produced any evidence capable of contradicting the applicant's allegations.

In particular, they have not refuted the applicant's argument that the planes N724CL, N787WH and N733MA that landed in Lithuania between 17 February 2005 and 25 March 2006 served the purposes of the CIA rendition operations and the conclusions of the experts heard by the Court, categorically stating that the aircraft in question were used by the CIA for transportation of prisoners into Lithuania. Nor have they refuted the applicant's assertion that the above rendition flights marked the opening and the closure of a CIA secret prison referred to in the 2014 US Senate Report as "Detention Site Violet", which was conclusively confirmed by expert evidence to the effect that Detention Site Violet was located in Lithuania and operated during the period indicated by the applicant (see also and compare with *Al Nashiri* v. *Poland*, cited above, §§ 414–415; and *Husayn (Abu Zubaydah)* v. *Poland*, cited above, §§ 414–415).

532. Consequently, the Court considers the applicant's allegations sufficiently convincing and, having regard to the above evidence from various sources corroborating his version, finds it established beyond reasonable doubt that:

(a) a CIA detention facility, codenamed Detention Site Violet according to the 2014 US Senate Committee Report, was located in Lithuania;

(b) the facility started operating either from 17 February 2005, the date of the CIA rendition flight N724CL into Vilnius airport, or from 18 February 2005, the date of the CIA rendition flight N787WH into Palanga airport; and

(c) the facility was closed on 25 March 2006 and its closure was marked by the CIA rendition flight N733MA into Palanga airport, which arrived from Porto, Portugal and, having disguised its destination in its flight plan by indicating Porto, on the same day took off for Cairo, Egypt.

(b) Whether the applicant's allegations concerning his rendition to Lithuania, secret detention at the CIA Detention Site Violet in Lithuania and transfer from Lithuania to another CIA detention facility elsewhere were proved before the Court

[...]

537. The Court further notes that the facts concerning the applicant's secret detention and continuous renditions from the time of his capture in Faisalabad, Pakistan, on 27 March 2002 to his rendition from Rabat, Morocco, in February 2005, including the names of the countries in which he was detained, the exact dates on which he was transferred by the CIA to and out of each country and the identities of all the rendition planes on which he was transferred have already been established conclusively and to the standard of proof beyond reasonable doubt in *Husayn (Abu Zubaydah)* v. *Poland* and in the present case (see *Husayn (Abu Zubaydah)* v. *Poland*, cited above, §§ 404 and 419; and paragraphs 489–532 above).

538. In particular, it has been established beyond reasonable doubt that until an unspecified date in February 2005 the applicant was held in secret detention in Morocco, at a facility used by the CIA and that on that date he was transferred by the CIA from Morocco to another detention facility elsewhere (see paragraph 497 above).

It has also been established to the same standard of proof, beyond reasonable doubt, that:

(a) The CIA secret detention facility codenamed "Detention Site Violet" in the 2014 US Senate Committee Report became operational in Lithuania either on 17 February 2005, the date of the CIA rendition flight N724CL from Rabat via Amman, which landed at Vilnius airport or on 18 February 2005, the date of the CIA rendition flight N787WH from Rabat via Bucharest, which landed at Palanga airport.

(b) The Detention Site Violet operated in Lithuania until 25 March 2006, the date of the CIA rendition flight N733MA from Palanga airport to Cairo (see paragraph 532 above).

[...]

546. Based on its free evaluation of all the material in its possession, the Court considers that there is *prima facie* evidence corroborating the applicant's allegation as to his secret detention in Lithuania, at Detention Site Violet, from 17 or 18 February 2005 to 25 March 2006. Consequently, the burden of proof should shift to the respondent Government.

547. However, the Government, apart from their above contention that there is no credible evidence confirming the applicant's detention in Lithuania, in particular in any border control records, and their general denial that any CIA secret detention facility had operated in the country, have not adduced any counter-evidence capable of refuting the experts' conclusions.

Having regard to the very nature of the CIA secret detention scheme, the Government's argument that there is no indication of the applicant's physical presence in Lithuania – which they sought to support by the fact that his name had not been found in the records of passengers on the flights in February 2005 – March 2006 (see paragraphs 426–428 above) – cannot be upheld. In the Court's view, it would be unacceptable if the Government, having failed to comply with their obligation to register duly and in accordance withthe domestic law all persons arriving on or departing from Lithuanian territory on the CIA planes and having relinquished any border control in respect of the rendition aircraft (see paragraphs 508 above), could take advantage of those omissions in the fact-finding procedure before the Court. When allowing the CIA to operate a detention site on Lithuanian soil the Government were, by pure virtue of Article 5 of the Convention, required to secure the information necessary to identify detainees brought to the country (see paragraphs 652–654 below, with references to the Court's case law). The Court cannot accept that the Government's failure to do so should have adverse consequences for the applicant in its assessment of whether it has been adequately demonstrated by the Government, against the strong *prima facie* case made by the applicant, that his detention in Lithuania did not take place.

548. In view of the foregoing, the Court considers the applicant's allegations sufficiently convincing. For the same reasons as stated above in regard to the date marking the opening of Detention Site Violet (see paragraph 514 above), the Court does not find it indispensable to rule on which of the two dates indicated by the applicant – 17 or 18 February 2005 – and on which of the two planes – N724CL or N787WH – he was brought to Lithuania.

Consequently, on the basis of strong, clear and concordant inferences as related above, the Court finds it proven to the required standard of proof that:

(a) on 17 or 18 February 2005 the applicant was transferred by the CIA to from Rabat, Morocco to Lithuania on board either the rendition plane N724CL or the rendition plane N787WH;

(b) from 17 or 18 February 2005 to 25 March 2006 the applicant was detained in the CIA detention facility in Lithuania codenamed "Detention Site Violet" according to the 2014 US Senate Committee Report; and

(c) on 25 March 2006 on board the rendition plane N733MA and via a subsequent aircraft-switching operation the applicant was transferred by the CIA out of Lithuania to another CIA detention facility, identified by the experts as being codenamed "Detention Site Brown" according to the 2014 US Senate Committee Report.

(iii) The applicant's treatment in CIA custody in Lithuania

549. The applicant stated that, as in *Husayn (Abu Zubaydah)* v. *Poland* on account of the secrecy of the HVD Programme and restrictions on his communications with the Court, he could not present specific evidence of what had happened to him in Lithuania. However, as the Court found in the above case, at an absolute minimum detainees in CIA custody,

whether in Lithuania or elsewhere, would have been subjected to the applicable standard conditions of detention at the relevant time, including solitary confinement, shackling, exposure to bright light, low and loud noise on a constant basis and the standard conditions of transfer, stripping, shaving, hooding, diapering and strapping down into painful crammed positions.

The Government have not addressed this issue.

550. The Court observes that, in contrast to treatment inflicted on the applicant during an early period of his secret detention, which is often documented in detail in various material (see paragraphs 92–97 above), there is no evidence demonstrating any instances of similar acts at Detention Site Violet. According to the 2014 US Senate Committee Report, the applicant from his capture to his transfer to US military custody on 5 September 2006 "provided information", which resulted "in 766 disseminated intelligence reports". The fact that nearly 600 such reports were produced between September 2002 and September 2006 indicates that he was continually interrogated or "debriefed" by the CIA during the entire period of his secret detention (see paragraph 156 above). However, in the light of the material in the Court's possession, it does not appear that in Lithuania the applicant was subjected to the EITs in connection with interrogations (see paragraphs 48–55 above).

[...]

552. As regards the Court's establishment of the facts of the case, detailed rules governing conditions in which the CIA kept its prisoners leave no room for speculation as to the basic aspects of the situation in which the applicant found himself from 17 or 18 February 2005 to 25 March 2006. The Court therefore finds it established beyond reasonable doubt that the applicant was kept – as any other high-value detainee – in conditions described in the DCI Confinement Guidelines, which applied from the end of January 2003 to September 2006 to all CIA detainees (see paragraphs 54–56 above; see also *Husayn (Abu Zubaydah) v. Poland*, cited above, §§ 418–419 and 510).

While at this stage it is premature to characterise the treatment to which the applicant was subjected during his detention at Detention Site Violet for the purposes of his complaint under the substantive limb of Article 3 of the Convention, the Court would point out that that regime included at least "six standard conditions of confinement". That meant blindfolding or hooding the detainees, designed to disorient them and keep from learning their location or the layout of the detention facility; removal of hair upon arrival at the site; incommunicado, solitary confinement; continuous noise of high and varying intensity played at all times; continuous light such that each cell was illuminated to about the same brightness as an office; and use of leg shackles in all aspects of detainee management and movement (see paragraphs 55-56 above).

5. As regards the establishment of the facts and assessment of evidence relevant to the applicant's allegations concerning Lithuania's knowledge of and complicity in the CIA HVD Programme

[...]

559. In *Al Nashiri v. Poland and Husayn (Abu Zubaydah) v. Poland* the fact that the national authorities had cooperated with the CIA in disguising the rendition aircraft's actual routes and validated incomplete or false flight plans in order to cover up the CIA's activities in the country was considered relevant for the Court's assessment of the State authorities' knowledge of, and complicity in, the HVD Programme (see *Al Nashiri v. Poland*, cited above, §§ 419-422; and *Husayn (Abu Zubaydah) v. Poland*, cited above, §§ 421-424). The Court will follow that approach in analysing the facts of the present case.

560. It has already been established that in respect of three rendition flights – N787WH on 18 February 2005, N787WH on 6 October 2005 and N733MA on 25 March 2006 the CIA used the methodology of "dummy" flight planning – an intentional disguise of flight plans for rendition aircraft applied by the air companies contracted by the CIA (see paragraph 507 above).

As the Court found in the judgments referred to above, the "dummy" flight planning, a deliberate effort to cover up the CIA flights into the country, required active cooperation on the part of the host countries through which the planes travelled. In addition to granting the CIA rendition aircraft overflight permissions, the national authorities navigated the planes through the country's airspace to undeclared destinations in contravention of international aviation regulations and issued false landing permits (ibid.).

561. Consequently, the fact that the Lithuanian aviation authorities participated in the process demonstrated that Lithuania knowingly assisted in the CIA scheme disguising the rendition planes.

[...]

(d) Circumstances routinely surrounding HVDs transfers and reception at the CIA "black site"

563. The Court considers, as it did in *Al Nashiri v. Poland* and *Husayn (Abu Zubaydah) v. Poland*, that the circumstances and conditions in which HVDs were routinely transferred by the CIA from rendition planes to the CIA "black sites" in the host countries should be taken into account in the context of the State authorities' alleged knowledge and complicity in the HVD Programme (see *Al Nashiri v. Poland*, cited above, § 437; and *Husayn (Abu Zubaydah) v. Poland*, cited above, § 439).

It follows from the Court's findings in the above cases and the CIA material describing the routine procedure for transfers of detainees between the "black sites" (see paragraphs 47–48 above) that for the duration of his transfer a HVD was "securely shackled" by his hands and feet, deprived of sight and sound by the use of blindfolds, earmuffs and a hood and that upon arrival at his destination was moved to the "black site" under the same conditions.

564. The Court finds it inconceivable that the transportation of prisoners over land from the planes to the CIA detention site could, for all practical purposes, have been effected without at least minimal assistance by the host country's authorities, to mention only securing the area near and around the landing planes and providing conditions for a secret and safe transfer of passengers. Inevitably, the Lithuanian personnel responsible for security arrangements, in particular the reception of the flights and on-land transit, must have witnessed at least some elements of the detainees' transfer to Detention Site Violet, for instance the loading or unloading of blindfolded and shackled passengers from the planes (see also *Al Nashiri v. Poland*, cited above, §§ 330 and 437; and *Husayn (Abu Zubaydah) v. Poland*, cited above, §§ 322 and 439).

Consequently, the Court concludes that the Lithuanian authorities which received the CIA personnel in the airport could not have been unaware that the persons brought by them to Lithuania were the CIA prisoners.

[...]

6. The Court's conclusion as to the Lithuanian authorities' knowledge of and complicity in the CIA HVD Programme

571. The Court is mindful of the fact that knowledge of the CIA rendition and secret detention operations and the scale of abuse to which high-value detainees were subjected in CIA custody has evolved over time, from 2002 to the present day. A considerable part of the evidence before the Court emerged several years after the events complained of (see paragraphs 22–24, 34–56, 287–294 and 296–303 above; see also *Al Nashiri v. Poland*, cited above, § 440; and *Husayn (Abu Zubaydah) v. Poland*, cited above, § 442).

Lithuania's alleged knowledge and complicity in the HVD Programme must be assessed with reference to the elements that its authorities knew or ought to have known at or closely around the relevant time, that is to say, between 17 or 18 February 2005 and 25 March 2006. However, the Court, as it has done in respect of the establishment of the facts relating to the applicant's secret detention in Lithuania, will also rely on recent evidence which, as for instance the 2014 US Senate Committee Report and expert evidence obtained by the Court, relate, explain or disclose facts occurring in the past (see *Al Nashiri v. Poland*, cited above, § 440 and *Husayn (Abu Zubaydah) v. Poland*, cited above, § 442).

572. In its assessment, the Court has considered all the evidence in its possession and the various related circumstances referred to above. Having regard to all these elements taken as a whole, the Court finds that the Lithuania authorities knew that the CIA operated, on Lithuanian territory, a detention facility for the purposes of secretly detaining and interrogating terrorist suspects captured within the "war on terror" operation by the US authorities.

This finding is based on the material referred to extensively above, in particular the evidence deriving from the 2014 US Senate Committee Report and, to a considerable extent, the evidence from experts.

The passages of the report relating the approval for the plan to construct the expanded detention facility given by the Detention Site Violet host country leave no doubt as to the Lithuanian high-office holders' prior acceptance of hosting a CIA detention site on their territory. Nor can there be any doubt that they provided "cooperation and support" for the "detention programme" and that, in appreciation, were offered and accepted a financial reward, amounting to some redacted sum of USD million (see paragraphs 554–557 above).

573. Furthermore, the experts, who in the course of their inquiries also had the benefit of contact with various sources, including confidential ones, unanimously and categorically stated that Lithuania not only ought to have known but actually did know of the nature and purposes of the CIA activities in the country.

[...]

574. The Court, as in previous similar cases, does not consider that the Lithuanian authorities necessarily knew the details of what exactly went on inside the CIA secret facility or witnessed treatment or interrogations to which the CIA prisoners were subjected in Lithuania. As in other countries hosting clandestine prisons, the operation of the site was entirely in the hands of the CIA and the interrogations were exclusively the CIA's responsibility (see paragraph 272 above; see also *Al Nashiri v. Poland*, cited above, § 441; and *Husayn (Abu Zubaydah) v. Poland*, cited above, § 443).

575. However, in the Court's view, even if the Lithuanian authorities did not have, or could not have had, complete knowledge of the HVD Programme, the facts available to them through their contacts and cooperation with their CIA partners, taken together with extensive and widely available information on torture, ill-treatment, abuse and harsh interrogation measures inflicted on terrorist-suspects in US custody which in 2002–2005 circulated in the public domain, including the Lithuanian press (see paragraphs 565–568 above), enabled them to conjure up a reasonably accurate image of the CIA's activities and, more particularly, the treatment to which the CIA was likely to have subjected their prisoners in Lithuania.

In that regard the Court would reiterate that in *Al Nashiri v. Poland and Husayn (Abu Zubaydah) v. Poland* it has found that already in 2002–2003 the public sources reported practices resorted to, or tolerated by, the US authorities that were manifestly contrary to the principles of the Convention. All the more so did the authorities, in 2005–2006, have good reason to believe that a person detained under the CIA rendition and secret detention programme could be exposed to a serious risk of treatment contrary to those principles on their territory.

It further observes that it is – as was the case in respect of Poland – inconceivable that the rendition aircraft could have crossed the country's airspace, landed at and departed from its airports, or that the CIA could have occupied the premises offered by the national authorities and transported detainees there, without the State authorities being informed of or involved in the preparation and execution of the HVD Programme on their territory. Nor can it stand to reason that activities of such character and scale, possibly vital for the country's military and political interests, could have been undertaken on Lithuanian territory without the Lithuanian authorities' knowledge and without the necessary authorisation and assistance being given at the appropriate level of the State (see *Al Nashiri v. Poland*, cited above, §§ 441–442 and *Husayn (Abu Zubaydah) v. Poland*, cited above, §§ 443–444).

576. The Court accordingly finds it established beyond reasonable doubt that:

(a) the Lithuanian authorities knew of the nature and purposes of the CIA's activities on its territory at the material time;

(b) the Lithuanian authorities, by approving the hosting of the CIA Detention Site Violet, enabling the CIA to use its airspace and airports and to disguise the movements of rendition aircraft, providing logistics and services, securing the premises for the CIA and transportation of the CIA teams with detainees on land, cooperated in the preparation and execution of the CIA rendition, secret detention and interrogation operations on its territory; and

(c) given their knowledge of the nature and purposes of the CIA's activities on their territory and their involvement in the execution of that programme, the Lithuanian authorities knew that, by enabling the CIA to detain terrorist suspects – including the applicant – on their territory, they were exposing them to a serious risk of treatment contrary to the Convention.

IV. ALLEGED VIOLATION OF ARTICLE 3 OF THE CONVENTION

[...]

A. Procedural aspect of Article 3

611. The Court, having regard to the fact that the Prosecutor General's Office opened the pre-trial investigation within a few days after the Seimas Resolution of 19 January 2010 endorsing the CNSD Findings and recommendations (see paragraphs 174 and 179 above), does not consider that the authorities failed to give a prompt response to the public allegations suggesting Lithuania's possible complicity in the CIA extraordinary rendition programme. Nor can it be said that during the subsequent six months the authorities failed to display procedural activity. From 10 February to 14 June 2010 the prosecutor took evidence from fifty-five witnesses, including some high political post-holders, the SSD officers, the SBGS, and the airport authorities and employees. Over that period numerous requests for information were addressed to various bodies, including the relevant ministries, airports, the aviation authorities, the Customs Service and others. The prosecution also consulted classified material of the parliamentary inquiry and carried out on-site inspections of Project No. 1 and Project No. 2 (see paragraphs 181–190 above).

612. However, it does not appear that, after June 2010, any further actions were taken, apart from responding to correspondence from Reprieve, which had addressed the prosecutor in connection with the suspicion that the applicant had been secretly detained in a CIA detention facility in Lithuania.

The first letter, of 20 September 2010, in which Reprieve asked the prosecution to investigate the matter, gave a fairly extensive description of the applicant's detention in other countries, before his alleged rendition to Lithuania. It indicated the putative period of his detention, which was situated between spring 2004 and September 2006 and matched the repeated movements of the CIA-linked aircraft through Lithuania's airspace, which were the object both of the parliamentary inquiry and current investigation. The prosecution replied that these circumstances had already been covered by the pending investigation. No action was taken.

In the second letter, of 18 November 2010, Reprieve asked the prosecutor to attempt to interview the applicant under the bilateral agreement on mutual legal assistance in criminal matters between the USA and Lithuania and, in addition, made eight motions for taking evidence from various sources, including the US CIA officials and Lithuanian officials listed by name, eyewitnesses, forensic evidence, companies involved in flights and many others. It also asked for information about the progress of the investigation On 13 January 2011 the prosecutor refused the request since Reprieve "was not party to the proceedings [with] the right to examine the material of the pre-trial investigation". None of the proposed actions were taken. The next day the prosecutor discontinued the investigation, finding that there had been no evidence demonstrating "illegal transportation of anyone", by the CIA, including of the applicant, into or out of Lithuania (see paragraphs 191–195 above).

613. The Court observes that the Government have stated that the prosecutor's decision was based on the fact that Reprieve had not provided any new evidence apart from the information already in the public domain and available to the authorities. This, however, does not explain the lack of any attempt to consider evidential motions which do not appear to have been unreasonable or unrelated to the object of the investigation.

614. It is not the Court's role to advise the domestic authorities about which evidence is to be admitted and which is to be refused, but their decisions in that respect are subject to the Court's scrutiny for compliance with the requirements of an "effective and thorough investigation". According to the Courts case-law, as stated above, the authorities must "always make a serious attempt to find out what happened and should not rely on hasty or ill-founded conclusions to close their investigation or to use as the basis of their decisions" (see paragraph 608 above, with references to the Court's case-law).

615. In that regard, the Court cannot but note that the prosecutor had in his possession personal details, including passports numbers, of the five US citizens who arrived on the CIA plane N787WH at Palanga airport on 18 February 2005 (see paragraph 371 above). Also, despite the fact that the case involved allegations of a large-scale rendition scheme operated by the CIA and that it was clearly established in the investigation that the CIA-linked aircraft "did arrive and did depart" from Lithuania at the material time (see paragraph 198 above), the prosecutor apparently made no

effort to identify, and to obtain evidence from, US citizens who could have been involved in the "partnership cooperation" with the SSD by means of formal requests for legal assistance to the US authorities. In the light of the material before the Court such formal requests were only made in the proceedings that were re-opened in January 2015 (see paragraphs 209–210 and 595 above).

616. The Court also takes note of concerns regarding the adequacy of the investigation expressed in the 2011 CPT Report. In particular, the CPT stated that, given that the investigation had related to a possible abuse of power, "the question [arose] whether [it] ... [was] sufficiently wide in scope to qualify as comprehensive". When the CPT delegation raised the issue of the scope of the investigation with the Prosecutor General's Office, they replied that "facts" were needed to launch a criminal investigation, not "assumptions" (see paragraph 353 above).

617. After the investigation was discontinued on 14 January 2011, in 2011–2013 the Lithuanian prosecutors received repeated requests from non-governmental organisations and appeals from the European Parliament to resume the proceedings in order to consider newly emerging evidence (see paragraphs 201–205 and 290–295 above). No response was given. Until the publication of the 2014 US Senate Committee Report and receipt of the detailed 2015 Reprieve Briefing – to which, according to Mr Black, the prosecutor has not so far responded either – the authorities remained totally passive (see paragraphs 206 and 395 above). Moreover, on the basis of the Government's summary description of the fresh investigation, ongoing since 22 January 2015, it does not appear that any meaningful progress in investigating Lithuania's complicity in the CIA HVD Programme and identifying the persons responsible has so far been achieved (see paragraphs 206–211 above).

618. Nor does it seem that any information from the 2010–2011 investigation or the fresh proceedings regarding their conduct has been disclosed to the public. The Government have argued that the 2010–2011 investigation was transparent and subject to public scrutiny since part of the material was declassified in the context of the proceedings before the Court (see paragraph 592 above). However, the Court notes that this material had not been publicly accessible until the public hearing in the present case held on 29 June 2016, at which the Government withdrew their request to apply Rule 33 § 2 to all documents submitted by them, except to

the extent necessary to ensure the protection of personal data (see paragraphs 11 and 13 above). It further notes that both Reprieve and Amnesty International were either denied any information about the progress and scope of the investigation or refused access – even restricted – to the investigation file, or had their requests to that effect left unanswered (see paragraphs 195 and 201–205 above).

Furthermore, as stated in the 2011 CPT Report, the CPT's delegation "did not receive the specific information it requested" about the investigation. In that context, the CPT also expressed doubts as to whether "all the information that could have been provided to [it] about the conduct of the investigation ha[d] been forthcoming" and whether the investigation was sufficiently thorough, "given the paucity of the information currently available" (see § 72 of the Report cited in paragraph 353 above).

619. The Court would emphasise that the importance and gravity of the issues involved require particularly intense public scrutiny of the investigation. The Lithuanian public has a legitimate interest in being informed of the criminal proceedings and their results. It therefore falls to the national authorities to ensure that, without compromising national security, a sufficient degree of public scrutiny is maintained in respect to the investigation (see *Al Nashiri v. Poland*, cited above, § 497 and *Husayn (Abu Zubaydah) v. Poland*, cited above, § 489).

620. The Court would further underline that the securing of proper accountability of those responsible for enabling the CIA to run Detention Site Violet on Lithuanian territory is conducive to maintaining confidence in the adherence of the Lithuanian State's institutions to the rule of law. The applicant and the public have a right to know the truth regarding the circumstances surrounding the extraordinary rendition operations in Lithuania and his secret detention and to know what happened at the material time. A victim who has made a credible allegation of being subjected to ill-treatment in breach of Article 3 of the Convention has the right to obtain an accurate account of the suffering endured and the role of those responsible for his ordeal (see paragraph 610 above; see also *Association "21 December 1989" and Others v. Romania*, nos. 33810/07 and 18817/08, § 144, 24 May 2011; *Al Nashiri v. Poland*, cited above, § 495; and *Husayn (Abu Zubaydah) v. Poland*, cited above, § 487).

621. Having regard to the above deficiencies of the impugned proceedings, the Court considers that Lithuania has failed to comply with the requirements of an "effective and thorough" investigation for the purposes of Article 3 of the Convention.

622. Accordingly, the Court dismisses the Government's preliminary objections of non-exhaustion of domestic remedies and non-compliance with the six-month rule (see paragraphs 413–417 above) and finds that there has been a violation of Article 3 of the Convention, in its procedural aspect.

B. Substantive aspect of Article 3

[...]

633. The Court has already found that the applicant's assertions concerning his secret detention in Lithuania from 17 or 18 February 2005 to 25 March 2006 and his transfer from Lithuania to another CIA "black site" on the latter date have been proved before Court and that those facts are established beyond reasonable doubt (see paragraph 548 above).

It remains to be determined whether the treatment to which he was subjected during his detention falls within the ambit of Article 3 of the Convention and, if so, whether and to what extent it can be attributed to the respondent State (see paragraph 587 above).

(α) Treatment to which the applicant was subjected at the relevant time

634. In the light of the material in the case file, as the Court has already pointed out, it does not appear that at Detention Site Violet the applicant was subjected to the EITs in connection with interrogations, although there are indications that he must have been continually interrogated or "debriefed" by the CIA during the entire period of his secret detention (see paragraphs 550–552 above). In that regard, the Court also notes that on 27 March 2007, at the hearing before the Combatant Status Review Tribunal in Guantánamo the applicant, after relating the ordeal to which he had been subjected in CIA custody, stated that "after the second – or second – after one complete year, two year, they start[ed] tell[ing] me the time for the pray[ers] and slowly, slowly circumstances [had become]

good". However, that statement must be read in the context of the treatment inflicted on him previously and in the light of what had happened to him before. The description of his plight given by the applicant at the above hearing and records of his statements in the 2007 ICRC Report give a shocking account of the particularly cruel treatment to which he had been subjected in CIA custody, from the waterboarding, being slammed against the wall and kept naked for days or months on end, through the confinement in a coffin-shaped box, to sleep deprivation, prolonged stress positions, exposure to cold temperature and food deprivation (see paragraphs 151–153 and 299 above; see also *Husayn (Abu Zubaydah) v. Poland*, cited above, §§ 102–107 and 508).

The Court considers that the applicant's experience in CIA custody prior to his detention in Lithuania is an important factor to be taken into account in its assessment of the severity of the treatment to which he was subsequently subjected (ibid.).

635. The Court has established beyond reasonable doubt that during his detention in Lithuania the applicant was kept – as any other CIA detainee – under the regime of "standard conditions of confinement" laid down in the DCI Confinement Guidelines. That regime included, as a matter of fixed, predictable routine, blindfolding or hooding of the detainees, designed to disorient them and keep from learning their location or the layout of the detention facility; removal of hair upon arrival at the site; incommunicado, solitary confinement; continuous noise of high and varying intensity played at all times; continuous light such that each cell was illuminated to about the same brightness as an office; and use of leg shackles in all aspects of detainee management and movement (see paragraphs 54–56 and 552 above). Conditions of confinement were an integral part of the CIA interrogation scheme and served the same purposes as interrogation measures, namely to "dislocate psychologically" the detainee, to "maximise his feeling of vulnerability and helplessness" and "reduce or eliminate his will to resist ... efforts to obtain critical intelligence" (see paragraphs 46–53 above).

636. A complementary description of the applicant's conditions of detention throughout the entire period that he spent in CIA custody can also be found in the 2007 ICRC Report. According to that description, based on the applicant's own account and on that of thirteen other high-value

detainees' they "had no knowledge of where they were being held, no contact with persons other than their interrogators or guards"; and "even the guards were usually masked and, other than the absolute minimum, did not communicate in any way with detainees". None of the detainees "had any real – let alone regular – contact with other persons detained, other than occasionally for the purposes of inquiry when they were confronted with another detainee". They had "no access to news from the outside world, apart from the later stages of their detention when some of them occasionally received printouts of sports news from the Internet and one reported receiving newspapers". The situation was further exacerbated by other aspects of the detention regime, such as deprivation of access to the open air and exercise, lack of appropriate hygiene facilities and deprivation of basic items in pursuance of interrogations (see paragraph 299 above).

637. Referring to the general situation in the CIA secret prisons, the 2014 US Senate Committee Report states that "the conditions of confinement for CIA detainees were harsher than [those] the CIA represented to the policymakers and others" and describes them as being "poor" and "especially bleak early in the programme" (see paragraph 84 above). It further states that in respect of the conditions of detention the DCI Confinement Guidelines of 28 January 2003 set forth minimal standards and required only that the facility be sufficient to meet "basic health needs". That, according to the report, in practice meant that a facility in which detainees were kept shackled in complete darkness and isolation, with a bucket for a human waste and without heating during the winter months met that standard (see paragraphs 54–56 and 77 above).

638. As regards the impact of the regime on the CIA detainees, the 2014 US Senate Committee Report states that "multiple CIA detainees who were subjected to the CIA's enhanced interrogation techniques and extended isolation exhibited psychological and behavioural issues, including hallucinations, paranoia, insomnia and attempts at self-harm and self-mutilation" and that "multiple psychologists identified the lack of human contact experienced by detainees as a cause of psychiatric problems" (see paragraph 77 above). In the CIA's declassified documents, adverse effects of extreme isolation to which HVDs were subjected have been recognised as imposing a "psychological toll" and capable of altering "the detainee's ability to interact with others" (see paragraph 56 above).

639. For the purposes of its ruling the Court does not find it necessary to analyse each and every aspect of the applicant's treatment in detention, the physical conditions in which he was detained in Lithuania or the conditions in which he was transferred to and out of Lithuania. While the intensity of the measures inflicted on him by the CIA might have varied, the predictability of the CIA's regime of confinement and treatment routinely applied to the high-value detainees give sufficient grounds for the Court to conclude that the above described standard measures were used in respect of the applicant in Lithuania and likewise elsewhere, following his transfer from Lithuania, as an integral part of the HVD Programme (see also *Al Nashiri v. Poland*, cited above, §§ 514–515; and *Husayn (Abu Zubaydah) v. Poland*, cited above, § 510).

640. Considering all the elements, the Court finds that during his detention in Lithuania the applicant was subjected to an extremely harsh detention regime including a virtually complete sensory isolation from the outside world and suffered from permanent emotional and psychological distress and anxiety also caused by the past experience of torture and cruel treatment in the CIA's hands and fear of his future fate. Even though at that time he had apparently not been subjected to interrogations with the use of the harshest methods, the applicant – having beforehand experienced the most brutal torture, (see *Husayn (Abu Zubaydah) v. Poland*, cited above, §§ 86–89, 99–102, 401 and 416–417; see also paragraphs 149–152 and 296 above) – inevitably faced the constant fear that, if he failed to "comply", the previous cruel treatment would at any given time be inflicted on him again. Thus, Article 3 of the Convention does not refer exclusively to the infliction of physical pain but also to that of mental suffering, which is caused by creating a state of anguish and stress by means other than bodily assault (see *El-Masri*, cited above, § 202; and *Husayn (Abu Zubaydah) v. Poland*, cited above, §§ 509–510).

Consequently, having regard to the regime of detention to which the applicant must have been subjected in Lithuania and its cumulative effects on him, the Court finds that the treatment complained of is to be characterised as having involved intense physical and mental suffering falling within the notion of "inhuman treatment" under Article 3 of the Convention (see paragraphs 630–631 above, with references to the Court's case-law).

(β) *Court's conclusion as to Lithuania's responsibility*

641. The Court has already found that the Lithuanian authorities knew of the nature and purposes of the CIA's activities on its territory at the material time and cooperated in the preparation and execution of the CIA extraordinary rendition, secret detention and interrogation operations on Lithuanian territory. It has also found that, given their knowledge and involvement in the execution of the HVD Programme the Lithuanian authorities knew that, by enabling the CIA to detain terrorist suspects – including the applicant – on Lithuania's territory, they were exposing them to a serious risk of treatment contrary to the Convention (see paragraph 576 above).

642. It is true that in the assessment of the experts – which the Court has accepted – the Lithuanian authorities did not know the details of what exactly happened inside Detention Site Violet or witnessed the treatment to which the CIA's detainees were subjected. The running of the detention facility was entirely in the hands of and controlled by the CIA. It was the CIA personnel who were responsible for the physical conditions of confinement, interrogations, debriefings, ill-treatment and inflicting of torture on detainees (see paragraphs 571–575 above).

However, under Article 1 of the Convention, taken together with Article 3, Lithuania was required to take measures designed to ensure that individuals within its jurisdiction were not subjected to torture or inhuman or degrading treatment or punishment, including ill-treatment administered by private individuals (see paragraph 632 above).

Notwithstanding the above Convention obligation, the Lithuanian authorities, for all practical purposes, facilitated the whole process of the operation of the HVD Programme on their territory, created the conditions for it to happen and made no attempt to prevent it from occurring. As held above, on the basis of their own knowledge of the CIA activities deriving from Lithuania's complicity in the HVD Programme and from publicly accessible information on treatment applied in the context of the "war on terror" to terrorist suspects in US custody the authorities – even if they did not see or participate in the specific acts of ill-treatment and abuse endured by the applicant and other HVDs – must have been aware of the serious risk of treatment contrary to Article 3 occurring in the CIA detention facility on Lithuanian territory.

Accordingly, the Lithuanian authorities, on account of their "acquiescence and connivance" in the HVD Programme must be regarded as responsible for the violation of the applicant's rights under Article 3 of the Convention committed on their territory (see paragraph 592; see also *El-Masri*, cited above, §§ 206 and 211; *Al Nashiri v. Poland*, cited above, § 517; and *Husayn (Abu Zubaydah) v. Poland*, cited above, § 512).

643. Furthermore, the Lithuanian authorities were aware that the transfer of the applicant to and from their territory was effected by means of "extraordinary rendition", that is, "an extra-judicial transfer of persons from one jurisdiction or State to another, for the purposes of detention and interrogation outside the normal legal system, where there was a real risk of torture or cruel, inhuman or degrading treatment" (see *El-Masri*, cited above, § 221; *Al Nashiri v. Poland*, cited above, § 518; and *Husayn (Abu Zubaydah) v. Poland*, cited above, § 513).

In these circumstances, the possibility of a breach of Article 3 was particularly strong and should have been considered intrinsic in the transfer (see paragraphs 579–580 above). Consequently, by enabling the CIA to transfer the applicant out of Lithuania to another detention facility, the authorities exposed him to a foreseeable serious risk of further ill-treatment and conditions of detention in breach of Article 3 of the Convention.

644. There has accordingly been a violation of Article 3 of the Convention, in its substantive aspect.

V. ALLEGED VIOLATION OF ARTICLE 5 OF THE CONVENTION

[...]

655. In the previous cases concerning similar allegations of a breach of Article 5 arising from secret detention under the CIA HVD Programme in other European countries the Court found that the respondent States' responsibility was engaged and that they were in violation of that provision on account of their complicity in that programme and cooperation with the CIA (see *El-Masri*, cited above, § 241; *Al Nashiri v. Poland*, cited above, §§ 531–532; *Husayn (Abu Zubaydah) v. Poland*, cited above,

§§ 525–526; and *Nasr and Ghali*, cited above, §§ 302–303). The Court does not see any reason to hold otherwise in the present case.

656. As the Court has held in Al *Nashiri* v. *Poland* (cited above, § 530) and *Husayn (Abu Zubaydah)* v. *Poland* (cited above, § 524), secret detention of terrorist suspects was a fundamental feature of the CIA rendition programme. The rationale behind the programme was specifically to remove those persons from any legal protection against torture and enforced disappearance and to strip them of any safeguards afforded by both the US Constitution and international law against arbitrary detention, to mention only the right to be brought before a judge and be tried within a reasonable time or the habeas corpus guarantees. To this end, the whole scheme had to operate outside the jurisdiction of the US courts and in conditions securing its absolute secrecy, which required setting up, in co-operation with the host countries, overseas detention facilities (see also paragraphs 22–23, 26–58 and 74–87 above).

The rendition operations largely depended on the cooperation, assistance and active involvement of the countries which put at the USA's disposal their airspace, airports for the landing of aircraft transporting CIA prisoners, and facilities in which the prisoners could be securely detained and interrogated, thus ensuring the secrecy and smooth operation of the HVD Programme. While, as noted above, the interrogations of captured terrorist suspects was the CIA's exclusive responsibility and the local authorities were not to be involved, the cooperation and various forms of assistance by those authorities, such as the customising of the premises for the CIA's needs or the provision of security and logistics, constituted the necessary condition for the effective operation of the CIA secret detention facilities (see *Al Nashiri* v. *Poland*, cited above, § 530; and *Husayn (Abu Zubaydah)* v. *Poland*, cited above, § 524).

657. In respect of the applicant's complaint under the substantive aspect of Article 3 the Court has already found that the Lithuanian authorities were aware that he had been transferred from their territory by means of "extraordinary rendition" and that by enabling the CIA to transfer the applicant to its other secret detention facilities, exposed him to a foreseeable serious risk of further ill-treatment and conditions of detention in breach of Article 3 of the Convention (see paragraph 643 above). These conclusions are likewise valid in the context of the applicant's complaint

under Article 5. In consequence, Lithuania's responsibility under the Convention is engaged in respect of both the applicant's secret detention on its territory and his transfer from Lithuania to another CIA detention site.

658. There has accordingly been a violation of Article 5 of the Convention.

[...]

VI. ALLEGED VIOLATION OF ARTICLE 8 OF THE CONVENTION

[...]

664. The notion of "private life" is a broad one and is not susceptible to exhaustive definition; it may, depending on the circumstances, cover the moral and physical integrity of the person. These aspects of the concept extend to situations of deprivation of liberty (see *El-Masri*, cited above, § 248, with further references to the Court's case-law; *Al Nashiri v. Poland*, cited above, § 538; and *Husayn (Abu Zubaydah) v. Poland*, cited above, § 532).

Article 8 also protects a right to personal development, including the right to establish and develop relationships with other human beings and the outside world. A person should not be treated in a way that causes a loss of dignity, as "the very essence of the Convention is respect for human dignity and human freedom" (see *Pretty v. the United Kingdom*, no. 2346/02, §§ 61 and 65, ECHR 2002-III). Furthermore, the mutual enjoyment by members of a family of each other's company constitutes a fundamental element of family. In that context, the Court would also reiterate that an essential object of Article 8 is to protect the individual against arbitrary interference by the public authorities (see *El-Masri*, cited above, § 248; *Al Nashiri v. Poland*, cited above, §538; and *Husayn (Abu Zubaydah) v. Poland*, cited above, § 532).

665. Having regard to its conclusions concerning the respondent State's responsibility under Articles 3 and 5 of the Convention (see paragraphs 643 and 657 above), the Court is of the view that Lithuania's actions and omissions in respect of the applicant's detention and transfer likewise engaged its responsibility under Article 8 of the Convention. Considering that the alleged interference with the applicant's right to respect for his

private and family life occurred in the context of the imposition of fundamentally unlawful, undisclosed detention, it must be regarded as not "in accordance with the law" and as inherently lacking any conceivable justification under paragraph 2 of that Article (see *El-Masri*, cited above, § 249; *Husayn (Abu Zubaydah) v. Poland*, cited above, § 533; and *Al Nashiri v. Poland*, cited above, § 539).

666. There has accordingly been a violation of Article 8 of the Convention.

Part Thirteen: IV.2.B. International Responsibility – International armed conflict – Consequences of responsibility – Consequences other than reparation

13/1

On 5 March 2018 during a meeting between Minister of Foreign Affairs of Lithuania Linas Linkevičius and the United States Special Representative for Ukraine Negotiations, Ambassador Kurt Volker which issues related to regional security, the importance of implementation of the Minsk agreements, UN peacekeepers in Donbass, and the future of Ukraine's reforms were discussed:

> The diplomats underlined that Russia's ongoing aggression against Ukraine hindered peacebuilding and reconciliation efforts in Ukraine. In the meeting between Lithuania's Foreign Minister and the Ambassador Volker, it was noted that as long as the Kremlin's aggression continued and the Minsk agreements were not implemented, sanctions must stay in place.
>
> Linkevičius and Volker discussed efforts to deploy the UN peacekeeping mission throughout the occupied Donbass. The U.S. Special Representative briefed the Minister about the ongoing talks with the Russian Presidential Aid Vladislav Surkov.
>
> Considerable attention was also devoted to the Western support for Ukraine, as the country was implementing reforms in a complex war-torn context in eastern Ukraine.
>
> "In 2014, Ukraine paid a high price for choosing democracy and its European path. It is important for the democratic world to be united and continue to consistently support Ukraine's reforms aimed at boosting economic growth and combating corruption", said Minister Linkevičius.

(Available in English at the Internet site of the Ministry of Foreign Affairs, <http://www.urm.lt/default/en/news/due-to-russias-ongoing-aggression-against-ukraine-sanctions-must-stay-in-place-say-linkevicius-and-volker->)

Part Fourteen: 11.C. Peaceful Settlement of Disputes – Means of settlement – Enquiry (fact-finding)

14/1

On 26 June 2018, the Ministry of Foreign Affairs made a statement on the joint investigation of the MH17 crash:

> Lithuania supports the efforts of the Joint Investigation Team and trusts the independent and impartial investigation into the causes of the crash of the Malaysia Airlines Flight 17 (MH17) of 17 July 2014 while it was flying over Ukraine.
>
> The Joint Investigation Team, set up by Australia, Belgium, Malaysia, and Ukraine, has concluded that the Malaysia Airlines Flight 17 was shot down over eastern Ukraine by a BUK-type missile which was brought there from the 53rd Anti-Aircraft Rocket Brigade of the Russian Federation deployed in the vicinity of Kursk.
>
> The perpetrators of the tragic crime must be identified and prosecuted.
>
> We urge the Russian Federation to cooperate with the investigator countries and the Joint Investigation Team.

(Available in English at the Internet site of the Ministry of Foreign Affairs, <http://www.urm.lt/default/en/news/statement-by-the-mfa-on-the-investigation-of-the-mh17-crash>)

Part Fourteen: 11.H.2. Peaceful Settlement of Disputes – Means of settlement – Settlement within international organisations – Other organisations

14/2

On 20 November 2018, during a meeting with Director-General of the World Trade Organization (WTO) Roberto Azevêdo the Minister of Foreign Affairs of

Lithuania Linas Linkevičius stressed the importance of settlement of trade disputes through the WTO system:

> "We must use the World Trade Organization as a platform to resolve international trade disputes through negotiation without escalating trade wars", said Lithuania's Foreign Minister.
>
> According to the Foreign Minister, Lithuania fully supports a stable and open international trading system. Rules established by the WTO are a guarantor of this system, as well as an effective supervision of their implementation. To this end, it is important to modernize the organization, update the rules and mechanisms for their implementation.
>
> Underlying causes of current trade disputes include state subsidies and unfair competition. Therefore, the WTO should mainly focus on addressing these issues. Lithuanian producers suffer significantly from Russia's dual energy pricing. Lithuania is actively involved in the drafting of EU proposals aimed at maintaining the WTO dispute settlement system and reforming the rules.

(Available in English at the Internet site of the Ministry of Foreign Affairs, <http://www.urm.lt/default/en/news/l-linkevicius-the-world-trade-organization-is-an-alternative-to-trade-wars>)

Part Seventeen: I.B.7. The Law of Armed Conflict and International Humanitarian Law – The law of international armed conflict – International humanitarian law

17/1

On 27 February 2018, the Vice-Minister of Foreign Affairs of Lithuania Darius Skusevičius attended a high-level segment of the opening of the United Nations Human Rights Council's 37th session that focused on the 70th anniversary of the Universal Declaration of Human Rights and expressed regrets about human rights violations in conflict zones in Syria and Europe:

> Due to Russia's systemic repressive policies in the occupied territories of Ukraine and Georgia, thousands of people live in the so-called grey area of legal regulation. Thus, they are struggling at the mercy of the whims of

fate" said Lithuania's Foreign Vice-Minister. According to Skusevičius, the protection of civilians in armed conflict is becoming increasingly complex, which results in the deaths of many civilians.

In his speech, the Vice-Minister Skusevičius also emphasized the need to strengthen the implementation of the international community's human rights commitments and to properly evaluate the daily work of human rights defenders and journalists in protecting human rights, ensuring their security in conflict zones.

The Council also discussed human rights violations in the occupied Crimea, with special attention paid to the consequences of the persecution of Crimean Tatars. More than 20,000 Crimean Tatars were forced to flee Crimea. Lithuania's Foreign Vice-Minister urged the participants not to leave the Crimean people to their fate and to keep up the international pressure on Russia demanding for an immediate cessation of the ongoing repression.

(Available in English at the Internet site of the Ministry of Foreign Affairs, <http://www.urm.lt/default/en/news/lithuanias-foreign-vice-minister-skusevicius-russia-continues-to-violate-international-law-in-occupied-territories-of-ukraine-and-georgia>)

Part Seventeen: 1.B.8. The Law of Armed Conflict and International Humanitarian Law – The law of international armed conflict – Belligerent occupation

17/2
On 26 July 2018, the Ministry of Foreign Affairs released a statement supporting US Secretary of State Mike Pompeo's Crimea Declaration of 25 July:

> Lithuania does not recognize and continues to strongly condemn the annexation of Autonomous Republic of Crimea and the city of Sevastopol by the Russian Federation. Our position is based on our unwavering commitment to international law and our conviction that Russia has blatantly violated one of its main principles, – to refrain from the threat or use of force against sovereignty, territorial integrity or political independence of any State. No country can change the borders of another by force.

Looking back at the 50-years of illegal occupation and annexation of the three Baltic States by the Soviet Union, we continue to deeply appreciate a principled stance by the US when 78 years ago the Sumner Welles Declaration was adopted condemning the occupation and refusing to recognize it. Throughout these 50 years, the Sumner Welles declaration has served as a backbone for the non-recognition policy of the occupation and – together with our continued diplomatic presence in the US, as well as in a number of other countries of the world, – contributed to ensuring the continuity of our statehood and eventually to the restoration of our independence.

We therefore very much welcome Crimea Declaration by the Secretary of State Mr. Mike Pompeo as released on 25 July, 2018, which once again reiterated that the Government of the United States of America continues to firmly stand with Ukraine and its people, and against the violation of territorial integrity of sovereign state of Ukraine by Russia. We also recall the established EU policy in this regard.

In concert with our allies and partners in the EU and NATO, and in coordination with the rest of the democratic community, Lithuania holds that Crimea is and will always remain a territory of Ukraine. We remain fully committed to upholding the sovereignty and territorial integrity of Ukraine within its internationally recognized borders including through the international instruments such as sanctions imposed on Russia, which should remain in force until the Ukrainian territorial integrity is fully restored.

Meanwhile we will continue supporting the Crimean Tatars, as well as other Ukrainian citizens residing in the annexed peninsula of Crimea, and will seek all those responsible for the violation of their fundamental rights to be held accountable.

(Available in English at the Internet site of the Ministry of Foreign Affairs, <http://www.urm.lt/default/en/news/lithuanian-mfa-supports-the-us-secretary-of-state-mike-pompeos-crimea-declaration-of-25-july->)

17/3
On 26 November 2018, the Ministry of Foreign Affairs released a statement concerning actions of the Russian Federation in the Kerch Strait:

The Ministry of Foreign Affairs of Lithuania strongly condemns actions undertaken by the Russian Federation on 25 November against Ukrainian navy vessels, which resulted in a physical blockade of the Azov Sea and the ramming of Ukrainian boats. In addition, the Russian coast guard vessels opened fire, injured Ukrainian sailors, and illegally seized Ukrainian navy vessels.

We stress that these provocative actions by the Russian Federation violate Ukraine's sovereignty, territorial integrity, fundamental principles of international law, and cannot be qualified otherwise than an act of open military aggression against Ukraine.

Lithuania does not recognize the illegal annexation of Crimea, condemns the illegal construction and maintenance of the Kerch Bridge, the militarisation of the Crimean Peninsula and the Sea of Azov by the Russian Federation, as well as the blockade of Ukrainian ports in the Azov Sea.

Lithuania calls on the Russian Federation to immediately end these aggressive actions against Ukraine, release seized Ukrainian navy vessels and their crews, and to restore the undisturbed navigation of the Sea of Azov.

We call on the international community to strongly condemn these illegal actions by Russia, to use all means in countering them, and to demand that Russia should immediately end them.

(Available in English at the Internet site of the Ministry of Foreign Affairs, <http://www.urm.lt/default/en/news/foreign-ministrys-statement-on-actions-by-the-russian-federation-in-the-kerch-strait->)

Part Seventeen: I.B.7. The Law of Armed Conflict and International Humanitarian Law – The law of international armed conflict – Conventional, nuclear, bacteriological, and chemical weapons

17/4

On 14 April 2018 the Ministry of Foreign Affairs of Lithuania issued the following statement on attacks against Syrian regime's chemical weapons facilities:

> Lithuanian MFA supports actions by the US, UK and France against the Syrian regime's chemical weapons facilities. Use of chemical weapons in Syria crossed all possible red lines. Those responsible for use of chemical weapons against civil population, including children, must be held accountable.
>
> Military response of the international community needed to send a strong signal to Assad's regime and its supporters. It is the only way to prevent the use of chemical weapons in the future.
>
> We are closely observing the ongoing developments in Syria.

(Available in English at the Internet site of the Ministry of Foreign Affairs, <http://www.urm.lt/default/en/news/lithuanian-mfa-statement-regarding-actions-in-syria>)

Part Nineteen: IX. Legal Aspects of International Relations and Co-operation in Particular Matters – Military and security matters

19/1

On 13 March 2018, the Ministry of Foreign Affairs released a statement regarding the poisoning case in the United Kingdom, wherein it called for a joint NATO and EU response:

> The Lithuanian Foreign Ministry expresses strong solidarity with the United Kingdom following an audacious criminal act – the poisoning of a former military intelligence agent Sergei Skripal and his daughter.
>
> There is never a justification for this type of attack – the attempted murder of private citizens on the soil of a sovereign nation.
>
> The Lithuanian MFA stresses that the use of a military-grade nerve agent within NATO territory represents an exceptional case, making it essential to identify the perpetrators and bring them to justice immediately.
>
> We call for a joint NATO and EU response.

(Available in English at the Internet site of the Ministry of Foreign Affairs, <http://www.urm.lt/default/en/news/lithuanian-mfa-statement-regarding-poisoning-case-in-the-united-kingdom->)

19/2

On 11 September 2018 in Tbilisi, Minister of Foreign Affairs of Lithuania Linas Linkevičius attended an international conference and discussed security in Europe and discussed European security and the progress of Sakartvelo:

> Lithuania's Foreign Minister drew the participants' attention to European security challenges, especially to Russia's aggressive actions and behaviour: "The continuing militarization of borders with Europe, the use of disinformation and cyber-attacks to stir up turmoil, and to undermine the values we cherish, such as the rule of law and democracy", said L. Linkevičius.
>
> According to Lithuania's Foreign Minister, in this context it is necessary to maintain a strategic partnership with Europe's natural ally – the United States of America – when strengthening Europe's capabilities and increasing defence spending. In addition, L. Linkevičius stressed the need to keep up pressure on Russia and to impose new sanctions in response to malicious cyber activity carried out by the country.
>
> The fourth annual international conference in Tbilisi: "World in 2018: Upside Down? was co-hosted by the McCain Institute for International Leadership at Arizona State University and Georgian Economic Policy Research Center (EPRC).
>
> In Tbilisi, the Minister L. Linkevičius also met with the President of Georgia Giorgio Margvelashvili, Chairperson of the Parliament Irakli Kobakhidze, Prime Minister Mamuka Bakhtadze, Minister of Foreign Affairs of Georgia David Zalkaliani, and representatives of the opposition. They discussed the progress of Sakarvelo in implementing the Association Agreement with the European Union, the situation in South Caucasus, important national and international political issues.
>
> "Sakartvelo is undoubtedly the leader of the Eastern Partnership countries, but it is very important to keep pace and further implement all the reforms needed for European and Euro-Atlantic integration", said the head of Lithuania's diplomacy in the meetings. He also urged the Government of Sakartvelo to ensure that the presidential elections on 28 October would be held transparently and democratically, and that the opportunity would be used to strengthen democratic processes and civil society.

(Available in English at the Internet site of the Ministry of Foreign Affairs, <http://www.urm.lt/default/en/news/in-tbilisi-linkevicius-focuses-on-european-security-and-the-progress-of-sakartvelo>)

19/3

On 19 June 2018, Linas Linkevičius, the Lithuanian Minister of Foreign Affairs, met with foreign ministers of the Nordic, Baltic and Visegrad countries in Stockholm (Sweden) and among other issues discussed hybrid threats and cyber security:

> We must improve and support societal resilience not only in Eastern Partnership countries but in our states, too, since the scope of disinformation and propaganda is growing", the Minister said. He also noted that both Europe and NATO needed to focus more on cooperation in the area of security which should embrace hybrid threats and cyber security.

(Available in English at the Internet site of the Ministry of Foreign Affairs, <http://www.urm.lt/default/en/news/linas-linkevicius-we-need-to-focus-more-on-cooperation-in-the-area-of-security>)

Appendices

ANNEX 1.A   Agreements signed by Lithuania before 2018 but entered into force in regard to Lithuania in 2018 – Bi- and multilateral agreements

Title	Conclusion	Entry into Force
Agreement between the Republic of Lithuania and the European Organization for Nuclear Research (CERN) concerning the Granting of the Status of Associate Member at CERN	27.06.2017	08.01.2018
Agreement between the Government of the Republic of Lithuania and the Government of the Republic of Kazakhstan on Mutual Protection of Classified Information	19.05.2015	25.03.2018
Minamata Convention on Mercury	10.10.2013	15.04.2018
Convention of 18 March 1970 on the Taking of Evidence Abroad in Civil or Commercial Matters between the Republic of Lithuania and the Principality of Andorra the Republic of Slovenia		21.04.2018 19.11.2018
Agreement between the Government of the Republic of Lithuania and the Government of Mongolia on the Exemption of Visa Requirements for Holders of Diplomatic and Official or Service Passports	18.09.2017	29.04.2018
Cooperation Agreement between the Republic of Lithuania and the Sovereign Military Hospitaller Order of St. John of Jerusalem of Rhodes and of Malta	04.09.2017	30.04.2018
Convention of 25 October 1980 on the Civil Aspects of International Child Abduction between the Republic of Lithuania and the Republic of Ecuador		01.05.2018
Agreement between the Government of the Republic of Lithuania and the Government of the Republic of Azerbaijan on the Exemption of Visa Requirement for Holders of Service Passports	27.10.2017	05.05.2018

ANNEX 1.A Agreements signed by Lithuania before 2018 but entered into force in regard to Lithuania in 2018 – Bi- and multilateral agreements (*cont.*)

Title	Conclusion	Entry into Force
International Convention for the Control and Management of Ships' Ballast Water and Sediments	13.02.2004	09.05.2018
Agreement between the Government of the Republic of Lithuania and the Government of the Republic of Croatia on Mutual Protection of Classified Information	17.07.2017	14.05.2018
Agreement between the Government of the Republic of Lithuania and the Government of Mongolia on Economic Cooperation	18.09.2017	05.06.2018
Agreement between the Government of the Republic of Lithuania and the Government of the United Arab Emirates on Economic and Technical Cooperation	01.11.2017	12.06.2018
Protocol No. 16 to the Convention for the Protection of Human Rights and Fundamental Freedoms (CETS 214)	02.10.2013	01.08.2018
Protocol amending the European Landscape Convention	01.08.2016	01.08.2018
Convention between the Republic of Lithuania and Japan for the Elimination of Double Taxation with respect to Taxes on Income and the Prevention of Tax Evasion and Avoidance	13.07.2017	31.08.2018
Protocol Relating to an Amendment to the Convention on International Civil Aviation [Article 50(a)] [Article 56]	06.10.2016	16.11.2018
Agreement between the Government of the Republic of Lithuania, the Government of the Republic of Estonia and the Government of the Republic of Latvia on Mutual Assistance and Cooperation in the Field of Disaster Prevention, Preparedness and Response	23.11.2017	24.12.2018

ANNEX II   Agreements signed by Lithuania in 2018 – Bi- and multilateral agreements

Title	Conclusion	Entry into Force
Protocol amending the Additional Protocol to the Convention on the Transfer of Sentenced Persons (CETS 222)	12.01.2018	
Agreement between the Government of the Republic of Lithuania and the Government of the Republic of Poland on Border Documentation Defining the Position of the State Border Line between the Republic of Lithuania and the Republic of Poland	17.02.2018	23.12.2019
Memorandum of Understanding on the Implementation of the EEA Financial Mechanism 2014–2021 between the Republic of Lithuania and Iceland, the Principality of Liechtenstein, the Kingdom of Norway	24.04.2018	25.04.2018
Agreement on the Terms of Accession of the Republic of Lithuania to the Convention on the Organisation for Economic Co-operation and Development	30.05.2018	05.07.2018
Amendments of 2018 to the Code of the Maritime Labour Convention, 2006, as amended (MLC, 2006) approved by the Conference at its one hundred and seventh session	05.06.2018	26.12.2020
Agreement among the Government of the Republic of Estonia, the Government of the Republic of Latvia and the Government of the Republic of Lithuania on the Automatic Academic Recognition of Qualifications concerning Higher Education	08.06.2018	07.01.2019

ANNEX II   Agreements signed by Lithuania in 2018 – Bi- and multilateral agreements (*cont.*)

Title	Conclusion	Entry into Force
Agreement between the Government of the Republic of Lithuania and the Government of the United States of America for Cooperation in Science, Technology and Innovation	25.06.2018	26.02.2019
Agreement between the Government of the Republic of Lithuania and the Government of the Sultanate of Oman on Economic Cooperation	25.06.2018	26.02.2019
Agreement between the Government of the Republic of Lithuania and Government of the State of Israel on Cooperation on Public Security and Fight Against Crime	12.06.2018	
Agreement on Economic Cooperation between the Republic of Lithuania and the Argentine Republic	13.07.2018	18.02.2019
Treaty on the Transfer of Sentenced Persons between the Republic of Lithuania and the Federative Republic of Brazil	26.09.2018	
Agreement between the Government of the Republic of Lithuania and the Government of the Republic of Latvia on the Cross-border Cooperation in the Provision of Ambulance Services in the Border Area between the Republic of Lithuania and the Republic of Latvia	03.10.2018	14.06.2019
Protocol Amending the Convention for the Protection of Individuals with regard to Automatic Processing of Personal Data (CETS 223)	10.10.2018	
Protocol amending the Agreement between the Cabinet of Ministers of Ukraine and the Government of the Republic of Lithuania on Cooperation in the Fields of Standardization, Metrology and Conformity Assessment	08.11.2018	

ANNEX II Agreements signed by Lithuania in 2018 – Bi- and multilateral agreements (*cont.*)

Title	Conclusion	Entry into Force
Agreement between the Government of the Republic of Lithuania and the Government of the Kyrgyz Republic on the Exemption of Visa Requirement for Holders of Diplomatic Passports	21.11.2018	04.12.2019
Agreement between the Government of the Republic of Lithuania and the Government of the Kyrgyz Republic on the Economic Cooperation	21.11.2018	11.12.2019
Protocol between the Government of the Republic of Lithuania and the Cabinet of Ministers of Ukraine Implementing the Agreement between the European Community and Ukraine on the Readmission of Persons	07.12.2018	01.01.2020
Agreement between the Government of the Republic of Lithuania and the Cabinet of Ministers of Ukraine on Employment and Cooperation in the Field of Labour Migration	07.12.2018	17.03.2020

Printed in the United States
By Bookmasters